AVID

READER

PRESS

10 to 25

The Science *of*
Motivating Young People

A Groundbreaking Approach
to Leading the Next Generation—
And Making Your Own Life Easier

DAVID YEAGER, PhD

Avid Reader Press

New York   London   Toronto   Sydney   New Delhi

AVID READER PRESS
An Imprint of Simon & Schuster, LLC
1230 Avenue of the Americas
New York, NY 10020

First Avid Reader Press hardcover edition August 2024

AVID READER PRESS and colophon are trademarks of Simon & Schuster, LLC

Simon & Schuster: Celebrating 100 Years of Publishing in 2024

For information about special discounts for bulk purchases,
please contact Simon & Schuster Special Sales
at 1-866-506-1949 or business@simonandschuster.com.

The names and identifying information of some people
discussed in the book have been changed.

Interior design by Ruth Lee-Mui

Manufactured in the United States of America

1   3   5   7   9   10   8   6   4   2

Library of Congress Cataloging-in-Publication Data

Names: Yeager, David S., author.
Title: 10 to 25 : the science of motivating young people : a groundbreaking approach to
leading the next generation-and making your own life easier / David S. Yeager.
Other titles: Ten to twenty-five
Description: First Avid Reader Press hardcover edition. | New York : Avid Reader Press, 2024. |
Includes bibliographical references and index.
Identifiers: LCCN 2024017510 (print) | LCCN 2024017511 (ebook) | ISBN 9781668023884
(hardcover) | ISBN 9781668023891 (paperback) | ISBN 9781668023907 (ebook)
Subjects: LCSH: Motivation (Psychology) in adolescence. | Motivation (Psychology) in
children. | Child psychology. | Adolescent psychology. | Mentoring. | BISAC: BUSINESS &
ECONOMICS / Leadership | PSYCHOLOGY / Developmental / Adolescent
Classification: LCC BF724.3.M65 Y43 2024 (print) | LCC BF724.3.M65 (ebook) |
DDC 153.8--dc23/eng/20240514
LC record available at https://lccn.loc.gov/2024017510
LC ebook record available at https://lccn.loc.gov/2024017511

ISBN 978-1-6680-2388-4
ISBN 978-1-6680-2390-7 (ebook)

For Margot, my spouse and best friend

For Susan and Scott, my parents

And for the fun and hilarious Yeager kids,
Scarlett, Tripp, Jack, and Ronan

Contents

Introduction

It seems like everywhere you turn, you hear older adults—Gen Xers, millennials, and boomers—describing *young people today* in dark and despairing terms. In my eighteen years as a developmental scientist, and thirteen years as a parent, I've heard it in the bleachers at my kids' games, in the boardrooms of major corporations I've consulted for, and by the watercoolers at schools I've visited. *They just don't care. They speak a different language. They're entitled. They're too sensitive.* But imagine a world in which older adults interact with young people, aged ten to twenty-five, in ways that reliably leave the next generation feeling inspired, enthusiastic, and ready to contribute—rather than disengaged, outraged, worried, or overwhelmed.

In this world, managers' work will be easier because their younger employees will be motivated and self-sufficient. Parents will be happier because they won't have to dread their children turning into teenagers. Educators will feel more successful and less burned-out because they can reach a stressed-out or disengaged generation of young people. And all the rest of us will be able to bridge the divide between the generations with confidence and without starting a war of words.

I've seen this world in the lives of great managers, parents, educators, and coaches. I've studied what they do and how they talk. I've used the scientific method—hypothesis, experiment, data, results—to understand why they're effective. I wrote this book because I want to share the secrets I've learned. This book is for anyone who wants to experience this better world firsthand in their interactions with young people aged ten to twenty-five. It shows how to stop clashing with the next generation and start inspiring them.

The idea for this book grew out of a simple observation I made about a decade ago: many beloved programs to promote youth health and well-being were shockingly ineffective. For example, in the mid-1980s, the U.S. federal government launched the "Just Say No" campaign encouraging young people to "just say no" when they were offered cigarettes, drugs, or alcohol. Not only did the campaign fail to curb teenagers' substance abuse, but studies found it *increased* the appeal of smoking and other drugs. Next, the government tried the Drug Abuse Resistance Education (D.A.R.E.) program. Uniformed police officers visited classrooms to communicate a zero-tolerance policy toward all illicit substances. D.A.R.E. officers lectured students and handed out freebies, such as neon pens, fanny packs, bumper stickers, and T-shirts. At the program's height, 75 percent of school districts in the United States were using it. The problem? It didn't work either. Some studies found that the D.A.R.E. program made students *more* likely to use drugs. In 2007, the Association for Psychological Science warned that D.A.R.E. was on a list of youth programs with the potential to cause harm. That hasn't stopped D.A.R.E. from continuing to be used in the majority of schools in the United States—including my own kids' schools.

The more I dug into the research literature, the more I saw a similar story. I looked at attempts to reduce bullying or teen obesity, programs to improve youth mental health, or efforts to promote healthier social media use. Programs touted by experts rarely yielded benefits. Interestingly, the same or similar programs were often effective with younger children. I became obsessed with a question: Why does our ability to positively influence the trajectories of the young suddenly disappear the moment puberty strikes?

It wasn't just a problem with formal programs. I learned that hardly anyone—managers, parents, educators, coaches—felt like they knew the right thing to say to a young person when it really counted. Young people were a mystery. Unfortunately, the advice most people got didn't help. People told me they felt ineffective, hopeless, or even angry. That obvious and palpable frustration made young people even less inclined to listen. Around the world, this cycle repeated itself over and over, leaving youth and adults exhausted. Two short stories illustrate this point.

The Mentor's Dilemma

One day, I was having coffee in San Francisco with an old friend, Dr. Alex Sweeney. He's a tall, handsome surgeon. The kind of person others listen to, which has been the case since his days as a high school and college quarterback. After he graduated from one of the country's top medical schools, he landed a prestigious fellowship. Now, he's a professor at a top medical school, specializing in ear, nose, and throat (ENT) medicine. Alex spends a lot of his time doing cochlear implants, which restore people's hearing—literally performing biblical-style miracles. He had a problem, though, and he wanted my advice. Alex supervised medical students and residents who were in their early twenties. When they messed up, he told me, he gave them clear and direct feedback, like that they needed to do an assessment differently or ask for a second opinion. But the residents didn't seem to fix their mistakes the next time. They kept making the same errors, as though he had never said anything to them. Alex couldn't figure out why. "It's frustrating," he told me. He spent all day helping his patients *hear*, but he couldn't make his trainees *listen*.

Here's another story. When writing this book, I followed one new manager and his twenty-three-year-old direct report for a year. They worked for a well-known large fashion-accessory company. (I agreed to mask their identities.) In fashion, young people are essential because they know what's trending better than older folks. In a very real sense, the manager's success depended on the young employee having the courage to provide honest opinions. But the direct report wasn't doing that. Her manager had read every management book, subscribed to every business-school professor's Instagram feed, and listened to every podcast. The manager cared about the direct report's career. But all that conventional wisdom wasn't working. One day in a meeting with senior management, the manager threw the young employee a softball question to solicit her opinion as a member of the target demographic. She flubbed it, and senior management was unimpressed. When the pair debriefed, the manager told her that she had missed an opportunity to share her thinking and get in line for a promotion. The direct report cried. The manager felt exasperated. As it turns out, the young employee felt unfairly criticized and put on the spot, as though the manager didn't believe in her. She thought he was trying to make her look bad in front of the higher-ups so that he wouldn't be blamed for her failure. There was a disconnect. The manager was trying to elevate her career, but she felt publicly shamed and privately unsupported. Nobody got what they wanted. A month later, she was gone from the company.

Both Alex and the manager were trapped by the *mentor's dilemma*. This refers to the fact that it's very hard to simultaneously criticize someone's work and motivate them because criticism can crush a young person's confidence. It's a dilemma because leaders feel like they're stuck between two bad choices. They could either put up with poor performance (but be nice) or demand high performance (but be cruel). Neither option is ideal. All too often, both sides—younger and older—tend to leave these interactions frustrated or offended, even though both sides might have entered the interaction with growth in mind.

The mentor's dilemma was first discovered by Geoffrey Cohen, a social psychologist at Stanford University. Cohen was studying college professors who gave rigorous, critical feedback to undergraduates on their writing assignments or presentations. He observed a puzzling trend: students took home their first-draft essays covered in comments but handed in their second drafts with barely any changes. Cohen saw that professors were frustrated and demoralized, thinking (like Alex did with his medical residents), *I've spent all this time giving them feedback, but it was a waste. They never fixed anything. What's the point?*

Coaches face this same dilemma when players don't correct their mechanics after direct feedback, partners at law firms face this when they mark up a junior associate's legal briefs, product designers face this when critiquing junior designers' work, and every parent faces this when children ignore what they've been asked to do. In each case, a leader feels torn between being too nice and too mean. No matter what they choose, things don't go the way they had hoped.

How can the mentor's dilemma be resolved? Many people swear by the compliment sandwich. This is where you bury your criticism of a young person between two pieces of bland praise, such as: *I like your enthusiasm* (positive), *your work is subpar and needs to improve* (negative), *but thanks for having a great attitude* (positive). It's not hard to see why speakers like the sandwich. The two compliments provide twice as many positives as the brutally honest negative. Applying simple arithmetic, the interaction was a net positive. What's not to like?

But here's the problem. Young people don't like the sandwich. The reason why is that they aren't asking themselves if their boss, coach, parent, or teacher is a positive person. Science tells us that when young people are being critiqued by an authority figure, they're asking themselves a deeper, more existential question: *Does this person who has power over my life think I'm incompetent?* Before they can hear the criticism for what it is—helpful advice on how to better meet their goals—they have to feel safe. The compliment sandwich is an attempt to create safety, but the problem is that the compliment is about something trivial. Bland praise for something unimportant and unrelated to personal or professional success doesn't address the young person's main fear. If anything, it confirms their fear that the leader thinks they're incompetent. The leader doesn't say anything good about their work, and even worse, the leader thinks their obvious attempt to placate the young person with hollow praise will work. Listeners just latch on to the criticism and view it as a personal attack.

The fact that common ideas such as the compliment sandwich persist despite their ineffectiveness suggests that we need a systematic science of motivating young people. This book will describe rigorous experiments that have been conducted to tell the difference between common sense and nonsense.

The Wise-Feedback Study

In 2014 I published a scientific experiment with Geoffrey Cohen (and others) on a simple but effective solution to the mentor's dilemma. We called it *wise feedback*. We had instructors be critical with their feedback but accompany that criticism with a clear and transparent statement about the reason they were giving that feedback—namely that they believed the student could meet a high standard if they got the right support. So-called wise feedback is wise (or attuned) to the predicament of young people who don't want to be held to an impossible standard and who also don't want to be talked down to.

We tested wise feedback in an experiment with middle school students in social studies classrooms. The seventh-grade students wrote first drafts of five-paragraph essays about their personal heroes. Next, teachers covered the essays with critical comments and suggestions: *You need to put a comma here. Explain this idea further. Rearrange that sentence.* Before the students got the essays, though, the research team attached handwritten notes from the teachers—either a treatment note or a control note. (Teachers wrote the notes, but they didn't know which student got which note or what the study was trying to test.)

Half the students, randomly assigned, got the treatment note with the wise feedback, which said, *I'm giving you these comments because I have very high standards and I know that you can reach them.* The other half of the students got a vague control-group note. *I'm giving you these comments so that you'll have feedback on your essay.* That note conveyed no clear reason for the feedback. Teachers handed back the essays in sealed folders so they couldn't see who got which note. Then, students were given a week to revise their essays or choose not to revise them.

We were hoping that the wise feedback would motivate students in the treatment group to work harder on their revisions. But even we were surprised by how strongly they responded. When students received the wise-feedback note, they were twice as likely to revise their essays: 40 percent of students in the control group revised their essays, but 80 percent did in the treatment group. The next year, when we ran the study with new students in the same teachers' classes, we required all students to revise their essays. We wanted to see if receiving the wise-feedback note would encourage the students who received it to push themselves to do better. Again, it worked. We found that students made more than twice as many of the teachers' suggested corrections, from 2.2 in the control to 5.5 when they got the wise-feedback treatment note.

What's more, the wise-feedback study led to more equitable outcomes. All students benefited from receiving wise feedback, but those belonging to minority groups (in this case, Black students) benefited most. Wise feedback drastically reduced racial disparities in the students' willingness to make revisions.

Here's the takeaway. When you hold young people to high standards

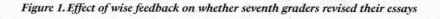

Figure 1. Effect of wise feedback on whether seventh graders revised their essays

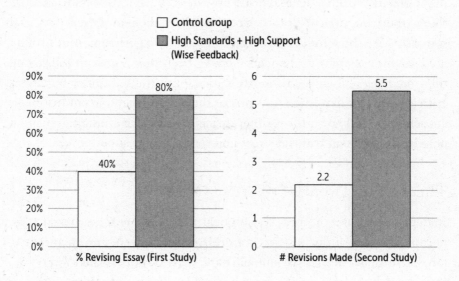

and make it clear that you believe they can meet those standards, you are respecting them because you are taking them seriously. Young people rise to meet the challenge because being respected is motivating. Further, you lift up *all* students and see greater equity.

In this book, I'll share many examples like wise feedback. These are simple, powerful ways of connecting with and motivating young people. They are scientifically proven to have a positive impact on a wide array of people. As I'll show, they work across gender, racial or ethnic, national, and religious groups. There's a simple reason for that. These practices get at the heart of what it means to be a young person, struggling to carve out a place in the adult world.

Employing the science-based strategies in this book may take a little bit of thought, but it doesn't have to take a lot of *time*. The wise-feedback note was just nineteen words. This makes it accessible to anyone.

Years ago, when I shared the wise-feedback study with Dr. Alex Sweeney, it helped him realize why he couldn't get his medical trainees to listen. They were intimidated. They saw his critical feedback as a sign that he thought they weren't good doctors, not as a sign that he was trying to make them *better* doctors. Alex changed his approach. He started explaining to the medical residents that he provides critical feedback because he thinks they can improve and that he was taking them and their potential seriously. Like the middle school students in our experiment, Alex's young medical trainees have responded. They've been more open to improving their medical skills in response to his feedback—and happier to get his criticisms. These days, Alex runs one of the top surgical units at his medical school. He's known for getting great medical outcomes *and* having a positive culture that trains doctors and retains the best employees.

The Ten-to-Twenty-Five-Year-Old Brain

It might seem like the best way to deal with a ten-year-old would have nothing to do with the best way for dealing with a twenty-five-year-old. At ten, kids usually don't show any outward signs of puberty; at twenty-five, they could have been in the armed forces for seven years. But looks can be deceiving. In fact, there are hidden neurobiological and motivational similarities across the age range from ten to twenty-five.

Age ten roughly corresponds to the start of pubertal maturation, which is biology's alarm clock for adulthood. Puberty starts a cascade of changes in hormones, the brain, the body, and in social life, all of which are aiming toward creating adults who can contribute to their group's survival. Neuroscientists know that this cascade continues to be influential well into the midtwenties. The connective architecture of the twenty-four- or twenty-five-year-old brain is still affected by its surroundings. This does not mean that the twentysomething brain is irredeemably immature. It means that it's still adapting, not yet stuck in its ways. This makes sense when you realize that the current global economy, which prizes ever-more-technical training, has caused the transition to a stable adult career to happen later and later in life, even later than for every prior generation of humans. Young adults' brains continue to adapt to the environment because it's good for their (and society's) survival. This means that the brains—and motivations—of young people ages ten to twenty-five have far more in common than most people realize. That's good news because we can draw lessons from a wide variety of situations to learn general principles that, when implemented, could make our interactions with the next generation go better—and make our lives easier in the process.

What is the important change in ten-year-olds that continues to shape their motivation at least until their midtwenties? It is the motivation to experience feelings of *status and respect*. Neuroscientists have shown that during puberty the brain becomes attuned to social status and respect. It craves socially rewarding experiences, sometimes even before the rest of the body has shown the other major signs of puberty. The onset of puberty—specifically gonadarche, which brings us to reproductive maturity and regulates hormones such as testosterone and estradiol—has a powerful effect on the reward-seeking regions of the brain (such as the region called the nucleus accumbens, which is rich in dopamine-receptive neurons). This gives our brains cravings for experiences such as pride, admiration, and respect and makes our brains averse to socially painful experiences, such as humiliation or shame. From the onset of puberty until we take on adult roles in society, we develop appetites for deeper and more meaningful experiences of respect—or, as the cultural anthropologists call it, *earned prestige*.

Any time young people interact with socially powerful people—managers, parents, educators, or coaches—status and respect come to the foreground. Because young people feel sensitive to differences in status, they are subtly reading between the lines with each thing we say, trying to interpret the hidden implications of our words, to find out if we are disrespecting or honoring them. This creates a pervasive disconnect between what adults intend to communicate when we speak and what young people can hear from our words. This is what happened in the control group in the wise-feedback study and in Alex's experiences at the hospital. Young people received critical feedback that came from a good place but they heard it as, *You're not good enough, and I'm looking down on you.* We say one thing, they hear another, and we fight over that misinterpretation, fueling one of the most common forms of conflict between the generations.

This *status-and-respect hypothesis*, which I first proposed with my collaborators Ron Dahl and Carol Dweck in the mid-2010s, contradicted society's popular view of adolescence as an inevitably frustrating developmental stage. Our hypothesis held that adolescents simply have a different set of needs that aren't being met. After all, we don't say that infancy is an inherently bad age because babies cry and fuss. Instead, we understand that they have developmental needs for sleep and food that must be met so they can grow and thrive. We find out if babies are hungry or tired, and then we feed them or put them down for a nap. Status and respect are to a young person what food and sleep are to a baby—core needs that, when satisfied, can unlock better motivation and behavior. Meeting young people's developmental needs prevents the worst kids-these-days behaviors that get under adults' skin. If we appreciate these needs, then as parents, teachers, managers, or coaches who support young people, we'll all be able to spend more time being proud of what they accomplish, assured that they are becoming capable members of society, and less time pulling our hair out.

The wise-feedback study pointed to a way to solve the mentor's dilemma: by conferring status and respect on young people. But it was also unsatisfying because it tested just one sentence. I wanted to know: How can leaders go from a onetime note to a whole relationship—or even a whole culture—characterized by high standards and high support? Once I walked out of my laboratory and started talking to real-life practitioners, I started seeing wise-feedback-like tactics making a real difference in young people's lives. One of the most unexpected places I saw this was in the world of coaching young National Basketball Association (NBA) players.

Chip Engelland's Story

When an NBA team selects a nineteen-year-old rookie in the first round of the amateur draft, the rookie usually feels confident and proud—not to mention flush with millions in cash. This confidence can be threatened when, soon after the player is picked, the team's shooting coach tells the player that they need to change their shot—the very thing that got them drafted in the first place. It leads to serious questions, such as: *Does the team think I'm not good enough after all?* Or even: *What if messing with my shot makes my shot worse—causing me to get benched or cut from the team?* The answers to these questions have huge implications, ranging from public humiliation to going broke. NBA coaches, therefore, face a version of the mentor's dilemma. If they critique a player's shot, it could cause the player to get defensive and refuse to change. If they don't critique the shot, the player may not live up to their potential—possibly causing both the player and the coach to get fired.

I was surprised at first when I discovered that a professional sports coach, of all people, had a satisfying solution to this mentor's dilemma. Many people think that the stereotype of a high-performing coach is a yelling, foaming-at-the-mouth chair thrower who enforces impossibly high standards, scares the daylights out of players, and breaks their wills, only to build them back up to be more obedient. After all, in the cutthroat world of the NBA, with enormous sums of money on the line, professional coaches don't have time to suffer fools. The NBA coach with perhaps the strongest reputation for being "heart-stopping" and "terrifying" is the legendary Gregg Popovich of the San Antonio Spurs. But did you know that Coach Popovich's Spurs organization is nothing like that stereotype? Although it's true that the Spurs maintain exceptionally high expectations, Popovich's coaching staff also supports players. They're like a family that quarrels but never doubts their mutual love. Over the decade and a half when the Spurs dominated the NBA, winning two championships, one of Popovich's assistant coaches was the walking, talking embodiment of the wise-feedback note. His name is Chip Engelland.

Chip Engelland just might be the best coach you've never heard of. Players and beat writers have described him as a "genius," a "master at what he does," a "guru," a "shot doctor," and a "legend" who's "recognizable by first name alone." Chip was the captain of Duke University coach Mike Krzyzewski's first conference-championship-winning team. At the end of his international professional career, Chip broke into coaching by hosting popular—but demanding—youth shooting camps. By the late 1990s and early 2000s, word of mouth got him gigs working with NBA stars Grant Hill, Steve Kerr, and Shane Battier. After two years on staff at a few NBA teams, Chip was hired by Gregg Popovich and the San Antonio Spurs as their full-time shooting coach. During his seventeen-year tenure with the Spurs, Chip improved dozens of players' shots, including those of NBA legends Tony Parker and Kawhi Leonard, and helped them win two NBA championships. Before Parker worked with Chip, Popovich used to think

That's a turnover every time Parker shot. Now, with years of Chip's coaching, Parker is a Hall of Famer. "He's the best," Grant Hill said of Chip. "And that's why the best team has him on their bench." These days, Chip works for a rival team, the Oklahoma City Thunder, who, after two years under Chip, have boosted three-point shooting by twenty percent and doubled their win total. Chip is a one-man *Moneyball* strategy. General managers can acquire undervalued players with mediocre jump shots, and after a year or so with Chip, they become all-stars or trade assets. Wherever Chip goes, team success follows.

Does Chip only ruthlessly focus on shooters' flaws? Does he try to break down a player's shot and rebuild it from the ground up? Is he all business, impossible to please? Not in the slightest. Here's how one Thunder player, whose free-throw percentage jumped from the mid-60-percent range to the lower-80-percent range, described him:

> Chip's hard to explain. He's a wizard with what he does. It's not unorthodox, but it's different to every other coach that I've had, who's said, "Shoot this way." . . . He's not trying to change my whole shot or make one big difference. It's just little things.

In the late 1990s, Steve Kerr was the sharpshooting veteran on Michael Jordan's Bulls, but his accuracy was falling. Chip helped him realize that he was releasing the ball off his middle finger, not his pointer finger. That was causing a wobble that made his shot unreliable. Soon, Kerr was back to his three-point-splashing ways.

When Chip turned Kawhi Leonard into a superstar by fixing his shot's release point, Chip said, "I felt his shot didn't need a full makeover. With just a tune-up, he could become a very good shooter, if not great shooter." When Leonard was drafted, nobody thought he needed a tune-up. They thought he needed a whole new shot (or a spot on the bench). But Chip saw it differently. Although he was demanding—forcing Leonard to stop slinging the ball over his shoulder—he was careful to support Leonard psychologically by never disrespecting him. Leonard is now a future Hall of Famer.

Shane Battier, former NBA and NCAA champion and Duke basketball player, explained to me what it's like to be on the receiving end of Chip's wise feedback. One summer Battier was working at Duke's youth basketball camp and Chip was in town. Chip offered to put Battier through a workout. At the end, Chip said, "Your shot is good. You're a great shooter." That made an impression because at the time NBA draft experts were doubting whether Battier's shot would translate to the NBA. Although Chip saw Battier's potential, he also thought Battier could be better with a few tweaks. An instant bond was formed. "He made me believe I could become an all-NBA shooter. That gave me the confidence to work on my shot," he told me. How so? Chip didn't puff up Battier with a compliment sandwich. Chip did it with high standards. He crafted sessions that gradually increased the level of challenge while requiring Battier to maintain the exact same form, whether he was coming off a pick or receiving a pass or shooting off the dribble. Chip's main goal was to strip away unnecessary motions that made Battier's shot unpredictable from one opportunity to the next. He was ruthless in changing small details, such as the position of the pointer finger on the ball or the spread of the thumb to control the ball throughout the shot. He was unrelenting in the need to practice new mechanics in increasingly difficult gamelike situations. While doing so, Chip was exceedingly supportive. After Battier took a shot that Chip knew wasn't great, he didn't yell, *Stop, what are you doing? Do it this way!* Instead he asked, "How did that feel?" Chip respected his players' autonomy and wanted them to do the thinking because they would compete in the game, not him. Often, Chip says to his players, "Hey, it's your script, not mine; you write it. I'm just helping you see how you want to tweak it."

Sometimes, changing a shot was a stressful, nonlinear, frustrating process. Chip didn't let players quit. He assured them of his support. When Chip first started working with the Spurs' Tony Parker, he said, "I'm with you for the ups, downs, and all-arounds. I won't ditch you if it doesn't work right away." Then he critiqued Parker's shot for the next decade, and it got better. Chip takes his players seriously by expecting a lot, but he's there to support them through the process. That's why his players trust him enough to take the terrifying leap of faith needed to change their shots.

In the end, Battier developed his shot and carved out a decade-long career in the NBA, capped by a transcendent performance in the decisive game seven of the 2013 NBA finals, during which Battier made six three-pointers, handing the Miami Heat an NBA championship—against Chip's Spurs. (The Spurs got revenge the next year.) "He's much more than a shooting coach," Battier told me. "He's a basketball psychologist."

After meeting Chip, I had to agree. "The mentor's dilemma resonated with me," Chip told me. "As a coach, I'm constantly trying to get young players to take feedback without feeling threatened." Chip explained that "it's fundamentally about the balance between challenge and safety." Challenge (higher standards) helps players grow in their areas of weakness, while safety (support) helps them trust that they won't be harmed, emotionally or physically, by stretching out of their comfort zones.

Chip even took the same approach—high standards, high support—with youth players. This reveals the similarities in optimal strategies from ten to twenty-five. At his youth summer basketball camp, Chip didn't just expect kids to *do* the drills. He expected them to *lead* the drills. By Tuesday of the second week of Chip's youth camp, the players led the drills, not the coaches. They upheld the camp standards for precision and timeliness, they provided critical feedback, and they held each other accountable. Chip did this because he was trying to give them more than a jump shot. He wanted them to have their own "coaches in their heads" that could keep helping them improve long after they left the camp.

Chip showed me that practices aligned with wise feedback can work even in high-pressure situations with serious constraints on our time. Of course, it took a bit of planning for Chip to teach the players how to run the camp, but the second week was a lot easier on Chip and his coleaders. In fact, when reporting for this book, I repeatedly saw that expert managers, educators, and parents tended to have independent, resilient, proactive young people who didn't need constant redirection to stay on task. That saved the adults' time (and frustration) in the long run. When leaders used the science and art of motivating the next generation, they felt effective *and* they got the satisfaction of helping others, making their lives both easier and more fulfilling. Furthermore, they could look back on a lifetime of personal success and meaningful contributions to others. It's a win-win proposition.

Pete and Leona's Story

It was July 2019. Around 150 people had gathered for Pete Sumners's memorial service at his old office building in Lufkin, Texas. They ate barbecue and peach cobbler on plastic plates and huddled near the air conditioner. Pete's family and friends told stories of his kindness and humor. His employees talked about the jobs he had created and the careers he had elevated. They also talked about how, eighty years earlier, Pete's contributions almost didn't happen.

One Friday in November 1939, Pete loaded all his belongings into a Ford Model A and started driving home to the family farm in the small town of Conroe, Texas. At the time, he was a sixteen-year-old student at Rice University in Houston, majoring in mechanical engineering. He had decided that morning to drop out.

Just three months earlier, Pete had driven to Rice with confidence and pride. He was self-assured, cocky even. After all, he had been a football player and star student at Conroe High School, with a 94.6 GPA (out of 100) and third in his graduating class. But Rice was not Conroe. When Pete received his preliminary grades, he was shocked. He was failing five of his six classes. He wondered if he deserved to be there. Indignant and despondent, stressed and anxious, Pete saw no choice but to give up on his dream.

As Pete drove home that day in 1939, he wondered what he would say to his mother, Leona, about his decision to drop out, and what she would say in return. Leona was a firm but loving woman who had guided her family through the Great Depression. Her warm and demanding demeanor had made her one of the most beloved teachers in the Houston Independent School District. But a few years earlier Leona had developed a chronic respiratory illness after working at an asbestos factory. Her health and strength were failing. Maybe she wouldn't put up a fight, Pete thought, if he explained to her that he wasn't cut out for college after all.

Pete arrived at the farm late on Friday night. The next morning, he was in for a surprise. "She may have been sick," Pete said in an oral history interview later in life, "but this Saturday she found the strength to work me over."

Smarts had nothing to do with it, Leona exclaimed. She didn't dismiss his fears, but she also didn't accept his excuses. He would persevere, she demanded, because he had potential. But she would also collaborate with him on getting support. He was having a hard time staying organized, so she arranged for him to find lodging in Houston with a prominent doctor. The doctor was married to an old friend of hers who would make sure he stayed on track—and keep him fed. By nightfall Pete was in the car, driving back to Rice. Leona hadn't even let him stay to wash his dirty laundry.

That fateful day marked an inflection point in Pete's life trajectory, one that would be on full display at his memorial service eighty years later. Pete went back to Rice and dedicated himself to his studies. At Rice, he met his wife, Opal, to whom he was married for seventy-five years, and with whom he had a large family. After Pete graduated in 1943, he was deployed to the Pacific theater of WWII. At just twenty-one years old, he used his engineering degree to lead maintenance for a fleet of B-29 bombers on Tinian that were pivotal to the Allied victory. He wouldn't have done any of that if Leona had let him drop out.

After the war, Pete's small engineering business brought air-conditioning to homes and offices around Lufkin. Pete liked to tell stories about what life in east Texas was like before air-conditioning. The air was unbearably hot and muggy. Men often changed their shirts three, four, five times per day. To sleep, you opened the windows and hoped for a breeze. But the open windows invited an onslaught of mosquitos. Such was your daily devil's bargain. It was a revelation when Pete's engineers showed up at your home or office and hooked up central AC. Pete was proud of the comfort he'd brought to thousands in east Texas. And he could only do that because Leona's timely, tough-but-loving guidance kept him on track to becoming an engineer.

Pete's biggest contribution of all, perhaps, was what he did for his employees. Pete's handyman, Tinker, went from being an unskilled teenager to a part owner of the business. Another employee, Jimmy, experienced depression. Pete was patient with Jimmy and never fired him for being unreliable, which could have sent him into a tailspin. But Pete expected a lot of Jimmy when he was feeling well. Jimmy thanked Pete for his life.

Pete hired Janice as a secretary at seventeen, straight out of high school. He gave her responsibility and an opportunity to learn. By the time she retired forty years later, she was managing the business. At the memorial service, Janice explained that because of Pete, she gave her kids something she never got: a college education. One is now a doctor, another a lawyer. "My kids can do what they do for so many other people because of what Pete did for me," she told me. Over the years, Pete treated his employees like Leona had treated him. He held them to high expectations, but he gave them his support as well. And it changed their lives, just like Leona had changed his.

The Pete-and-Leona story represents something bigger than just a college-dropout decision. It exemplifies what adults can do for young people at any major fork in the road that leads to a better future for them and their communities.

I'm also drawn to Pete's story for a personal reason. You see, Pete was my grandfather. Leona was my great-grandmother. I never knew Leona because she died in 1941, but I am a product of her tradition. Leona is the reason why Pete met my grandmother, Opal, who gave life to my mother, who has a similar disposition and powerfully influenced me.

I was immersed in these stories growing up, but I never really understood them. We always laughed that Leona was so tough on old Pete. We focused on how harshly she enforced her high expectations. We downplayed her support. I didn't realize it until recently, but our blindness to the true meaning of Leona's actions says something profound about our culture. Our society tends to think that there are only two ways to interact with young people: tough or soft, mean or nice, authoritarian or permissive. We don't realize that you can have a bit of both: you can have high standards *and* high support, like the wise-feedback note. Because we don't realize that, we often emulate only half of what Leona did—either kick her son out or lavish him with free housing. Then, because we get it only half-right, we miscommunicate with young people, preventing them from fulfilling their potential. It's an infuriating cycle. What if we could break out of it?

That day in Lufkin at Pete's office, talking to Janice, my journey of learning became personal. I became determined to find the Leonas and the Petes of the world. I wanted to study their secrets. I would scour workplaces, homes, schools, and scientific journals to find out: How do the best managers, parents, and educators get the most out of young people, pushing them to be the best without crushing their spirits? I wrote this book to share what I've learned.

Note that I'm on the same journey of learning as you are. I need this information as well. I manage young people in my research lab. I'm a parent of four, with the oldest just starting her teenage years. I coach baseball and basketball. I used to teach middle schoolers and now I teach in college. I've tried all the ideas in this book. Although I can't say I did them perfectly, I can promise that on the occasions when I got them right, it was worth it.

Those of us on this journey want actual, practical knowledge of how to interact effectively with young people. That's why, for each chapter, I've written questions and suggestions for how to take the ideas and put them into practice. They appear sequentially at the end of the book.

With that, I'd like to welcome you to your continuing education about the wonderful, vexing, and inspiring world of motivating and influencing young people.

Section I

Understanding
Ten-to-Twenty-Five-Year-Olds

Chapter 1

What We Get Wrong

Terrie's Deathbed

This hospital room in Winston-Salem, North Carolina, was normally reserved for patients on end-of-life care, but on September 8, 2013, it was used as a makeshift video-production studio. The U.S. Centers for Disease Control and Prevention (CDC) had come to record the parting advice of a woman, Terrie Hall, who would die of cancer two days later. In 2000, Terrie Hall found a small sore on the inside of her cheek. A biopsy showed that it was a tumor, and further testing showed the cancer had already spread from her mouth to her throat. Over the next thirteen years Terrie would undergo radiation therapy, chemotherapy, and surgeries that would remove parts of her jaw and her larynx (voice box), leaving her in need of an electronic prosthetic larynx to speak. She used this raw, wheezing, synthetic voice to share her final lessons with the CDC and the world.

Terrie developed cancer because she was addicted to cigarettes. Like 90 percent of adult smokers, she became hooked before she was eighteen. "I had my first cigarette at age thirteen, and age seventeen is when I really started being a regular smoker," she said. In 1964, the U.S. Office of the Surgeon General had released a blockbuster report titled *Smoking and Health*, which informed the world that smoking was, globally, the leading cause of cancer and cancer-related deaths. It was a lost battle for the tobacco companies, but they were winning the war. They had invested millions in making smoking look cool. There was the Marlboro Man—a rugged cowboy who tamed the wild terrain, always with a cigarette in hand—and Joe Camel—a classy, "smooth character" who lived the high life surrounded by beautiful women and a cloud of smoke. When the government said that smoking was *dangerous*, it may have helped the tobacco companies' situation. It showed teenagers that smoking was a way to be rebellious and win the admiration of their peers.

As a junior at Forbush High School in 1977, Terrie was a popular cheerleader, constantly invited to parties. Her friends smoked, and she wanted to be with them, so she started smoking too. "It was the cool thing to do," she told the CDC. Soon she was smoking two packs a day, every day, for decades, until her larynx was surgically removed. On her deathbed, she said, "My fear now is that I won't be around to see my grandchildren graduate or get married." And she lamented that "this [raspy synthetic voice] is the only voice my grandson knows. I miss being able to sing lullabies to him." But Terrie was also full of purpose. She wanted the future to be different. She hoped, she prayed, that the CDC or anyone else listening might come up with a better way to prevent young people from ending up like her.

In 1998, after a landmark legal decision against the tobacco industry, the tobacco companies were pressured by the federal government to launch anti-smoking advertisements on television, in newspapers and magazines, on billboards, and on the radio. Suddenly, the same advertising agencies that had made millions coming up with ways to get teens to smoke were charged with doing the opposite. One campaign's tagline said, "Think. Don't smoke." Another tagline said, "Tobacco is whacko if you're a teen." Everyone expected that the more teens saw these ads, the less likely they would be to smoke. But that's not what they found. When a rigorous independent study evaluated the tobacco companies' campaigns, they found that "Think. Don't smoke" and "Tobacco is whacko" caused young people to be *more* likely to think that smoking was cool and rebellious, to think *more* favorably of the tobacco companies, and to trust the companies *more* to look after their health. The anti-smoking campaigns also made teens *more likely to try smoking*. Public health experts were baffled, and the tobacco companies continued making money.

Anti-tobacco programs aren't the only efforts that flop. Did you know that the most common effect of anti-obesity programs for young people is weight *gain* compared to those who didn't get a program? And did you know that antibullying programs for late middle school and high school students tend to *increase* bullying? As a society, we want to target those age groups to prevent extreme events like suicide or school violence, but the most common programs either backfire or prove useless.

If we want to help the millions of people like Terrie who suffer for decades due to preventable choices made by their younger selves, then we need to confront our society's inability to understand and influence young people. The overwhelming failure of so many of our society's youth-serving programs should be a sign that we need to look more deeply at our fundamental mental models about young people. We owe it to young people to ask the hard question: What if the problem has more to do with us—and how we treat the next generation—than it has to do with who they are?

Taking Your Pills

Dr. Steven Alexander has been a professor of pediatrics for decades at Stanford University's number-one-ranked youth kidney transplant center in the United States. When I met him not long ago, he told me about a fascinating set of challenges his nephrology clinic was facing.

Like all medical professionals involved in kidney transplants, Dr. Alexander is a merchant of happiness and freedom. The kidneys filter out the toxins in your body that you normally excrete through urination. When kidneys lose their function, you need to use a dialysis machine to filter those fluids instead. You endure this agonizing treatment three times per week, for three and a half hours per day. The day before dialysis you're puffy and short of breath because your body cavities are filled with waste liquids. On the day of dialysis, you suffer the pain of having gallons of waste drained out of you. When Alexander's clinic gets you a kidney transplant, you're finally freed from the chains of the dialysis machine, capable at last of living a mostly normal life.

When Dr. Alexander started in nephrology in 1976, the transplant procedure was still new. Children and adolescents rarely kept their transplanted kidneys for very long. Back then, fewer than 30 percent of children lived for three years or longer. Now the survival rate after three years is closer to 95 percent. The medical profession has spent billions developing new surgical techniques and medications, they have created a vast infrastructure to keep organs viable long enough to make it to a recipient, and they have trained world-class surgeons. The most important discovery of all was highly effective drugs to prevent the body from rejecting the transplanted kidney. These drugs, called immunosuppressants, stop the immune system's attacks on a new kidney that came from someone else's body. The miracle of taking an organ out of one person and sewing it into the body of a child in need has now become routine.

And yet, every year, scores of Dr. Alexander's patients lose transplanted kidneys when they shouldn't. The reason why is simple to diagnose but hard to solve: *doctors can't get ten-to-twenty-five-year-old patients to take their immunosuppressant pills regularly.*

"I think I'm so clear, as clear as can be, and then two weeks later, they're taking their pills completely wrong," one exasperated doctor told me.

"Surgeons would have a record of one hundred percent kidney survival if they could get the young people to take their meds," Alexander told me. Indeed, a study of every transplant in the United States to date showed that kidney rejection is almost at zero for children under ten years old because their parents make them take their pills. But every year from age ten to seventeen, when young people seize more freedom and autonomy, rejection rates inch up. The rates stay high until age twenty-five, when they start going back down dramatically. Thus, ten to twenty-five are the problem years.

Here's a story I once heard from a nurse at Stanford's pediatric nephrology clinic. She called parents of patients whose blood tests indicated problems. The nurse would say, "Your son's blood tests say there is zero medication in his bloodstream, and he's having symptoms. Are you sure he's taking his medications?" She would hear the mom ask her son, "You're taking your pills, right?" followed by a loud and obnoxious "*Of course, Mom!*" from the son. The nurse would calmly explain that it's biologically impossible for the patient to show no trace of the medicine in his blood if he's taking it, unless he has a rare disorder that perfectly and completely metabolizes the medicine before it works. In either scenario, the patient would need to come into the clinic immediately for further testing. After a long pause, the nurse would hear the mother come back on and say, "Okay, he told me he's not taking the meds. He'll start. Thanks for calling."

Parents may be compassionate, but kidneys are not. Without the immunosuppressant, the body starts to reject the kidney within a day. "Kidney transplants are unforgiving. You absolutely must take immuno-suppression every day," Alexander explained to me. After a few days the transplanted kidney is rejected by the body. The young person goes back on dialysis for years—or forever.

This isn't just Dr. Alexander's problem. In fact, 35 to 45 percent of all adolescents and young adults who receive transplants—kidneys, livers, hearts, stem cells—don't take their pills as prescribed. And this problem hasn't gotten better over time, despite improved surgical techniques and medication. A prominent physician recently reviewed the entire history of pediatric kidney transplants and reached a dismal conclusion: "We appear to be no closer to solving the problem of nonadherence than we were forty years ago. . . . It remains a critical and often unsurmountable detriment" to transplant survival. When it comes to changing the behavior of young people during the critical window of ten to twenty-five, medicine has not delivered results. What's going on?

One clue comes from deeper reflection on the flaws in the "Think. Don't smoke" and "Tobacco is whacko" anti-smoking campaigns. Both campaigns tell youth what to do (i.e., "Don't smoke" is a command). That's potentially a poor fit with how adolescents want to feel at a neurobio-logical level. Likewise, transplant-education sessions involve telling, telling, telling. Doctors, nurses, and pharmacists hold three separate conversations with young patients and their parents. The authority figures describe the consequences of not taking the immunosuppressant pills and make the young person repeat everything back to them, like a comprehension quiz. It's the young person's job to listen and obey.

"You don't get educated on how to talk to adolescents," one experi-enced doctor told me. "Doctors are trained to communicate scientific in-formation, not pay attention to what's stopping humans from acting on the information. So everything we say comes across as a threat, like, 'If you don't do this, then I'm going to have to increase your meds.'" Indeed, one transplant recipient gave a keynote to doctors and nurses at a professional conference. "The doctors tried many fear tactics on me," he said. "It didn't work." He lost his first kidney and was by then on his second.

The limited scope of this conversation could come across as disrespectful to young people because it fails to seriously address how the medication will affect the patients. "I hated the pills. I didn't seem to take my pills seriously," one transplant recipient said. "People don't realize how hard it is to take your medication twice a day," another patient told me.

Here are some of the side effects of immunosuppressants: diarrhea, weight gain, numbness, and a fruity smell on your breath. "One of them made me hairy," a patient told me. "I kind of looked like a werewolf and had a unibrow." Another told me, "I feel like I'm a fat kid. I can't take my shirt off with a girl." Oh, and the doctor tells you not to drink alcohol. Think about how those side effects conflict with your plans for a teenage social life. The kidney doctor with a clipboard and a white lab coat was telling you to accept your new life, with no objections, as an overweight, hairy kid with digestive problems, numb extremities, and stinky breath who can't party and is embarrassed to swim shirtless. Skipping the pills—and their side effects—allows a young patient to temporarily forget that they're different. It gives them a way to feel socially normal, however briefly.

The medication itself, therefore, is a potential threat to social survival. Maybe some young people do listen. Many others nod along, making their body language look like they're listening, but they're faking it. Their neurons are not processing the information. This is a reason why the standard patient-education process doesn't always convince young people to adjust their habits and routines so that they take their medication seriously.

And that is why, after billions of dollars spent over the last forty years to turn the miracle of pediatric organ transplants into a routine surgical procedure, the single biggest unsolved scientific puzzle has nothing to do with nephrons or the immune system. It has everything to do with navigating the complex world of adolescent behavior change.

Dr. David Rosenthal, a pediatric heart-transplant doctor at Stanford University, told me that his experience working with teenagers makes him feel that he is "living in an alternative universe from my patients. I cannot imagine what they're thinking." Likewise, Dr. Steven Alexander warned that "we need to understand what young people need and give them what they need—or get ready to pay the consequences."

Questioning Our Model of Young People

Failed attempts to motivate and influence young people—like "Think. Don't smoke" or the conventional patient-education approach in most transplant clinics—come from what I call the *neurobiological-incompetence model*. According to this model, a young person is a flawed and deficient thinker who can't comprehend the future consequences of their actions. Thus, young people need to be told what to think and do repeatedly by adults who know better. Consider, for example, that the tagline "Think. Don't smoke" is a command from a supposedly wiser and smarter and more responsible adult public health expert, implying that young people aren't currently thinking.

Over the last two decades, a scientific revolution has been brewing in the study of young people. It's pushed back against the neurobiological-incompetence model. This revolution asserts that youth are not *problems to be managed* but instead are *resources to be cultivated*. This new scientific consensus was spelled out in two major reports. One was issued in 2019 by the National Academies of Sciences, Engineering, and Medicine titled *The Promise of Adolescence*. Another more digestible summary was issued around the same time by the UCLA Center for the Developing Adolescent (CDA) and the FrameWorks Institute. Combined, the reports pulled insights from more than twenty-five leading neuroscientists, hormone experts, psychologists, anthropologists, and more.

The UCLA report explained why much of the behavior of young people that worries or annoys us does not come from ten-to-twenty-five-year-olds being inherently incompetent. Rather it comes from this age group's attempt to learn how to be socially successful in the world. This usually means having social standing in the eyes of their peer groups and their communities' adult authorities. Said differently, young people want *status and respect from peers and mentors*, earned by making meaningful contributions. This suggests that if we can understand their perspectives and what they really want, then the same motivational drives that lead to problematic behaviors such as smoking, unhealthy eating habits, or bullying can be channeled instead into important contributions to our organizations, families, schools, and society.

Dr. Ron Dahl, a University of California, Berkeley physician and neuroscience researcher and cofounder of the Center for the Developing Adolescent, likes to tell a story to illustrate the main takeaway of the landmark UCLA report. The story involves a discussion he had with a diverse group of education scholars, including the Dalai Lama and scholars in Tibetan Buddhist traditions. After Dahl shared some of the emerging insights from the science about puberty and adolescents' increased motivation to gain status and respect, he heard them chuckle. Through the translator Dahl learned that they often observed young boys demonstrating a hilarious version of the hunt for status and respect. In the Buddhist monastery, the best way to gain prestige and respect is by showing kindness, compassion, and empathy. This led youth to try to outdo each other in these values. I imagine them saying, *After you! No, after you!*, each trying to one-up the others' loving-kindness. This was an example where the boys had discerned the cultural currency of status and respect—living a principled spiritual life in service of others. They were intrinsically motivated to distinguish themselves and earn prestige that garners the respect of their community, considering the values of the group. This shows that puberty isn't destructive; it's instructive. It fuels young people's desire to become contributing members of the group. "We shouldn't fear puberty. We should help youth learn to harness it for good," Dahl told me.

Interestingly, one of the best illustrations of this new scientific consensus comes from one of the only public health efforts to have ever shifted smoking behavior: the "Truth" campaign.

The "Truth" Campaign

One day in the spring of 1998, the public health establishment's old guard faced off against the new guard in a meeting that would ultimately drastically improve one of the United States' longest-standing public health crises.

The meeting was called by officials from the state of Florida, who were trying to select an advertising agency for a multimillion-dollar campaign to reduce teenage smoking. The money would come from a settlement to a class action lawsuit between Florida and the tobacco companies, as compensation for the cost to the state of treating smokers for cancer.

On one side of the conference room sat a platoon of conventionally trained government epidemiologists, the scientists who specialize in stopping the spread of diseases. The old guard had been invited to make sure that the winning ad agency upheld the CDC's so-called *approved strategy* for stemming the tide of teenage smoking. Across the table sat Alex Bogusky, the creative director at then-upstart advertising agency Crispin Porter + Bogusky, which was trying to win the business. The leader of the new guard, Bogusky was in his midthirties but looked ten years younger. He wore an impish grin, and the twinkle in his eye gave the impression that a wild idea lurked just around the corner. His frame was fit and lean from decades of mountain biking and other adventure sports. Next to Bogusky sat his artistic directors, all in their early twenties.

What was the CDC's approved strategy? It involved three messages for teenagers: (1) smoking causes cancer, (2) smoking makes your teeth yellow, and (3) smoking isn't sexy. The CDC wanted Bogusky's ads to drill this information into as many teenage heads as possible.

This approved strategy was the result of the epidemiologists' hyperrational way of thinking about youth behavior, rooted in classical economic thinking. In this model, people decide something by weighing the relative costs and benefits, as well as an outcome's likelihood and the time horizon. That is, if teenagers thought that smoking gave them a near-certain likelihood of a benefit in the immediate term (e.g., a nicotine buzz) but a very unlikely cost in the long term (e.g., cancer), then they would tend to choose to smoke. From this perspective, the appropriate public health response is to (1) make long-term costs seem far more certain (e.g., smokers would definitely get cancer) and (2) make near-term costs also seem more certain, such as changes to the teenager's appearance (yellow teeth) or social life (unsexiness).

Bogusky thought this whole theory—and the CDC's implementation of it—was doomed to fail. Weeks earlier, he had sent his young art directors undercover to skate parks and malls to test out the CDC's approved strategy. Fully 100 percent of the teens they talked to could already eloquently describe, lit cigarette in hand, how smoking caused emphysema and cancer. They didn't need someone to explain that. Were they worried about yellow teeth? Maybe when they were fifty! But not now. And by the way, smoking seemed to them to be a main reason why they were having lots and lots of sex. Smoking made their lives great! This research showed Bogusky that even if his ad campaign brought the CDC's approved strategy to millions, it wouldn't stop teens from smoking. It was conveying information that they either already knew to be true or already knew to be false. Not only was it redundant, it was also insulting. Telling a teenager something that they think they already know—especially when it's an adult doing it "for their own good"—comes across as an affront to their autonomy and competence. It's disrespectful.

Back in the conference room, Bogusky watched his words carefully. His firm needed the work. They were small but talented, working with midlevel clients to sell mountain bikes or shoes. The Florida anti-teen-smoking campaign had the potential to be a multimillion-dollar breakthrough. The approved strategy was throwing a wrench in Bogusky's plans, however. It wasn't just bland—it was harmful. "This is a double cross from the tobacco companies," Bogusky told the Florida team. "It's a backhanded way for the companies to hire me to increase smoking." He said this because the tobacco settlement had one stipulation: the money had to be spent on *telling kids not to smoke.* Bogusky thought that strategy would drive millions of teens to smoke *more*, putting the money back into the tobacco companies' pockets. "If that's how you're spending the settlement money, I don't want to be a part of it," Bogusky told them.

Bogusky said this because he noticed a far more subtle, but just as fatal, flaw in the CDC's approved strategy. As far as Bogusky could tell, it was not informed by what young people wanted. Usually the first question ad executives ask themselves is: Do people already want the product, or do they not? There is a reason why cars, beer, and fast food are the crown jewels of most ad executives' portfolios. These are products that most people already want. The ad just needs to give them permission to buy them, and everybody makes money. Ad campaigns to get people to take health precautions, by contrast, aren't nearly as successful, for the simple reason that most people don't want to take health precautions. The CDC's approved strategy was encouraging teenagers to use self-control to deny themselves something they wanted. Bogusky, and any ad executive worth their salt, knew that a self-denial strategy would lose every time to a strategy geared toward giving people permission to pursue what their hearts most desired.

Bogusky suspected that the CDC experts had no idea what teenagers wanted out of smoking. Therefore they had no idea how to give them an alternative that could displace smoking. That's why he prodded them, "Have any of you ever asked a teenager why they smoked—like, what they got out of it?" They were silent. Bogusky was disappointed, but he understood why. "They thought teenagers were dumb," he told me. The CDC experts were coming from what we now know to be the neurobiological-incompetence model—like most public health experts at the time. In that model, the only reason a young person would choose the long-term certain harm (e.g., cancer) over long-term certain health is because of incompetent decision-making. In this view, the teenage brain was myopic, unable to weigh long-term risk correctly. It wouldn't matter *why* they made irrational choices. It simply mattered that they were carrying out their mental utility-maximization calculations incorrectly. According to this model, any new ad campaign should feature adults telling them what choice to make.

Bogusky's starting assumption was different. He thought, fundamentally, that teens were smart. They only smoked, he reasoned, because the companies had found a way to present smoking to them as a solution to a problem they cared about. A key fact driving his logic was that about 30 percent of Americans smoked at the time, and just like Terrie Hall about 90 percent of them had started when they were teenagers. Further, most adults wanted to quit but couldn't because of their addictions. Thus, Bogusky and his team concluded that smoking must have met a uniquely *adolescent* need, not an adult one. After all, most adults didn't want to be doing it.

What was that adolescent need? In Bogusky's analysis, smoking served as a public, visible way for young people to declare their adultlike status.

As young people moved from an age at which all their decisions were made for them into an age at which they took charge, teen smokers wanted to communicate to anyone around them that *I make my own decisions about my own body*. The tobacco companies understood this on a deep level. They knew—and used marketing research to confirm—that smoking shows the world that you are in total control of your life and death. Therefore you have the status and rights afforded to adults. The fact that smoking could kill you in the distant future didn't make teens feel dumb. It made them feel like courageous advocates of their right to self-determination.

Anthropologists like to point out that our human ancestors often had ceremonies—rites of passage—in which youth declare, in front of their communities, that they were adults. Outside of a few religious and cultural traditions, modern society has lost the rite of passage ceremony. But that doesn't mean that the underlying need that it served in our evolutionary past has been erased. Smoking filled that void. "Cigarettes were the best product ever to meet teens' needs to demonstrate their status as adults," Bogusky told me. "Once we understood that, we were like: *Why wasn't the teen smoking rate one hundred percent?*"

This helps explain why the conventional anti-smoking strategy would never work. You can't tell a young person to ignore their vital need to demonstrate their competence and status in front of the people whose opinions they care about any more than you can tell a baby to stop being hungry or needing to sleep. If you want to prevent the problematic behavior, you need a replacement that meets the need underlying the behavior. That realization never occurred to the CDC experts. They were blinded by a simplified rational-actor model.

Bogusky assembled a new approach. He would embolden youth to fight back against the greedy, predatory corporate forces that lured teens into a deadly addiction. "If we were to turn the tables on tobacco, we surmised that we could not take away their tool of rebellion without giving them an alternative," CP+B's president, Jeffrey Hicks, wrote in a 2001 article. "Attacking the duplicity and manipulation of the tobacco industry became 'truth's' rebellion." That day in Miami, like a scene out of *Mad Men*, Bogusky pitched a brilliant series of ads. The "Truth" campaign, as he wanted to call it, would depict young people exposing the lies of the tobacco companies, acting as passionate agents of change who wanted to be forces for good. The suits from the CDC, so entrenched in the rational-actor model from economics, responded with skepticism. "How do you know it will work?" they asked. "I can't guarantee it will work," Bogusky told them, "but I can guarantee that everything you're planning on doing now will backfire." He got the green light.

One of Bogusky's first "Truth" commercials in Florida showed actors portraying tobacco executives stalking the halls of a hospital on their way to thank a customer who, like Terrie, was on their deathbed. The executives in the commercial wonder aloud, "What are we going to do to replace you?" The executives then turn and stare longingly and creepily at a teenage girl in the waiting room. Another commercial asked, "What's the connection between a fifty-one-year-old executive and a bunch of teenagers?" Then they cut to a boardroom full of middle-aged executives saying, "They're our only source of replacement." An initial evaluation found that Bogusky's Florida "Truth" commercials reduced middle schoolers' smoking rates by 19 percent and high schoolers' by 8 percent.

One year after the Florida lawsuit was settled, all fifty states signed a master settlement agreement with the tobacco companies, which created a billion-dollar fund to support continued anti-smoking advertising, institutionalizing "Truth" into a lasting initiative. Soon CP+B was making national ads that ran on MTV and during the Super Bowl. The money again had to be spent on telling teens not to smoke, but the settlement added a new stipulation. The ads could not personally attack the tobacco executives. Bogusky's creative talent got to work. Soon they developed the "Truth" campaign's most well-known ads. One depicted twelve hundred young people outside a major tobacco company's high-rise tower. On cue, the young people dropped to the ground, looking dead. The camera panned over the motionless bodies. Silence. Then one young person dramatically held up a sign saying, *Tobacco kills 1200 people a day.* He told the tobacco companies to "tak[e] a day off."

The "Truth" campaign was a stroke of genius. They took the marketing tactic that got teens to start smoking and flipped the script. If a teenager refused to smoke, it didn't mean they were doing what grown-ups said.

It was showing the world they were a rebellious and autonomous person worthy of an adultlike status. By rejecting cigarettes, they could fight back against injustice and protect the vulnerable by joining a chorus of hundreds of peers who approved of them. The campaign ensured that the underlying adolescent needs for belonging, connection, status, and respect were fulfilled by a healthy behavior (not smoking) rather than an unhealthy one (smoking).

Think about how "Truth" signals respect for young people in a way that "Think. Don't smoke" doesn't. The latter has an insulting implication that the problem is young people's inability to think clearly. The "Truth" ads, by contrast, depicted young people as the only ones who could think clearly enough to fight back against the manipulation that the establishment failed to protect them from. Adults who stand on the sidelines are complicit in a horrifying scheme perpetrated by the tobacco companies, which kills thousands of Terries annually.

When researchers evaluated the national "Truth" campaign, they found striking results. Wherever the ads played, teenagers' desires to try or continue smoking declined. Crucially, the campaign made young people think that smoking wasn't cool—the only approach to have ever done so. These attitude changes translated into better public health outcomes. Starting with the launch of the "Truth" campaign, teen smoking rates declined every year, from about 28 percent to under 6 percent. Teen smoking was almost eliminated as a public health problem. To this day, public health experts consider the "Truth" campaign to be (along with seat belt ads in the 1970s) one of the two most successful public health efforts in U.S. history.

What lessons can we take from the story of the "Truth" campaign? It shows that young people can in fact make choices that are good for their long-term health if we give them a route to status and respect. "Young people are not idiots," the current CEO of the "Truth" initiative told me. "They make decisions about what's valuable to them, so it's our job to make nonsmoking a valuable decision, on their terms." Instead of trying to get young people to care less about status or respect and more about their long-term self-interest, we should spend more time figuring out how to present choices to them in a way that aligns with the social rewards they already value.

The "Truth" campaign raises the possibility that similar solutions could prove effective for other challenges that adults face with adolescents, perhaps even medication adherence. As parents, educators, and managers, we are perennially frustrated with young people who don't keep themselves safe, do their homework, or take the initiative at work. But what if we could choose a different way? The answer to that question comes from a scientific revolution in the science of young people.

A Scientific Revolution

Dr. Ron Dahl is one of the leading minds in the science of adolescence. He may be in his midfifties, but he acts young at heart—brimming with energy, and daring to raise big questions that nobody else would touch, a lot like the adolescents he specializes in. Dahl has spent decades conducting research on the basic workings of the adolescent brain. But he can hardly keep himself from bouncing from human neuroscience to animal research on puberty to the cultural anthropology of adolescence in preindustrial societies to the behavioral experiments in my research. Dahl's eclectic and driven style of research is partially the result of experiences from his youth. He grew up in a working-class family in Kane, Pennsylvania, over one hundred miles from any major city. His brother went down a tragic path of addiction, but Dahl didn't. He attributes this in part to the influence of a mentor in high school, his humanities teacher Arlene Heath. She lived and breathed the wise-feedback note, demanding excellence and having vigorous debates with him but always caring for him. For thirty years until she died in her nineties, she wrote him letters to challenge him to think more broadly, beyond the boundaries of science, and to ask the bigger questions about what it means to be human. Dahl dislikes the negative incompetence view of adolescence in part because he knows how young people can be inspired and empowered by mentors like Arlene.

Dahl cofounded the Center for the Developing Adolescent with colleagues like Dr. Adriana Galván at UCLA to spread a more accurate—and optimistic—science of adolescence. (I am a member of the center's scientific steering committee.) Dahl, Galván, and the rest of the scientists at the Center for the Developing Adolescent are on a mission to explain why the neurobiological-incompetence model is wrong—and how to use this more accurate view of youth to better society.

According to the incompetence model, young people's brains are incapable of correctly weighing the future consequences of their behaviors—such as how an impulsive action now could lead to poorer health later. In this model, young people lack working prefrontal cortices, which is the part of the brain that controls planning. What's more, their brains are swimming in hormones that make them impulsive and ready to jump on any short-term pleasure or avoid any short-term pain, regardless of the long-term consequences. Young people's feeble prefrontal cortices, according to the incompetence model, are no match for their appetites for reward. A popular metaphor for this model suggests that young people are driving a car that's "all gas" (a hormone-induced, neural impulse for reward) with "no brakes" (lacking a reasonable brain that can stop the impulse). Due to this supposed lack of a prefrontal cortex, it's unwise to ask young people to make consequential decisions that could affect their future.

The incompetence model has ancient roots. Plato wrote in the *Phaedrus* in the fourth century BCE that the process of transitioning from youth into mature adulthood is like a charioteer struggling to control two powerful winged horses, like Pegasus. In this metaphor, the charioteer represents our reason or logic, and the unruly horses our passions. According to Plato, we must learn to discipline and suppress our youthful passions, and only then can we ascend to the heavens and see what is true, good, and beautiful. The basic contours of Plato's argument persisted for centuries and were later adopted by neuroscientists. By the turn of the twenty-first century, our prefrontal cortices took the place of the charioteer and our limbic systems symbolized the unruly team of horses to be controlled. "The prefrontal [cortex] became the aspiration for how adolescents should develop," Galván told me.

A key actor in this intellectual history was the MacArthur Foundation Network on Adolescent Development and Juvenile Justice. Started in 1995 and continuing until 2017, this was a network of leading neuroscientists, developmental scientists, and legal scholars. They were brought together for a noble purpose. They aimed to reverse a trend, started in the 1990s, toward increasingly harsh and punitive sentencing for severe crimes committed by youth under eighteen, such as the death penalty or life without parole. Such sentences rested on an assumption that the adolescent's brain would not continue to mature later in adulthood. The MacArthur network argued that the adolescent brain was still maturing and that irreversible punishments (e.g., the death penalty or life without parole) should not apply to teenagers because they should be withheld for people who are fully responsible for their actions. The network's research explained how "adolescent immaturity in higher-order executive functions such as impulse control, planning ahead and risk avoidance" was no match for the emotional, impulsive reward-sensitive regions of the brain. A 2012 Supreme Court amicus curiae brief summarizing the network's research described the "relative deficit in mature self-control" among young people and concluded that "expecting the experience-based ability to resist impulses . . . to be fully formed prior to age eighteen or nineteen would seem on present evidence to be wishful thinking." With this evidence, the MacArthur network successfully lobbied the Supreme Court to change federal policy about sentencing juveniles to the death penalty and later life without parole, first in 2005 (*Roper v. Simmons*), then in 2010 (*Graham v. Florida*), and later in 2012 (*Miller v. Alabama*). The neurobiological-incompetence model, therefore, could be used for good, even though it wasn't the whole story.

The MacArthur network's take on the adolescent brain soon spread beyond the narrow use case of adolescent criminal sentencing. It was applied to any and every youth decision-making process. One kidney transplant doctor I talked to heard a presentation on the network's research. He soon concluded that asking an adolescent to use their prefrontal cortex to remember to take their immunosuppressants "is like asking someone without triceps to do pushups—it's impossible." Outside of the legal context, the incompetence model urges adults to try to take control of young people since we can't trust their judgment. The same kidney doctor joked that we should just implant a chip in young patients' brains to remind them to take their meds, and shock them if they don't, to make up for the hole where their prefrontal cortex is supposed to be. That's the incompetence model taken to its logical conclusion.

Was the MacArthur network's incompetence model founded on solid evidence? One key study in support of it came from none other than Adriana Galván. In Galván's well-known 2006 study, she and her colleagues scanned the brain activity of thirty-six children, adolescents, and adults as they made gambles to get small, medium, or large financial rewards. When the adolescents won large rewards, the reward-sensitivity regions of their brains lit up more than any other age group. The region of the brain implicated in planning for the future (the prefrontal cortex) didn't show the same activation. This finding has taken on a legendary status in the field. It seemed to show a maturational imbalance in which the adolescent brain is hijacked by a lust for rewards to the detriment of the rational, temperate parts of the brain. Galván stands by the study's results but no longer thinks the field has interpreted them correctly. Her study didn't show that adolescents have a puberty-induced frontal lobotomy. "Of course adolescents have prefrontal cortices," Galván told me. The prefrontal cortex helps you with goal-directed behavior, "and young people are really good at goal-directed behavior."

Think about it. Young people do lots of complex things—they learn calculus, they become elite athletes and compete in the Olympics, they figure out how to get their crushes to fall in love with them, and they master new trends, technologies, and programming languages months or years before adults. These skills require functioning prefrontal cortices. Even "deviant" behavior takes planning. Do you remember making plans to sneak out, organize a house party, or hide something from your parents? If you were like most teens, you were like Patton in the European theater. Likewise, teens who smoke must clear many logistical hurdles. They need to own and remember a lighter; they have to convince a twenty-one-year-old to buy them cigarettes; they have to hide the evidence, wash the scent out of their clothes, and more. These accomplishments—good and bad—would be impossible without a functioning prefrontal cortex.

In newer laboratory experiments, Galván explained, young people often do *better* at goal-directed behavior than adults, when incentive structures are right. "They're not always deploying their prefrontal cortices in ways that adults want them to," Galván explained, "because they've got different motivational priorities." Specifically, young people value social rewards—experiences like status and respect—from both peers and adults.

When they sense that their social status and respect are under threat, or when they see a route to feeling more like socially valuable people, then they switch what they pay attention to more rapidly than adults do later in life. These newer studies made this discovery in part because they broadened their view of what a reward is. Foundational studies like Galván's in the early 2000s involved a financial gamble as a reward when the participants were humans. When the participants were rats or hamsters they involved hedonic rewards such as sugar water or cocaine. Hedonic rewards are very different from complex social emotions such as pride, belonging, shame, or humiliation. Once neuroscientists (including Galván's students) started experimenting with social rewards, then a far more complex pattern of evidence began to emerge. Ultimately it showed important prefrontal abilities in adolescents who were properly motivated.

The Parental-Nagging Study

Kevin is in his early twenties, and he's on his second kidney transplant. When asked what it's like to be a teenager needing to take his meds twice daily, he was quick to say that his main memory was of his mom yelling at him. He didn't like this because he already felt guilty enough. He felt bad that his aunt gave up her kidney for him, and he worried that his expensive medications were a financial burden on his single mother. When his mom told him to do something he already felt guilty about, he said "It feels like an accusation, like a lack of trust." Did it motivate him to be independent? Take his medications? "Not at all," he told me.

Kevin's experiences were consistent with the results of a study that Ron Dahl published in 2014 with Jennifer Silk and a team of researchers at the University of Pittsburgh. Their landmark study answered a simple yet profound question: What happens in the teenage brain when you're being nagged by your parents?

Silk and her team brought a few dozen healthy boys and girls aged nine to seventeen into the research laboratory to have their brains scanned in a functional magnetic resonance imaging machine, or fMRI. The fMRI is a machine that can detect which parts of your brain are engaged at what time and which parts of your brain are tuning out. (It does this by detecting changes in blood flow in regions that reflect different patterns of neural activity.) The week before the study, the subjects' mothers recorded themselves completing this sentence: "One thing that bothers me about you is . . ." The researchers took these clips and played the one for each subject while the fMRI magnet circled their brain. Here's an example of what a teenager heard from their mom:

> One thing that bothers me about you is that you get upset over minor issues. I could tell you to take your shoes from downstairs. You'll get mad that you have to pick them up and actually walk upstairs and put them in your room. You'll get mad if I tell you that your room is a little dirty, and it just needs sweeping and dusting. You get upset if your sisters want to do something that you don't agree on but three of them do, and you don't want to do it. You get upset too easily, and you just need to calm that down.

Imagine that you're a teenager. Then try reading this out loud. Your hormones are raging. Your mom is constantly on your case. And she says to you, *You just need to calm that down*. How would you feel? You might feel angry, disrespected, and offended. It diminishes your feelings, telling you that you shouldn't feel the way you feel. Your mother's attitude also threatens your autonomy, treating you like a child who just needs to do as they're told. Young people hate being made to feel like that.

What did the brain-activation data show? Silk and Dahl's team found that during the parental nagging, the regions of the brain that were associated with feeling intense emotions were on fire (more blood flow in the lentiform nucleus and the posterior insula), a neural signature showing that the youth were angry. How about the thinking-and-planning region of the brain (the dorsilateral prefrontal cortex, DLPFC) and the region of the brain related to listening to a speaker and inferring their meaning (the temporoparietal junction, TPJ)? In a perfect world, those regions would be lighting up more, which would signal that the subjects were listening to the criticism, processing it, and planning out how to respond. But the opposite happened. The planning regions of the brain showed dramatically lower activation, suggesting there were no plans to do what the parent

Figure 1.1. The parental-nagging study's results.

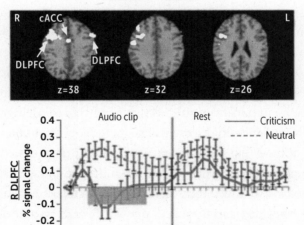

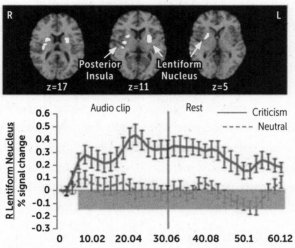

said. The "mind-reading" regions (the TPJ) showed lower activation, suggesting the youth weren't trying to understand what their parents really wanted from them. Thus, the parental nagging triggered no listening or planning how to change—only fury and frustration.

Interestingly, the researchers also had the young people in the same study listen to their mothers talk in a more neutral tone. No accusations, no diminishment, no controlling demands. When that happened, the brain scans of the young people looked fine. They took in the information, and their thinking-and-planning brain regions were engaged. That is, their brains performed competently when their mothers talked to them neutrally. This is not the data you would see if their brains were biologically deficient. Instead, these are the results you'd expect to see if young people are highly responsive to whether adults speak to them disrespectfully.

Overturning the Incompetence Model

Silk and Dahl's parental-nagging study provided an interesting crack in the foundation of the neurobiological-incompetence model. It suggested that some of the perceived teenage incompetence might result from how teens respond to our words, not from a fixed biological inability to reason. But to really overturn the model, more evidence would be needed.

From 2010 to 2012, "it started to feel like this [incompetence model] couldn't be the whole story," Galván told me. The missing evidence, Galván explained, came in part from studies that were able to use newly available technology to understand the brain. The technology examined the *connectivity* in the brain—that is, the extent to which one part of the brain talked to and influenced other parts of the brain. In the old studies, an fMRI scan could only assess whether there was any activation at all—whether people used their prefrontal cortices or their reward systems more in one circumstance or another. It couldn't tell the difference between an adolescent being *incapable* of maturity versus *unmotivated* to think in a way that adults think is more mature. But new studies applying better technology—first with animal brains and later with human brains—started to show how the motivational, reward-system networks worked together with the prefrontal, planning networks. As it turned out, they were talking to each other in exactly the opposite way predicted by Plato's chariot metaphor in *Phaedrus*.

The newer evidence showed that the logical, reasoning part of the brain (the prefrontal cortex) doesn't teach the emotional and passionate regions of the brain (the limbic regions, like the nucleus accumbens) how to be more rational. Instead, the emotional regions serve as the teacher, and the prefrontal regions are the student. "Emotion is a learning tool," Galván explained to me. "It teaches you what to retreat from and what to approach; that's so important in establishing that the emotions are not secondary to the reasoning parts of the brain."

In particular, an adolescent's prefrontal regions and regions related to memory (such as the hippocampus) are focused on learning how to feel like a socially accepted and successful individual in their culture. Evidence for this came from studies showing that adolescents could show all the hallmarks of a mature, adult brain—planning ahead, weighing multiple options, accurately conducting complex value calculations—when it was for social rewards, such as helping others or looking good in front of a peer. After all, psychologists such as Erik Erikson have argued for almost a century—without neural evidence—that a central task of adolescence is to gradually become an independent social actor who can contribute to the community. One of the most noticeable effects of this developmental process is that young people become highly attuned to social status and respect.

Let's think about what this looked like in our evolutionary history. How did our ancestors survive? If you were a young person wandering the savanna, the single greatest threat to your daily survival, and to your potential to ever have children, was to be disrespected and excluded from the group. The group would only keep valuable contributors around—the ones who could hunt with the group, care for children, or acquire other resources. If our evolutionary ancestors didn't pay very close attention to what gave them status and respect in their communities, then they'd run the risk of being ostracized, which meant eventual death. As a result, what looks like a problem of neurobiological incompetence is in fact a question of *motivational prioritization*. Young people deploy their considerable cognitive resources to attend to and protect their immediate social status and respect. If the information they get from adults threatens their social survival by robbing them of the status and respect they crave, they'll likely tune it out. This isn't because they're immature. It's because it's part of learning how to survive.

Puberty drives this process. As your body starts preparing to develop sexual maturity, it pumps testosterone throughout your bloodstream, which affects many neural systems. "This spike in testosterone, in both boys and girls, contributes to adolescents' hypersensitivity to signs of social status and respect," Dahl told me. "It catalyzes the reward systems in the brain," Galván added. Of course, being disrespected feels bad at any age. But Dahl explained that the start of puberty triggers "an amplification of the salience of gaining social value. It makes it extra thrilling, and extra intense, when you're admired, respected, or loved. And it's extra painful when you're diminished and disrespected."

Anyone who has spent time with a young person aged ten to twenty-five has probably seen this hypersensitivity play out. It dramatically changes what young people pay attention to and what things mean to them. My four-year-old doesn't yell *I know, Dad!* when I ask him to put on his coat. My eleven-year-old does.

Dahl wants people to stop fearing the hormones of puberty, especially testosterone. In Shakespeare's play *The Winter's Tale*, a wise shepherd wished that "there were no age between ten and three-and-twenty, or that youth would sleep out the rest" because all youth is for is "getting [women] with child, wronging the ancientry, stealing, fighting." Sound familiar? Dahl wants to rehabilitate puberty's reputation. He thinks young people's testosterone-induced hypersensitivity to status and respect is not a design flaw in the human condition. It's a feature. It helps to motivate young people to learn and explore socially, seeking ways to contribute and gain social value. This probably aided survival throughout human history, such as learning how to navigate complex and unpredictable social groups. If, as *The Winter's Tale* suggests, we just put adolescents to sleep, how would they learn to be competent adults? They would miss out on critical aspects of social and cultural learning, and particularly the trial-and-error learning that's so crucial for growth.

To drive this point home, Dahl points to studies of songbirds. When researchers block puberty and the associated changes in testosterone from happening, the birds never go through the arduous process of learning to sing a song that will attract a mate. Then they die alone. Puberty, Dahl believes, isn't a threat to survival. It's the means of survival.

In retrospect, Galván and Dahl appreciated the contributions of the MacArthur network, but they thought it went too far in promulgating the neurobiological-incompetence model. The network didn't have to say that puberty causes adolescents to lack mature decision-making abilities. Perhaps something closer to the truth of the matter—that young people have different motivational priorities, which would likely shift as they age—could have been as effective at achieving the valuable policy goal of promoting more humane sentences for convicted youth.

The Adolescent Predicament

When society fails to appreciate the power of the situation young people are in, it leads to the neurobiological-incompetence model. This results in ineffective solutions like "Think. Don't smoke" or the same old transplant-patient-education model. Tell, tell, tell. Blame and shame. I call it *grownsplaining*. Bogusky calls it the *tale of woe*. But when we understand young people's situational predicaments, then we can feel more compassion for them. That helps us come up with more effective solutions, like Bogusky did with the "Truth" campaign.

What is the powerful situation that young people are in? It's what I call the *adolescent predicament*. This is simply defined as the mismatch between young people's neurobiological needs for status and respect and the level of status or respect afforded to them by their current circumstances (e.g., relationships, roles, jobs). This predicament is what happens when adults force young people to choose between social survival (and risk to long-term well-being) versus social harm (but better long-term well-being). Lots of things provoke the adolescent predicament. Being nagged by a parent. Receiving critical feedback on writing. Feeling berated by a superior at work during a performance review. Or being talked down to by a doctor. In all these examples, there's a power imbalance between a young person and an authority figure. At the onset of puberty you become biologically attuned to being treated like a competent adult, but some new challenge always threatens to jeopardize your adultlike status. This predicament doesn't just arise when you start middle school or high school. It happens any time you experience a change in roles, when you transition from one set of expectations and job descriptions to another, when status is on the line.

The adolescent predicament can last well into your twenties, even after puberty is done. The reason why is that our society, with its ever-increasing demands for advanced, technical skills, keeps young people in a holding pattern for so long. Consider that some early-maturing youth might be biologically prepared to reproduce by age thirteen, but they might not get a well-paying, full-time job until they are twenty-six, twice the age of biological maturity. That's a long time to be waiting to be afforded status and respect, and it can raise serious questions in a young person's mind about their social standing. Because of this predicament, it's possible for over-twenty brains to still choose behaviors that seem immature from an older adult's perspective. This is what makes the motivational priorities of the ten-year-old brain surprisingly similar to the priorities of a twenty-five-year-old brain, despite the differences in neural architecture. Thus, even a twentysomething employee can experience a gap between how they want to feel at a biological level and how their environments treat them. When the gap widens, then young people tend to pay much closer attention to whether they feel respected by those who have the power to shape their reputations.

This explains why the UCLA report said that the brains of ten-year-olds and twenty-five-year-olds were similar, despite the many obvious differences. Both groups face an adolescent predicament. The specific details of their predicaments might differ—the younger ones might worry about humiliating themselves in front of their friends or romantic partners; the older ones might worry about looking bad in front of their first bosses—but the underlying principles remain the same.

Notably, the UCLA report doesn't conclude that twenty-five-year-olds are immature and need to be treated like children. Quite the opposite. It's saying that twenty-five-year-olds want to be taken seriously and treated like meaningful contributors to the organization's success, and ten-year-olds want to be taken seriously as well.

The adolescent predicament helps us understand complex issues like why kidney-transplant patients don't take their pills, and it can suggest novel solutions that work with our pubertal hormones, not against them. To narrow the gap at the center of the adolescent predicament, we can increase experiences that grant status or respect. Consider a study I conducted involving the nutritional supplement Vegemite.

The Vegemite Study

Of all the chaos and devastation that World War I sowed around the globe, one of the least important consequences was an interruption in the Australian supply of Marmite.

Named for the French word *marmite* ("cooking pot"), Marmite is a sticky, dark-brown food paste made of concentrated, bottled brewer's yeast. The salty, powerful flavor can only be described as distinctive. Though Marmite was developed in the early 1900s as a way of monetizing the yeast by-product of the Bass Brewery in Staffordshire, England, it was later discovered to be rich in the vitamin B complex, and so it became a standard part of British soldiers' rations.

As a part of the British Empire colonized by many British settlers and veterans, then, Australia had a demand for Marmite that the original manufacturer could no longer supply, both because of the war demand and because of long-term disruptions to international trade. So in 1922, Melbourne businessman Fred Walker hired food chemist Cyril P. Callister to develop a home-brewed replacement, Vegemite. Today it is still considered a taste of home by many Australians.

To most non-Australians, however, Vegemite is revolting. Just a taste prompts gagging, retching, keeling over, and exclamations of *Oh no, what did I just eat?* If someone took a picture of your facial expression at the exact moment when a spoonful of Vegemite touched your tongue and showed the photo to an expert psychologist who could spot any emotion, they could identify the telltale signs of disgust. Your cheek muscles would lift, your eyes would squint, your nose would scrunch, your lips would widen into a frown (see figure 1.2). The taste of Vegemite is so mind-bogglingly unpleasant to non-Australians that in 1988 the famous Stanford philosopher

Figure 1.2. Non-Australian research participants disgusted by a spoonful of Vegemite.

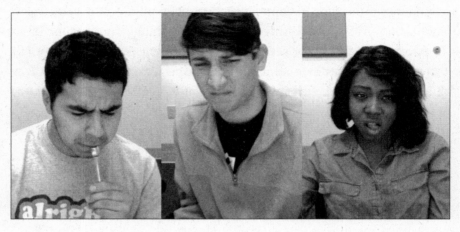

David Lewis coined what has been called the Vegemite Principle, which states that some things are so indescribably unpleasant that they must be experienced to be understood.

Vegemite has played many influential roles in the last century—as a nutritional supplement, as a dare for teenagers, and as an anchor for serious works of philosophy. For me personally, the most consequential was Vegemite's starring role in a scientific test of how the feeling of respect can inspire young people to take their medication. Our experiment used Vegemite to directly test the link between the language adults use when instructing youth and their adherence with unpleasant medications.

Vegemite was an excellent candidate for our experiment on the causes of medication nonadherence because of its unpleasant taste and its high nutritional value, being chock-full of vitamins. If you put those two facts together—nobody wants to eat Vegemite, but eating it is possibly good for you in the future—then eating Vegemite sounds like just about everything adults ask young people to do for their well-being. Avoid junk food. Get enough sleep. Factor trinomials. Learn from critical feedback. And, most critically, take your immunosuppressants. That's why Vegemite let us safely study problems like the kidney-transplant patients' nonadherence. Failing to take Vegemite, unlike failing to take your actual anti-organ-rejection pills, doesn't have real health consequences. But it's a good stand-in for the adolescent predicament—where a young person is deciding how to behave based on how much the authority figure is showing them status and respect.

We brought 184 young people aged eighteen to twenty-five into the lab, and we asked them to sample a nutritional supplement (a small amount of Vegemite on a spoon). They tried it and learned that it was disgusting (see figure 1.2). Next, a medical professional instructed them to take a larger dose of the medicine—a heaping spoonful—in order to improve their own well-being and contribute to nutritional science.

We randomly divided the participants in half and gave them two different versions of the instructions. One group was asked to take the Vegemite respectfully by the medical professional (see the left side of figure 1.3). The other group was asked disrespectfully (see the right side of figure 1.3).

Medical professionals helped us write the disrespectful instructions on the right in figure 1.3 so they sounded like the normal way they talk to patients. The speaker positioned themselves as the authority ("based on what I know about medicine and disease") who told the patient what to do ("you should take this medicine"). *Should* is a key word. It implies that *I know what is best for you to do, despite what you personally may be experiencing.* It presumes the young person lacks agency, like the "Think. Don't smoke" campaign. Furthermore, the speaker diminished the importance of the patient's feelings ("try to ignore" the disgusting taste of Vegemite).

The instructions on the left in figure 1.3 are worded with more respect. Try reading them out loud. Hear the difference? We followed four principles when writing them. First: ask, don't tell. This respects the young people by treating them as adultlike. Adults are asked; children are told. Second: find ways to honor the young person's status—for example, point out their competence and expertise—rather than simply appealing to your own authority. Speaking respectfully means avoiding an I-know-better-than-you attitude. Although professionals might indeed know more about the medicine, they don't know more about the young person's own feelings or barriers to *taking* the medicine. Third: validate whatever negative experiences young people may have had. Treat their feelings as real and legitimate. Then look for a way forward. For instance, one can mention that negative feelings are a sign that they're trying something worth

Figure 1.3. Respectful versus disrespectful instructions in the Vegemite study.

	Respectful Instructions Group	Disrespectful Instructions Group
	Hello. My name is . . . and I'm a second-year medical student finishing basic sciences at one of the system medical branches. I'm here to . . .	
1. Ask, don't tell.	**Ask whether you might consider** taking this medicine.	**Tell you that you should** take this medicine.
2. Honor their status, don't invoke yours.	**You are a university student,** so I figured I would explain the scientific reason why it would be helpful for you to take it.	**Based on what I know** about medicine and disease, the smart thing to do is to take this medicine.
	Some people have reported that this medicine is unpleasant to take because of the bitter taste . . .	
3. Validate and explain, don't diminish.	**You might find it helpful** to think of that slight discomfort as doing your part to help others.	**Try to ignore that.**
4. Presume agency.	Thank you for **considering this request.**	Thank you **in advance for your cooperation.**

doing. Fourth: presume agency. Acknowledge that the young person can make up their own mind, and then make it clear that you are rooting for them to make the healthy and positive choice. Another part of presuming agency is pointing out how their actions can have broader consequences (e.g., "doing your part" to help others).

After participants were instructed to take the Vegemite in one of these two ways, we left them alone to make their choices. What did we find? In the respectful-instructions group, 66 percent of young people picked up the spoon and ate the Vegemite, while only 47 percent of the group that heard the more disrespectful message did so. That's a huge difference. Consider that nearly all our study's participants found Vegemite disgusting and did not want to eat it. And yet nearly two-thirds did so when they were asked respectfully, even though there were no consequences for them if they refused.

This is just one study, not the be-all and end-all. We haven't yet proved that respectful language helps young people keep their kidneys. But the Vegemite study offers a critical takeaway: When we see data showing that too many young people take up smoking, don't take their medication, or make some other unwise choice, we shouldn't blame "kids these days" for acting irresponsibly. Instead, we should try to appreciate their adolescent predicament. They're communicating to us that they want the same dignity and respect that we have as adults—and what's irrational about that?

Rethinking the Hormones of Puberty

What I haven't told you yet is that the Vegemite study was also designed to test Ron Dahl's hypotheses about the pubertal hormone testosterone. We did this to demonstrate the limitations in a foundational part of the neurobiological-incompetence model, which holds that young people's surging testosterone makes them fundamentally immature and irrational. If we could show that testosterone is just something that makes people more sensitive to respect, then we could turn the model on its head.

In the Vegemite study, we divided each of the two instruction groups in half, so there were four groups in total. Half of each instruction group got a dose of testosterone before they received the Vegemite instructions, and half got a placebo (in this case, a harmless drug that they were told was testosterone but actually wasn't). The testosterone, which the subjects took by spraying it up their noses like an allergy inhaler, wears off in a few hours and doesn't have any long-term effects. But it does temporarily put you in a heightened teenager-like state, awash in pubertal hormones. Notably, we did this among the young adults (eighteen to twenty-five) whose testosterone levels were measured ahead of time and shown to be low. These were the people who might not have been as attuned to status and respect at that time if not for our dose of testosterone. We wanted to know: If you took a low-testosterone young adult and infused them with testosterone, would they react more negatively to disrespect, and more positively to respect, like a teenager would?

The results were astounding. See figure 1.4. When low-testosterone young people got a placebo, with no additional testosterone (the two bars on the left), they only slightly distinguished between respectful and disrespectful instructions. But when they got a nasal shot of testosterone, the instructions made a big difference (see the two bars on the right). Less

Figure 1.4. Respect harnessed the power of hormones to promote healthy behavior.

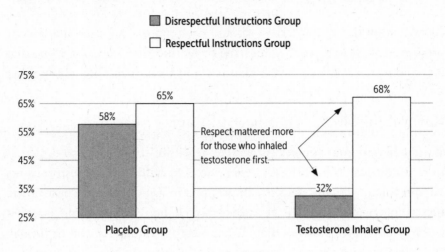

than a third of the young people on testosterone complied with the disrespectful instructions (32 percent). But when asked respectfully, the young people on testosterone proved the most willing to comply of any group (68 percent)—an increase of more than two times.

The Vegemite study showed that the hormone-sensitized defiance that we've come to expect isn't young people's destiny. Instead, defiance is one response to the adolescent predicament—provoked by a mismatch between how youth want to feel (respected) and how we make them feel (disrespected). Young people try to narrow the respect gap by asserting their autonomy. But we don't need to put them in this position at all. We can encourage healthy autonomy if we can satisfy their needs for status and respect through what we say and how we say it.

Of course, I'm not saying that disrespectful language is the *only* reason why young people don't take their medications. But I *am* saying that harnessing young people's desire for status and respect is a promising way to get their attention and keep them focused on behaviors that are good for their well-being. Imagine how much better our lives would be if hormonal young people were twice as likely to make a wise choice, all from a small shift in our language.

Berquist's Initiative

Dr. Steven Alexander hadn't heard about the recent scientific revolution in adolescent neuroscience. When I told him about it, he was excited to learn that the incompetence model promulgated by the MacArthur network wasn't the whole story. He asked: What if we took adherence to medication and turned it from something where you're punished if you don't do it to something that makes you feel respected? He was asking, in effect, how to give medication nonadherence "the full Bogusky."

Interestingly, the start of an answer to Dr. Alexander's question could be found just a few doors down at Stanford University's liver-transplant clinic. They have one of the best teen organ-retention rates in the country. Dr. Bill Berquist's group educates their pediatric patients thoroughly, like any other clinic, but that's only part of what they do. "There's also a social aspect to not taking your medication," Berquist acknowledged. He adds a twist by telling the transplant recipients they have a "special gift" that makes them unique. Every time they take their medication as prescribed they are doing their part to honor the memory and life of the person who donated a liver to them. They are honoring the work of the medical professionals who sacrificed so much to get them out of the intensive care unit and into a normal life. Berquist doesn't guilt or shame his patients. He gives them identities as people of worth, high-status people who make a difference. Berquist and his team reframe the pill-taking decision from one that pits short-term social well-being against long-term physical well-being to one that lets an adolescent feel like a socially worthy person *right now*.

To pull this off, Berquist's liver-transplant team takes great care in *how* they talk to patients. They avoid the pitfalls highlighted by the parental-nagging study or the Vegemite study. Berquist's team educates the adolescent patients directly, separately from their parents, so doctors aren't awkwardly talking to parents about how to get their child to listen to them in front of the child. Berquist's clinic also invites the transplant patients together at summer camps, so they feel like a part of a community. Finally, Berquist's team takes a very respectful approach in their communications with patients, one that I call *collaborative troubleshooting*.

They say, "What are the things that will get in the way of you honoring

this gift by taking your medication? Okay, let's talk about those and troubleshoot." They are direct and clear—they aren't pushovers—but they
never dismiss or invalidate the young person's feelings or barriers. They
mimic the respectful instructions in the Vegemite study. Their tone is collaborative, not condescending. The attitude they exude is respectful, effective, and empowering.

Berquist's team is tough but supportive. They take the young people
seriously, they don't baby them, they don't look down on them. They understand the adolescent predicament. They listen to the constraints young
people are under and don't act like they are invalid or irrational. And their
approach works.

There's a word I like to use for adults who successfully pull off this
kind of interaction with young people. They are *mentors*. Berquist's team
might not think of themselves that way, but I do. Like any great mentor,
they align their communication style with a young person's needs, and set
them up for long-term success. It's not always easy to be a mentor, but it's
a role that anyone can fill if they communicate in ways that are attuned to
the adolescent predicament, and that satisfy young people's appetites for
social status and respect.

Chapter 2

The Mentor Mindset

Status Games

Just before dusk in late July, a dozen or so teenage boys and girls gathered in the hot neighborhood square. The boys were flexing, preening, showboating, intimidating, punching, feign punching, and flinching. They were jockeying for position on the ziggurat of status like fighter pilots in *The Right Stuff* or *Top Gun*.

On the sidelines of that square stood an uncertain, geeky teenage boy named Melvin. He was conflicted. He longed to cruise the square with confidence, but he was terrified that he would step on a social land mine. Melvin's concern was legitimate. He was an easy target for boys higher on the ziggurat. He was sleek and skinny with fluffy hair. His mom was his best friend. Melvin was at the bottom of the social ladder. He watched the status Olympics from afar like a kid who couldn't muster the courage to hop into a game of double Dutch.

This was a problem for Melvin. To most adults, status work among teenagers seems frivolous. An anthropologist like Dr. Rachna Reddy, who observed the scene, sees it differently. She sees status work as essential for survival. How else can boys learn who's dangerous, who's an ally, whom to approach, and whom to avoid? And how else can they signal they bring something of value to the group? Status work is as healthy for adolescents as play is for toddlers.

But here's the thing. Status work can be subtle. To understand the nuances, you need to see it up close. In Michael Lewis's book *Liar's Poker*, the author's firsthand account of twenty-two-to-twenty-four-year-old trainees in high finance in 1980s New York City, he explained status competition in that milieu. The bond-trading floor, Lewis wrote, "was a minefield of large men on short fuses just waiting to explode. . . . There were a million little rules to obey," but trainees "knew none of them," and so they were "impossibly out of step with the rhythm of the place." They were constantly at risk of being ridiculed or, even worse, ignored (and eventually fired). Melvin's task was like that of a new bond trader in the eighties. He needed to discern the difference between an alpha who would pummel him at every opportunity and one who would accept him once he'd proved himself. To learn this, he couldn't stay a bystander. He had to throw himself into the mix. The longer Melvin stood on the sidelines, the worse off he would be.

A few weeks prior, one of Melvin's friends tried to join the group. He got beat up by a dominant guy. Later, another friend tried to join. He was ignored and soon retreated. For whatever reason, that afternoon Melvin got lucky. Dexter, a much older guy with nothing to prove and the freedom to be benevolent, noticed him. Dexter had the kind of cool confidence that came from having earned a safe place on the ziggurat of status. Dexter allowed Melvin to follow him around, to join the fray. Dexter wasn't necessarily affectionate. He tolerated Melvin's presence and subtly guided him away from behaviors that could evoke the ire of the older, stronger boys. This provided all the opportunity Melvin needed, Reddy explained to me. Dexter took Melvin from the nosebleed section at the status Olympics to the bench of the winning team. He saw the social-status land mines and learned from Dexter how to avoid or defuse them. With Dexter as a mentor, Melvin became a social learning machine. What did Dexter get out of it? He got an ally, and it cost him next to nothing.

Years later, Reddy checked back in with Melvin. She was amazed by his transformation. He was confident, respected, strong, and well-adjusted. Not too aggressive, not a pushover. He had learned to climb the ziggurat of status. He was doing better than ever. "I'm so proud of him," Reddy told me, even though she hardly knew him.

What Dexter did for Melvin is *mentoring* in its most basic, most primal form. I say *most primal* because Melvin and Dexter are chimpanzees. They live in Uganda, at Ngogo in Kibale National Park. There, anthropologists like Rachna Reddy and Aaron Sandel have been making striking discoveries about the evolutionary roots of mentorship and other forms of social relationships. Reddy and Sandel, to the surprise of their entire field, discovered that the closest ape species to *Homo sapiens* relies on mentors like Dexter for survival during the critical transition from adolescence into young adulthood.

Let's take that in. *Chimps mentor.*

This finding has profound significance. It contradicts the popular idea, growing in some circles, that mentoring is new age, fluffy nonsense invented by millennials to appease Gen Z. In fact, mentorship is not a recent invention. It allowed our evolutionary ancestors to survive and thrive.

Of course, humans use forms of mentorship that chimps can't. Human mentors spend more time jointly problem-solving. They patiently listen while mentees get something off their chests. Chimp mentors, by contrast, don't spend much time talking about feelings or directly teaching their mentees how to do things. But chimps' indirect form of mentoring gives us a powerful new lens for understanding human behavior. Dexter used the comfort provided by his social status to benevolently provide protection and permission to Melvin. That enabled Melvin to get close enough to peers to understand the subtleties of social success. Sometimes, it seems, a good way to use our status and privilege is just to protect others' right to be in the room.

Melvin and Dexter's story helps us strip away the cultural baggage of mentoring. According to a 2019 report from the U.S. National Academy of Sciences, all mentoring means is that a powerful or established person aligns their resources and actions with the long-term best interest of a young person. That's different from how most people think about mentoring. They think it's a formal job obligation, like when we're the designated mentor to a new person at work. Or it's a volunteering gig, like Big Brothers Big Sisters. If we're not drawn to these roles, we might be tempted to say, *Oh, mentoring isn't for me.*

Reddy's study of chimp mentoring shows that you don't have to be like Mentor, who in Homer's *Odyssey* was an avatar for Athena, the Greek goddess of wisdom. Lowercase *m* mentoring is more informal. You use your position to help someone younger than you resolve their adolescent predicament. You support them as they try to earn status and respect. This mentorship addresses the mismatch between a young person's currently low level of status and what they need to be a respect-worthy contributor to the group. That is probably why mentorship was so critical to the survival of our evolutionary ancestors.

The Mentor's Dilemma at Work

Stef Okamoto, a manager at ServiceNow (a large technology company), was about to email her team's presentation to a senior executive. To her, it was a mundane action, like ones she had taken countless times in her long and decorated career. To her direct report Melanie Welch, twenty-three years old and five months into her first real job, it was the most nerve-racking moment of her short professional life. The presentation represented months of Melanie's work summarizing mounds of data—surveys, interviews, and more—to inform the company's strategy. Once Stef clicked send, the senior executives would know whether Melanie's work was any good—and possibly whether she belonged at the company. Melanie's mind was racing. What if she had made a mistake? Would the executives question her work? How would that affect her reputation? Without a track record at the company, Melanie thought, the moment could define her.

According to our culture's dominant narrative about young people—that they're shortsighted, fragile, and neurobiologically incompetent (see chapter 1)—Melanie was overreacting. *She's a Gen Z snowflake*, some might think. If you knew anything about Melanie's background, however, you'd realize how far that attitude was from the truth.

In college, Melanie was an honors student and an athlete. And not just any athlete. She was a three-year starter and defensive stalwart for the Boston College (BC) women's lacrosse team. Every year of Melanie's career, BC dominated the competition, playing for the national championship six years straight, as one of the most successful dynasties in all of college athletics. Just nine months before Stef sent the fateful email to her supervisors, Melanie's BC team played Syracuse University with a trip to the championship game on the line. With eleven minutes left in the fourth quarter and trailing by two goals, BC had virtually no chance of coming back if they allowed Syracuse to score. A wide-open Syracuse player got the ball. Melanie promptly locked her down. Seconds later, Melanie was flattened by Emma Ward, one of Syracuse's top scorers. Ward had already scored two goals. If Melanie didn't recover, Ward would almost certainly have scored another. Melanie never flinched. She blanketed Ward, who didn't see the ball again that possession. Moments later, BC got a turnover and struck quickly. BC scored three goals in the remaining minutes, defeating Syracuse and sending BC to the championship. Melanie's isolation defense, with all eyes on her, had turned the tide.

Twentysomething Melanie Welch is not one to wilt under pressure. On the lacrosse field, she never backed down from a challenge. Not even in the face of long odds and a crushing collision with a powerful adversary. It's not likely that Melanie's strength and resilience, cultivated over a decade of playing her sport at the highest level—all while maintaining an honors-level grade point average at an elite school—evaporated the moment she entered corporate America.

Why, then, was Melanie so anxious about a work email? Because of the adolescent predicament (see chapter 1). As a new hire at a large company, Melanie experienced a mismatch between how she wanted to be seen (as a valuable, worthy contributor to Stef's team and to the company) and how she was currently seen (as an unproven new hire). This adolescent predicament brought Melanie's concerns about her social standing to the forefront of her mind. Her past successes on the lacrosse field or in the college classroom couldn't shield her from this predicament. After all, the company wouldn't evaluate her on whether she caused a turnover in a lacrosse game a year ago. This is why even supremely talented and confident young superstars still have reasonable doubts about their positions and potential, especially early in a transition. Indeed, anyone who starts a new position or role, in which they must earn a new reputation that impresses people who have power over them, would be concerned about their social status, just like Melanie was.

The adolescent predicament faced by young employees like Melanie sets up a mentor's dilemma for managers like Stef. Should managers be tough (potentially harming reports' confidence) or supportive (compromising the quality of the work)? Managers who are stuck in the old neurobiological-incompetence way of thinking tend to resolve this dilemma in a way that is blind to the adolescent predicament. Therefore, they fail to correctly manage young employees like Melanie.

Some managers tend to think, *If she was a high performer, she wouldn't need any support.* I call this an *enforcer mindset.* In this mindset a manager focuses solely on enforcing a high standard, not on supporting a young person's potential to meet that standard.

Other managers tend to think, *If she's going to be so sensitive, then it means she can't handle the pressure.* I call this a *protector mindset.* In this mindset a manager focuses on protecting the young person from distress by lowering their expectations.

Neither the enforcer nor the protector mindsets are a fit with what Melanie told me she wanted most. She wanted to be a high performer— an overperformer, really—but she also wanted a sense of validation. She wanted to do a good job, worthy of respect from her supervisors, and she wanted feedback on how close she was to that goal. Leaving her to her own devices, without a feedback loop, wouldn't meet this need. Nor would lowering expectations.

Luckily, Stef Okamoto doesn't believe in the incompetence model. She is deeply committed to the idea that young people are capable of important—even astonishing—contributions when they are managed correctly. Because of that, Stef tends to use something I call a *mentor mindset.* This is a mindset in which young people are held to high standards, but they are also given the support they need to meet those high standards. Ultimately, Stef's mentor mindset transformed an anxiety-provoking moment for Melanie into one that made her feel proud and valued.

What did Stef's mentor mindset look like? First, she maintained exceptionally high standards for the work. The project Stef assigned Melanie to was not busy work. It was vital to gaining support from senior management for Stef's new strategic agenda at ServiceNow. Although Stef cared deeply about the quality of the work, she never stepped in and did it for her. She expected Melanie to own it, which means she trusted Melanie to take it seriously and do a good job. When Melanie shared drafts or ideas,

Stef was critical. She said things like, "Hmm, what would happen if we tried this another way?" No detail was too big or small to consider doing over. Melanie needed to be held to those standards because she didn't yet know how the senior executives tended to think. Stef's expectations, therefore, allowed Melanie to anticipate and avoid common criticisms. Further, because it was a real project—not an intellectual exercise—Melanie felt an authentic sense of accomplishment when she met a truly high standard.

Second, Stef was supportive. Rather than expecting Melanie to sink or swim, Stef was a lifeboat. Stef happily jumped on Zoom when puzzles arose, even rearranging meetings so they could have a quick troubleshooting session. When Melanie needed a second opinion on how to present to a specific senior executive, Stef made sure she got critical feedback from colleagues who'd pulled off strong presentations to management recently. Stef wasn't just a cheerleader—although she was constantly affirming Melanie's job well done. She also used her connections and time to protect Melanie's right to be in the room. When Stef clicked Send, Melanie was nervous, but Stef wasn't. She knew the work had been through the ringer already. Stef was confident that the final product would make Melanie look good in the eyes of management.

Stef was right. The senior vice president loved it and was impressed. Already, the presentation is influencing the company's strategy. Stef made sure Melanie got all the credit.

I talked to Melanie the next day. She told me it was her best day at the company so far.

"Stef expects a lot of me," Melanie explained, "but she's also there to pat you on the back. That's something I need right now because it's my first full-time job." This makes sense. In lacrosse, Melanie got immediate feedback. She either stopped a player from scoring or she didn't. At work, there's rarely such feedback. That makes it harder to know whether she's doing a good job, and therefore whether she's worthy of her team's respect. Stef's high standards and high support allowed Melanie to get cycles of feedback, both critical and supportive, on an almost-daily basis, eventually building up to the ultimate payoff of earning a reputation as a strong contributor. Stef didn't *grant* Melanie status and respect. Using a mentor mindset, she cleared a path for Melanie to *earn* it.

The Three-Mindsets Framework

Soon after we published our wise-feedback study in 2014—demonstrating the importance of combining high standards with high support—I noticed a problem. The problem wasn't with the science (we replicated our results). The problem was with how the study was being interpreted. More and more, I saw people describe my interventions as simple, cheap fixes to complex problems. The author Daniel Coyle, in his book *The Culture Code*, called it "magic feedback." This bothered me. The secret sauce in wise feedback wasn't what was written on the note. It was the dignity and respect afforded to young people at a time when they were vulnerable. That's not magic; it's the human condition. I began worrying that companies would start selling Post-it Notes with wise feedback prewritten on them, claiming they could magically erase the achievement gap.

My worries turned into a mission soon after I wandered into Uri Treisman's calculus classroom at the University of Texas at Austin. Uri is a legendary math educator (among other things). I visited his class soon after I was promoted with tenure, simply because that was as good a time as any to start getting better at college teaching. What I saw influenced me profoundly. Yes, Treisman was the walking, talking embodiment of the wise-feedback note. But it wasn't like he gave students a Post-it and a differential equation and then left them to their own devices. He had an elaborate system of supports that helped all students—no matter their backgrounds—to master calculus and have the option to become professional mathematicians, engineers, or scientists. Watching Treisman made me realize how much those of us in the ivory tower of academia can learn from observing expert practitioners in their natural habitats. Craving more examples, I met Stef Okamoto because, at the time, she was the best manager at Microsoft, according to several internal metrics. Later, I found Chip Engelland, the NBA's best shooting coach. Then I found one of the most successful secondary school teachers in the United States, the top PhD mentor for astrophysicists, a highly effective parenting coach, and many more experts.

Through years of observing and interviewing these leaders, I discovered what distinguished them from their less-successful colleagues: their mentor mindsets. This mindset is consistent with the lesson of the wise-feedback note, of course, but it is also more profound and nuanced. I called it a mindset because it was a worldview and suite of behaviors. It went beyond simple statements and included concrete actions. What's more, these mentor-mindset leaders were far more effective than peers who used enforcer and protector mindsets.

The simplest way to understand these mindsets—enforcer, protector, and mentor—is to examine the framework presented in figure 2.1. The first thing to notice is that there isn't just one axis—rigor—that organizes leaders' approaches with young people. It's not the case that we can only be low-rigor pushovers (i.e., the protector) or high-rigor dictators (i.e., the enforcer). In fact, there are *two* axes. You can have high standards *and* high support. You can be a mentor.

Think of two perpendicular dimensions, as shown in figure 2.1. One is standards (i.e., rigor or expectations) and the other is support (social, emotional, or material). High standards, low support: that's the enforcer mindset. High support, low standards: that's the protector mindset. High standards, high support: that's the mentor mindset. (There's a fourth quadrant in the bottom left, the *apathetic mindset*. These checked-out people tend to end up in either the enforcer or protector quadrants when they reengage anyway, so there isn't much use in describing them.)

Figure 2.1. The mentor-mindset framework.

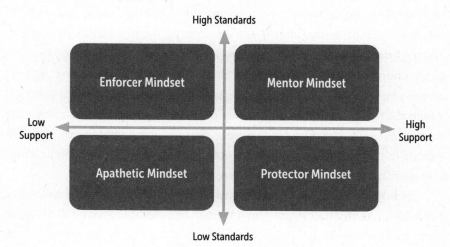

As I spoke with dozens of managers, parents, and educators, I started wondering: Why does anyone resort to the enforcer or protector mindset? Because these suboptimal leadership styles come from valid fears and worries. On the enforcer side, people worry that immature and defiant young people could wreak havoc on society. They need accountability. They need discipline. They need standards. *That's the price of excellence*, we tell ourselves, and, *I'm either willing to inflict pain on people to get their very best performances or I'm not.* If that's their starting assumption, then it's obvious why an enforcer can feel like they're doing what's best for young people (and society). Unfortunately, enforcing a standard without providing support means punishing or failing young people far too often, especially the most vulnerable.

On the protector side, it can seem cruel to hold young people to standards we don't think they can meet, like we're failing fifth graders for not knowing calculus. We fear being too demanding. *They aren't mature*, we say, *so it's unfair to expect too much of them.* Because we care for young people, we do everything for them. *I should care more about the person than their performance.* Then we end up prioritizing self-esteem boosts rather than legitimate accomplishment. While this approach usually comes from a caring place, it doesn't push young people to grow. What's more, it can come across disrespectfully because it is rooted in a belief in young people's incompetence.

The third way, the mentor mindset, is to have high standards plus high support. Upholding high standards can help maintain order and prevent the feared descent into chaos. Simultaneously, the high levels of support convey how much we care for young people. By taking young people seriously and giving them the support they need to earn impressive reputations, we give them a route to status and respect. They get to earn prestige, which they need far more than a self-esteem puff-up. Thus, we can begin to resolve the adolescent predicament. Decades of scientific research, reviewed in the following pages, shows that the mentor mindset is the most effective leadership style for the broadest group of young people.

Luckily, there's hope for those of us who use the enforcer and protector mindsets. Each is half-right. The enforcer has the standards. Great! Now let's add the support. The protector has the support. Great! Now let's add the standards. If we want to change ourselves or others, we can't blame or shame. We can tweak our styles and become more effective leaders.

Box 2.1. A Preteen's Summary of the Three Mindsets

One day my daughter Scarlett, in seventh grade at the time, asked me, "Daddy, what kind of middle school teacher were you?"

"What do you mean by that?" I replied, pretending like I wasn't writing a book about that exact topic.

Scarlett shocked me with an authentic description of this book's three mindsets.

"Well, were you the very strict teacher that nobody likes, so strict that nobody learns anything? Where there's no time to talk, and they don't help you, and the only reason you listen to them is so you get a good grade and don't get yelled at?"

That's the enforcer mindset!

"Or were you the teacher where everyone is talking when you're doing stuff, and you don't really care, and they're free to do whatever they want, and you still kind of get a good grade?"

The protector mindset!

"Or were you the teacher where even if nobody likes the subject, you make the kids actually like it, where everybody's quiet because they want to work hard, where you get freedom, but you know when it's too far, and we don't disrespect you because we think your rules make sense? Like, a good teacher that everybody loves?"

What a description of the mentor mindset!

Scarlett had spontaneously generated the best 150-word summary of this book I could imagine. Without answering, I asked, "Scarlett, did you make those up? Or did you read about them somewhere?"

"I made it up in my brain," she assured me. At that moment I realized that the three mindsets I saw in my observations—enforcer, protector, and mentor—have a basis in how young people make sense of the world.

Although the terms *enforcer*, *protector*, and *mentor mindsets* are new, the ideas are rooted in more than eighty years of research. As I examined this research literature, however, I was struck by a troubling observation. Each different subfield—about managers, parents, educators, and more—had its own vocabulary and intellectual history. Nobody had worked out the parallels. There were best practices for managers and best practices for parents of teenagers and best practices for teachers. There *had* to be an overlap. Neurobiology doesn't change when young people go from home to school, from school to work, or from work to home. But the literature didn't link these different contexts.

This disconnected scientific literature was a problem. It meant that knowledge about how to perform one role wasn't being shared with the others, and that was a shame. Consider, for example, how much managers and parents could learn from great educators. A teacher restarts their culture every year or semester with a new group of students, and they often teach one hundred or more students per year. They see the arc of a relationship unfold many times. This gives them many opportunities to learn what works by trial and error. The average parent, by contrast, will parent only two or three young people. They will hardly ever feel like they got a relationship do-over. New managers usually have only a handful of direct reports. Until now, there hasn't been a way to cross-reference the key terms from educators to managers or parents and back. What follows is my attempt to do this—to tie this intellectual history into a single coherent story that's based on the neurobiological realities of youth—their need for status and respect.

The Three-Mindsets Framework: An Intellectual History

Kurt Lewin was a Jewish scientist who was forced to flee Nazi Germany before WWII. He came to the United States and settled at the University of Iowa, where he founded the discipline of social psychology. His experiences with anti-Jewish discrimination gave him a long-standing interest in leadership styles that promote freedom and democracy. In 1939, Lewin published a revolutionary experiment.

Lewin's experiment contrasted leadership styles in an unlikely setting: after-school arts and crafts clubs for preteen boys. The boys in Lewin's study were assigned to one of three different kinds of adult leaders. One group got a leader who used an enforcer mindset (which Lewin called authoritarian). This leader demanded, yelled, shamed, cajoled, embarrassed, and prodded. A second group got a protector mindset (which Lewin called laissez-faire). This nice and friendly leader expected little, gave no structure, and acted cool with anything and everything. A third group leader had a mentor mindset (which Lewin called democratic). This leader expected students to work hard and accomplish a lot and provided emotional and material support. The leader gently guided students to improve their projects using Socratic questioning. He didn't tell the boys how to create their projects, and he didn't praise them if the work wasn't adequate. Crucially, Lewin had the same adult facilitators play the different roles in different weeks, so that he could more precisely assess leadership *styles*, not just the personalities of the facilitators.

What happened? A few weeks in, the enforcer-mindset club was "dull, lifeless, submissive, repressed, apathetic; [there was] little smiling, joking, freedom of movement." Children hated the enforcer-mindset club, even though they complied and dutifully made their art projects. What were the mentor-mindset clubs like? "The interactions in the [mentor-mindset] club were more spontaneous, more fact-minded, and friendly. Relations to the leader were free and on an 'equality basis,'" Lewin observed.

Lewin examined which club created more internalized motivation. He did so by having the group leaders let students vote on disbanding the clubs. In the enforcer-mindset groups, students immediately voted to discontinue. One by one students threw their projects on the ground and tried to destroy them. They were giddy, like the last day of school in a teen movie. Students "chased each other around the room wildly" with toilet paper rolls, Lewin observed: "Rather clearly, the work products of this [enforcer-mindset] atmosphere seemed to be objects of aggressive attack rather than prideful ownership." What about the low-expectations protector-mindset group? Students hadn't created very much, but what they did they discarded. They also voted to discontinue. How about the mentor-mindset leader? There, the students were invested in their art projects, which were often of higher quality. They wanted to keep working on them even though they didn't have to because they were proud of what they had created.

Which leader did the youth like the most? The enforcer-mindset leader topped the most *disliked* list, with 95 percent of kids. Few kids liked the protector-mindset leader, although they appreciated that "he wasn't strict" and "we could do what we pleased." Still, "he had too few things for us to do." The protector didn't push them as hard as they wanted to be pushed. In the beginning, it was fun to have no rules, but ultimately the students yearned for structure and attention.

How about the mentor-mindset leader, with his combination of high expectations and high support? He was "just the right combination," students concluded. "He was a good sport, worked along with us, and thought of things just like we do." And "he never did try to be the boss, but we always had plenty to do." "We all liked him," they said.

A few decades later, Diana Baumrind showed that Lewin's leadership styles applied to parenting as well. Baumrind completed her PhD in 1955 under the direction of Hubert Coffey, who was one of Lewin's students at the University of Iowa in the 1930s. Baumrind noticed that parents, like Lewin's leaders, tended to differ on the same two dimensions in figure 2.1 above: how demanding they were (their high standards) and how warm they were (how responsive and supportive).

Baumrind called parents who were very demanding but unsupportive authoritarian. This is akin to the enforcer mindset. Baumrind also saw lots of parents who were not demanding but very warm. She labeled them permissive. This group was similar to the protector mindset. Baumrind's research, conducted over decades, showed that enforcer and protector parents were both more likely to raise poorly adjusted children. There was a third group, however. The parents who raised the most well-adjusted children scored high on both demandingness and warmth. They were called authoritative. This was similar to the mentor mindset (see figure 2.2). To complete the square, the psychologist Eleanor Maccoby later named the low-standards, low-warmth style neglectful; I have called it apathetic.

To illustrate what enforcer and protector parenting looks like today, I recently conducted a small study in which I briefly described Baumrind's parenting styles to parents and youth. Then I asked them to tell me about times when they've seen these styles in their own lives.

Sam, a seventeen-year-old, told me his father takes an enforcer approach.

"He's always expecting me to get nothing but A-pluses in every class no matter what." Sam feels like he's using every resource available to him to do well in school, but he's never perfect. After all, he's taking college courses like calculus and physics. Sam's dad tells him he's just not applying himself. "Go figure it out," his dad told him. Sam is overwhelmed by the absence of support. "Not being able to keep up with his high standards affects your mental health," he told me. Sam is starting to feel alone and helpless.

Here's another example. When Alicia's parents saw her struggle to try something new—a sport, a game, or even a new friendship—they would rush in to protect her. They told her, "That's okay, you don't have to do it if it's too hard." She saw it on their faces: their fear and anxiety when she expressed the smallest amount of frustration. Her parents were motivated by a genuine desire to protect Alicia until she grew old enough to fend for herself. However, the age at which they would stop protecting her kept getting pushed back (fourteen, fifteen, sixteen, seventeen . . .). "While it made me comfortable," Alicia told me, "it also made me really scared. I felt like I was unprepared for being independent or going out in the world."

Later in her career, Baumrind realized that many people were misinterpreting her research in a critical way. Because her "authoritative" (mentor mindset) parenting style had its roots in Lewin's democratic leadership, people thought that the ideal leadership style was one that ceded all control to young people, allowing them to debate endlessly and control the group's agenda with a consensus vote. Naming it "democratic" was bad branding on Lewin's part. Baumrind spent much of her later years clarifying that "authoritative" (mentor mindset) leaders often appear quite tough and demanding to observers—even setting out the agenda and expecting young people to follow it. Importantly, they are always supportive enough so that young people can meet the high standards.

The parenting expert Dr. Becky Kennedy, in her book *Good Inside*, echoes this sentiment: "I can parent in a way . . . that involves firm boundaries and warm connection, that gives my kids what they need today and sets them up for resilience in the future." The key to doing this, she says, is to realize that upholding high standards (e.g., setting firm limits on screen time or not letting your kids go to an unsupervised party) is entirely separate from caring about their feelings about our standards (e.g., their fear of missing out or facing peer rejection). We don't have to choose standards or support; both can work together.

At around the same time Baumrind's work started getting noticed, the same basic principles were independently discovered in the context of teaching by a scholar in an entirely different field, using entirely different methods. Dr. Rosalie Wax was a prominent cultural anthropologist in the middle of the twentieth century. After Wax completed her PhD dissertation at the University of Chicago, her brilliant career was derailed by sexism. The university didn't pay her a salary because of a rule that said women could not be paid if their husbands already had a salary. (Wax's husband was a professor at the University of Chicago.) Her experiences with bias spurred her to try to help others, eventually leading to a study of the dire educational conditions on the Pine Ridge Reservation in South Dakota. There, Wax found that the most common educational approach was an enforcer mindset. The enforcer teachers saw it as their duty to uphold the intellectual history and cultural ideology of mainstream American culture, to the detriment of Indigenous culture. Wax observed that the Native American students hated these cold expectations, and they rebelled. They created a "silent classroom," refusing to do any work.

Wax observed a few warm and friendly teachers with low expectations. They had a protector mindset. These teachers weren't mean, but they harbored negative views of students' potential. They acted as though Native students' minds were "meager, empty, or lacking in pattern," only capable of rote memorization. Students didn't engage in deep thinking. They learned very little.

Wax also found a small handful of teachers who created classrooms full of wonder, learning, and of course, discipline and hard work.

There are a few teachers who develop fine classrooms and teach their pupils a great deal. These teachers are difficult to describe because they are remarkably different in background and personality and some are "real characters" in the sense that this word was used fifty years ago. In general, they differ from the less successful instructors in that they respect their pupils. By this, we mean that they treat them as if something worthy of respect was already there.

These teachers . . . do not tolerate nonsense. . . . All are very fair and all are extremely skillful in avoiding a situation which would embarrass a shy student before the class. They tend to place a heavy emphasis on scholastic work.

Later authors would label Wax's superteachers *warm demanders*. They demanded, and gave, *respect*, but they were also warm in that they cared about the students' welfare. This is a strong parallel to the mentor mindset. In Wax's study, the mentor-mindset teachers' respect for the Native American students was rooted in their belief that they had something of value to contribute and should be taken seriously. In general, when that respect comes from someone in a powerful position—like a teacher—it leaves an impression, especially for young people who experience the adolescent predicament and crave status and respect. With mentor mindsets, adults lay a foundation of respectful relationships. Then they take young people seriously and expect them to live up to their potential, while providing the necessary supports. Young people subsequently find the motivation to do the right thing.

More recently, business leaders have begun to study styles of leadership, and they have similarities to the work of Lewin, Baumrind, and Wax. The popular business author Kim Scott laid out different styles for how managers can give feedback to their direct reports, and these have fascinating parallels with the mentor mindset, the enforcer mindset, and the protector mindset. According to Scott, managers who practice *radical candor* give their direct reports honest critical feedback and voice clear statements that make their positive intentions transparent. This is like the mentor mindset. Scott contrasts this with *obnoxious aggression* (analogous to the enforcer mindset) and *ruinous empathy* (analogous to the protector mindset). Scott argues that these feedback styles can have a powerful impact on employee morale; for example, during performance management conversations. I agree.

A Mentor-Mindset Exemplar

Sergio Estrada teaches at Riverside High School in El Paso, Texas. I found Sergio through an analysis of the data from around 1,100 teachers across

Texas delivering rigorous college-level courses in high schools. We located the forty or so teachers that the statistical model said had the most surprising success. This means that the model thought students would do poorly, but for some reason they did well. We called these teachers *bright spots*. They were proof that ordinary teachers could consistently use the mentor mindset to achieve extraordinary results even in places many people had given up on. We convened these bright-spot teachers for three days to study what they did and how they taught. In this group of superteachers, Sergio stood out. He, more than anyone, achieved top performance for all students from all backgrounds. At a school at which just 2 percent of students were ready for college according to their standardized tests, 95 percent of Sergio's students pass college-level physics each year.

Here is what Sergio *doesn't* do. He doesn't enforce an impossible standard for performance without guiding or assisting his students. He's the opposite of his colleague Mr. Trimmer, the math teacher.

Trimmer is a lover of math who sees himself as the gatekeeper to the field. He has very little patience for students who fail to grasp the basic concepts. *I can explain math to you, but I can't understand it for you*, he says. This comes from Trimmer's belief that his students are unruly, unmotivated kids who tend to disobey him, disrespect him, and learn nothing.

Figure 2.2. Mapping the mentor-mindset framework onto previous frameworks.

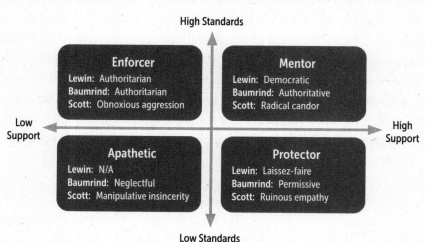

Therefore, his class is an exercise in compliance. He governs with fear. Any sign of disrespect or disobedience is met with threats of harsh discipline. Signs of laziness are met with public shaming. *I teach, you listen* is the social contract. Trimmer is a true enforcer. Most students fail, and those who pass do so by memorizing (and often later forgetting) the content, not by mastering it. Few of Trimmer's students are prepared for college-level work.

Many of Sergio's colleagues in the district are the opposite. They don't enforce standards. Take the pre-AP English teachers, so called because their courses put students on track for Advanced Placement (AP) courses. "They aren't *real* pre-AP students," the teachers said. They accused the administrators of putting unqualified students in their advanced courses simply to boost the school's ranking on district metrics for course-taking. In the teachers' eyes, the students are too frail, too far behind, to be held to high standards. "They are going to fail and lose confidence" if students took the district's challenging college-preparatory tests. Therefore, the teachers rebelled. They reverted to methods that required much less critical thinking, such as telling students to write formulaically or regurgitate facts on tests. Lowering standards to protect students from distress, however, produced roughly the same results as Trimmer's enforcement strategy: rampant student disengagement, shallow learning, and eventual failure. A Riverside student named Yvonne told me, "My English teacher, she doesn't believe we can do anything. So, she doesn't try to teach us. She just gives us worksheets and tells us to memorize them. She doesn't respect us." The English teachers use a protector mindset.

What does Sergio do? He uses the mentor mindset: high standards, high support. His physics class is demanding. He covers the hardest concepts. He expects students to master them. But his class is also highly supportive. His lessons are interesting, involving hands-on labs and activities. Although his tests are very hard, students can retake them and recover points. He makes himself available to go over missed problems with students. When students come before school or during a free period to get help, he lavishes them with praise: "Selena is rocking it today because she came in and talked about problems she missed. She's really improving!" Quick, correct answers aren't praised nearly as effusively as having the courage to troubleshoot mistakes with Sergio.

During the 2021–2022 school year, Sergio and Trimmer shared a troubled student, David. David was retaking Trimmer's math class after having failed it during the prevaccine COVID-19 year. He was disruptive and noncompliant. By the end of August, David had just a 13 percent in Trimmer's class. It was a level of failure that takes creativity and sheer force of will given how much work early in the year consists of easy in-class assignments. One day Trimmer came to Sergio's classroom to warn him that David would be a handful. Sergio was confused. "David's doing awesome in my class," Sergio told me. David had an 85 percent. The morning I talked to Sergio, David had come in to apologize for missing an assignment. He turned it in by lunch. "I have no discipline problems from David." In fact, Sergio has never sent a student to the office in all his years at Riverside. Sergio's success with David is a kind of treatment group to Trimmer's control. He got remarkable learning and growth from the same students, in the same school, when he used a different, more respectful mentor-mindset approach.

Why the Mentor Mindset Works

As I encountered this fascinating breadth of research on leadership, parenting, and teaching styles, I was dissatisfied by three major factors. First, there was a lack of a coherent vocabulary across different literatures that seemed to mostly be reaching the same conclusions. That's why I proposed the framework shown in figure 2.2. Second, the literature wasn't clear on why the mentor mindset was more effective. I needed to tie the ideas about how best to lead young people with the new science of adolescents' neurobiological realities—their desire for status and respect. Third, the literature didn't show where the mentor-mindset approach came from or why people held on to the less-effective enforcer- or protector-mindset approaches. Such knowledge would be crucial for figuring out how to shift leaders from enforcer or protector into the mentor-mindset group. My contribution to the literature was to solve these three issues.

Here's why the mentor mindset works in education, parenting, and management. It offers a way of resolving the adolescent predicament. Consider that young people don't acquire their social standings by having status given to them. They get them by *earning prestige*—a unique kind of respect that only comes from having demonstrated their worth and value to socially powerful others, be they peers or leaders.

To be respected, in the language of the Tsimane, an Indigenous tribe in the Bolivian Amazon, means "worthy of admiration." Thus, to say that the young want respect is to say that they want to be admired by people whose opinions they care about. They obtain this admiration by showing their skills to other members of the group. In our evolutionary history, this would mean that the young person successfully foraged or hunted or cared for an infant or protected the tribe from aggressors, and other members of the tribe noticed it. What did an effective mentor do, then? The Maori tribe in New Zealand has a beautiful term for it: *whakamana*, which means "to give prestige to, give authority to, confirm, enable, authorize, legitimize, empower, validate." (*Mana* means "power," and *whaka* means "to give.") *Whakamana* is what leaders need to do to resolve the adolescent predicament and satisfy young people's sensitivity to status and respect.

An effective mentor creates opportunities for young people to learn about, and begin to acquire, what counts for status in a valued social group. This is what Stef did, as shown at the outset of this chapter, when she gave Melanie a challenging project, helped her to perform well, and then gave her the credit in front of management. Like with chimp mentoring, Stef protected Melanie's right to be in the room and earn a positive social reputation. It's what Sergio does when he requires his physics students to complete ambitious hands-on activities—but he supports them until they master them. Mentors don't take over and do things for young people, like the protector. Nor do mentors uphold impossible standards so that few are successful, like the enforcer. Instead, they find ways for young people to earn respectworthy reputations.

Harvard University psychologist Dr. Joseph Henrich explains that prestige comes from one's reputation for being competent and valuable to the group. Prestige offers a different route to status from dominance. Dominance is a show of force. It grants the kind of status where people listen to you because they must. Prestige, on the other hand, is the result of your actions and skills. Prestige bestows the kind of status where people listen to you willingly because they trust your competence and your knowledge. The enforcer mindset relies on dominance. Young people reluctantly follow because of fear of severe consequences but stop following as soon as the leader loosens their grip. That's what we saw the boys do in Lewin's authoritarian groups. The mentor mindset applies prestige-based leadership. Young people willingly follow the leader because of the exciting prospect that they can earn a better reputation. (In the protector mindset, young people don't listen to the adult at all.)

Why is the prospect of earning prestige a powerful motivator? Not everyone has the strength or desire to dominate the group, so it's not always a viable route to status. But prestige? That's a universal option. Prestige is accessible. Anyone can learn and develop the skills to contribute to their group in some way. When young people do that, they feel an incredible sense of self-respect. The feeling of having *earned prestige*—rather than having something unearned given to you—ranks among the best feelings in the world, especially during an adolescent predicament. That's why Melanie, Stef's young direct report, said the day her presentation was well-received was one of her best days at the company.

By giving young people the thrilling opportunity to earn prestige—and satisfy their needs for status and respect—mentor-mindset leaders offer them the chance to feel amazing. Young people soon learn that if they want to keep feeling that way (and avoid feeling humiliated), they should follow the mentor-mindset leader. The enforcer- or protector-mindset leaders, by shaming, blaming, judging, evaluating, and controlling young people, deny the opportunity to earn prestige. That's demotivating. The result is what Rosalie Wax saw on the reservation: passive or active teen rebellion.

Beliefs Play a Role

Read the sentence below and fill in the blanks:

Given that young people are _____,
the best way to motivate them is to _____.

Suppose you filled out the first blank with this: *lazy, shortsighted, entitled, overly sensitive wimps.* How would you fill out the second blank? I've asked hundreds of adults this question. Most people say something like,

Threaten them with the consequences of their poor behavior, or *bribe them with rewards for good behavior*. They don't say, *Treat them like responsible adults who can independently make wise decisions*. Now suppose you filled out the first blank with: *capable of incredible persistence, resilience, and accomplishment if they are given the proper support and encouragement*. An entirely different set of actions would come to mind.

This exercise shows us the importance of *beliefs* in shaping our leadership styles. With one set of beliefs, one set of actions follow. With another set of beliefs, you get different actions. This simple fact helps answer an important question in the literature: Where do the different leadership styles come from?

Where the Three Mindsets Come From—and How to Change Them

For a long time, the different leadership styles were thought of as just that: personal preferences, almost like personality traits, which couldn't be changed. Research on the authoritarian personality, for example, seemed to imply that some people are just bound to be enforcers, some are bound to be permissive protectors, and there's nothing that can be done about it. My research with my collaborator Carol Dweck shows that's not the case. The different styles don't solely come from immutable characteristics or ossified childhood experiences. They come, in part, from people's beliefs. Because beliefs can be changed, then so too can the way we lead and inspire young people. This is the biggest reason why I don't talk about *styles*, but instead talk about *mindsets*. Mindsets are worldviews that shape behavior and grow out of specific, fundamental, alterable beliefs. Beliefs are the antecedents of leadership styles.

I haven't just seen this in my scientific studies. I've also directly experienced this in my own life.

In my early twenties, before I became a scientist, I lived and worked in an orphanage in Talagante, Chile, called the Hogar de Niños San Jose. I ran day care and educational programs for kids aged two to eighteen, working twelve-to-fifteen-hour days. In my mind, I was there to love and support the kids, not discipline them. I thought, *They've been through so much, they don't need me there getting them in trouble or telling them what to do.* For example, one morning we took out every toy and created a massive obstacle course. For an hour it was joyous chaos. When it was time for lunch, nobody wanted to clean up. I let it slide. They went to lunch, and I stayed to clean. From then on, the kids walked all over me. I hadn't upheld high expectations for collective responsibility, and they took advantage of it. Looking back, I had a deficit view, not an asset-oriented view. I thought of the orphaned children mainly in terms of what they lacked—love or a stable home—not in terms of what they could do if it was expected of them. This deficit belief pushed me into a protector mindset. I sought to protect them from anything unpleasant.

A woman in her forties, Tía (Aunt) Carmen, worked there too. (We went by *tío* or *tía* at the Hogar). She had experience and could command a room. Her kids didn't break the rules, they cleaned up, they didn't fight. Tía Carmen never raised her voice. And the kids adored her. I vividly remember her legs enveloped in hugs from three-to-five-year-olds.

One day Tía Carmen took me aside. She said, "Tío Davíd, yo soy *así*," which means, "I'm like *this*." Then she put her left hand out flat, like a road. With her right hand she did a karate chop on her left hand, making a perpendicular shape. She was showing me that she held kids to straight and narrow rules. "Pero les cariño." But I love them, she said. She was telling me to be firm but loving. She wanted me to have high standards and support. A mentor mindset.

A few years later, I had another opportunity when I took a job as a middle school English teacher in Tulsa, Oklahoma. About half my students came from neighboring farms, while the other half were recent immigrants from Mexico. My students had a wide range of English skills. I had the Tía Carmen mantra in my mind: Yo soy *así*. I would show them the straight and narrow and hold them to it because I cared about them. I still focused too much on what struggles the kids faced—their poverty or low family education levels—but this time, I had different cultural role models in my mind. I thought about the tough, demanding teachers in poor schools, like in the movies *Dangerous Minds* or *Stand and Deliver.* My pendulum had swung in the other direction.

I spent each Sunday grading essays. I wanted my students to meet a high bar for excellence. I gave them lots of feedback. Even when their essays checked all the boxes for getting high Bs, I pointed out how their writing could be even stronger, more unique, publishable even. I imagined students would love me for it. I was treating them like adults who could have intellectual debates, not kids. I even had dreams of them celebrating me for those red marks on their essays! I was dead wrong. From their perspective, what did it feel like to get back the essays dripping in ink? They hated it. They felt mad. Wounded even. Usually, only about half my students revised their essays at all. The other half were content with their scores. They didn't even want to look at my comments. I had failed the classic mentor's dilemma, years before I knew about Geoffrey Cohen's breakthrough research on wise feedback.

There was a mismatch between my intentions and students' perceptions. I tried to push my students to improve. When they didn't revise, I thought they didn't want to learn. But they perceived something different. They thought I was a jerk who disliked them and hated their essays and could never be satisfied. I misunderstood them; they misunderstood me. We all left the interaction crushed and defeated.

People trying in earnest to do their best can easily fall into the enforcer or protector mindset if they hold on to neurobiological-incompetence beliefs. I suspect that many people fall into the enforcer and protector mindsets with the best of intentions. We love our children, and so we are tough on them—or we go easy on them. These unhelpful mindsets don't come from disdain or apathy, but from faulty beliefs, like my deficit belief about the children at the orphanage. These faulty beliefs set up entire worldviews that ensnare us, making it difficult for us to see the mentoring alternative.

The decision tree depicted in figure 2.3 shows how the enforcer and protector mindsets both grow out of the neurobiological-incompetence model. The belief that young people are incompetent leaves us with only one binary choice: Do we want to be tough or nice? Either we're a drill sergeant or a softy. We prioritize either self-reliance or self-esteem. *Full Metal Jacket* or *Ted Lasso* (in the first season, at least).

Sometimes the same person can move through this decision tree in different ways. I see people (myself included) shift back and forth from enforcer to protector, or vice versa. Maybe we start out wanting to be nice,

Figure 2.3. A three-mindset decision tree.

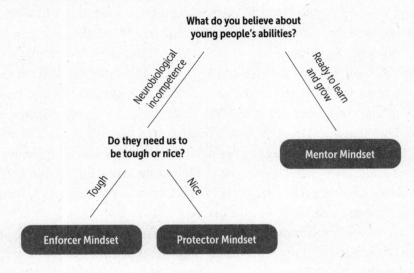

using the protector mindset, but then young people walk all over us. Then we slam the door shut and impose our will, using the enforcer mindset. Then we feel bad and return to the protector. Nobody likes this cycle, but it's hard to escape when our starting point is neurobiological incompetence. Even great mentors slip now and then. They have their protector and enforcer moments.

We can reject the neurobiological-incompetence model, as the new wave of scientists have. We can focus on young people's strengths and assets, not their deficits. If we do this, then a third way—the mentor-mindset way—shows itself to us. Enforcers can build on their high standards by adding more support. Protectors can build on their care and concern by adding higher standards. Both are half-right, and so both just need to add one element to get it all the way right.

Different children can even evoke different mindsets. One mother of two sons in their early twenties told me that she catastrophizes when it comes to her older son, worrying that nothing will go right for him. She takes the protector mindset with him, trying to solve his problems. Her younger son is independent and resilient, and nothing fazes him. She can take a mentor mindset with him more naturally. She worries less about his immediate safety. This mother is working on using the mentor mindset with both of her sons, but that means different things for different kids. With her older son, she needs to acknowledge his competence more. With her younger son, she needs to maintain appropriate supports to not veer into enforcer territory. The route to the mentor mindset can sometimes depend on the child.

See table 2.1. It shows how a focus on *beliefs* solves the puzzle of where Lewin's and Baumrind's and Scott's styles come from. The three different styles come from core beliefs, which lead to semicoherent worldviews and in turn set up patterns of interacting with young people. One idea flows into the other, which flows into behavior. That's the power of a mindset.

Table 2.1. The Three Mindsets: How Worldviews Flow into Behaviors

	ENFORCER MINDSET	PROTECTOR MINDSET	MENTOR MINDSET
Beliefs about young people	Immaturity makes them dangerous risks to themselves and others.	Immaturity makes them fragile and vulnerable if they struggle.	Young people are ready to accomplish impressive things with the right support.
Our role relative to young people	Insist on high standards and establish consequences for failing to meet them.	Protect them from discomfort (and don't stress them out with high standards).	Form an alliance to help them meet a high and personally relevant standard.
Interpretation of a young person's failures	Failures are signs of laziness, inattentiveness, or low ability.	Failures are debilitating and should be avoided.	Failures mean I didn't provide the supports (social, emotional, or material) needed to meet the high standard.
Responses to a young person's failures	I did my job, but they didn't do theirs; dole out consequences and expect them to improve on their own.	Show compassion (and even provide excuses) but don't pressure them to improve.	Presume positive intent and collaborate on finding the needed resources to improve.

The notion that the different mindsets are *worldviews*—in that the lower rows in table 2.1 follow from the beliefs in the top row—is important because it suggests how we can start to change from enforcer to mentor or protector to mentor. We can adopt a different belief—a neurobiological-*competence* belief. If we do that, then the rest of the mentor mindset starts to flow naturally into our interpretations and behaviors.

Chapter 3

The Generational Divide

A Generational Conflict

A few years after Whole Foods CEO and founder John Mackey sold his company to Amazon for $13.7 billion, he gave a series of interviews in what amounted to a grievance-airing tour. He reserved his harshest and most unfiltered criticism for the next generation. These were the sixteen-to-twenty-five-year-olds who worked in the checkout lines and the stockrooms, and whose labor had built Mackey's fortune. Whole Foods had a terrible time hiring and retaining them. And that baffled Mackey. To his mind, he offered a good wage and purposeful work. After all, Whole Foods's philosophy was aligned with many of the values of the next generation, such as environmental sustainability and ethical sourcing of products. Mackey even developed a term—*conscious capitalism*—that would seem to appeal to the Gen Z workforce. Even so, "we're really straining to get people hired," Mackey lamented. "I don't understand the younger generation. They don't seem to want to work."

After interviews with Whole Foods employees, I've learned that Mackey got one thing right: he doesn't understand young people.

A simple comparison of U.S. supermarkets on the job-review site Indeed.com reveals that Whole Foods is one of the lowest-rated employers in its category. Approximately 24 percent of retail employees give it the lowest ratings (a one or two out of five). Compared to several competitors,

Whole Foods received twice as many negative ratings. One former retail employee's review said, "No respect for any employees, literally could not care if you lived or died." What's happening?

According to Mackey's interview for *ReasonTV*, when he and others from the baby boom generation started out in the workforce, people expected to dislike their jobs for at least the first ten years. Pay was compensation for suffering. Mackey didn't necessarily think people should expect to feel a sense of meaning or purpose or fulfillment at work. That's what you spent your money on—or what you got in your thirties, if all went well. The relationship between managers and young employees was transactional. Thus, in the Mackey worldview, you waited to find meaning, purpose, and fulfillment when you were older. When you're young, you put up with nonideal working conditions.

Mackey's attitude neglects teenagers' and young adults' developmental needs for status and respect. What seemed to Mackey like a decline in the work ethic of "kids these days" could just as likely be a consequence of how Whole Foods was treating their young employees. Mackey sounded oblivious to the fact that, for the current generation and likely future generations, dollars are a poor replacement for self-respect. He offered a clear example of how our culture's neurobiological-incompetence model could leave leaders bewildered and employees bitter—even CEOs who had a vested financial interest in motivating the young.

If our society could solve the Mackey problem and stop retail jobs from being disrespectful dead ends, we could transform the industry and its workforce. Roughly 68 percent of adults in the United States have not completed a college education, and many of them work in retail. In the Global South, the numbers are even higher. That's a lot of young people who feel like they don't have a future in our economic society and who could possibly turn to more destructive means to reassert their self-respect.

Mackey's complaints serve as an example of a broader problem called the *generational divide*: older generations feel like they are constantly catering to the needs of young people, only to be shamed or blamed for not doing enough.

Parents, for instance, describe feeling daunted by the emotional dramatics of their kids. One mother told me about reminding her teen-age children to put on their shoes or grab their coat, only to get yelled at for daring to tell them what to do. Educators told me about young people who acted insulted at being asked to meet the minimum standard, such as coming to class, turning in assignments, and passing exams. Managers told me about times when they believed they used the correct terms for a hot-button social issue of the day, only to be told by a twenty-three-year-old that they were a bigot. Our fear of young people's unpredictable volatility silences us, which leads to even more misunderstandings and therefore more shouting. This cycle seems destined to repeat itself, making our lives worse and worse with each revolution.

The cycle of finger-pointing, blaming, and shaming is so infuriating, in part, because we want so badly to avoid it. Parents go through existential crises when their children start adolescence. Just two or three years earlier, we had finally figured it out. Our kids were reading, riding bicycles, and putting on their own pants. They laughed at our dad jokes and mom jokes and mostly behaved well. Then puberty struck. Suddenly the same kids started acting like aliens. What's more, they seemed to reserve their most outrageous behavior for an audience of other parents who judged us for having such disrespectful and ungrateful offspring. It's humiliating and disempowering.

Likewise, educators usually enter the profession because they want to help kids. When every day turns out to be the opposite of how they imagined their lives as educators, they eventually start wondering whether they're in the wrong profession.

Does this have to be our destiny? Or can we do something about it?

The Origins of Our Generational Divide

Each generation tends to think of the generational divide as a problem limited to, and indicative of, their specific moment of time. We blame our current frustrations on superficial things like social media or smart-phones and never really fix the deeper problem. In fact, the clash between the generations has repeated between almost every "ruling" generation and every "upstart" generation throughout recorded human history.

Aristotle, the Greek philosopher from the fourth century BCE, trashed the young in his work *Rhetoric*:

The young are in character prone to desire and ready to carry any desire they may have formed into action. They are fickle in their desires, which are as transitory as they are vehement. . . . They are passionate, irascible, and apt to be carried away by their impulses. Their ambition prevents their ever tolerating a slight and renders them indignant at the mere idea of enduring an injury. . . . Finally, they are fond of facetiousness, facetiousness being disciplined insolence.

Much later, in 1937, the prominent psychotherapist Anna Freud (the daughter of Sigmund Freud) wrote this:

Adolescents are excessively egoistic, regarding themselves as the center of the universe and the sole object of interest. . . . They form the most passionate love-relations, only to break them off as abruptly as they began them. . . . They oscillate between blind submission to some self-chosen leader and defiant rebellion against any and every authority. They are selfish and materially-minded and at the same time full of lofty idealism. At times their behavior is rough and inconsiderate, yet they themselves are extremely touchy. Their moods veer between light-hearted optimism and the blackest pessimism.

When each successive generation grows up, we look down on the next generation, as though we have forgotten what it feels like to be young. Then we call the next generation immature. When most adults think about their own youthful indiscretions, they do so with a wink and a laugh. But when they think about today's generation doing something similar, they ring the alarm bell about the decline in morality in "kids these days."

New research has shown that this generational moral decline is mostly a cognitive illusion. Harvard University social psychologists Dr. Adam Mastroianni and Dr. Dan Gilbert analyzed responses to public opinion survey questions from 1949 to 2019 that asked U.S. adults about the moral character of each generation. Older people thought the next generation lacked the moral values of their own generation but didn't say that their own generation made their own youthful mistakes. The older the survey respondents, the more they convinced themselves that the moral fabric of society was being ripped to shreds by the younger generations.

This illusion of moral decline causes us to think that if only we could stop the young from straying from the path of their elders—for example, by undoing progress in culture or technology—then we could return our society to its moral glory days. But focusing on a generation-specific solution blinds us to the underlying cause of our conflict with young people.

In a clever scholarly paper published in 1987, Dr. Daniel Lapsley and Dr. Robert Enright compared public writings about adolescence going back to the 1880s. During a depression or recession, adults endorsed the incompetence model, presumably to disparage youth who were competing with adults for jobs and status. During wars? We see "a more rugged, adult-like portrait of youth," Lapsley wrote. After all, we need them to work in factories, fight in battles, and maintain stiff upper lips.

For example, influenced by rhetoric about young people serving in the Vietnam War, the United States passed the Twenty-Sixth Amendment, confirming the right to vote for citizens aged eighteen or older. In 1968, President Lyndon B. Johnson said:

> Throughout our history as a young nation, young people have been called upon by the age of eighteen to shoulder family responsibili-
> ties and civic duties identical with their elders'. . . . Reason does
> not permit us to ignore any longer the reality that eighteen-year-
> old young Americans are prepared—by education, by experience, by
> exposure to public affairs of their own land and all the world—to
> assume and exercise the privilege of voting.

Each year since the passage of the Amendment, the incompetence model has worn away at LBJ's progress.

The changes in attitudes about young people from era to era have shown us that the neurobiological-incompetence model—and the pre-dicament it creates—is not a fixed reality. It's a tool used by society when adults need to regain control. Luckily, we can choose another way to view young people and find new solutions to bridge the generational divide.

The War over Meaning

> Human beings live in the realm of meanings. We do not experience pure circumstances; we always experience circumstances in their significance.
> —Alfred Adler, *What Life Could Mean to You* (1931)

When Stanford University psychologist Geoffrey Cohen discovered the quintessential mentor-mindset practice—wise feedback, with its appeal to high standards and high support—he was trying to overcome what he and his collaborator Claude Steele called the *barrier of mistrust*. The barrier of mistrust applies to people who have less power in a setting, and then have their status or respect questioned. When this happens they tend to assume the most unfavorable and antagonistic reasons for the questioner's behavior. With status at stake, they will dissect each word, looking for deeper meaning. When a student gets the compliment sandwich, they may think, *My teacher praised me for my effort but not my ideas—does that mean they think I'm bad at school?* Or they may think, *They said I need to get better at presentations. Does that mean they think I'm incompetent in general and don't belong here?* This barrier of mistrust can lead to a breakdown in communication when a higher-power person initiates a challenging conversation with a lower-power person. This is especially likely to happen to groups of people who have a good reason, based on past experiences of unfair treatment, to suspect they could be treated poorly. Because of the barrier of mistrust, small and seemingly minor details of the conversation can carry outsize weight and can powerfully influence motivation.

Take the example of criticism on an essay. That's not an objectively bad event. One could even argue that it's objectively good. An expert has taken the time to help a novice improve, just like a good coach would. But the status-sensitive student will probe for signs of disrespect behind the criticism. They will assume the worst possible meaning—that they are being looked down on or disrespected—unless they are given a good reason to switch their default assumptions. The wise-feedback note was designed to take this problem off the table. It clarified to young people that they could presume positive intent behind the critical feedback. The note broke through the barrier of mistrust.

The barrier of mistrust helps explain the frustrating generational divide. It's a *war over meaning*. Mistrust makes young people subtly read between the lines of each comment their elders make, trying to interpret the hidden implications of our words, to determine if we are disrespecting them or not. Young people focus more on the *unsaid* part than the *said* part. For instance, when a teenager's mother asks, "Did you brush your teeth?" the child interprets it as, "I think you're so incompetent that you won't even remember something so simple as brushing your teeth"—even though the mother never said the second part. Given that interpretation, anger makes sense. It's humiliating to be told you're incompetent—even if the mother said no such thing. Likewise, if a manager asks a young employee to speak off script in a meeting with senior management, the employee may think it means, *I'm trying to show everybody how much smarter than you I am*, although the manager never said or meant that.

There persists a disconnect between what higher-power adults intend to communicate when we speak and what young people hear us say. On the adults' side, we think we're doing everything for them while they don't appreciate it. On their side, they think we're disrespecting them and looking down on them. Young people reject adults' advice, and adults cite moral decline among the young as the reason why.

Can *both* sides—the adults and the adolescents—win the war over meaning? They can with the mentor mindset.

The Definition of Mentoring

As I alluded to previously, here is how the U.S. National Academy of Sciences defines *mentorship*:

> Mentorship is a professional, working alliance in which individuals work together over time to support . . . personal and professional growth, development, and success.

There are three things to notice about this definition and how it expands our understanding of the mentor mindset. First, consider the word *alliance*. In an alliance, both parties (the mentor and mentee) maintain their own independent goals and roles and identities. Mentorship is not a conquest in which one party (the manager or teacher) dominates the lower-power party (the employee or student), which is the intent of the enforcer mindset. A mentor-mindset manager such as Stef Okamoto (chapter 2), for example, does not coerce her employees to conform to *her* version of their goals, although her group does set (and meet) lofty goals. She and her mentees form an alliance.

Second, a mentor assumes future growth. Stef's direct reports said that she saw them for *who they could become*, not who they were right then. A mentor wants you to meet a high standard, but they realize it takes time and development to get there.

Third, a mentor provides support—both material (time, staff, coaching) and psychological (seeing someone *as a person*, not as a number or as a responsibility). This definition of mentoring anticipates how we can use the mentor mindset to help both sides win the war over meaning.

Treaties, Not Truces

If the mentor mindset involves forming an *alliance*, then the natural response to the cross-generational war over meaning is to aim to sign a *treaty*, not a *truce*. With a truce, there's usually a conquering victor and a surrendering loser. In that event, one side's meaning has won out, usually through a show of force. A treaty is much better. With a treaty, both sides have assessed their needs. They have an awareness of what's necessary for both parties to thrive despite potentially competing interests. They mutually agree on terms. Then they renegotiate as necessary, which means they must keep the lines of communication open.

Bridging the Generational Divide in the Workplace

Who is the opposite of former Whole Foods CEO John Mackey? Meet Ole. He's in his late thirties, he didn't go to college, and he manages the most overperforming branch of the Obs supermarket chain in Norway. Under Ole's management, his branch climbed from the fiftieth percentile in total profits to the third-ranked store nationwide, despite having a much smaller client base than other stores. Ole doesn't have Mackey's problem of slacker teens, and if he does, they shape up quickly. In extensive interviews with Ole, his assistant managers (both of whom were former prison guards, interestingly), and his frontline employees, I saw an eager and resilient young staff, always ready to seek out feedback. Nobody was staring blankly forward, leaving customers helpless. No one sneaked into the stockroom to smoke or take a nap. Ole created an independent work ethic because he formed a treaty over meaning. That made his store impressively profitable while also making it the kind of place where people wanted to work.

Ole's twenty-three-year-old employee told me a story that drove this point home. When she first started working at the store straight out of high school, she was paired with an older woman who was jaded and wanted to game the system. The older worker taught her bad habits, like hiding in the break room or waiting to be told to do anything. Ole called the young employee into the office one day and gave her a tough talking-to. He said she wasn't living up to the standard in the supermarket and she needed to shape up. I asked the young employee if she'd felt offended or threatened to quit. After all, that's basically what happened in the control group in the wise-feedback study (see the introduction). The young employee looked at me like I was a lunatic. She told me that Ole was right. She hadn't been living up to her potential, but she wanted to. Ole also made it clear to her that she had the potential to be a leader at the store. Now she's an eager and proactive employee. She's shadowing her manager to prepare for a promotion and attending a leadership academy that Ole sent her to. Apparently, Ole's high standards didn't provoke a war of words because his meaning was clear: *I care about you and your future, and that's why I'm upholding this high standard.* "It's fundamentally about trust," Ole told me. And how does he build it? "Everyone knows I want the best for the store and the people," he answered. Even when he's harping on the day's sales numbers on the walkie-talkie, the meaning is clear: "I care about you too much to give you no standards," he says to his employees. It's the grocery store version of the mentor mindset.

Is Ole's success just a by-product of the socialist culture in Norway? No, because similar supermarkets in other countries also do a much better job motivating their young retail employees than Whole Foods. For example, Wegmans, a grocery store chain on the East Coast of the United States, leads with this philosophy: "Every day at Wegmans, you'll have the opportunity to learn and grow. Because when good people get together and work toward a common goal, they can achieve anything." That sounds like wise feedback—and a whole lot more. Wegmans has half the proportion of one- or two-star reviews that Whole Foods has on Indeed.com. Frontline retail workers attest that Wegmans "respects you as a person" and is "the best place I've ever worked" and "made time fly by." Why? Because, as they said, they were "surrounded by great coworkers and friendly managers. They treat their employees extremely well. . . . It taught me a lot about people and respect."

Think about that. In Mackey's worldview, he's paying you for your time, so he doesn't have to respect you as a person. When you don't work hard, then you're lazy and violating the terms of his contract. It's a fair economic exchange that he plans to enforce. But in Wegmans' worldview each party's needs are valued. They respect people and their purposes first. Then people are willing to work so hard that they lose track of time. That could explain why Wegmans is number one on the *Forbes* list of best employers in retail and Whole Foods isn't even on the list.

The Generational Divide over Social Issues

Disparities over meaning between the generations come to the foreground especially when we look at hot-button social issues. The prominent sociologist and psychologist Dr. Stephen Russell, an expert in the healthy development of LGBTQ+ youth and the adults who interact with them, sees this a lot. He hears from adults who fear that because the terms and acronyms used to describe sexuality and gender change so fast, they'll get them wrong. According to Russell, adults don't know if they should say lesbian or gay or queer, if there should be a plus or not, or what order the letters go in. They worry that if they say something wrong, they'll be labeled bigots. That worry means they say nothing at all. But young people interpret adults' silence to mean they're biased and unsupportive, which harms youth even further. Adults feel paralyzed. By the way, this isn't a problem faced only by straight, cisgender people. I heard the same thing when I interviewed people in their midtwenties who identified as queer and worked full time at LGBTQ+ youth support centers. They told me it's hard to keep up with teenagers using the latest terminology even when it's their own or similar identities in question.

Dr. Melissa Thomas-Hunt sees a similar reluctance to talk about race or ethnicity among CEOs and senior management. A distinguished professor of business at the University of Virginia, Thomas-Hunt formerly served as the head of global diversity and belonging at the home-rental company Airbnb. She told me that, especially since the killing of George Floyd in 2020, employers feel stuck. If they said something about race- or ethnicity-based injustices, then young people (and politicians) would find a problem with it no matter what. It was not forceful enough, or too forceful, or not appropriately nuanced. Employers also worried that if they made a statement once, they would have to make a statement about every issue or event. They would then spend an eternity writing press releases to placate the twentysomethings.

On the other hand, Dr. Thomas-Hunt told me, employers often have a strong economic incentive to get it right. The competition for young talent can be fierce, especially in the technology and engineering fields, and young talent is harder to recruit to a company with a PR problem.

This conflict doesn't have to be intractable. Dr. Thomas-Hunt found that when employers, like Airbnb, showed a willingness to listen, learn, and change—for example, by elevating voices from minority groups rather than complaining about them—they've had more success at having meaningful conversations. Why did this work?

In 2012, the Stanford social psychologist Dr. Priyanka Carr (who later became the COO at SurveyMonkey) published a fascinating series of experiments that helped us understand this conflict. Carr's experiments showed that some people believed that the world could be divided into prejudiced versus unprejudiced people. They thought that prejudice was a fixed trait (a fixed mindset about prejudice). Other people believed that people could learn to reduce prejudice over time; for example, by educating themselves about another group's experiences. To them, prejudice could change (a growth mindset about prejudice).

Carr found that the research participants who thought prejudice was fixed tended to also think that small missteps in group relations would mark you as an -ist (e.g., racist, sexist). Then the prejudice-is-fixed believers avoided cross-group conversations because of what they might reveal about them. By contrast, the participants who thought prejudice could be reduced with education were more open to talking with someone from a different group. They didn't worry as much that a lack of knowledge right now would mean they would always be an -ist.

Carr's study helps us understand how the fight over meaning plays out across the generational divide—and how it might be resolved. Young people often act like Carr's participants who thought that prejudice was fixed. They seem determined to label older adults, based on very little information, as sexist, racist, homophobic, and hateful. Of course, they sometimes have a good reason for this. Young people in an adolescent predicament are often in a perpetual state of status threat detection, coming from the barrier of mistrust. Their sensitivity causes many young people to quickly sort the world into harmful/bad/unsafe people versus helpful/good/safe people to avoid further hurt. This barrier of mistrust can worsen the very problem young people want to solve, however. It leads adults to stay silent for fear of being outed as -ists. Furthermore, when adults say or do something that's out of step with how they are supposed to talk about group differences, their punishments (e.g., getting canceled) seem out of proportion with their supposed crimes. Then adults dismiss young people as immature, complaining wimps. Both sides end up labeling the other, and neither side learns from the other.

Think back on our metaphor of an authentic treaty, not a truce. People don't willingly sign a treaty (i.e., without threat of force) if they believe the other party is fundamentally evil and untrustworthy. Therefore, as a starting point for any treaty between the generations, both sides must abandon the tendency to apply fixed labels. They must have an earnest desire to learn. Successful companies have done just that, as Thomas-Hunt told me.

Let's conclude with a remarkable case study of an organization that took this principle to heart.

Encircle

Who has succeeded at de-escalating the war between the generations over diverse gender and sexual identities? Meet Encircle, an after-school program and therapy provider for LGBTQ+ youth and their parents.

Encircle originated across the street from the Mormon Tabernacle in Salt Lake City, Utah. Tragically, suicide is the leading cause of death for young people in Utah. LGBTQ+ youth are three times more likely to contemplate killing themselves. This high suicide rate means that even conservatively religious Mormon parents, who tend to oppose differences in gender and sexuality, care deeply about the question of how to talk about LGBTQ+ identities—especially when it involves their own children. They see it as the only way to prevent an unimaginable catastrophe. But they feel helpless, worried that they will make matters worse. So they often say nothing. Because of a barrier of mistrust, this leaves LGBTQ+ youth to imagine what their parents think—and they often imagine the worst.

Dr. Stephen Russell explained to me how this cycle can lead to death. He's often consulted by communities who have experienced an LGBTQ+ youth's suicide. On one occasion, he was on a panel with a mother who had lost her child to suicide. The child's suicide note said she thought her parents would never accept her. The mother, in tears, claimed she never said anything of the sort. Sure, maybe she had made an offhand comment about LGBTQ+ characters showing up in too many sitcoms these days. She couldn't remember anything hateful. But she also never had a direct conversation with her daughter. Her daughter then had to guess what her mom thought. Without any other information to overcome the barrier of mistrust, her mother's offhand comments led her to presume the worst. And that led the daughter to despair.

In Utah the situation can be even worse because there are many messages in the religious community about sex and sexuality. A key issue, the staff at Encircle told me, is that most youth feel condemned as bad and shameful by the Mormon church. Even when their families or church leaders don't shame them, they report feeling intense guilt that the church might excommunicate their parents for accepting their queer identities. They would have deprived their parents, whom they love, of eternal life.

That's a big weight on a young person's shoulders, and it can lead youth to depression and suicidal thinking.

Amazingly, in Encircle's six years of operation, with thousands of youth served, they haven't lost a single kid to suicide. Encircle must be doing something right to bridge the generational divide. What are they doing?

Encircle's motto is "no sides, only love." They don't encourage LGBTQ+ kids to think of their parents as monstrous bigots. Nor do they tell parents to abandon their religious views, or demand they review *Urban Dictionary*'s list of gender identity terms. Instead, Encircle focuses on common goals and values: parents want their children to survive, while their children would prefer not to feel suicidal. Then, through group and individual therapy, they focus on finding a *treaty* that ends the battle over meaning. Encircle's staff helps kids and parents understand that the source of their conflict usually stems from the meaning of something that was left *unsaid*, and rarely from something explicitly said.

Most of the time, Encircle has discovered, parents aren't afraid of the kid's actual sexual or gender identity. They fear what the identity *means* for their child's future. After careful questioning, most Mormon parents at Encircle eventually admit that they worry their child will grow up to be sexually promiscuous. Thus, the true root of their worry is that their child will never have the joy of a committed relationship and a family, and will lack the moral character they tried to instill in their child. These parents are surprised to discover that their kids, especially young ones who recently came out, are often thinking about exactly what their parents want them to be thinking about: what kind of person they want to be in a long-term, committed, loving relationship with when they grow up.

"Our culture has totally overlapped promiscuity with sexuality," Russell told me. His research finds that "young people usually aren't even especially interested in sex when they first come out. They're thinking about love, not sex." Parents, for their part, are also usually thinking about love, specifically hoping for their child to be loved by someone unconditionally. Parents meant to say, *I don't want you to be promiscuous*, and kids heard, *We'll never accept the love of your life*.

Encircle helps both sides understand each other, lower the temperature, and jointly problem solve, for instance by setting fair dating rules.

Parents realized that they could accept their child's identity without abandoning their responsibility to impart moral values and uphold a high standard of conduct. In turn, children learned that their parents could accept
them unconditionally while still setting personal boundaries and expecting responsibility and integrity.

Encircle's method provides a strong example of the mentor mindset.
Parents send a clear signal that they will value, respect, and give dignity
to the child, while also fulfilling their own vision of a good parent as one
who upholds high standards for behavior. Interestingly, although Encircle
never actively encourages it, they find that highly religious parents tend to
become significantly less dogmatic and judgmental as time passes. This
attitude change gives their children more hope that the feelings of shame
could improve, leading to less despair and suicidal ideation. The parents
become almost like a living, breathing argument in favor of Carr's belief
that prejudice can change. That, in turn, can make both sides more open
to the honest dialogue that's needed.

Chapter 4

Acquiring the Mentor Mindset

Stef and Sergio

Stef Okamoto was born in the late 1960s in Longview, Washington, a small mill town between Seattle and Portland, Oregon. "My parents had no money to pay for college. People called us trailer trash," she told me. Stef is now the director of manager excellence at ServiceNow. Before that, she spent twenty-three years at Microsoft, the last seven of which she served as the director of manager capabilities in Global Learning & Development. That is, she trained more than thirty thousand managers who were collectively running one of the world's most profitable companies. As we'll see, she's a paragon of the mentor mindset in management.

Sergio Estrada was born in 1991 and raised in El Paso, Texas. His parents emigrated from Mexico. They divorced when he was young, and his mother raised him. She had less than an eighth-grade education. Sergio, his mother, and his brother, Kevin, lived in a women's shelter until they moved into a friend's home. All three (and Sergio's grandmother) slept on a mattress on the floor and lived out of a suitcase. They eventually settled into a house close to the Rio Grande, which marks the U.S. border with Mexico, to be nearer to his mother's family. Sergio attended Riverside High School, so named because it's directly on the border. People in the Riverside community are proud, but they recognize that there are many challenges. In 2023, a student was stabbed and killed in a robbery just outside the high school. Sergio graduated from Riverside High in 2009, and after he graduated from college he came back to teach college-level physics at the school. Like Stef, Sergio is a paragon of the mentor mindset in education.

Stef and Sergio emerged from very similar childhoods to enter very different professions. But their mentor mindsets have much in common. Stef and Sergio both have very high standards. They also provide generous, human-first, respect-forward support.

"My direct reports are humans, not productivity robots," Stef told me.

"I don't teach courses, I teach humans," Sergio said on the first day we met.

The question I asked myself after meeting Stef and Sergio was this: Were they just naturals? That is, were mentor-mindset exemplars simply born that way?

As I got to know them both better, I learned the answer: They weren't just naturals. They had to learn how to use the mentor mindset. Their stories reveal how even good people with the best of intentions can fall into the protector and enforcer mindsets due to misguided beliefs that are common in our culture. Their stories also show how anyone can escape those unhelpful beliefs and learn to adopt a mentor mindset—making their own lives, and the lives of young people, much easier in the process.

Stef's Story

At R.A. Long High School in Longview, Washington, Stef Okamoto was the captain of the varsity volleyball team; she started on the softball team that played in the junior Olympics; and she graduated in the top 5 percent of her class. "I knew education was the only thing that was going to save me," she said, "but not a single counselor said anything about college or guided me in any way." When she told people at R.A. Long that she wanted to go to college, everyone—even her coaches—told her, "You'll be back in Longview one day." But Stef persevered.

She couldn't afford tuition at the University of Washington (UW), which is in Seattle. She accepted an academic scholarship and a scholarship to play volleyball nearby at Lower Columbia College, a school from which very few students graduate. There, Stef earned her associate's degree, the first postsecondary credential of anyone in her family.

Stef next transferred to UW to pursue a bachelor's degree in psychology. She lived with her aunt and uncle forty-five minutes away. She took two morning classes, and then drove an hour to a job behind the cash register at a local office-supply store, working until it closed. Then she drove back to campus to take night classes or volunteer in a research lab, finally getting home around midnight. The lab work fulfilled a requirement she needed to graduate with a bachelor's in science.

Stef's first job wasn't in science, however. She got a job at a Seattle-based company that published books on traveling and working internationally. When the company told her she had to move to Michigan or lose her job, she talked to a friend who worked at Microsoft. The friend said that Stef would be great at testing software. As a tester, her job would be to serve as a stand-in for thousands of users, to find the bugs before they did. Her experience publishing books that gave people instructions for navigating foreign countries made her unusually skilled at climbing inside other people's minds and seeing through a novice's eyes how they will make sense of something new and different. That prepared her for discovering how a beginner might try (and fail) to use a piece of poorly designed software.

Stef taught herself what she needed to know. This was the 1990s, so she had to learn how the Internet worked from For Dummies books. She took night classes. Soon she landed a job at S T Labs, the vendor that Microsoft outsourced their software testing to. For four years, Stef tested the software that trained developers for the Microsoft Windows operating system. By 1999, she was leading that team. In 2000, Microsoft decided they wanted control over the testing and resulting publications. They hired the best people from S T Labs. That included Stef.

When Stef joined Microsoft, CEO Steve Ballmer had created what many have described as a toxic corporate culture. Subsequent Microsoft CEO Satya Nadella recounted in his book *Hit Refresh* that when he took over from Ballmer, employees had grown used to hearing "What a stupid question!" in meetings. There was a "fear of being ridiculed." They were terrified of "not looking like the smartest in the room." Nadella summed up the situation, and his own philosophy, by saying Microsoft had "a bunch of know-it-alls, when we really needed to be a bunch of learn-it-alls."

Microsoft's mindset under Ballmer could be encapsulated by two words: flipping tables. During the Ballmer era, on more than one occasion an executive literally flipped a table over and screamed at a young employee who made a mistake. "Flipping tables" became Microsoft's shorthand for a toxic culture. "You had meetings where people would cry because you were made to feel that you would be pummeled. It was such an environment of fear," a veteran manager told me. "Young people would get peppered with condescending questions from senior leadership," I heard from another manager. "Did it happen once? No, it happened all the time." This abusive culture stifled positive risk-taking, especially for young engineers just starting out, trying to make a name for themselves.

Microsoft's culture during the Ballmer era harmed the bottom line because it drove away young talent and led the retained talent to underperform. Microsoft began the millennium as the largest company in the world according to market capitalization. When Steve Ballmer took over from Bill Gates as CEO in 2000, he promptly ushered in a "lost decade," during which Apple, Google, and others zipped by. In 2012, a single product from Apple—the iPhone—generated more revenue than all Microsoft's products. The company was losing. Ballmer's culture had alienated top engineers, who often went to Google, where they could be valued contributors on meaningful projects—not to mention enjoy free lunch, play volleyball, and ride scooters all day.

Stef hated the old, flipping-tables culture at Microsoft. "Young engineers and project managers were in total fear of presenting to leaders," she told me. "Leaders would make you feel like an idiot if you weren't perfectly buttoned up. Even in private, you couldn't ask for feedback without them making you feel stupid. It was their way of upholding Ballmer's 'high expectations.' Sometimes new employees would present and then you'd never see them again." The employees who remained barely spoke up in meetings.

A major contributor to Ballmer's enforcer-mindset culture was a performance management policy he implemented called *stack ranking*. In stack ranking, managers ranked each employee's performance in one of three tiers: exceeded expectations, met expectations, or failed to meet expectations. Critically, the ranking was not calculated relative to any objective level of accomplishment, like shipping a new product or discovering a new algorithm. Ballmer's policy forced a curve. For each stack of twenty to sixty employees, 10 percent or so had to be labeled low performers, even if they performed objectively better than employees ranked high in other stacks. Low performers got no bonuses, and if you earned low ranking twice, you lost your job. *Rank and yank* it was called.

Stef despised stack ranking. Her team frequently overperformed compared to other teams, which meant her worst performers were usually better than top performers in other "stacks," but they still had to be ranked compared to their own "stack." She thought it was inefficient and cruel to fire competent people she had trained and supported just because of an artificial curve that unjustly rewarded people in mediocre stacks.

According to many young engineers, stack ranking wasn't just unfair, it was dumb. It incentivized them to sabotage their teammates' work. It "creates competition in the ranks, when people really want community," one former Microsoft vice president told *Vanity Fair*. Stack ranking perpetuated the outdated, toxic culture at Microsoft.

How did Microsoft come to adopt this quintessential enforcer-mindset policy? Stack ranking comes from the *mythology of the demanding leader*. Picture the football coach who makes the slackers run laps, the high school principal who roams the hallways with a baseball bat to keep rowdy students in line, the professor who fails half the class to protect the prestige of theoretical chemistry, the technology executive who crushes everyone's spirit for the sake of the perfect product, or the music instructor who isn't satisfied until you've practiced so much that your hands are bleeding.

For Ballmer, the demanding leader of lore was Jack Welch, the larger-than-life CEO of General Electric in the 1980s and '90s. Welch invented rank and yank. In his book *Jack: Straight from the Gut*, Welch explained his enforcer mindset. He made it his goal to "sort the A, B, and C players." If Welch deemed you an A player, you deserved a bonus two to three times larger than B players. If he deemed you a C player, you deserved nothing. You should get fired. Welch was "heavy on yelling and short on empathy."

Early in Welch's tenure, GE was bloated and bleeding money. They needed to trim the head count. Rank and yank might have made sense for a while. But Welch continued the harsh policy past when it was necessary. He maintained exacting standards but was blind to the need for support. He fired more than one hundred thousand employees during his twenty-plus-year tenure, shipping many of their jobs overseas and accelerating the destruction of the working-class economy that had created so much upward mobility in post–WWII America.

In his book about Welch called *The Man Who Broke Capitalism*, *New York Times* journalist David Gelles noted that although rank and yank reduced costs and raised short-term stock prices, it proved a bad long-term policy. It pushed away talent and stifled innovation, just like Ballmer did later at Microsoft. (GE recently split into three smaller companies with collectively far lower value than its year-2000 peak.) Nevertheless, copycats mostly paid attention to GE's stock market run during the nineties. They concluded that Welch's impossible standards and ruthless firings formed essential ingredients in his ascent to the top of the pyramid of American capitalism. Human-oriented supports did not play a part in Welch's calculus, except for a tiny sliver of A performers.

Rank and yank took on a mythological moneymaking status that persists to this day. Adam Neumann, former CEO of the disgraced startup WeWork and a disciple of Jack Welch, famously used rank and yank—firing about 10 percent of the company's workforce after performance evaluations—even when they had had billions in cash flow surpluses. Neumann's toxic work culture took part of the blame for WeWork's spectacular implosion after its attempted IPO in 2019.

Boeing CEO Dave Calhoun used to lead GE's aviation division under Jack Welch. In early 2023, following a downturn in the U.S. economy, Calhoun announced that Boeing would return to stack ranking. Managers were forced to tell roughly 10 percent of employees that they did not meet expectations, even if just a few months earlier they had been evaluated as having met expectations. But it was a false standard. "I've had to flat-out lie to staff members who were rated low and were not deserving of it," a manager said. On a Facebook group for "Microsoft old-timers," a sarcastic veteran of Ballmer's Microsoft quipped, "I'm sure this will work out well for them." A year later, Calhoun and his engineers were under fire when a

Boeing plane's escape door flew off while Alaska Airlines Flight 1282 was in the air. Calhoun stepped down as CEO soon after.

When Ballmer took over as CEO of Microsoft, Welch's influence and the myth of the demanding leader had never been stronger. Buoying that myth was a powerful and pervasive ideology that management theorist Douglas McGregor famously called *Theory X* in his essay titled "The Human Side of Enterprise." Stef would spend her entire career fighting against Theory X. (McGregor chose the name Theory X simply because he wanted to avoid the debates that a more descriptive name would evoke.)

Theory X is the management version of the neurobiological-incompetence model (see chapter 1). Under Theory X, people (especially the young and immature) are assumed to be fundamentally lazy and selfish. Theory X says that people can be motivated only by the allure of gaining material rewards (e.g., money) or the threat of losing rewards (e.g., wage cuts or termination). Accordingly, the way to motivate people is to rank them so that they strive to climb to the top and get the best rewards. If they don't respond to that system, then you should fire them. This approach exemplifies the enforcer mindset. Although Microsoft's Ballmer-era rank-and-yank policy may sound barbaric today, it was simply the logical extension of a long-standing belief in Theory X among demanding leaders in industry.

Theory X contributes to a self-perpetuating cycle that reinforces enforcer-mindset practices like stack ranking and table flipping. Stack ranking failed to motivate employees at Microsoft to do their best work throughout the Ballmer years. Managers ranked underperformers in lower tiers and eventually fired many of them. Those few people whom the system failed to crush were rewarded. Thinking themselves better and smarter than everyone else, they thought stack ranking had done its job—weeding out the slackers, rewarding the superstars. They didn't realize they were wasting enormous amounts of talent by creating a motivational problem that didn't have to exist.

It's easy to imagine a similar dynamic playing out among parents. Think about a parent who subscribes to Theory X and notices their teenager refusing to do their math homework. If the parent believes that teenagers are lazy, then they're more likely to use tools of control: threats of punishment for noncompliance (yelling, telling, blaming, shaming, grounding) or rewards for compliance (bribes, promises, relaxed curfews, lower expectations). These tactics don't inspire the teen to work diligently and independently. Therefore, the parent will be left with even more evidence that young people are lazy, reinforcing Theory X in a recurring cycle that generates an ever-more entrenched enforcer dynamic.

This self-perpetuating enforcer-mindset culture running at Microsoft dominated when Stef was promoted to her first management position. Stef rejected Theory X. She instead believed in what McGregor's 1957 essay called *Theory Y.*

According to Theory Y, people are not inherently selfish, lazy, and driven by material reward and punishment. Perhaps they can be made to look that way by poor management, but that is not their nature. Instead, they can be motivated by what the psychologist Dr. Abraham Maslow called higher-level needs: social connection, social status/prestige, or meaning/purpose. When motivated through such means, people can work proactively and independently without needing constant direction or supervision. This makes workers more productive and it makes managers' lives easier because they don't have to constantly surveil their employees.

McGregor's Theory Y offers different explanations for poor performance and different ways to motivate high performance. Performance can suffer when people's higher-level needs are threatened. Under Theory Y, therefore, a manager's goal is to help people address their fundamental needs for respect, dignity, and meaningful reputations.

Stef vowed to be a manager who had nothing in common with the Theory X–believing, stack-ranking, table-flipping enforcer-mindset managers that surrounded her at Microsoft. She decided to represent a sliver of humanity in an inhumane culture.

Stef had pure intentions, but she struggled with execution. That caused serious problems for her direct reports. When she became a manager without much prior training, she rejected Theory X. She unfortunately also adopted a shallow understanding of Theory Y. That made Stef bring a protector mindset to work. She thought she needed to protect people's egos and self-esteem. By rejecting Microsoft's enforcer culture she ended up avoiding difficult conversations.

One of her rookie mistakes was to treat her young direct reports like they were her buddies rather than her supervisees. She gave them high support but insufficient standards. In particular, she worried that the professional feedback she gave them might feel too personal, and the last thing she wanted to do was attack her young colleagues. Therefore, she withheld criticisms of their performance. However, stack ranking was alive and well, so when performance-evaluation time came around, the committee had to put some of her direct reports in the lowest-performing category. She had avoided having the hard conversations with them, and now it was too late to help them out. As a result, she had jeopardized the bonuses, career velocity, and even job stability of people she cared about deeply.

Another early mistake came from Stef's way of helping her direct reports solve problems. During one-on-one meetings, her team members would sometimes complain about another manager or teammate. Stef's naturally protective instincts drove her to confront the offender. That didn't solve the problem; it made it worse. That was her protector mindset in action. Deep down, she harbored doubts about whether her reports could solve their own problems. She had to start respecting her employees' competence. She changed her approach. When direct reports brought complaints to her, she began by asking them if they needed to vent, or if they wanted her to step in. If the latter, she made sure they were okay with how she planned to get involved.

Stef, like many of us, had to learn to reinterpret Theory Y and see its more profound implications. She had to learn that you can simultaneously challenge people *and* address their needs for status, respect, and dignity. Mangers can do it by having a conversation that takes young people's abilities seriously while also helping them access the resources they need.

Eventually, Stef crafted performance-management conversations that I call *collaborative troubleshooting*. That's a way of responding to mistakes or errors that makes people feel safe confronting and overcoming their limitations.

Consider an example of how Stef used collaborative troubleshooting via a performance evaluation she shared with me for someone in the lowest category of her stacked rank:

I want to give you a heads-up that we finished your performance review. Unfortunately, you were in the lowest category. I get it. It stinks. But I want to be clear with you. I don't think that your performance in this cycle is a reflection of your trajectory. I know what you are capable of. Six months from now, I don't want you to have a narrative that you're a persistent low performer. I want you to control the narrative, to show that you're a high performer. I have some ideas for what we can do over the next six months to get there. But I'd like to hear from you. What is your vision for how we can get you in a position to take on the right high-profile projects? How can we impress the right people so that you can recover your reputation for being someone with high career velocity? Once we figure that out, then we can make a plan for how to get there.

This is bread-and-butter mentoring. She's collaborating to meet high standards while supporting personal growth.

Notice what Stef didn't do. She didn't chastise the low performer with an enforcer mindset. Nor did she say, *You are a low performer because you had too much on your plate, so I'm going to lower expectations for you or do your job for you*, with a protector mindset. She *raised* expectations. But then she offered meaningful support. She offered herself as a coconspirator, a collaborative troubleshooter. She's not a judge of her employee's overall worth as an employee.

Stef's experiences at Microsoft planted the seed for her growth into a successful manager. Other managers recognized how tough—fierce even—she could be, especially when it came to her direct reports' growth. Young employees adored her. Dozens now say that they owe their successful career trajectories to her mentorship in their early to midtwenties. Stef's LinkedIn page looks like a bulletin board of unsolicited love letters from former direct reports. Her direct reports maintained promotional velocity. For example, Salonee Shah, her former direct report, is now in a senior position setting management strategy for all of HR at Microsoft. (Since talking with Stef, I've tried out collaborative troubleshooting in my own parenting, as shown in box 4.1.)

> **Box 4.1. Trying Out Collaborative Troubleshooting when Parenting**
>
> I gave Stef's collaborative troubleshooting a try with my daughter. Scarlett had to prepare an eight-minute-long TED-like speech for her seventh-grade English class. Like many twelve-year-olds, she waited until two nights before it was due to start writing it. She was freaking out.
>
> If I was an enforcer, I would have said, *You made your bed, now lie in it.* Her low score would be the price she had to pay for her procrastination. If I was a protector, I would have said, *Okay, let me dictate it to you, and then you can edit it.*
>
> Instead, I channeled Stef's mentor mindset. "Well, let's talk through what you have in your outline so far. You do a first draft, then we'll look at it. Then we'll fix all the problems with it. If we do that once, it'll be a lot better. And then you'll know how to edit your own text in the future," I told her. The problem stopped feeling so big. I saw Scarlett's shoulders release. She took a deep breath. She grabbed her pencil. "Okay, let's see how it goes after a first draft, and then we'll fix it."
>
> It took a little bit more time out of my evening, but it was worth it. A few days later Scarlett crushed her presentation. She was proud. "That was the right kind of hard," she told me. The mentor mindset strikes again!

When Satya Nadella took over as CEO of Microsoft in 2014, he steered the culture away from Theory X to the authentic version of Theory Y. Nadella and his colleague Kathleen Hogan eliminated stack ranking and brought in a more humane system of performance evaluations called a *Connect*.

Stef wanted to help Nadella, Hogan, and their team undo the toxic Ballmer culture. She wanted to take Theory Y company wide. To do that, she would have to move to HR. She had no experience in HR, but that kind of thing had never stopped her before.

Stef decided to make her own luck. She started an aspiring-manager forum to train the next generation of managers within her engineering group. The forum covered topics like *Courage in critical conversations* (something she herself struggled with initially), *How to coach employees on their career development plan*, or *Growth mindset: Building a team that achieves its true potential*. The forum was wildly successful. It became the de facto route to management excellence at Microsoft's top units.

Stef applied to transfer to HR and scale up her ideas and was rejected—until HR came to their senses and brought her over. Soon, Stef's small but powerful team led all new employee onboarding and all manager training for the company's global workforce of 190,000 people. Their framework had three parts: *model*, *coach*, and *care*. Stef was instrumental in making sure *care* was in the final framework.

Accolades soon followed. By 2023, as a result of Nadella's top-down cultural transformation and Stef's bottom-up leadership, Microsoft was ranked as the best company to work for in the world by Statista and *Time*, with 95 percent of employees saying they were proud to work there—a far cry from Ballmer's "lost decade."

Soon after, the technology company ServiceNow took note of Stef's accomplishments and aggressively recruited her away to a new opportunity. There, she could own the company's manager-development and -evaluation strategy. At ServiceNow, Stef continues to thrive.

Sergio's Story

When Sergio Estrada attended Riverside High School, he was a top-ten student who excelled in all subjects, especially math and science. "I had a bit of a fixed mindset at the time," he acknowledged. He was highly competitive. It bothered him that his high school girlfriend, Jasmine, seemed to be better than him at everything. Jasmine got higher SAT scores *and* higher grades, and excelled in speech, debate, and theater. She was valedictorian; Sergio wasn't. When Jasmine beat him at something, he was upset for days. Now they're married and his fixed mindset has faded. Sergio still hates losing to Jasmine at board games though.

Sergio's fixed mindset started to change as a student in Nancy Arroyo's AP Calculus class. Arroyo was the chair of the math department at Riverside and a winner of the Presidential Award for Excellence in Mathematics and Science Teaching, the highest award for teaching from the National Science Foundation (NSF). According to both Sergio and Jasmine, it was because she didn't put up with nonsense. Her class was rigorous. One day midway through the semester, Sergio got a 2 out of 5 on a practice AP test—a failing grade. Arroyo looked at him and said, "Sergio, how could you be sad or surprised? You're not trying. You do your homework the morning of. You rush through it." She told him that he had a ton of potential, but he just wasn't applying himself. Her words stunned Sergio, but they didn't offend him. She was right. He was slacking, coasting on ability. "Arroyo was one of those change-your-life teachers, like Jaime Escalante from *Stand and Deliver*. It was a turning point in Sergio's life," Jasmine told me. Arroyo even used to show *Stand and Deliver* to the class every year to inspire them. It worked on Sergio. A few months after his fateful conversation with Ms. Arroyo, Sergio got a 4 (a high pass) on the AP Calculus test. (Jasmine got a 5.) He stopped underestimating the students who had to try hard to do well. Arroyo's mentor mindset begat Sergio's growth mindset.

Sergio, like Stef, received no advice about applying to college. He started to form his first concrete plans in eleventh grade when a recruiter from Yale came to Riverside. He looked at Sergio's test scores and grades and told him to apply. Sergio got excited—then he looked at the price tag. Nobody told him about scholarships. He never applied to Yale.

Jasmine knew more about college. She wanted to go to Texas A&M, which boasts outstanding academic programs at an affordable price for Texas residents. Sergio learned that with his grades and class rank, he wouldn't have to pay anything. He applied and was admitted to the honors program. "I made a spontaneous decision," he told me. "I had never been to campus. All I knew was that the valedictorian, my girlfriend, thought it was a good school." Jasmine's mother didn't like the news. "There was no way I was going to let her go to college with her boyfriend," Jasmine's mother told me recently. Jasmine enrolled at the University of New Mexico on a scholarship instead.

Sergio's first year in A&M's honors program challenged him. The other honors students had studied at fancier high schools. Sergio had to work twice as hard to get the same grades. After much effort, he started doing well. A year later, Jasmine transferred to A&M. They soon got married and had a baby. Day care was expensive, so Sergio and Jasmine traded off watching the baby, working, and going to class. Sergio stopped worrying about his ego and started thinking about making a living.

During his sophomore year, Sergio took a job that he could do from anywhere between classes: working the customer-service phone lines for Apple. On nights and weekends, Sergio answered your call if you dropped your iPhone in the toilet, didn't have AppleCare, but still wanted a free replacement. Or if your phone ate your pictures and you couldn't log in to iCloud. "They would call in angry and yell at me. But my philosophy was this: They just wanted to be heard. They are okay with a bad outcome as long as they feel understood." Sergio never caved in to the callers—he wasn't handing out free iPhones!—but callers always left the conversation feeling validated and respected. They still wanted to be Apple customers. How did he do that? Sergio always apologized to the customer, even if the issue wasn't Apple's fault, because that was Apple's protocol. Then he would repeat what they said, rewording it so the customer knew he'd listened. "The hardest thing was to take time to understand how they were feeling. They are talking to me ugly, but the only way to fix the situation was to make them feel understood. To do that you have to listen." Last, he would *collaboratively troubleshoot.* He would try to fix the issue, but *with* them. He educated them about why they had a problem and showed them how to avoid it in the future. He wouldn't just tell people what to click to recover their lost photos on iCloud. He would explain it to them patiently like they were peers or colleagues. People would end the calls feeling like they'd made a friend for life. It was like therapy. Sergio's mentor mindset and collaborative-troubleshooting style was forged in the crucible of Apple's customer-service-training program.

While Sergio was still working for Apple, he had never considered being a teacher. But Jasmine knew that she wanted to be one. At Riverside, she had been on a special teaching pathway that helped her land a teaching job back at Riverside after graduating from college with a leg up on tenure.

Sergio could not have taken a more different path.

Sergio started at Texas A&M University with the goal of working for a "three-letter organization," such as the FBI or the CIA. He initially majored in psychology and Russian. He thought that mastering human behavior and foreign languages would make him a good candidate. During his junior year, he learned that he had a rare eye condition. His corneas were thinning out. Eventually he would lose his sight. Therefore, he couldn't use or carry a gun. Any field job for the FBI or CIA was out of the question.

Sergio switched to premed. He dropped Russian, picked up neuroscience, and started taking as many science classes as he could. He aced them. His new plan was on track.

His senior year, Sergio signed up for a program where students could shadow A&M alumni in medicine. He shadowed three doctors. Two told him they only started making money and enjoying their jobs much later in life. They also had poor work-family balance. A third doctor didn't like his job or the money he made doing it. Sergio was thinking of providing for his young son right away and enjoying his life with Jasmine. Ultimately he decided against going to med school.

Sergio felt like he'd dodged a bullet. But by then he was a fifth-year student at A&M. His major wasn't leading him to a future he could envision. Jasmine had returned to El Paso with the baby, living close to her family, preparing to teach at Riverside, already on a career path. "I was lost and confused. In the wilderness," he told me. "I panicked."

After graduation, Sergio got a job at the Verizon call center in El Paso. He had loved his time at Apple, and he thrived at helping people in a crisis, so he thought he'd do it for a little bit more pay closer to home. Eventually, he thought, he could move up in the company and perhaps have a leadership role in customer service. Immediately, Sergio felt exploited by Verizon. They paid him poorly and pressured him to upsell people calling in with tech problems. He wasn't helping people. He hated it and quit. Now Jasmine and the baby had to live on one public school teaching salary. Sergio longed for the days when he felt optimistic about his future.

Jasmine talked him out of his funk. She told him, "You have the two most important qualities to being a great science teacher. You know science well, and you're really good at listening to people and helping them solve their problems." She knew that he felt most confident and most alive when he was crushing it in his science classes or helping people at Apple. Helping a sexagenarian master a dizzying array of logins and devices is not that different, she told him, from helping sixteen-year-olds understand a complex physics concept. She thought he would be an excellent teacher.

In his first year, Sergio was not an excellent teacher.

The spring after he quit Verizon, Sergio completed an online alternative teacher certification. He learned nothing of value. "All I did was memorize things and click boxes on easy quizzes."

In the fall, he taught three sections of regular physics, two sections of biology, and a section of engineering at Riverside High School. He put his Apple call center skills to use. His students liked him. Then, two months into the school year, the AP Physics students staged a revolt against their teacher. They were the highest-achieving students at Riverside, just like Sergio had been six years earlier. But they weren't learning anything. In Sergio's engineering class (which they also took) they had to get tutored in physics by Sergio's regular (non-AP) students. The AP exam was coming in April, and the class was running out of time. Raul, who would later attend Yale on a full scholarship, knew that Sergio was a good teacher. Raul went to the principal and demanded that Sergio become the AP Physics teacher instead. Thus, with essentially no training in how to teach and having taken only a couple of physics classes, Sergio found himself teaching an entire year of college-level physics to underprepared students with two months less than the normal time.

To Sergio, the stakes for the AP Physics job could not have been higher. After years lost in the wilderness, worried about how to provide for his family, he finally had a chance to prove himself, to feel like he had a path. He needed a permanent job. *Teaching had to work out.*

Sergio also cared deeply about his students. He'd sat in those same desks six years earlier. Like him, they so rarely received guidance in their academic careers. Now it was his turn to change their lives.

Desperation set in. Sergio needed to equip his students to pass the AP test, which required a score of 3 or above. But how would he learn how to teach successfully?

He first turned to Jasmine. She reminded him of Arroyo, their favorite teacher. What did it mean to go "full Arroyo"? Sergio remembered her as tough, demanding, and rigorous. Driving students forward. Assigning tons of problems, expecting work daily. Sergio decided to copy her—like his life depended on it.

Next, Sergio asked his principal if he could shadow the best AP Physics teacher in the city. He planned to watch the class and copy what they did. He had no time to spare.

The principal directed Sergio to Oscar, who taught at one of El Paso's richest and highest-achieving schools. Oscar's students scored more 5s (out of 5) on the AP exam than anyone else in the district. "There are two important things about teaching AP Physics," Oscar told Sergio on the first day. First, you have to go superfast through the content. Second, you have to teach to the top of the class only. If you slow down and if you try to teach everyone, then you're going to hurt the kids at the top because you're not going to cover the material they need. And the kids at the bottom won't get it, anyway, so there's no use teaching to them.

Sergio nodded and took copious notes as he watched Oscar's class. "The main thing that stood out was how intense he was with kids," Sergio told me. One day the class was doing a hands-on physics experiment. A kid made a mistake. "Oscar really got into the kid's face, yelling, 'Why are you doing that? We've gone over it *five times*. How could you be making this mistake?'" Oscar was Microsoft-flipping-tables mad. "I thought, *Oh man, Oscar is being shown to me by the district as the standard that I should emulate.*" Sergio returned to his classroom not quite ready to give it the full Oscar. But he had a strengthened resolve to act tough.

"That year I was really strict about deadlines, a sink-or-swim kind of guy," Sergio told me. "I thought that rigor was good, hard was good, you had to push kids." He was trying to copy Arroyo and Oscar. He gave a lot of homework: Two hard problems every day, five days a week. Each problem would take the students thirty or forty-five minutes to solve even if they were keeping up. Most of his students were not keeping up. Sergio did not accept late work, and his students couldn't revise homework or tests if they figured the concept out later. His grading was punitive. "Everything was really high stakes," Sergio recalled. Most of the class had Cs, Ds, or Fs. Sergio pushed onward. He reminded himself of what Oscar told him: *Go fast. Teach to the top. Make students take the class seriously.* He pushed through new content every day, even if students didn't understand a concept. Students fell further and further behind. "I wasn't focused on building up their skills so that they could do well. I was focused on blazing through content." To all but a few students, earning an A in the course seemed more and more impossible. Students started cheating. There was so much cheating. Sergio held the line. He thought that students needed to work harder. He remembered his own experience in Arroyo's class. They needed the Arroyo kick in the pants, just like he'd gotten.

As the AP exam approached, Sergio hoped that his students would pass and love him for it. But even though he had held students to very high standards—higher than many AP teachers—his students didn't know the content well enough. He tried to keep the class light to keep his students' spirits up. He joked with them. He convinced himself that his friendly demeanor made up for being tough on them. Then Sergio asked his students to write letters about the class to future students. He hoped for ringing endorsements, despite the low grades. In his mind, he hoped he was Arroyo reincarnated. He soon learned how wrong he was. "I had this student Adam, and I thought we were cool. But in the letter he explained he hated my class. He told everyone not to take it. He was a nice, smart kid with no reason to lie. I was shocked. I'll never forget how my class made him feel." This crushed Sergio's confidence.

Why did the students hate Sergio's class? Because no matter what they did, they couldn't succeed. They felt stressed, overwhelmed, and helpless. They weren't inspired by the high standards. They were defeated by them. Sergio thought he was being Mr. Teacher of the Year by instilling personal responsibility. But the students got Cs and hated him.

A great example of his failed approach came from a physics lab assignment. Sergio put students into groups, gave them Hot Wheels cars and tracks, and said, "Find the force of friction." Then he crossed his arms and walked away. He smugly thought, *Oh, they're thinking critically and independently. I won't help them at all.* Students would raise their hands to ask for clarity. He would give no more than small hints and walk away smiling, thinking, *I'm a good teacher.* In reality, his students were sitting there lost, frustrated, and upset. They had none of the skills they needed to do the task. They knew that the lab would count as a major part of their grade and that they wouldn't have any opportunity to get the points back if they figured it out later. Not only did Sergio's students despise the class, they didn't learn the material. More students failed the AP exam that year than any future year. Their failures haunt him to this day.

How did it go so wrong, despite Sergio's positive intentions? Sergio fell into the enforcer mindset through a series of misunderstandings that could happen to any of us.

Exhibit A: Arroyo. Jasmine was right to suggest he imitate her, but he'd completely forgotten two key facts. First, Arroyo covered so much content and expected so much work *because she had a double-block period* for calculus. She had ninety minutes, while Sergio only had forty-five. She literally had twice as much time. Time is a supportive resource. She used that resource to meet with students, go over their work, and make the workload manageable, so her high supports matched her high standards. Sergio had Arroyo's expectations but gave only 50 percent of her support. That's the enforcer mindset.

Second, Arroyo served as the chair of the math department. She overhauled the curriculum, from ninth through eleventh grade, to prepare students for the demands of AP Calculus in twelfth grade. By the time students walked into Arroyo's class, she had already helped them master the fundamentals. They had learned to walk before she forced them to run. Sergio neglected this. He thought he could push students to their limits in a single year without addressing any of the foundational skills they might not have learned under the non-mentor-mindset teachers in ninth through eleventh grade.

Exhibit B: Oscar (the AP Physics teacher). Oscar's students succeeded *despite* his classroom practices, not because of them. Their successes didn't come from his teaching style. Oscar taught at a school with abundant resources. His students came to class well prepared. When he pushed them, they could go home to parents who were engineers or who had majored in physics in college and they could explain the concepts to them. Or students' families could afford private tutors. What's more, at Oscar's school many students are weeded out of AP Physics if, after the first midterm, Oscar thought they couldn't cut it. That's not effective teaching. That's selection bias. By asking Sergio to copy Oscar, the district made a common error. It was like asking him to examine CEOs such as Steve Jobs or Elon

Musk and conclude that their successes came from how they belittled or emotionally abused their subordinates. Those CEOs succeeded *despite* their hostility, not because of it.

Furthermore, Oscar's reputation rested mostly on his ability to prepare a handful of students to earn 5s. He wasn't trying to prepare marginal students to pass with 3s, which conferred college credit. Nor was he trying to prepare all students to major in science in college, regardless of their AP scores. Oscar almost treated most of his students as though they didn't exist. That didn't help any students—except for a hand-selected privileged few—to learn. When you cherry-pick the top scores from among the richest and most-prepared students at the richest school, then of course teachers like Oscar look good. Oscar's apparent teaching success was a false signal. Thus, his practices shouldn't be emulated.

Why did Sergio, armed with clear talent and a gritty determination to excel at teaching, get misled by his memory of Arroyo and his observations of Oscar? Because of the mythology of the demanding leader.

In education, the mythology of the demanding leader takes its greatest inspiration from Jaime Escalante, hero of the film *Stand and Deliver*. Jaime Escalante was, in fact, one of America's greatest teachers. Like Sergio, he taught predominately Latinx students experiencing poverty. He prepared them to pass college-level courses, and his top students often went on to attend elite universities. Uri Treisman, who created UC Berkeley's famous calculus workshop in the late 1970s and '80s, taught many of Escalante's former students (see chapter 11). "They really stood out from the other Latino students in my class," Treisman told me. Escalante's success was real. But the story of how Escalante achieved his success was a lie.

In *Stand and Deliver*, Escalante takes students who are at a seventh-grade math level at the beginning of the year (i.e., pre-algebra) and brings them up to speed through calculus by the end of the year—six years of math in one. To explain this, the film focuses primarily on Escalante's philosophy that "students will rise to the level of expectations." His approach is all expectations, not much support. The enforcer mindset. Film Escalante is unrelenting, refusing to accept any excuses for late work, just like Sergio was in his first year. His character is often harsh, telling his female students that if they fail they will end up "barefoot, pregnant, and in the kitchen."

The wild success of *Stand and Deliver* inspired a genre of copycat films, including Michelle Pfeiffer's *Dangerous Minds* and Hilary Swank's *Freedom Writers*. In the latter, Swank's character famously berates a student who failed an assignment, "You know what this is? This is a 'f*** you' to me!"

For the last four decades, the lesson for any aspiring teacher has been clear. If you want to whip a ragtag group of minority youngsters into shape, you need to maintain exceptionally high standards, regardless of how you make them feel. This myth of the demanding leader valorizes the enforcer mindset.

Since the release of *Stand and Deliver* in 1988, it has been played countless times to motivate students of color in low-income public schools across America. Adriana Heldiz is a young Latina journalist who grew up in Southern California, near Escalante's real-life school. Her essay titled "Please Stop Talking About *Stand and Deliver*" describes how the movie became a substitute teacher on days when teachers had to grade papers and didn't want to give whole lessons.

By the time Sergio was a first-year teacher with little experience or training, he had seen the movie dozens of times. That myth of the demanding teacher likely influenced how he recalled the lessons from Arroyo's class. But it leaves out an important fact: the high supports that matched Escalante's (and Arroyo's) levels of demand.

Did you know that in real life Escalante didn't run his program alone but ran it with two other incredibly talented math teachers—Ben Jimenez and Angelo Villavicencio? A team, not a solitary superteacher. And did you know that their program never took students from pre-algebra to calculus in a year? They achieved that progress over three or four years—still impressive—and they managed it in the same rather mundane way that Sergio's AP Calculus teacher Ms. Arroyo did. They refashioned the entire math department to have a complex system of prerequisites throughout the pipeline, so that by senior year Escalante could push students to their limits. The key was never sheer will or brute force from a solitary teacher. Jasmine was right that Arroyo taught like Escalante. But not for the reasons depicted in *Stand and Deliver*.

Most importantly, the Escalante team didn't demand excellence out of thin air. They lavished students with supports, including intensive eight-week summer programs taught by award-winning teachers, starting the summer after eighth grade; former successful students as paid tutors; visits from alumni who were now attending elite universities to share tips about how to be successful in calculus; before-school tutoring (starting at 7:00 a.m.) and after-school tutoring (until 7:00 p.m.); improved training of seventh- and eighth-grade math teachers; and an exceptionally supportive principal, Henry Gradillas, who among other things allowed Escalante to hire staff—eventually up to nine new, handpicked super-teachers—to remake the entire math pathway.

Yes, it is true that at one of the poorest schools in Los Angeles, Escalante's program at its height had more than one hundred students in AP Calculus. But not because of a reality-distortion field of irrationally high standards from one insane man. Instead, the supports matched the level of demand. The Escalante team owed their success to the mentor mindset all along, not the enforcer mindset.

Our society has learned the wrong lessons from films like *Stand and Deliver*. So did Sergio when he learned the wrong lessons from Arroyo and Oscar. So do many other teachers, parents, and managers when they learn similarly wrong lessons from Jack Welch and other Theory Xers. These cultural role models make us think that the solution to yearslong neglect of young people's skills is simply to enforce high expectations. When we try to imitate these models, we find ourselves disappointed by their (and our) ineffectiveness.

Sociologist Erving Goffman, in his influential 1956 book *The Presentation of Self in Everyday Life*, compared everyday social behaviors such as teaching in front of a classroom to being an actor in a theatrical performance. We are not "ourselves" when we are "on stage," he argues, but rather we become actors playing roles—or rather, our understandings of our roles. How we understand these roles—for example, whether we act tough or lenient, warm or cold—depends on our mental *scripts*. Goffman defined scripts as our hunches about how to perform those roles based on our past experiences. Goffman's thesis holds that the less expertise and direct experience we have in a role, the more we rely on stereotypes to define our scripts.

Cultural scripts help us fill in the blanks when we lack direct experience. For example, when European college students want to throw an

America-themed party, they dress up in backward baseball hats and drink out of red Solo cups. Those customs stand out to them the most in coming-of-age films about U.S. teenagers. European partygoers *perform America.*

Inexperienced teachers like year-one Sergio who are working with low-income youth tend to *perform Escalante,* especially when they're desperate. *If I want to become a superstar teacher who gets the most out of kids, I need to copy what Hilary Swank did in Freedom Writers.* Year-one Sergio Estrada assigned impossible physics labs and told students to figure it out without support. This enforcer mindset can persist even though both researchers and exemplary teachers have pointed to the importance of the mentor mindset. The mythology of the demanding leader gives us a comforting script while distorting the facts in front of our eyes.

We can find our way out of this problem by understanding students' perspectives. Recall that in a mentor mindset, students' perspectives are not trivial complaints or entitled demands. They are useful sources of information that adults should take seriously. Young people can help us adopt a mentor mindset. Adam's feedback note at the end of Sergio's first year caused Sergio to reevaluate his assumptions about his students—and therefore his entire teaching philosophy. Adam was a smart, good kid who liked working hard. His mediocre grades and dislike of the class couldn't be chalked up to teenage laziness, rebellion, or incompetence. Theory X couldn't offer a satisfying explanation. Sergio realized he needed to take Adam's criticism seriously. Adam, therefore, helped Sergio escape from the mythology of the demanding leader and become the mentor-mindset exemplar he is today.

Sergio started copying what Arroyo *actually* did, not what he remembered her doing. Arroyo had spent a whole year forming a respectful relationship with him, like the warm-demander teachers on the reservation in Wax's study (chapter 2). She made time to explain the concepts to him. Arroyo didn't apply a go-try-harder-alone mentality. She didn't use grades punitively. She used them more like temporary measuring sticks. Low scores didn't equal dumb students. Students' mistakes presented opportunities to collaboratively troubleshoot. These realizations brought Sergio to a plan of action. He would maintain his Arroyo-like expectations, but he would overhaul the way he supported students.

Sergio's life became like a training montage from a Rocky movie. He attended an AP summer institute for teachers and learned that you need to break the labs up into parts and teach foundational skills. He repeated his Hot Wheels lab about friction, but prior to that he added several labs that taught the essential components: how to formulate a hypothesis, how to turn it into a testable prediction, how to carry out reliable observations, and how to use intuition and data to check your conclusions. He still expected students to own their thinking, but he made time for them during his off periods and after school to go over their work.

Within a few years, Sergio had become the most effective equity-promoting teacher in the state. His was a master class in inclusive excellence. Sergio prepared far more of his students to pass college-level physics. His school soon adopted a program called OnRamps, which offers college courses taught by public high school teachers across Texas. (It's a more rigorous, more affordable, and more equitable competitor to the College Board's AP program.) In OnRamps, Sergio's high school students took college-level exams that were graded by the actual physics professors at UT Austin. Every year, more than 90 percent of his students passed this rigorous college-level physics course. And unlike Arroyo, he did it with a regular class period, and without overhauling Riverside's entire curriculum.

Although Sergio improved his teaching through many impactful practices (detailed in section II of this book), I want to focus on how he independently developed a collaborative-troubleshooting approach that is strikingly parallel to Stef's management version.

I usually interviewed Sergio during his Friday off periods. Sometimes students came in for homework help. One day a senior came in. Sergio asked her, "How do you feel about that test today?" "Nervous and behind," she said. "Okay, well let's see how it goes, then you'll come in and we'll fix it. Go get it, girl." His words demonstrated a simple case of collaborative troubleshooting.

It's *collaborative* because he shows that he's on the same journey of learning as the student. He uses *let's* and *we* language. He implied he'd walk the journey with his student, not leave her to her own devices, even though the responsibility for doing the thinking would be hers.

Next, *troubleshooting* avoids all-or-nothing language. He doesn't say, *We'll see whether you're a good student*, or *whether or not you learned anything*. He simply suggests they'll have to tinker with her knowledge afterward. What happened next? She earned a C, then came in for test corrections, got a B+, and with some more work was on track to pass the final.

Sergio's collaborative troubleshooting is the opposite of what many Riverside students get. One day while I was talking with Sergio, in walked Santiago, a junior at Riverside in Sergio's class. I asked him to describe a typical experience with a non-Sergio teacher. This is what he said.

The English teacher assigned Santiago to write a persuasive essay that considered both sides of an argument. Santiago could come up with one side of the argument but not the other. He had 50 percent of a strong essay and 50 percent garbage. He came after class to get help from his teacher. "Can you help me with the other half?" Santiago asked her. She shook her head no. "Tiene que focate," she said. *You have to pay attention.* "Y no paga atención porque no quiere paga atencion." *And you don't pay attention because you don't* want *to pay attention.* She pushed a pile of worksheets across her desk for him to complete on his own. "Traemelos." *Do them and bring them back to me.* She gave him no help, only busy work. It was high standards, no support. Not collaborative. Not troubleshooting. *Blaming, shaming, humiliating.* The enforcer mindset.

"Dr. Yeager," Santiago told me, almost in tears, "she didn't try to understand where I was coming from."

"What do you mean?" I replied.

"Well, I have ADHD. I only understand fifty percent of what *anyone* tells me. I was coming to her after class to get help with the other fifty percent. She says that I don't want to pay attention. This is literally the only way I can show that I want to pay attention. And she's blaming me for it." He was hurt, but also defiant and indignant. Santiago wanted me to understand how unjust the situation was. He felt disrespected, diminished, and unmotivated. "She's probably trying to teach us to be responsible. But she's going about it all the wrong way," Santiago told me.

The story is very different from the perspective of Sergio's mentor mindset. In Sergio's class, each assignment captures a reflection of what students can do that day, not a measure of their abilities overall. His role is to troubleshoot their confusion and help them get unstuck so they can meet a higher standard. He doesn't want a solitary failure to define them. "You are more than a number," he says constantly. And it works. One student told me, "In Mr. Estrada's class you never feel stupid when you ask a question. My classmates are all very supportive. I feel it is because Mr. Estrada doesn't allow anyone to feel less than anyone else."

Section II

Mentor-Mindset Practices

Chapter 5

Transparency

A lack of transparency results in distrust and a deep sense of insecurity.
—His Holiness the Fourteenth Dalai Lama

You've got a mentor mindset. You maintain high standards. You're support-ive. But do the young people in your life know it? If they don't understand how your leadership can help unlock their potential, then your actions won't motivate them nearly as much as they could. *Transparency* about mentor-mindset actions makes a difference, and anyone can start being transparent right away. You simply explain what you're doing and why.

Two Transparency Problems

Junior Teachers

Today Andrew is a public school principal, but years ago, when he was an inexperienced and insecure first-year teacher, his principal terrified him. Stone-faced. Impossible to impress. Every other week the principal came to his class to watch him teach. He would slip in from a back door and sit in the back, taking notes. He did not smile. After about twenty minutes, he would leave without saying a word. His visits disturbed Andrew. *Why was he there? Does he think I'm no good? That he has to keep an eye on me?* Andrew felt judged.

Eventually, Andrew's principal would debrief with him. He offered inci-sive and useful advice. But Andrew still never knew what he was thinking.

Andrew never let his guard down, and never fully implemented the feedback as a result.

A few years later, Andrew's principal retired. At the party, dozens of colleagues stood up to give toasts. One after another praised the principal's mentorship—his rigorous standards, his empathic concern. Suddenly, Andrew realized the principal didn't visit the classroom to evaluate him—he was just showing how much he cared about the details of instruction. The principal had assumed Andrew would understand that by spending valuable time visiting the classroom, he clearly cared about Andrew's growth. But that wasn't transparent to Andrew at all.

Due to a lack of communication, Andrew spent years feeling crushed and unmotivated, like he could never measure up to the principal's impossible standards. He was ultimately grateful for the principal's mentorship but resentful of the wasted mental energy. Now as a principal himself, he takes care to be transparent about his mentor-mindset approach each time he observes a teacher.

Junior Lawyers

Jane is a successful mid-career attorney at a large firm with offices all over the world. She hasn't made partner yet, but she's responsible for authoring key legal briefs and supervising junior attorneys.

Recently, she realized she had a problem. One of her twenty-four-year-old junior associate attorneys couldn't take critical feedback. The junior associate would look at Jane's comments on her draft brief, which almost always involved a near-total rewrite, and get offended. The junior associate would complain to peers, to HR, or to more senior attorneys, but she wouldn't fix her work. On some level, Jane understands her colleague's prickliness. The legal profession has a notoriously toxic culture. You're either a genius or an idiot. If you write exactly the way the senior partners want you to, you're the former; if you don't, you're the latter. The junior associate breezed through a top college and top law school. Now, when Jane asked her to do something meaningful and gave her real feedback, the criticism made her feel like an idiot. She couldn't handle it. So rather than take the criticism seriously, she believed Jane disliked her.

"She's interpreting my criticism as a sign that I think she'll never make partner," Jane told me, "but it's her inability to take feedback, not her performance, that's the biggest red flag for me." Jane feels especially baffled because she thinks she's a *really, really nice person.* She works hard to be so. She reads books on management at night. She strives to sound superpositive. But to no avail. After several months, Jane stopped giving feedback altogether. She would rather let the junior colleague think she's a great lawyer—but keep her off important cases—than deal with the taxing emotional labor. "She's just hurting herself." The junior associate wasn't promoted, and the firm wasted hundreds of thousands of dollars on a failed hire.

What Do These Problems Have in Common?

Both the teacher-principal problem and the junior-senior lawyer problem are versions of the mentor's dilemma. They also have the same underlying solution: *transparency.*

In both cases, the mentors cared about their mentees and provided support (in the form of feedback) to help them meet a high standard. That's a good start. The mentors had the right mindset. In both cases, however, they miscommunicated with mentees, who felt threatened. Then the miscommunication spiraled into hurt feelings and distrust. To resolve this problem, each could have been *more transparent about their meaning.* After all, if the root of the generational divide is the fight over meaning, then we need to make the meaning of our mentor-mindset practices exceptionally clear.

We can see how this works in a powerful study conducted in an entirely different context: police officers talking with civilians on the street.

The Transparent-Policing Project

Kyle Dobson is now an award-winning assistant professor of public policy at the University of Virginia. In 2021, he led a landmark study along with Andrea Dittmann, a lauded assistant professor at Emory University's Goizueta Business School. (I collaborated on the study as well.) Dobson and

Dittmann's simple yet profound study, focused on community policing, compellingly illustrates the power of transparency.

When officers are engaged in community policing, they're encouraged to get to know the community and proactively solve problems with community members, rather than only stepping in to investigate crimes. By taking this proactive and positive approach, in contrast to a more aggressive stop-and-frisk approach, officers hope to build more trust in the community. However, many experiments have evaluated community policing, and they found, on average, that it's unreliable and rarely effective. Civilians frequently continued feeling threatened. Crime rates stayed high. And as far as Dobson and Dittmann could tell, nobody could explain why.

The Threat Cycle

Dobson and Dittmann first decided to get to the bottom of the community policing conundrum when they were graduate students at Northwestern University's Kellogg School of Management. They didn't start out by judging all officers as bad or untrustworthy, nor did they consider officers blameless. Instead, they presumed that the officers' well-intentioned efforts were somehow getting lost in translation.

To diagnose the issue, Dobson and Dittmann rode along in the backs of police cars with officers in the community policing units in Evanston and Chicago, Illinois. Out in the field, the problem immediately presented itself to them, even though it wasn't apparent to the criminologists and policymakers examining spreadsheets in their offices. Dobson and Dittmann quickly observed that when officers approach citizens on the street and start making small talk, people feel intimidated. They get evasive, give short answers, and try to exit the conversation as quickly as possible. Officers, noting people's evasiveness, sometimes go into gumshoe mode and start investigating them for crimes. These dysfunctional interactions trigger a cycle of threat, suspicion, and interrogation that undermines the very trust the officers hoped to nurture.

One day, a pair of officers bragged to Dobson and Dittmann that they were about to charm some members of the community. They walked up to a family, all Black adults, having a picnic at the park. Supremely confident, the officers, both white, unloaded a barrage of questions: *What are you doing here? What are you eating? Do you live nearby? Where are you going next?* The officers stopped when they felt satisfied and walked back to their patrol car, high-fiving each other for doing a good deed. Dobson, who is Black, snuck back around and asked the adults at the picnic what the interaction was like for them. They told him that they didn't feel at ease. They felt violated, threatened, at risk of being arrested, and lucky to have escaped with their lives. Why did they experience so much apprehension? Because they knew all too well that police officers, especially in the city of Chicago, have a history of misusing their power, either by making unnecessary arrests or by physically harming civilians who have not committed a crime.

You can see this dysfunctional cycle in a transcript from a conversation in Dobson's experiment (described later) between a fully uniformed and armed on-duty female police officer and a twenty-one-year-old woman she questioned on the street. As you read it, ask yourself: Is the officer creating the kind of rapport she's aiming for?

OFFICER: Can I talk to you for a second?

CIVILIAN: Yes.

OFFICER: I'm Officer [Last Name] with the [town/city] Police
    Department. What's your name?

CIVILIAN: [Name].

OFFICER: [Name]? Um, are you a student?

CIVILIAN: Yes.

OFFICER: Yeah, is it okay if I sit down and talk to you?

CIVILIAN: Yeah.

OFFICER: Cool.

CIVILIAN: **Did something happen?**

OFFICER: No, no. I just wanted to talk to you.

CIVILIAN: Oh ...

OFFICER: Just wanted to say hey.

CIVILIAN: **Something happen?**

OFFICER: No something, nothing happened. No. Just wanting to talk to
    you, say hey.

CIVILIAN: Hi.

How would you characterize this exchange? Most say awkward—or cringe, as younger people would put it. Also, note the fear in the young civilian. She asks twice if something (a crime) has happened, highlighted in bold. Dobson knows for a fact that this officer *wanted* to put the civilian at ease and have a nice conversation because Dobson interviewed her after. What went wrong?

The Transparency Observation

After a year of ride alongs, Dobson observed that a few officers had simply and elegantly solved the threat cycle. Any time they approached a civilian on the street, they explained in clear words that they were just going to ask some questions to get to know and help the community. (And they meant it.) They announced their benevolent intent up front. That's all. Amazingly, the officers engaged in pleasant conversations and sometimes helped solve people's problems. After one interaction in a low-income housing project—where residents often come to distrust the police—Dobson overheard a civilian exclaim, "Now *that's* what policing should be about!"

Dobson called this solution a *transparency statement*: a simple and clear declaration of your intentions at the start of any potentially threatening interaction. In a way, it functions like a wise-feedback note. Recall that in the Post-it Note study, wise feedback helped students feel less threatened by critical feedback. Teachers clarified that they intended to support students' growth, not blame or condemn them. Because students so often feel judged, evaluated, and shamed, they needed to hear the teacher's intentions stated clearly. Dobson realized that officers practicing community policing needed to overcome the same apprehension. In general, people feel threatened by officers wearing weapons who ask them questions. When people feel threatened, it puts up the barrier of mistrust. Then they assume the worst—unless they are given clear reasons to think differently. Only then might they be open to a new and different narrative.

The Transparency Experiment

Dobson, Dittmann, and I decided to put their clever observation to the test in a rigorous experiment. We recruited young adults from eighteen to twenty-five years old, the age group that has the most encounters with law enforcement, to participate in an experiment about "real-life interactions." We didn't tell the young people that they'd be interacting with officers. They sat in different places where people in the community were likely to encounter police officers, as we knew from prior scouting. They wore physiological-stress-detection devices on their wrists, and hidden microphones recorded their conversations. After a few minutes of waiting, Dobson arranged for a fully uniformed and armed on-duty police officer to approach the young people and start asking them questions.

Dobson instructed half the officers, the control group, to interact with the civilians as they normally would. (The transcript above is an example from the control group.) He instructed the other half of the officers to start with a short transparency statement, such as, "Hi! I'm Officer [name]. How's it going? *I'm walking around trying to get to know the community.* Can I talk to you for a minute?" See the study setup in figure 5.1 below.

Figure 5.1. The procedures for Dobson's transparency experiment.

Transparency condition:
"Hi, I'm Officer [Last Name], how's it going? *I'm walking around trying to get to know the community.* Can I talk to you for a minute?"

Control condition:
"Hi, I'm Officer [Name], how's it going? Can I talk to you for a minute?"

N = 232 interactions

Baseline	Interaction & Recovery	Survey
~2–5 min	~2–3 min	~1–2 min

Continuous skin conductance monitoring

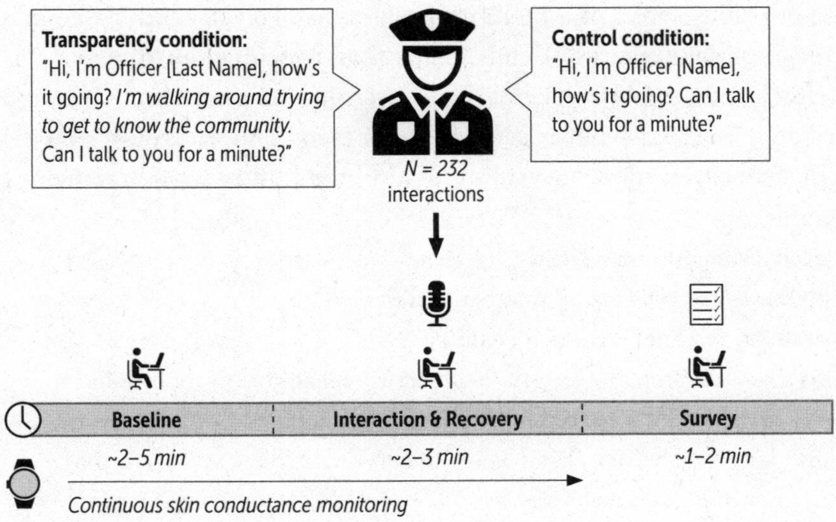

Would that transparency statement really make a difference? Prior to the experiment, Dobson's partner officers told him that it wouldn't. After all, they thought it seemed obvious that they were trying to get to know the community (rather than trying to harass people). Their department shield says KEEPING YOU, YOUR FAMILY, AND THE COMMUNITY SAFE. Why would people think anything differently? But if civilians come to the interaction with a barrier of mistrust, maybe the officers' positive intentions wouldn't be so obvious.

In the control condition, the stress monitor showed that people felt threatened. Informed by electrical signals from the sweat on people's skin, we found that people went into fight-or-flight mode, trying to escape. We also used complex statistical procedures to analyze their language. In the control condition, people used short, evasive, formal language—all signs that they felt threatened and wanted the conversation to end as quickly as possible. On a survey at the end of the study, fully 70 percent said that they felt threatened.

How about the transparency condition? Starting with a short transparency statement transformed the officers' interactions with young people. The stress-physiology signals showed that the participants were emotionally engaged. Linguistic analyses found more positive words in the transparency group. The officers and the participants engaged in more complex back-and-forth conversations (that were ultimately twice as long). And both sides spoke in a more informal tone, like you tend to see in a conversation between two friends, rather than two antagonists.

Here's an example transcript of a conversation between an officer and a civilian in the transparency group, both women. (This excerpt is from the end of the conversation, a few minutes after the transparency statement.)

[Minutes after the transparency statement]

CIVILIAN: Are you here all summer?

OFFICER: Yes, I'm here 365 it feels like.

CIVILIAN: I'll probably see you then because I'll always be at [my job] every day for some reason. Working those doubles.

OFFICER: [Laughter] Yeah, I'm going to come in and just say hey to you now because I feel like—

CIVILIAN: Yes, I'm at the front desk. Just come.

OFFICER: You'll just like need it to, like—

CIVILIAN: To get through the day, honestly.

OFFICER: Yeah, to like just switch it up, flip it up.

CIVILIAN: No, you should. You should definitely come in. I'm always at the front desk.

OFFICER: I will. I will. Next time, I'm, I'm working tomorrow. You work tomorrow?

CIVILIAN: Yeah. No, I actually do.

OFFICER: I'm going to come say hey.

CIVILIAN: Yeah, come say hi. Literally. Okay.

OFFICER: Well, it was nice to talk to you.

CIVILIAN: It was nice meeting you. I'll see you later.

What difference do you notice? Most people notice the easy, serve-and-return dynamic between the officer and civilian. Prior to this study, the civilian said that she distrusted police officers. But with the transparency statement, we see a striking shift. She's asking the officer to come visit her at work!

People may assume, *Oh, well the officer in the second transcript was just a nicer person than the officer in the first transcript.* But in fact, *it was the exact same police officer in both transcripts.* In the latter conversation, the officer gave a ten-word transparency statement about the reason why she was striking up a conversation. Nothing else changed.

Another common objection I hear is *Well, what if the officer just pretended to be nice to get the civilian to put her guard down so the officer could take advantage of her?* Sure, that's a possibility in the real world. Sometimes officers could have poor intentions. In this case, however, the officer said prior to the study that she wanted to form good relationships with civilians in the community. Her efforts in the control group failed. But when she added the transparency statement, she succeeded in meeting her goals. In general, transparency works best when you seek to achieve positive relationship goals, not when you aim to manipulate people.

Note that the transparency statement can be flexible. It's not one-size-fits-all. In Dobson's study, he allowed the officers to customize a statement for each interaction so it didn't feel fake or forced. Even with different wording, the transparency statement proved effective so long as (1) it came right at the beginning of the interaction, to build trust swiftly; (2) it made a clear declaration of benevolent intent; and (3) it referred to the officer's own intentions and behavior, not something abstract about their role. An officer had to say, "*I'm* out trying to get to know the community," rather than "Officers are out here getting to know the community."

The Sergio of Policing

Dobson is a relentless scientist. After completing his transparency experiment, he started planning how he could get transparency training into the hands of more officers. He found a collaborator in the police force: Officer Jeremy Bohannon, who works on community policing initiatives for the Austin Police Department. Bohannon is Black, in his midthirties, and deeply reflective about his role in the community. He's fair and equitable and against racialized divisions in criminal justice. Dobson found Bohannon by analyzing the department's statistics, similar to how we found Sergio. Bohannon has the lowest rate of civilian interactions that escalate into arrests. He told me that some of his colleagues consider that a bad thing. They measure success by how many arrests officers make. Bohannon thinks their attitude comes from an enforcer mindset—the belief that young people are fundamentally risks to manage, and so the more of them you put away, the better off society is. Bohannon doesn't think that way. He believes that many young people make mistakes and end up in tough situations, sometimes escalated by the arrival of police. Confronted by officers, young people might run away or act suspiciously. But if officers start off an interaction the right way—for example, with transparency about their mentor-like approach—then they can prevent many criminal behaviors from happening.

What does a transparent mentor-mindset approach look like for officers like Bohannon? One Friday, Dobson and I got Officer Bohannon and Sergio Estrada together for a beer in Austin to find out. Bohannon told us about the time he and his partner were called into a convenience store where a Black teenager was loitering. The clerk behind the desk, concerned about shoplifting or an armed robbery, had called 911. How would the officers respond? Their training had taught them to prioritize safety by incapacitating the suspect as quickly as possible. A typical officer might start yelling, *On your knees!* or *Lie down!* immediately upon entering the store. Alternatively, they might come up behind the suspect and wrestle him into handcuffs. Once they had handcuffed the subject and contained the threat, they would ask questions such as, *What are you doing in the store?* and assess him for shoplifting. Bohannon's partner expected him to take the enforcer-mindset approach their training had instilled in them. But Bohannon took a drastically different approach. He made eye contact with the teen and walked up slowly. He did not touch or draw his weapon. Then he explained his intentions. "I'm here because of a 911 call," he said. "But I want you to know we're not accusing you of anything. My goal is to understand what you need and help you get it. If you wouldn't mind, could you tell me what's up and then we can see if I can be helpful?" Note what he didn't say. He didn't ask, *Did you shoplift?* or *Are you going to rob the store?*—questions that would have put the teen on high alert. Even if the teen was innocent, he might have worried that the officers would unfairly accuse him of a crime, and he might have fled. If he had run, officers might've shot or arrested him. Instead, Bohannon's transparency statement put the teen at ease.

What happened next? The teen told Bohannon that he was trying to take the public bus home. He'd missed the free school bus because he had to run an errand for his mom that afternoon. He walked to the corner store to catch the city bus, but he didn't have any money to pay the fare. He was waiting for someone who might be willing to give him the $1.50 for the bus. Yes, he was loitering, but he didn't know what else to do. Bohannon listened intently. He said, "Okay, thanks. I do still have to check your pockets because it was a 911 call, but after that we'll figure out how to get you home." Sure enough, the kid's pockets were empty. No stolen goods. No weapons. Note that because Bohannon made it clear that his job was to help the kid figure out his situation, the kid had no problem with the routine search. What happened next shocked Bohannon's partner. *Bohannon gave the kid a ride home in the squad car.* As the teenager got out of the car, he said, "No cop has ever treated me with respect like that before. Thanks."

Lessons from Dobson's Transparency Studies

Power disparities. Transparency statements prove especially important in situations that involve both a *power disparity* and a *history of conflict or poor treatment.* Those are the circumstances that cause the barrier of mistrust. In the policing example, an officer has the authority to use lethal force. Quite literally, a civilian's life rests in the officer's hands. Naturally, the civilian feels threatened and on high alert—unless given very good reason to feel completely safe and secure from harm. Unfortunately, public opinion surveys show that trust in the police has fallen to an all-time low. Given this history, officers need to use transparency statements to hit refresh for each interaction.

Likewise, Andrew, the junior teacher, needed a transparency statement from the principal who was observing his class. A power disparity exists between an established principal and a new teacher. The former has authority to fire (or reward) the latter. Moreover, teachers in general tend to distrust administrators, in part because admin no longer interacts with kids in the classroom on a day-to-day basis. When a principal walks in the room to observe a teacher, a teacher will reasonably suspect that the principal will use their power to evaluate or potentially reprimand the teacher. A transparency statement could take that possibility off the table and set the stage for a more trusting interaction.

The same logic applies for the senior attorney, Jane, who had more power than her firm's junior associates. Jane can't hire or fire junior associates, but she can tell the partners if they've performed poorly. Her negative reports could get them fired or at least kept off important cases until they're laid off. Mired in law firms' toxic, all-or-nothing, genius-or-idiot cultures, a junior associate would reasonably presume that negative, critical feedback was just thinly veiled code for *you're an idiot*—unless Jane made it crystal clear that she did *not* mean her feedback as an insult.

In short, transparency statements are needed when, in the absence of additional information, a lower-power person feeling vulnerable and uncertain of their status has a legitimate reason to suspect reputational or physical harm from a higher-power person.

Timing. Dobson's policing study also offers the lesson that that early distrust breeds future conflict or withdrawal. Transparency enabled the officer to break the cycle of threat and mistrust. Instead, we got a high-quality relationship in a short amount of time. To demonstrate the importance of timing, Dobson did an extra analysis of the officer-civilian transcripts. In cases where officers made transparency statements at the end of three-minute conversations, the transparency came too late. People didn't say, *Oh, I'm totally fine with being terrified for my life for three minutes now that you explained what you were doing.* They needed to hear it in the first few sentences.

How can adults craft transparency statements to reach the young people in their lives? For the last few years, we have worked with Sergio Estrada to find an answer. Our findings appear in a new experiment that we call the first-day-of-class-speech study.

Transparency Speeches

Sergio Learns to Be Transparent

Even Sergio Estrada didn't automatically come across as a mentor-mindset superhero. Some students looked at his exceptionally high standards—pushing students to the limits of their understanding, requiring them to own their learning and fix their mistakes—and thought he was being mean. After all, *other* Riverside teachers don't expect very much. To avoid losing students, Sergio had to learn to infuse his class with supportive messages about why he held them to high standards, and how his class provided opportunities for all to meet these standards. He did this from day one and continued it throughout the year. One experience that instilled this practice in him came from Mia, a student in his college-level physics class in the 2021–2022 school year.

Mia Lagunas was a straight-A student. When she was young, her family moved from Mexico to El Paso. Nobody in her family had gone to college. She cared a lot about doing well in school and making her parents' sacrifices for her worthwhile. But in Sergio's class, "the first two months were so brutal for me," she said. "I had never been so academically challenged as I was in that class." Unlike in her other classes, Mia routinely earned Bs and Cs in Sergio's class—or even worse. She struggled to adjust to the first school year back in person after the COVID-19 pandemic. "My brain was working at only twenty-five percent during online school." That quarter-power brain ran head-on into the high expectations of Sergio's mentor mindset. "There were times where I felt so lost." She hated the class at first.

Sergio's experience with Adam (recall chapter 4) had taught him to listen to students and be self-critical. He decided to change his approach. Working with me and my team, Sergio wrote a speech that would transparently and succinctly lay out his philosophy of instruction. Rather than make students like Mia guess why his class was different from every other class at Riverside, we would make his mentor mindset abundantly clear to them.

Sergio organized his speech around five key questions that he knew students were asking themselves.

1. **What is it like to learn in this class?** Sergio started off by explaining that learning isn't supposed to be easy. It's not all As and 100 percents. It will require hard work at first, but the effort pays off. He said, "By the end of the unit, questions that once seemed impossible will feel manageable."

2. **What is the meaning of struggle in this class?** Students assume that teachers look down on them for mistakes. Sergio had to clarify that "everyone will make mistakes in this class, and we will make those mistakes into teaching moments for the class. It helps me be a better teacher when you make mistakes."

3. **Can I ask questions?** Most students refrain from raising a hand to ask a question because they fear broadcasting their ignorance in front of the class. Sergio had to explain that "you are never wasting class time with questions. Don't look around and say, 'Why is nobody else asking a question?' I guarantee you are not the only one with that question." He even makes questions high status by praising students who ask them: "You might be the only one who's courageous enough to ask it."

4. **Why do we have to redo our work so much?** Sergio doesn't let the first quiz or test grade stand because he wants students to fix their misunderstandings. He says, "You are allowed to

redo any assignment in the class [because] analyzing your mistakes is an important step in learning to not make that mistake again."

5. **What do my test scores mean?** Lastly, Sergio knows that most students walk into a classroom thinking that tests represent an all-or-nothing opportunity to confirm whether you are a good student or a bad student. He says, "Tests are checkpoints in time. Tests do not determine your future, your potential, or even what you truly know at that moment. You are more than a number."

In addition to delivering this speech to the class, he printed it out and re-reads it all the time. He referred to it at the start of each new unit and before and after each big exam.

By the end of the fall semester, Mia and the other students in Sergio's class began to come around. They started to appreciate his mentor-mindset approach. "When we failed a test—and believe me we did that all the time," Mia told me, "instead of giving us that grade, he would call us in during advisory and say, 'Okay, let's look at the mistakes you made, try to see why you made them, and fix them.'" *Collaborative troubleshooting!* "Now I appreciate those teachers who value you as a student," Mia said. "I knew he cared about us, and he was going to give us the tools and resources to be successful. That's why I didn't drop the class."

Because of Sergio's mentorship, Mia was admitted to a prestigious summer internship at NASA. A year later, she was selected as a QuestBridge scholar and received a full scholarship to Boston College, where she is now the first in her family to go to college.

Messages and Opportunities

Dr. Cameron Hecht is an award-winning scholar at the University of Texas at Austin who's worked under top psychologists like Stanford's Carol Dweck and the University of Wisconsin–Madison's Judy Harackiewicz. Hecht and I have conducted experiments on the Sergio transparency speech with thousands of teenagers.

Hecht identified the two critical pieces to this type of speech. One piece is mentor-mindset *messages*—the statements about what you believe. For example, Sergio says he believes that all his students can understand physics deeply if they learn from their mistakes. For the second piece of the speech, his class needs to hear about *opportunities*—the possibilities for growth and improvement given to students and the structural decisions that enable them. Sergio's examples include his revision policy—anyone can revise any test, quiz, or homework—and his availability during off periods to go over assignments with students. Following up messages with opportunities is critical, Hecht found, because not doing so amounts to hypocrisy. A teacher would look like a jerk or a liar if they said *Everyone can improve!* but then had a grading policy where you're stuck as an F student for the whole semester if you fail at the beginning. After all, teenagers are evolution's perfectly designed hypocrisy detectors.

This two-pronged approach aligns with what I saw when observing Stef Okamoto as a manager at ServiceNow and Microsoft (chapters 2 and 4). She transparently explained to her direct reports that she provides critical feedback because she thinks they can meet a higher level of performance. The opportunities, however, are the incentive and bonus structures. If people were praised for growth but only rewarded for absolute performance on their first try, there would be a misalignment. As we seek to be transparent about our mentor mindsets, it's important to remember the value of both *messages* and *opportunities*.

The Importance of Repetition

Dr. Stacy Sparks, who teaches introductory chemistry to nearly three thousand college freshmen each year, opened her class with a clear message about her beliefs ("In this class everyone is capable of meeting the high standards") and opportunities for growth ("You can come to office hours to talk about your confusion or mistakes"). But then the first exam rolled around. Students avoided office hours. They didn't ask questions. They felt like Stacy was sorting them into med-school material or not.

Stacy approached me with this problem. We realized that she couldn't assume that clarifying her mentor mindset once would suffice. She needed to repeat her message at difficult moments, such as hard exams. Those are the moments when students doubt themselves the most. They're feeling vulnerable and so they fall back into their old default assumption that professors don't care about them and just want to sort them into genius or idiot buckets. Timely and repeated transparency statements can reassure students of our mentor-mindset intentions.

Once Stacy reasserted her transparent message about her mentor mind-set—far more often than she initially thought she should have to—then she saw more and more students coming to office hours and improving.

Chapter 6

Questioning

I shall only ask him, and not teach him, and he shall share the enquiry with me.

—Socrates in Plato's *Meno*

Two Challenges

Kate's Story

Kate is a mom of two and lives in Chicago. One night, her oldest son, Jared, then a high school sophomore, came home from a party drunk and high on marijuana. Kate responded with a combination of yelling and prosecuting. "What were you thinking? Where were you? Don't you know how mad this makes me? Don't you know how scared we are? Don't you know how grounded you'll be?" She instigated an interrogation, not a two-way conversation. What happened next? Jared knew that he couldn't have an honest discussion about alcohol or marijuana with his mother, so he got better at hiding his substance use. He snuck around her. Then his habit got worse. A few years later, Jared dropped out of college because of his low grades.

Gary's Story

Gary lived alone with his teenage daughter, Charlotte, after his wife moved out and stopped communicating with them. For years, Charlotte had struggled with eating disorders, self-harm (e.g., cutting), anxiety, and depression. Increasingly, Charlotte spent her time online, eventually starting a relationship with an older boy who lived in Canada. Gary worried about the relationship and wanted Charlotte to find someone closer to home. What did he do? Nothing. He feared any conversation about her dating life would turn into a fight. With Charlotte's mom gone, his was the only positive adult relationship his daughter had left. A fight would jeopardize that. He didn't want his daughter to lose her relationships with her mom, dad, and boyfriend all at once. So he adopted a protector mindset and avoided the topic altogether. Over the next few months, Gary saw Charlotte lose sleep, sacrifice more of her face-to-face friendships, show less interest in field hockey, and become more depressed. Feeling isolated and alone, Charlotte spent even more time late at night with "the only person who understood" how she felt: her Canadian boyfriend.

Meet Lorena Seidel

Kate's and Gary's stories share one important feature: both are examples of the mentor's dilemma. Kate and Gary, like many of us, feel a tension between critiquing our children's choices and maintaining a good relationship with them. Interestingly, this commonality means that the mentor mindset can help in both situations. Indeed, Kate and Gary learned what to do next from the same parenting coach, an expert in the mentor mindset.

Kate and Gary's parenting coach, Lorena Seidel, is the Sergio of parenting. She is one of the most in-demand parenting coaches in the United States. If you desperately want a household free of slamming doors, *I hate you*s, shaming, blaming, guilt, or embarrassment, then you call Lorena.

Lorena was born in Brazil to an enforcer-mindset mother. Lorena told me that her most vivid memory as a child was a time when she and her brother broke a valuable item while playing. After a verbal lashing, her mother forced the children to literally kiss her feet as a sign of deference and respect. Then and there, Lorena vowed to be nothing like her mother.

Twenty-five years later, Lorena was living in Connecticut. She was a mother of two young children. A successful teacher. A master's-educated professional. She thought parenting would be a breeze. She considered herself an expert. One day, after her children broke a rule, she blew up. "Respect your mother!" she screamed. When the tornado of rage died down, she surveyed the wreckage. Tears. Fear. Humiliation. She had become her mother! That day she made a new vow. She would figure out what she had learned as a child, and she would unlearn it as a parent. She would have to learn how to change her mindset. A decade later, she has succeeded, and she's on a mission to share her insights with others.

As a scientist, I am often skeptical of parenting experts—and really anybody peddling secret knowledge about the next generation. Sometimes, it feels like parenting is the only area of self-help that's worse than dieting, which is notoriously driven by fads and contraditions, not science. When it comes to mentor-mindset parenting, how can we tell the difference between common sense and common nonsense?

Over the last three years, I became confident in Lorena's advice for three reasons. First, I have personally witnessed, with envy, one of her clients' households. They have four children just as energetic and difficult as my own, but in that house the children modeled proactive helpfulness and respectful independence. Second, her advice aligns well with the behaviors of the mentor-mindset exemplars and decades of research. Her philosophy is not a fad—it's a more practical version of what Baumrind (chapter 2) has been saying for decades about mentor-mindset (i.e., authoritative) parents. Nevertheless, she has a new way of tying powerful ideas together into a sensible framework that even busy, stressed-out parents can pull off. Third, I've tried her advice with my own children, and it's helped quite a lot. Of course, most parents, myself included, don't want to spend a lot of money on a parenting coach or can't afford to. Here I've tried to identify the principles of Lorena's methods so that anyone can access this information.

What did Lorena say to Kate about her enforcer mindset and Gary about his protector mindset? She started by helping them see why their initial responses, while growing out of their love for their children, were nevertheless short-term strategies.

Kate, for example, saw the danger of drugs and alcohol. She wanted to nip the problem in the bud. She was also offended that her son would so flagrantly disrespect her house rules. She wanted to teach him a lesson about respect. Her enforcer mindset taught him the wrong lesson. It taught him that he should not get caught. The enforcer mindset backfired in the long term.

Gary wanted to protect his daughter from the distress of feeling like she lost both parents—one physically, one emotionally. Therefore, he avoided a difficult conversation. But this short-term strategy never helped his daughter cope with her deeper issues of loneliness or abandonment.

Lorena feels compassion for parents who resort to these short-term strategies. She understands how parents can succumb to the urgency to look like a good parent, and how this can lead to the enforcer or protector mindsets. Whether our kids partake in drinking, unhealthy dating, or something else—cutting, disordered eating, or suicidality—we feel like terrible parents for having out-of-control children.

We also fear the invisible audience of parents who judge us for being *public* failures, either because we are too firm on poor behavior (in Kate's case) or too soft (in Gary's case). We internalize this imaginary jury of our peers from the moment we learn we're expecting a baby. Parenting judgment starts with our choice of name-brand versus generic prenatal vitamins and continues through each developmental milestone, from the amount of plastic in your baby's first stroller to where your teen goes to college.

Lorena thinks parents rush to solve problems with the quick-fix enforcer and protector mindsets partially because these approaches send a clear signal to the imaginary jury of our peers that we're not being neglectful. We obsess over what our child's behavior *means* for us as parents, in the eyes of this imaginary audience, rather than considering what our child actually *needs* for healthy development.

Of course, the audience is *imaginary*. Therefore, parents often fixate on their *guesses* of what others might be thinking, not what they've actually heard. "The problem is never the problem," Lorena is fond of saying to clients. "It's what we *think of the problem*." When we think the problem is that other parents will condemn us, then we can fall into the quickest short-term mindsets.

In a strange twist of irony, Lorena thinks parents often act like teenagers. We react impulsively with enforcer or protector mindsets to look good in front of peer parents, just like our own children who take huge risks because of what they imagine *their* peers might think of them if they don't attend a party or do something dangerous.

Lorena explains that we're mostly fighting over the *meaning* of a situation, not the situation itself. It's a version of the battle over meaning (chapter 3). To kids, the situation means they're not getting what they need. To parents, it means they're the kind of people who get disrespected by their kids. Meanwhile, nobody fixes the underlying conflict.

This problem is simple to understand but difficult to overcome. Here's an example. Lorena's kids, aged ten and twelve, sometimes bicker loudly at home, like all kids. It doesn't bother her that much. When they fight in public, however, she feels mortified. One afternoon, her kids fought on a crowded train car full of strangers. Humiliated, she panicked. In enforcer mode, she ordered one kid to stop acting selfish, the other kid to stop overreacting. Stop! Stop! Stop! Stanford emotion scientist James Gross calls this strategy *suppression*. Lorena told her kids to suppress the feelings they were having because their conflict made her uncomfortable. Suppression is a classic enforcer-mindset tactic—it follows from the idea that your kids' emotions are illegitimate, so you can simply tell them to stop. In a moment of clarity, Lorena flashed back. She had turned into her mother again!

Determined to try something different, Lorena addressed her kids in a low voice: "I don't know what to do right now, and I need your help to find a solution. I feel uncomfortable. I feel embarrassed, like all these people are thinking I'm a not a good mom and that my kids are running the show. I know your priority right now is to figure out who's right about your argument, but my priority is to be considerate to all these other people on the train. Can you help me figure this out?" She spoke in a puzzled, curious voice without a hint of anger or sarcasm. "I'd like us to get on the same page so we all get what we want. Do you have any ideas?" Note that she opened up to the kids about *her own* feelings, then she *asked* them about *their* actions. She invited them to join her in the collaborative-troubleshooting mode. It's a treaty-coauthorship session. They figured out how to resolve the conflict without going down the path of shaming, blaming, punishing, and bribing.

Asking *questions*—particularly ones that launch us into joint problem-solving, collaborative-troubleshooting mode—can show young people that we need to work together to understand the mismatch of priorities. Questions also send a respectful signal that we as parents aren't simply demanding that our children comply and suppress their feelings. Instead, we legitimize children's perspectives and demonstrate a willingness to work with them. In sum, Lorena shows us that *it's better to ask than to tell.*

Question Asking and the Mentor Mindset

What does legendary NBA coach Chip Engelland say when a player misses a shot in practice? He doesn't yell, *Wrong, stop, do it this way!* He asks, "How did that feel?" and he waits for an answer.

How does Sergio Estrada react when a student misses a physics problem? He doesn't say, *You got this wrong because you forgot to multiply the force.* He asks, "Can you tell me how you got this answer?" Then he starts collaboratively troubleshooting, building on the student's understanding.

And what does Stef Okamoto say to an employee on track for a poor performance review? She doesn't declare, *You're doing everything wrong.* She asks, "Can you tell me where you're getting stuck and what you've tried so far so we can try to fix the problem?" Then she runs interference.

Again and again, I saw that *questioning*, rather than *telling*, constituted a core mentor-mindset practice. And it reminded me of the best manager I ever had: Jennifer (Jen) Wu.

Jen Wu is now one of Silicon Valley's most influential education-technology venture capitalists. She controls a portfolio worth hundreds of millions of dollars at Reach Capital. Fifteen years ago Jen worked at an underfunded nonprofit in the San Francisco Bay Area dedicated to educational equity, called Partners in School Innovation. For one amazing summer, I interned there. With Jen as my manager, it proved the most productive summer of my life.

What made Jen so great? Here's what she didn't do. She didn't show up every morning and tell me how to organize my day (even though she was a trained project manager). Nor did she leave me alone to do whatever I felt like, which would have been a disaster. As a twenty-five-year-old PhD student, I usually had complete control over my time—so nothing forced me to be organized. I was inefficient and unrealistic. I didn't need a manager to babysit me, but I needed help working on a team deadline. Jen decided that she would meet with me for fifteen minutes every morning throughout my twelve-week internship to help me prioritize. Our meetings usually went like this:

JEN: So, David, what are you planning on working on today?

I describe something that was unrealistic and would take three weeks.

JEN: Okay, so which part of that is most important to do now?

I say that nothing I had just said was that important, but something else would be more important.

JEN: Great, so if you did that more important thing, would you have the resources you need to get it done?

I say I don't have what I need at all.

JEN: Interesting. If I got you what you needed, and you worked on the first step toward the big project, how much could you get done today?

I finally put it all together and lay out a well-organized and reasonable plan that links to what I would need to pull it off.

JEN: Try that and then come check with me. If you get stuck I'll see if we can get you what you need to stay on track.

Without fail, I accomplished my entire list and then some by about 3:00 p.m. each day. I finished my project weeks ahead of schedule, without much stress. What's more, I learned to ask myself Jen's questions. She gave me the enduring gift of a "manager in the head."

Why did it work? Look back at Jen's questions in the transcript. They sounded curious and authentic. They weren't judgmental or condescending. They built on my answers until she fully understood what I was saying. Further, Jen was no pushover. She could be demanding—she squinted and looked at me sideways when I said something unrealistic—but she was never adversarial. Her demeanor made it clear to me that she just wanted to understand how in the world I planned to fit everything into eight hours. Her challenging questions made me feel like she was taking me seriously, as though I had it in me to make a strong plan, not like she was undermining my competence. These questions motivated me because I wanted to impress her.

This style of questioning is a mentor-mindset practice. Jen demonstrated high standards (because she expected me to explain my thinking logically) and high support (because she responded nonjudgmentally and tried to understand my thinking while troubleshooting with me until I had a realistic plan).

What makes Jen Wu's mentor-mindset questions especially important today? Millions of new graduates, after spending years in college with total control over their time, entered a mostly work-from-home workforce during and after the COVID-19 pandemic. They needed a mentor-mindset manager. They rarely got one.

When I interviewed dozens of Gen Z employees for this book, I heard about managers' apathetic mindsets. The new hires reported that their managers neglected them for months, then fired them for underperformance. Many managers practiced extreme enforcer mindsets, even mandating nanny-cam software to track employee productivity so that they could punish truants. Derisive CEOs such as Elon Musk accused at-home employees of pretending to work.

I wonder how many of these supposedly lazy young people just needed a manager like Jen Wu. If a mentor sets aside fifteen minutes a day (or even fifteen minutes a week) to ask you authentic, open-ended questions about how to optimize your time, you'll feel motivated. On the other hand, having a manager who doesn't give you any meaningful time or attention is demotivating. Who knows how much money businesses could save—and how much more respected young employees would feel—if new hires got the Jen Wu treatment. They would probably work more efficiently, overperform, and want to stick around at their jobs.

When Lorena Seidel went back to school to complete her master's degree, she read a century's worth of parenting advice. Individual psychology,

Alfred Adler, 1927. Attachment theory, Mary Ainsworth, 1978. Positive discipline, Jane Nelsen, 1981. Positive psychology, Martin Seligman, 2000. And so on.

Lorena's tour through the history of parenting research surfaced two themes. First, just about every expert said some version of the same thing: *Understand and address the underlying cause of the child's behavior; don't just respond to the behavior.* Second, parents rarely do it. Positive parenting and addiction have a lot in common, Lorena noticed. Everybody's constantly falling off the wagon.

A hundred years' worth of research on parenting has granted us important theories that have proved frustratingly difficult to apply to the complexities of our daily lives. By and large, child psychologists' big theoretical insights in the twentieth century didn't occur to them when the macaroni was burning on the stove, the repairman was knocking at the door, and four kids were fighting over an iPad. Their revelations occurred in quiet offices, surrounded by books. Parenting advice therefore tends to be impractically tailored to hypothetical parents who have endless attention and patience, no constraints on their time, and logical, compliant children. That's not the reality most parents live in.

I admire the expertise of people like Lorena, who took the scientific evidence and said, *How can I actually use this? And how can I get other parents to use it?* She spends time in many households. She sees parents at their most honest and vulnerable, not how they'd describe themselves in therapy sessions. She swears by questioning as a mentor-mindset practice because she's seen it work in all manner of families.

How does Lorena coach parents to ask questions effectively? She focuses first on parents' mindsets.

Even before I told her about the premise of my book, Lorena said to me, "We know how to be kind and firm. We are naturally one or the other. It's the *nice-and-nasty dance.* But we can't find the sweet spot of being kind and firm at the same time." Lorena knew that we're inclined to become either enforcers or protectors. When circumstances are calm, parents cater to kids' needs. We fill the piggy bank with kind deeds, hoping our kids will show their gratitude by listening the first time we ask. We're protectors. Then when we need some behavior to change (e.g., pants on or punches pulled), we ask once. We ask twice. We give a warning. We give a second warning. We ask a third time. We're ignored. Then we go nuclear. We yell, we threaten, we blame, we shame. We take away privileges. Screens are gone. Then we go back to acting nice again because we feel guilty. The nice-and-nasty dance. Protector to enforcer and back again.

Sometimes, both parents feed into the problem. One parent is the enforcer, the other the protector. They're partners in the nice-and-nasty dance.

Lorena thinks that a mindset shift is the key to escaping this dance because she sees parents trapped in the dichotomy of good parent versus bad parent—a fixed mindset of parenting. Parents think, *I went to the seminar, and I read the book, and I still ended up blowing up at my kids. I guess I'm a bad parent.* They fall back into the protector mindset. But the protector's indulgence prevents kids from learning how to be self-directed—which inevitably leads to repeated behavior, another enforcer explosion, and more guilt.

Lorena wants to free parents from that cycle, using a simple but profound concept: the *do-over*. Lorena teaches parents that after they fall into either protector or enforcer mode, they can try again. They're not stuck being bad parents. They could knock on their kid's door and apologize for failing to uphold the family's standards and for failing to help the kid meet the standard. They can explain that they should've tried to figure out what their child needed because they care about the child's welfare and the health of the family. By taking this approach, do parents cede too much control to young people? No, because parents lead the conversation with a tough-but-loving mentor mindset.

During the do-over, Lorena coaches parents to ask *authentic questions with uptake*. For example, "I know you yelled that you hate your brother. Although I don't want that behavior in our house I also suspect it's coming from somewhere important. Can you help me understand what you *really* needed in that moment so that I can help you get it next time?" This outreach opens the door for collaborative troubleshooting and treaty writing.

Sometimes the kid responds obstinately. They might say, "I really needed my brother to feel pain because I hate him." You can answer that easily by countering, "Could it be anything else?" This is important because most kids get mad about what something *meant*, not what happened. For instance, the parent might learn that the siblings started fighting over an injustice, rooted in the parent being too permissive with screen time for one child (who needs to be distracted) versus another (who is more self-directed). Kids are effective hypocrisy detectors, after all. The parent might then ask, "Now that I understand what you needed, what could I have done to make sure you got it?" In that moment, the child feels heard, validated, and supported. But the child also has to think. Next, Lorena coaches parents to plan for the future so kids own this process next time. "What can I say to you next time so that we just quickly figure out what you need, rather than having a fight? I want to say it in a way that doesn't offend you, so could you tell me what you'd like to hear from me?" Now the parent and child have insider shortcuts for cutting straight to the problem-solving, skipping the *I hate you*s. This strategy works better than the paternalistic approach of saying "Cut it out."

Allow me to emphasize something profound about Lorena's questioning. She doesn't assume that parents can stop while their hair is on fire and suddenly turn into a mix of Mary Poppins and Atticus Finch. She thinks that most parents, even great ones, have bad instincts and tend to resort to using an enforcer or protector mindset, largely because the culture they grew up in gave them two bad options. Thus, most parents will need do-overs. The do-over, in turn, lays the groundwork for solving the next crisis more efficiently. A do-over takes a bit of time—five or ten minutes—but it offers a much better alternative to having another forty-five-minute meltdown four times a week. If you do it enough, then kids start knowing what you're going to say to them. You can give them their own "coach in the head" like Chip Engelland or Sergio Estrada. This tactic doesn't prevent all conflicts, but it makes de-escalation easier.

These days, when Lorena hears bickering two rooms over, she announces, "Girls, what am I going to ask you?" After a pause, a sigh, or a grunt, they say, "You're going to ask us if we're fighting over what we really need . . . and if we could find a way to have both of us get what we need . . . and that in our house we're supposed to solve our own problems respectfully . . . because you love us and you want us to be successful adults after we grow up and move out." "Okay," Lorena replies, "can you have that conversation and work it out?" "Fine!" they yell and huff off, better friends than before and more equipped for the future. What used to be an exhausting forty-five minutes—followed by hours of guilt for having such acrimonious children—became fifteen seconds. A little questioning saved far more time and grief in the long run.

"I got tired of refereeing," she told me. Her kids would fight, and she'd take away the toy or whatever. But her mindset was wrong. She was depriving her kids of the chance to learn skills like resilience and responsibility. "I resolved to never referee a fight again," she said. That decision to shift toward a mentor mindset and start asking questions (mostly during do-overs) saved her hours and countless headaches. That realization inspired her to coach parents to *ask, not tell* when they're in a conflict.

Although questioning can prove highly effective, many people instinctually pursue the opposite approach. They do so because of something I call the *compulsion to tell*.

The Compulsion to Tell

The compulsion to tell is the tendency to tell young people exactly what to do. Although this compulsion comes from a good place, it gets in the way of respecting young people. Our failure to show respect then feeds into the adolescent predicament, widening the generational divide.

Where does the compulsion to tell come from? Telling someone information is efficient. If we adults have relevant expertise or wisdom, we can quickly impart what we know by telling it to another person directly, rather than gradually building a young person's understanding via questioning. Giving information also feels polite. We rush to tell someone the information they need when they are confused, stuck, mistaken, or in distress. For example, if a stranger became lost in the neighborhood and pulled over to ask for directions, most people would tell them how to find their way. Or if a child asked a question about how to do fractions, most people would explain it to them. Withholding the answers would seem cruel. By contrast, it feels good to offer people information that helps them out.

Telling clearly works well in many circumstances. But we're fooling ourselves if we think that telling is always a good deed. Consider this:

Although *telling* usually feels good, *being told* often feels bad. Especially when someone tells you what you should do in the domain of personal choice.

Let's think about it. How would you feel if someone told you whom to befriend, which joke to tell, or how to dress? Many people would feel disrespected, like they were being talked down to or treated like children. When we impose our will on adolescents, we thwart their desire to be agentic learners who figure out how to have meaningful, respectworthy roles in their cultures. They need to learn *for themselves* how to gain and maintain status and respect—how to earn prestige—in their milieu.

Being told undermines that. You can't *tell* an adolescent what will get people to respect them any more than you can tell a child how to ride a bike. Status and respect have to be experienced and adjusted across many small interactions, just like the tiny muscles that have to adjust to keep your balance on a bike. *Telling*, in many cases, can deprive young people of valuable learning experiences. Further, it can be demotivating because it feels disrespectful.

Kate's compulsion to tell didn't help her son find a different way to fulfill whatever needs he was trying to meet by partying, such as his need to have social status in his friend group. A parent can't wish away a teenager's need for affiliation with friends, or any other need, any more than they can wish away a crying baby's need for milk or sleep. Kate *told* and didn't ask questions. So she didn't find out how her son's needs were driving his behavior. Then his behavior got worse.

How can we overcome the compulsion to tell?

Lorena believes we must acknowledge where this compulsion comes from, such as our need to impart our knowledge to young people to keep them safe. That's a good thing, and we should hang on to it, she says. Then we must choose a different way to meet our needs, one that better aligns with adolescents' needs: *questioning*.

When we *ask* instead of *tell*, we can indirectly accomplish the same goal of imparting knowledge. Young people are less likely to interpret our desire to help them as a desire to control them, making them more open to our (indirect) suggestions. Although questioning feels unnatural at first—because it goes against the compulsion to tell—it eventually becomes unconscious. In fact, most of the mentor-mindset exemplars I talked to didn't even realize how frequently they asked questions.

To build that unconscious habit, we need to understand the styles of questioning that engage young people effectively.

The Science and Practice of Questioning

The question—aka the interrogative clause—has many purposes.

The question's most obvious function is information exchange. A knowledgeable answerer educates an ignorant questioner. The question also has a secret double life when wielded for social purposes. A question can befuddle and belittle, or it can elevate the unknowledgeable. Questions can harass and prosecute, or they can grant agency and power and form the bases of meaningful relationships.

These diverse social purposes of questions are on display in Plato's famous work of philosophy named the *Meno*. In that dialogue, a haughty know-it-all named Meno poses a puzzle to Socrates: Is virtue (*areté* in the Greek) something that is *taught* (i.e., told to you by a teacher) or something that is *acquired* (i.e., learned through experience)? Over the next ten thousand or so words, Socrates never answers this question. Instead, Socrates asks questions that twist the prideful Meno into a pretzel, until Meno admits he doesn't even know what virtue is. Socrates's purpose was to reveal Meno's ignorance and, by implication, enhance Socrates's perceived wisdom. Socrates used questions for a social purpose: to put Meno in his place (Plato, the author, knew Meno would later condemn Socrates to death).

Plato's *Meno* also shows the kinder social purpose of questioning. In the most memorable section, Socrates asks questions of an uneducated servant until the boy understands a complex proof of a geometric theorem. Socrates purports to show that we all have knowledge in us already, and with the right experiences—in this case, leading questions—we can build on our assets and become smarter. "There have always been true thoughts in him," Socrates says, "which only need to be awakened into knowledge by putting questions in him." Socrates's questions enhance the status of a child because they reveal underappreciated knowledge.

Plato could've just had Socrates answer Meno's question by saying,

Virtue comes from a mix of knowledge we already have and experiences we have, which can be guided by a good teacher or mentor. The lesson could have been a lot shorter. Plato wrote it as a dialogue, however, to demonstrate how questioning as an *experience* leads to deeper learning. He shook the audience out of their compulsion to tell by showing them *how* to construct knowledge. By contrast, declaring *that* knowledge is constructed wouldn't work. People, in general, are so committed to the compulsion to tell. Thus, questioning in the *Meno* serves as a classic example of the English teacher's advice that it's better to *show* than to *tell*.

Not all questions are created equal. Although some brands of popular psychology tend to spread oversimplified, one-size-fits-all versions of practices like questioning, it's important to remember my refrain: most common sense is in fact common nonsense.

Think about Kate, the mom from Chicago whose son came home drunk from partying. Kate asked questions alright, but not the mentor mindset kind. *What were you thinking?* is a question, but it's not an authentic question. When we ask, *What were you thinking?* we mean, *You're an idiot who wasn't thinking. I don't care what your excuse was because it was wrong and you should listen to me.* Young people respond to what we mean, not what we say.

Think about teenagers getting grilled by officers during flawed community policing outreach, like in the control group in Dobson's study described in chapter 5. Peppering people with questions about their present, past, and future usually didn't endear the police to their community. To the contrary, civilians felt threatened.

To solve the puzzle of questioning, we can turn to decades of reliable research in the field of linguistics. The large and diverse field of linguistics has identified a particular type of question with special power: an *authentic question with uptake*.

Authentic Questions with Uptake

In an *authentic question*, the question asker does not know the answer and legitimately wants to know the answer. Kate yelling, "What were you thinking?" at her son is not an authentic question because she thinks she knows the answer (*You weren't thinking*), and she's not interested in his answer. A more authentic question would ask the child to explain their thinking.

A question *with uptake* means that the asker has been influenced by, or incorporated, information from the answerer. The asker has tailored their questions to that conversation—and ideally to the answerer's needs. Authentic questions with uptake can initiate collaborative troubleshooting. For example, if Kate had asked her teenage son, *I hear you that you were desperate to be with your friends tonight, but can you explain to me why it made sense to you, at the time, to break the family rules to be with them?*, that would have been an authentic question with uptake. For maximum effectiveness, she could use the question as a launching-off point for a serious conversation about status and respect in the peer group.

Authentic questions with uptake are effective, in part, because they build *relationships*. Linguists such as Dora Demszky, a professor at Stanford University, note that authentic questions with uptake create a common ground and a sense of collaboration. That's important because young people are constantly trying to make sense of how they're being treated. When asked a question, a young person wonders: *Does the questioner want ammunition to use against me, or do they want to work together as equals?* Authentic questions with uptake imply the latter, which serves as a foundation for a better relationship.

Authentic questions also have a beneficial effect on *cognition*. Young people have to think harder to answer authentic questions. Putting their brains to work helps them learn more and own the ideas.

Note that these two benefits work together. Authentic questions build trust, and that in turn helps young people feel safe enough to embrace the challenge to think deeply. This helps explain why asking authentic questions with uptake is a mentor-mindset practice. Authentic questions with uptake provide high support (because the questions don't directly challenge or threaten a young person's status by telling them that they're wrong) so that young people can meet high standards (because the questions demand original thinking from the young person).

How do authentic questions with uptake help leaders bridge the generational divide? Asking questions is the starting point when negotiating a treaty (rather than a truce) in the war over meaning. A successful treaty is built on an understanding of what each party needs. Asking questions surfaces that understanding; dictating terms doesn't. When we *tell*, we launch a conquest of meaning. We are saying: *my meaning matters; yours doesn't.* We leave kids to choose either compliance or rebellion. We don't open a negotiation; we issue an ultimatum. That ultimatum fails when our kids won't respect it. They will do what they want as soon as we turn our backs, possibly hurting themselves or humiliating us. Therefore, we need to negotiate a treaty that both parties can live with. Asking authentic questions with uptake is critical to this process because it allows both parties to negotiate successfully.

This is why negotiation experts excel at asking questions. A good example comes from Chris Voss, who for a time was considered the best hostage negotiator in the world. He shares many of his secrets in his popular book *Never Split the Difference* (and in his excellent MasterClass videos).

Voss's most interesting practice is *mirroring*. When you mirror someone, you repeat the last three or so words that they said, turning them into a question. (If you mirrored me now, you would say, *Into a question?*) Voss's mirroring constitutes the purest and simplest form of an authentic question with uptake. It takes very little effort. You just repeat words you've heard. Therefore it works for busy or frazzled parties of a negotiation. Mirroring also builds relationships, communicating, "I heard every word you said word for word, and I'm proving it because I just repeated it back to you," Voss says. And it makes the other side think because they have to explain themselves. Mirroring is a simple mentor-mindset practice anyone can do.

Mirroring works because of a basic principle of communication described by sociolinguist Gail Jefferson in 1972. Jefferson observed that a *repeat*—or mirroring a word or phrase back to someone—is interpreted by the other person as a correction or a request for clarification. Jefferson gives the example of two young children talking to each other. The first, still learning to count, says, "Six, eleven, eight, nine . . ." and the second child, noting the error, simply says, "Eleven?"—prompting the former to offer the correction of "Seven, eight, nine . . ." A repeat, phrased as a question, is an indirect and subtle way to call attention to a mistake. Even very young children understand it.

Voss uses mirroring to prompt the other side to tell him how they might be mistaken about their preferences. Then they reveal what they really want out of the negotiation, so Voss can offer a deal they'll accept. By repeating the subject's words back to them, Voss subtly implies that their previous explanation was insufficiently detailed. That prompts them to say more, while avoiding a direct request. Voss finds mirroring useful because two adversarial sides in a negotiation often have different pictures of what's at stake. This makes the different sides unlikely to comply with a demand for more information.

For example, imagine a parent who said, *Why do you care so much about spending time with your friends?* Their meaning would be clearly insulting. The kid could respond, *How dare you question my priorities!* By mirroring the child instead, the parent could avoid directly challenging them to explain themselves because the child would understand the unspoken question (*Why did you say . . .*). When children are mirrored, they pick up on the subtle expectation to communicate clearly. They humor the parent, and they share the critical information for the negotiation.

The mirroring technique can help adults reach across the generational divide when they are at risk of misunderstanding what young people are thinking. Consider this example from a negotiation between a mother and her teenage daughter:

TEEN: Mom, why won't you let me go to the party? I need to spend time with my friends!

MOM: [Mirroring] *Spend time with your friends?*

TEEN: Yeah, I'm worried they're going to do something fun without me, and then I won't be invited the next time!

Before initiating this conversation, the mom might have believed that her daughter wanted something wild out of the party: to cut loose, to act irresponsibly, maybe to drink or get high. But look at how much she learned from her mirroring question! Mirroring prompted her daughter to admit to the fear of missing out (FOMO). She worried that her friends would have an epic time, make a million memories, and then try to recreate those memories in a small group that excluded her. Terrified of social death, she felt like going to the party represented a do-or-die ultimatum. After questioning, the mother had good information to negotiate with. She might next try to address the source of her daughter's acute FOMO (e.g., through Socrates-like questioning of her assumptions). Or she might offer a compromise, such as going to the party for a limited period of time or inviting some of the girls over that night. One bit of mirroring put the mother in a stronger negotiating position, while making her daughter feel heard, valued, and respected.

Questioning works in other settings beyond parenting. Stanford psychologist Mark Lepper, who pioneered the concept of intrinsic motivation, made a fascinating observation about expert tutors in the mid-1990s. Expert tutors used authentic questions with uptake in two ways. First, they always started off the tutoring session with questions about how the kid was doing and what they were up to. To novices, this small talk seems like a waste of time. But the expert tutors knew that they needed to establish a relationship of trust before they could push the students. Authentic questions with uptake help them do that.

Second, expert tutors asked questions to collaboratively troubleshoot a student's misunderstanding. Tutors never directly pointed out students' errors. They didn't say, *That's wrong, do it over.* Instead, when a student got the problem wrong, tutors spoke indirectly. They would say things like *Hmm, does that work?* That question encouraged kids to try out the formula or calculations themselves. Or the tutor would say something like *That's interesting. Is that the right answer?* Here, the question achieved the exact same communicative intent as saying *Wrong, try again.* Students clearly understood when they had gotten something wrong. But students didn't feel offended. Tutors also used the indirect-questioning method because it put the onus on the students to do the thinking. It helped students develop a "coach in the head" going forward. After all, most tutors only work with individual students for one hour per week, but students do many hours of homework. Tutors can't possibly do everything for students. So if they're doing their jobs correctly they instill in young people skills to use on their own.

Evaluations of classroom teachers have likewise found that questioning can promote learning. In the mid-1990s, University of Wisconsin–Madison researchers Martin Nystrand and Adam Gamoran observed over

110 English/language arts classes four times per year for two years. They examined hundreds of hours of footage, tracking how much time teachers spent asking questions that built on a student's contribution and took the student seriously. The more a teacher asked those kinds of questions of students, the more those students learned. The Nystrand study wasn't an experiment, however.

In an experiment published in 2023, Dora Demszky and her team randomly assigned teachers to use an online tool that incorporated natural-language-processing technology to give them a simple statistic: the percent of the class time they spent asking authentic questions with uptake. This tool increased teachers' use of the questions, and the students learned more. Demszky's experiment proved that authentic questions with uptake can have a causal effect on student learning.

Mentor-Mindset Exemplars' Questioning

We can see the power of questioning at work in the practices of Sergio Estrada, mentor-mindset exemplar. I often saw Sergio question his students rather than tell them information. He didn't answer when they asked, "Is this correct?" Instead, he asked them what they thought. He did this even when talking with students who were stressed and at their limit.

One evening, an earnest but vulnerable physics student contacted Sergio through Remind, the class's secure online homework tool.

"I'm so lost and confused. I don't understand this problem at all. I'm crying," she typed.

"Okay, show me what you've done so far," Sergio said. She uploaded a screen capture of her work. Then, Sergio typed, "I see that you have the first part, but what happens if you [describes physics concept]?"

The time stamp shows a fifteen-minute break. Then a reply: "Okay, I see it now. I got it. Thanks so much. I was so overwhelmed but I'm fine now."

The restraint! How in the world did Sergio manage to not answer the question of a crying student at night? How did he ask, not tell?

"I would never deprive a student of an opportunity to know that they're capable of understanding the hardest concepts in physics," Sergio explained to me.

Three months later, after the COVID-19 pandemic shut the world down and locked this student in her house, away from her friends and teachers, she passed Sergio's course and became the first in her family to earn college credit.

Sergio's example shows why authentic questioning with uptake is a manageable practice that anyone can do. His response to his student cost little in terms of time and effort. He merely had to tap out a question on his phone while watching Netflix on the couch with his wife. But his support proved massive in terms of its psychological effect. It made the difference between his student spiraling out of control with anxiety all night, worrying that she would disappoint her teacher and fail a college-level course, versus going to bed confident and poised. Questioning, like transparency, shows that the mentor mindset often depends on small but mighty acts.

Managers like Stef Okamoto also use authentic questions with uptake. Stef's former direct report Salonee Shah described a conversation with Stef early in her time at Microsoft. Stef had given Salonee a big job with high expectations for a junior employee: overseeing the onboarding process for every new Microsoft employee—eight thousand people per year at the time. Stef could already tell that running the logistics of a big organization wouldn't satisfy Salonee, an overachiever. About a month after they started working together, Stef asked Salonee what her stretch project should be. At first Salonee felt taken aback. Wasn't she already on track for a great performance review, doing something impressive that benefited the whole company? Sure, but she could do more, Stef explained, and her current job would eventually make her bored. Stef asked, "What's something you'd want to brag about on your performance evaluation? What kinds of skills do you want? And what skills do you want to build on?" After some negotiation, they landed on a new data dashboard that would enable Microsoft to keep better track of every new employee's onboarding progress. With Salonee as the lead, they developed the new tool, creating a game changer and a money saver. More importantly, the project built on Salonee's experience with data dashboards from her previous job as a teacher. It also gave her valuable new experiences leading a software-development project. Later, Stef made sure Salonee presented the new tool to senior management and got the credit for it.

Think about the important role questioning played in this case. If Stef had simply *told* Salonee, *I'm adding tons of work to your already full plate*, the extra responsibility might have felt crushing and unjust. But because Stef *asked*, together they could design a new project to build on Salonee's interests and experiences, align with her goals, and give her the chance to earn prestige. Questioning proved core to Stef's respectful mentor mindset.

Organizational scholars Dr. Edgar Schein and Peter Schein call Stef's questioning approach *humble inquiry*. (Others have called it *respectful inquiry*.) The Scheins define humble inquiry as "the fine art of drawing someone out, of asking questions to which you do not already know the answer, of building a relationship based on curiosity and interest in another person." Many successful managers commonly practice this kind of inquiry.

Parental Questioning Routines

Lorena Seidel has a beautiful little routine she teaches parents to follow when in conflict with kids. She gives them a six-question guide for coauthoring a treaty in the war over meaning. Her guide reflects clinical psychology advice (e.g., cognitive behavioral therapy and motivational interviewing), and it's simple enough for any parent to use when their kids are upset. See it below in table 6.1.

The first three questions help the child recognize that their way of seeing things poses a problem. The second three questions help them come up with a better, more motivating way of seeing things. Lorena finds that changing how we see things helps us resolve problems because kids (and adults) tend to react to the meaning of a situation, not its reality. They think, *I'm upset because the situation is objectively terrible.* They rarely consider, *I'm upset because how I'm seeing the situation is a problem, but I could choose to see the situation differently, and that would help me achieve my goals.* With Lorena's guided questions, however, we can train our kids to do the mental work to get to the latter place. Not only does this approach help in the moment, it also equips kids to think in a more optimistic, troubleshooting-oriented way in the future.

Table 6.1. A Questioning Routine for Parents to Use with Young People in a Crisis

PART 1: QUESTIONS ABOUT THE OLD, BAD MEANING OF THE SITUATION	
Question: *What does this mean to you?*	Typical answer: *You think I'm bad./You're bad./They're bad.* (i.e., overgeneralization)
Question: *How is that meaning making you feel?*	Typical answer: *It makes me feel worse.*
Question: *Is that serving your goals?*	Typical answer: *No, it's getting in the way of what I want.*

PART 2: QUESTIONS ABOUT THE ALTERNATIVE, BETTER MEANING OF THE SITUATION	
Question: *What's something else it could mean?*	Typical answer: *You love me, and that's why you're saying no./ We had a misunderstanding.* (positive reappraisal)
Question: *How would it make you feel if you thought that?*	Typical answer: *I'd feel a lot better/more optimistic.*
Question: *Would that serve your goals?*	Typical answer: *Yes, it would be motivating.*

As I said, I'm skeptical of most parenting advice, so I had to try this one out myself. I chose my third child, Jack-Jack, as my test subject. See box 6.1.

Box 6.1. What Happened When I Used Lorena's Questioning Routine with Jack-Jack

Like his namesake, the lovable character from Pixar's *The Incredibles*, my third child, Jack-Jack, is mostly adorable but sometimes turns into a fire-breathing beast when provoked. The day after one of my interviews with Lorena, I took Jack, who was six at the time, to a busy park downtown. As we were leaving the park, he demanded a toy. "Absolutely not," I told him. "You just played with the best toy in the world: a pile of sand and a slide." "*I want a toy!*" he screamed. Jack's precocious skill is his volume. We once took him to the doctor to see if he had a hearing impairment. The doctor reassured us it was not a physical problem, it's just a character flaw.

At any rate, that day my imaginary audience was massive. Every parent-ing instinct said, *Scoop him up and hide him in the bathroom until he stops crying*, or *Buy him the damn toy!* I decided to give it the full Lorena, even though I felt like a phony. Here's more or less a transcript that I wrote down immediately after:

Me: Jack-Jack. I see that you're really angry. What do you think it means that I'm saying no to the toy?
Jack: *It means you hate me!*
Me: Hmm, okay. Could it mean anything else?
Jack: *It means you're a terrible father!*

[Ten to fifteen spectators start googling the number for child protective services.]

Me: Okay, and how does it make you feel when you think that's why I said no?
Jack: *It makes me feel sad that my only father doesn't love me!*
Me: Wow, and does thinking that serve your goals? Like, is it helping you feel happier?
Jack: Ummm . . . [decrease in volume]

[Ha! He wasn't ready for that question!]

Me: Here's a question. I'm curious. Is there anything else it could mean? Like, another reason for why I'm not buying the toy, but that doesn't mean I don't love you?
Jack: Well . . . [long pause] . . . Maybe you want me to be a good and grateful person who appreciates the nice things I already have. . . . And maybe you don't want me to buy a plastic toy that I'm going to break and cry about later. . . . And maybe you don't want to put more plastic in the landfills. . . .

[I had definitely scolded him with these lines in the past, but all of a sud-den they were his ideas?]

Me: That's interesting. And how would it make you feel if those things were true?

Jack: I guess it would mean that you love me so much that you care how I grow up . . . and you care about the environment because you want the earth to be clear for me.

Me: Wow, and if that was true, then would it serve your goals? Would it help you be happier?

Jack: Yeah it would make me feel good to know that my dad is a good person who's always looking out for me.

[Game, set, match, Lorena Seidel! I couldn't believe it had worked. Five-star review.]

Me: Cool! Want some ice cream?
Jack: Yes!

Sometimes, parents need to be asked the authentic questions, not the kids. Why? Because in the war over meaning that causes our generational divide, parents can get it wrong. Sometimes, parents need to come around to a new way of seeing things in order to help their child change their behavior.

An extreme illustration of this point comes from research conducted by Dr. Daphne Bugental at the University of California, Santa Barbara. Bugental's 2002 study focused on new parents with a high risk of engaging in infant abuse. She divided these parents into three groups: a control group that received no treatment, a standard treatment group that received about seventeen visits from a health care professional each year, and a group that received the standard treatment plus an enhancement—which involved training the home visitors to ask authentic questions with uptake.

Bugental designed the questions to give parents new ways to make meaning out of their own or their child's behavior when problems arose. For instance, if a child cried excessively, the moms might say that the child cried so much because *I'm a bad mother* or *the baby is mad*. These negative ideas could lead to hopelessness in the first case or reciprocal anger at the baby in the second, followed by neglect or abuse. During the enhanced home visits, the specially trained health care professionals asked questions until the parents came up with different, better explanations for their babies' challenging behaviors. When parents eventually landed on explanations such as, *The baby is tired*, or *The baby has gas*, or *I haven't been responding to the baby quickly enough*, then the home visitor would build on that until the parents had their own plans for doing better the next time. Each visit continued this collaborative troubleshooting. One year later, when the researchers visited the families' homes, they found that the control group and the standard-treatment group both showed serious levels of abuse: 23 percent to 26 percent, with no difference between the treatment and control groups. In the enhanced-visit group, the rate of abuse was just 4 percent. The questioning had made a striking difference.

Asking parents the right questions can prevent child abuse. Can it prevent teen suicide? That's what I observed happening with the counselors at Encircle, the LGBTQ+ after-school center in Salt Lake City, Utah (see chapter 3).

One senior administrator at Encircle told me, "We want the most religious parent in the world to walk through the front door and say, 'I want my kid here.' " To achieve this goal, the Encircle team begins by asking, not telling. "We don't say, 'You're so dumb for thinking your child is screwed up for being gay,' " one counselor told me. Instead, they start with questions to establish common ground: the importance of family, loving one another, and happy relationships. Agreeing on the importance of these values goes a long way with parents who arrive suspicious that Encircle wants to indoctrinate their child into an anti-family agenda. The counselors don't greet skeptical parents with lectures. "I don't like to be told what to believe," one counselor told me, just like parents don't want to be told what to think. "So the only thing that works is to give someone space to question."

Counselors ask parents, "As you think about your child being gay [or trans, or nonbinary, etc.], what does it mean to you?" Usually, parents respond with something extreme: their child's identity means they won't have eternal life, or their child's identity is "just wrong." But the Encircle team keeps asking, just like in the Bugental study. They don't convey judgment, only curiosity. They mirror. Eventually they ask a question like, "What scares you about your child being gay?" At this point, parents usually open up. They say things like, "My kid will never be happy because they won't get married and have a family," or "It means that all my parenting for fifteen years was wrong, a waste, and a failure because they have no morality." That meaning scares most parents.

The Encircle team then moves into the second stage of Seidel's guide, using questions to shift the meaning while staying authentic. The counselors say, "Okay, could you ever imagine a future where your [gay/trans/nonbinary] child is happy? What would that look like?" Usually, the parents land on a vision of their child in a loving and committed relationship, confident that their parents accept them. An Encircle counselor who grew up in the Mormon faith told me, "The best parents hold them accountable and create boundaries, in a healthy environment with unconditional love." Encircle's internal mantra is as profound as it is psychologically wise: "Do the right thing [of loving your child], for *your* reasons."

Gary and Kate

Gary's Story, Part Two

Charlotte was staying up later and later to chat online with her Canadian boyfriend. She started missing even more assignments, skipping more field hockey practice, and even staying home from school to sleep. The consequences loomed large. Would she quit field hockey—and lose her chance for a scholarship to college? Would she fail her classes? Gary's instinct told him to avoid the whole issue, but he suspected that instinct was wrong. He turned to parenting coach Lorena Seidel for help.

Lorena started by asking Gary why his daughter might be so committed to this relationship. They realized that because Charlotte is socially anxious, this one-on-one online relationship felt safe and comfortable for her. It gave her an easy way to feel accepted. Once Gary understood that her online relationship came from a reasonable place, he saw that it wouldn't work to come to her with shaming, blaming, yelling, and telling. He couldn't delegitimize her by demanding she stop wanting a way to feel accepted. That's an enforcer tactic. It wouldn't make her social anxiety go away. He'd have to find another way.

Lorena and Gary planned to say two things to Charlotte. Gary first needed to acknowledge all the good things that came from her online relationship. He didn't have to worry about her going out with a drunk driver or getting STIs. "I'm glad that you're not out partying, drinking, and driving. You're such a responsible teenager," he said when they finally talked. By leading this way, he didn't put her on the defensive.

The second step was for Gary to ask questions. Rather than directly commanding her to break up with her boyfriend, they'd collaboratively troubleshoot around her health and well-being. "You know that I love you so much," Gary said to her, "and because I love you so much I need you to get the sleep you need, to get your grades up, and to feel good about field hockey. I also want to make sure you have friendships and relationships here as well as online. I'm concerned that you're losing out on friendships here. Can we talk about some solutions that make me feel good and at peace with your happiness but that also work for you?" Gary didn't feel that confident going into the conversation. To his surprise, it went shockingly well. They collaborated on some guidelines for screen time and in-person friend time that worked for Charlotte.

What happened? Six months later, she'd broken up with the Canadian boyfriend and started dating someone Gary liked, in the real world. Not only that, but she was more competent and responsible in her relationships because she was the one exercising her agency. They had curfew rules that Gary felt good about.

Their progress offered a beautiful example of what I've been calling treaty coauthorship, not truce signing. Nobody's meaning dominated. Questioning was, in Voss's terms, key to *the art of letting the other side have your way.*

Kate's Story, Part Two

Kate knew that her problems were just beginning. Her other son, Damien, was just a few years younger than Jared, and he'd soon be starting high school. Kate turned to Lorena for coaching. They debriefed the Jared experience and prepared a plan for responding better in the future. Sure enough, a few years later, Damien repeated his brother's behavior. This time, his parents felt ready. "Yeah, we got this," Kate's husband said. "I'm so glad this happened while he's at our house." Most parents, me included, live in fear of terrible scenarios like an out-of-control teenager coming home drunk from a party. But Kate and her husband relished the opportunity. Why? Because their mentor mindsets set Damien up for success in the future. They did that by troubleshooting collaboratively, using authentic questions with uptake.

Kate and her husband put their drunk son Damien to bed. The next morning, they started the conversation by saying that normally they would ground him for two months, and that would be the end of the conversation. If they did that, however, then he wouldn't learn any skills that would help him handle the situation differently. They loved him too much to let him keep behaving the same way, they said, so instead they would have a series of conversations with him over the next two months. "You might wish that we had just grounded you, rather than talk about it," they told him. He would have to be honest with himself, and that would be uncomfortable. But they promised to listen to what he said and work with him on a solution.

For the next two weeks, Damien wasn't grounded per se, but he was effectively grounded. He had to talk honestly and openly with his parents, answering questions about what he was trying to accomplish by going out and getting drunk and staying out past curfew.

This series of conversations helped Kate and her husband see that Damien's partying behavior came from a good place. He's a very social kid who thrives on connecting with friends. Damien was afraid that his friends would all have fun without him and realize that they don't need to invite him places anymore. To him, the *meaning* of missing a party is the beginning of a long, slow social death that ends in him having nobody to turn to for the rest of his life. "Telling a teenager not to want to go to a party is like telling a baby to not want to play with toys," Kate told me. With that understanding, she and her husband didn't fall into their typical good cop/bad cop, protector/enforcer dynamic. Instead, they sought to *mentor* Damien so he could find other ways of meeting his need to be social, while living within the family rules.

First, they told Damien they admired his social side. They reminded him of the time, a year earlier, when he went to a New Year's Eve party and talked to a girl who felt suicidal. Damien talked her off the metaphorical ledge. The girl's mother called Kate to say thanks for helping her keep her daughter alive. Thus, Kate didn't shame or blame Damien's social side. She honored and respected it.

Second, Kate and her husband entered collaborative-troubleshooting mode. They told Damien their goal was for him to earn back their trust. "We want to be able to go to sleep at night and not worry that you've snuck out and are in danger of being killed. We can't deal with that stress and fear. And you probably want our trust so you can have more freedom. So we're ready to talk with you and understand you for as long as you need until we figure this out." They started troubleshooting by debriefing the fateful night a day or two after it happened. How did he get so drunk so quickly? The authentic questions gave them a new insight. That evening Damien had brought a backpack filled with hard seltzers to the party. Normally he could only fit a few seltzers in his pants. But that night the extra storage space in the backpack made it easier for him to drink too much. They came up with a solution: don't ever take a backpack. They came up with a few other principles, some of them mundane and logistical, that Damien agreed could work for him. After a few weeks, when he started going out with friends again (with a short leash), they continued to debrief and renegotiate the rules and expectations. They started having the most honest conversations they'd ever had. Damien stopped hiding or lying or sneaking. He began sharing. He didn't have many other problems throughout high school. He grew into a happy, healthy, mature kid. This mentoring approach ultimately made him far more prepared for the free-for-all of college than most of his peers were.

What happened to Damien's older brother, Jared? Lorena helped Kate realize that she could get a do-over. Kate took the opportunity. Once Jared moved back home during the COVID-19 pandemic, she didn't blame or shame or yell or tell. She asked authentic questions about his plans and about what wasn't working for him. They now have the best relationship they've ever had.

"I'm so grateful to have him home," Kate told me, because "the parent-child relationship gets frozen in that rough high school phase, and you never have time and space to live together as adults in a relaxed environment." They've had time to heal. Kate's newfound mentor mindset made all the difference.

Chapter 7

Stress

Although stressful experiences feel unpleasant in the moment, they are the path through which everyone who ever became really good at something got to where they are.

The synergistic-mindsets intervention

Talking About Stress

The last decade has ushered in a revolution in the science of stress, revealing that most of us take the wrong way of thinking and talking about stress. To see the old and new way of thinking, consider this message sent from an undergraduate student named Hawi to her college professor in the spring of 2022:

I am emailing you to let you know that after nine months of fighting, my mother lost her battle to cancer this weekend and has passed away. Being back home knowing that my family is not doing well, and that my mother just died, my mental health is at an all-time low. She is literally the closest person in my life. I do not have the emotional capacity to attend class for the rest of this week, or possibly more. I let my group know about my situation, and they understand. I will not be able to do any of the daily assignments (including the one due last night), so I sincerely hope that this will not negatively impact my grade in your class. Please understand.

If you got this email, how would you respond? Obviously as a first step we need to acknowledge the incredible grief and loss Hawi must be going through. But we also have professional roles that involve deadlines, expectations, and grades. On any given day a student will experience many different outside stressors that have nothing to do with our class—with the loss of a loved one being among the most rare and extreme. How should we balance our responsibilities regarding those academic stressors in the midst of Hawi's broader experiences of grief?

Many people feel like they have two options. Should we reduce stress by telling Hawi not to worry about the class? This option extends compassion, but if we made it our policy to let students off the hook for any and every stressful situation, it could lead to chaos. Should we hold Hawi responsible for completing her assignments? Trapped in this tough dilemma, we feel like we can either choose to accommodate young people's stress (while harming their learning and growth) or help them move along their professional trajectories (while suffering poorer mental health). But it doesn't seem like we can do both.

Leaders face this dilemma more and more frequently, not just with their mentees' experiences with grief but with many other serious outside stressors. In the years since the fall of 2020, my university colleagues and I have received more than triple the number of emails regarding stressful nonacademic issues that could legitimately derail a promising student's career.

Our students' experiences are part of a bigger trend. Scientific surveys of mental health in the United States show that every year since 2008, the year the Great Recession began, youth mental health problems have risen. In the two years after the start of the COVID-19 pandemic, the rate of clinically significant anxiety rose another 300 percent. That's an astonishing change. An international survey sponsored by Salesforce found that 76 percent of students named well-being as their top concern; well-being was also the most pressing issue named by 73 percent of university administrators in a survey from the American Council on Education.

Stef Okamoto described the same concern among managers at Microsoft. With greater regularity, young employees email managers asking for flexibility on deadlines, responsibilities, or time at work due to stress or mental health challenges. So many of Microsoft's managers struggled to respond appropriately, Stef told me, that her team had to create emergency manager trainings.

Even trained psychologists have a hard time with problems like Hawi's. I learned that when I gave a talk to a large group of PhD-level social psychologists. These experts have spent years studying the subtleties of human emotion and social relationships. I asked them what they would have said to Hawi. Without exception, they gave some form of the answer: *Don't worry about the class. Just focus on your family and mental health. Take an incomplete and finish later.* I get it. It seems like the safe thing to say. But if you knew anything about Hawi and what she was trying to accomplish, you would realize that nothing could be further from the right answer. I know this because I interviewed Hawi a year later to ask her what she appreciated and what she didn't about her professors' responses, and she said she wouldn't have wanted the PhD social psychologists' reactions.

Interestingly, people's ideas about stress can be just as wrong when we move from intense, life-altering stressors to everyday stressors, such as feeling excluded, judged, or left out by others. There, too, much of our society's common sense about stress is nonsense.

Contemporary Western culture has tended to give people problematic beliefs about stress. Stanford University psychologist Dr. Alia Crum, a key architect of the scientific revolution in the study of stress, calls it the *stress-is-debilitating* belief. This is the belief that stress inevitably harms our performance and health. That belief in turns leads to the conclusion that we should avoid stress whenever possible.

Often, the stress-is-debilitating belief leads us to a protector mindset. If someone we care about is experiencing stress and we believe stress is bad, then it makes sense to encourage them to take action to reduce their stress (e.g., scaling back ambitions). Or we intervene to protect them from stress (e.g., taking away their responsibilities). The social psychologists sought to protect Hawi from stress by giving the advice to focus on mental health rather than classes.

Other times, the stress-is-debilitating belief can make us enforcers. We say or think something like, *I know that what you're doing is very stressful, but you need to be gritty and power through it [or give up] because I can't do anything to help you.* Stress is either a bad thing to avoid or a bad thing that one must suffer through alone.

Crum's work has shown that our culture's stress-is-debilitating belief is both untrue and unhelpful. It's untrue because stress is often the natural by-product of us choosing to do something hard that's important to us. Examples include getting a college degree, giving an important presentation at work, or having a difficult conversation with a loved one. In fact, stress can often help us for the better. For example, our worries about passing a class, giving a good speech, or having a difficult conversation could make us prepare more thoroughly.

The stress-is-debilitating belief is unhelpful because when we believe that stress is debilitating, and then we notice our stress, we feel even more worried. We may think, *What is wrong with me that I am the kind of person who gets so stressed?* We stress about being stressed.

What ideas can replace our culture's stress-is-debilitating belief? Crum has proposed a *stress-can-be-enhancing* belief. With this belief, stress can serve as a source of energy to fuel improved performance. With that belief, you can encourage people to lean into their stress—to use it as an asset. You're not lowering standards. You're just helping them see how their body's stress can act as a resource to help them meet a higher standard.

When we teach a stress-can-be-enhancing belief, it can convince young people to see some forms of stress as a positive resource. What's more, when we emphasize that stress can be enhancing, *and it actually helps them do well*, then they remember it. This mentor-mindset approach to stress—embracing stress, rather than running from it or getting crushed by it—helps impart a nugget of wisdom that reinforces resilience in the long run. An example of how I've tried to apply this in my own parenting with my daughter, Scarlett, appears in box 7.1.

Box 7.1. Applying the Stress-Is-Enhancing Mindset in Parenting

On the morning of her big sixth-grade cello audition, my daughter, Scarlett, got in the car and said, "Daddy, I'm worried I'm not going to do well on the audition. I feel so stressed and nervous that my stomach hurts." I didn't want her to suffer. Should I tell her that she didn't have to do the audition? No, then she wouldn't get the satisfaction of a job well done after the months of rehearsal. The protector mode was out. Should I tell her to just ignore it? No, suppressing bad feelings, pushing them down, usually doesn't help you and could do harm. Besides, girls in our culture are already told far too frequently to ignore intense feelings. I didn't want to perpetuate that. Enforcer mode was out. How could I respond with the mentor mindset?

I turned to Scarlett and asked, "What do you think I'm going to say?" To my surprise, she replied, "Oh, you're going to tell me that the fact that I'm nervous means that I really care about doing well on the audition. I've chosen to do something important. And you're going to say that my racing heart is just getting more oxygen and adrenaline in my blood to my muscles and my brain so that I can remember what I practiced and do my best." I was shocked. She said it better than I could! "Yes, that's exactly what I was going to say. How did you know that?" I replied. Scarlett said, "Oh, you told me that two years ago when I was about to water-ski, and I was nervous and floating in the water with butterflies in my stomach. You said that the stress would make my muscles strong enough to hold on to the rope. Then I got up and had the most fun skiing ever." "Okay, wow," I replied, "so do you think you can keep that in mind when you go to your audition today?" "I guess so," she said. And guess what? She nailed the audition!

Because the stress-is-debilitating belief is so pervasive—and the stress-can-be-enhancing belief is relatively unknown—teachers, parents, and other youth-serving professionals face a seemingly impossible version of the mentor's dilemma. This dilemma was at the heart of the question of how to respond to Hawi's situation in school.

On the one hand, many of young people's most potent stressors come from school, or more generally the challenge of keeping their skills relevant in an ever-changing labor market. Young people need to work hard and persist in gaining advanced technical skills, not only to have a career path but also to have a foundation of logical reasoning and problem-solving for any career path. We shouldn't tell young people to give up on their most demanding courses. But if we maintain impossible demands, as in an enforcer mindset (bottom left of figure 7.1), the chronic stress could crush them.

Figure 7.1. Three alternative responses to a young person's stressful situation.

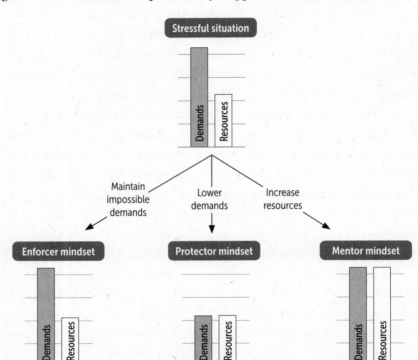

On the other hand, youth today are experiencing exceptional levels of stress and mental health problems. Spurred by our culture's stress-is-debilitating belief, adults feel compelled to take stressful demands off the table. Teachers, managers, and parents resort to the language of self-care: take a break, focus on mindfulness, deprioritize your achievement goals. The protector-mindset response (middle of figure 7.1) is often the opposite of what young people need to hear. It doesn't help them to persevere through the normal and inevitable negative feelings of confusion or frustration as they grow and develop in school or at work.

What if we didn't have to choose? What if we could maintain rigorous standards without causing unbearable stress—for example by increasing support (bottom right of figure 7.1)? Let's return to Hawi and see what the mentor-mindset approach to stress could look like.

When Hawi was in elementary school, her family emigrated from

Amhara, a region in northern Ethiopia, to a suburban neighborhood near Dallas, Texas. She excelled in high school, making the honor roll each semester, while leading the debate team and playing in the chamber orchestra. She was elected president of the student council during her senior year. Hawi's mother was proud when Hawi was admitted to a selective honors program at the University of Texas at Austin. In college, she threw herself into her studies and her leadership roles. She joined the University Leadership Network, the Black Business Student Association, and many other clubs. She studied urban economic development in South Africa. Her senior year, while she was living at home with her dying mother and caring for her brother and father, she finished both an honors thesis and an independent research project to help Black students feel comfortable and be successful when studying abroad. She had lined up a job at a large financial services company in their competitive two-year program. It would rotate her around every major consumer division and launch her career into the stratosphere.

Hawi was competent, motivated, and goal driven, and she had a vision for her future. The class in question was the last one she needed to graduate in her major, and she wanted to graduate on time to start her job. After all, Hawi's mother wouldn't have wanted her death to derail her daughter's bright future. But of course, Hawi was still grieving. She needed flexibility on the assignments along with reassurance that she wouldn't be made to feel guilty or ashamed for falling behind or letting her group down. She didn't need a handout—*a fake A*. Hawi viewed this class, and her final project in it, as a step toward achieving her career goals and making an impact in the world.

How did Hawi's professor reply? The professor maintained the high standard for the most meaningful part of the course—the final project—but supported Hawi by relieving her of most small assignments—the daily work. Said another way, the professor maintained *intellectual* rigor while offering *logistical* flexibility. The daily assignments served to keep students on task, but Hawi was already self-motivated, so it made sense to emphasize the rigorous thinking needed to complete a high-quality final project. Rather than just telling her to forget about the class, the professor emphasized to her that during a time of crisis, doing something that matters to you and the world around you can provide a sense of meaning that can help you cope with stress. The professor paired the high standards of the mentor mindset with high supports: the professor met with Hawi and her classmates multiple times to give feedback on their group project, sharing resources to help them refine it.

What happened next? Hawi came back to class after a few weeks and got to work on a superb final project. She and her team developed a novel method for coaching teachers to have a more understanding and empathic approach to discipline in middle school, allowing them to practice using large language model technology (e.g., OpenAI's GPT-4), over a year before most of the public knew about generative AI. Her group's presentation became *the* model shown to new students in subsequent semesters in the class. Hawi's contributions proved integral to the project, and the content she learned in class also helped her finish her senior thesis. A few weeks later, she graduated with honors. The graduation celebration was everything she could have asked for, as she was surrounded by her loved ones, bittersweet tears in her eyes, knowing that her mom would be proud of her.

This is what the mentor-mindset approach to embracing (rather than fearing) stress can be about. Hawi wouldn't have made it to that moment if her professor had taken a protector approach to stress or mental health (*you're too stressed, take an incomplete*) or an enforcer approach (*suck it up*).

The New Science of Stress

We don't always realize it, but the purpose of the human stress system is fundamentally good. It keeps us alive. Imagine a person crossing a busy intersection when a car suddenly speeds toward them. If the person experienced no stress response, they wouldn't jump out of the street and out of danger. A well-functioning stress response mobilizes energy to help us get to safety. To experience stress is to be fit for survival.

The way people tend to talk about stress obscures this point because it confuses different terms. Affective scientists—the experts who specialize in stress and emotions—are careful to distinguish a *stressor* from a *stress response*. A *stressor* is simply any demand that your body or mind responds to. You can have a material demand, such as a speeding car, or a psychological demand, such as an important presentation for your boss at work. A *stress response* is how your body or mind reacts to a stressor. Stressors, especially psychological stressors, are often neither good nor bad. The ways in which we *respond* to our stressors, however, can be better or worse. A person can stand frozen in the street and get crushed (a negative response), or they can jump out of the way (a positive response). Similarly, someone can feel completely overwhelmed by a presentation (a negative response), or they can focus on their excitement to show what they've accomplished (a positive response).

Common ways of talking about stress conflate these two. When people say, *I'm stressed out*, they usually mean, *I'm having a negative response to this stressful demand*. A listener, however, can mistakenly interpret that statement as, *This person's stressor is bad and needs to be removed*. Due to that miscommunication, people default to the stress-is-debilitating belief and the protector mindset that follows from it.

What causes a negative stress response? People's appraisals, or interpretations, of stressful situations lead them in positive or negative directions. Figure 7.2 shows a simple pathway building on the work of Stanford University affective scientist James Gross. First, when people encounter a stressor, they must appraise the *severity* of how demanding the task is. Factors that make a stressor more demanding include how much effort a task requires, how uncertain the outcome is, or how many things we have to deal with. Second, people also appraise the *resources* available to cope with the stressful demand. Examples of resources include skills, preparation, time, or the amount of help people get from others.

Importantly, people's appraisals of demands and resources aren't fully determined by the situation. They're subjective, and subjective perceptions can differ. For example, a calculus exam might feel highly demanding for someone just learning calculus. It's less demanding for a professional mathematician. The questions on the exam are the same, but the subjective level of demand differs. People perceive resources subjectively as well. A shy calculus student might think they can't turn to their peers for help. An outgoing student might think the opposite. Both individuals are surrounded by the same number of classmates to possibly study with, but the appraisals of whether those peers are helpful resources can differ.

Figure 7.2. The path from stressors to stress responses goes through appraisals.

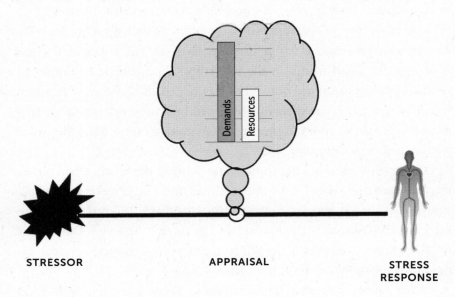

STRESSOR   APPRAISAL   STRESS
                                                        RESPONSE

What makes appraisals the key to good or bad stress responses? After people have appraised demands and resources, they can respond to a stressor in one of two ways: a *threat-type* or a *challenge-type* response. See figure 7.3.

The human stress system shows a *threat-type stress response* when a person makes an appraisal that the high level of demand from a stressor exceeds the available resources for coping with it (left side of figure 7.3). This threat-type stress leads the body and the mind to prepare for *damage and defeat*. First, the blood vasculature becomes more constricted, keeping more blood centrally and less blood in the extremities. This vascular constriction is a holdover from our evolutionary ancestors. They primarily faced physical threats. Preparing for damage and defeat meant minimizing blood loss by keeping more blood in the body's core. Next, with a threat-type response, people release more of the hormone cortisol. Cortisol reduces inflammation in damaged body tissue. Threat-type stress evokes a cortisol response because the mind expects to suffer physical harm, and therefore have damaged tissue to attend to. Threat-type stress also tends to reduce testosterone because being defeated tends to decrease

Figure 7.3. Demand/resource stress appraisals lead to threat- versus challenge-type responses.

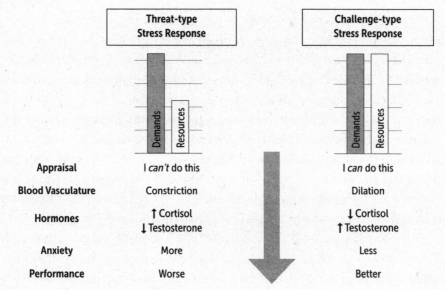

testosterone, in both men and women. Further, people experience more negative emotions, such as anxiety, because they worry about their survival. Finally, people underperform because the neurons in their brains receive less-oxygenated blood.

As shown on the right side of figure 7.3, the human stress system can instead show a *challenge-type stress response.* This happens when people make an appraisal that they have sufficient resources to meet the high demands of a stressful situation. When the mind expects to rise to meet the challenge, then the heart pumps more blood throughout the body. That brings more oxygenated blood to the muscles and the brain. The body doesn't produce as much cortisol because the mind doesn't expect damage and defeat. Instead, the body produces more testosterone because the mind expects to earn the prestige that comes from being successful at something difficult. Challenge-type stress also tends to make people feel less anxiety and more confidence. Motivation and performance go up. This is why affective scientists seek to promote challenge-type responses as a solution to threat-type responses—and as an alternative to giving up (which would eliminate the stressor altogether).

Simple (but Powerful) Interventions

Jeremy Jamieson, now a professor of psychology at the University of Rochester, grew up in a working-class family in the Boston area. He's the kind of scientist with a rare ability to apply his considerable work ethic to a single-minded focus on technical details that most other people find too mundane. He applied this personality quirk to his two passions: Boston professional sports teams and the minutiae of the body's cardiovascular and neuroendocrine responses to stress. He hit the jackpot when he landed a postdoctoral fellowship in Boston, working with one of Harvard University's top affective scientists, Dr. Wendy Mendes. Jamieson arrived at Harvard eager to test a simple idea with profound implications. Why not tell research participants that their stress responses are fuel to improve performance?

Jamieson's reasoning aligned with Crum's research on the stress-can-be-enhancing belief. It contradicted society's typical view, which is that when we feel stressed—when our hearts race and our palms sweat—it means we don't have the resources to cope with our demands. Jamieson wondered: What if he could convince people that their stress responses weren't additional demands, but additional resources? By changing their appraisals, he might help people realize that they had the resources they needed to meet their demands. That is, if he gave people a challenge-type *appraisal* of their stress, it might lead to a physiological challenge-type *response.* This idea was too good not to try.

Jamieson wrote a scientific article for research participants to read before they took a stressful exam. The information was basically what I've said in this chapter (see box 7.2).

Box 7.2. Excerpts from Dr. Jeremy Jamieson's Stress-Can-Be-Enhancing Scientific Article

- People generally think that feeling anxious will make them do poorly. However, our research indicates that being nervous does not hurt performance, but actually helps because our body releases hormones called catecholamines which are associated with better cognitive functioning.

- When people are stressed or anxious, the sympathetic nervous system (SNS) tells the body to release energy. This results in an increased heart rate, which is vital because it delivers oxygen to the brain. Thus, a racing heart rate signals that your body is moving blood to where it is needed.
- The SNS also affects breathing. Breathing becomes faster and deeper because of our body's need for more oxygen. Sometimes, breathing can become irregular and cause harmless but unpleasant symptoms, such as breathlessness.
- Finally, SNS activation increases sweating, which cools the body to prevent it from overheating and allows the person to address the anxiety-provoking situation without collapsing from heat. So, sweating during stressful situations is perfectly normal and helped our ancestors survive.
- During the test today it is important to remember that your body's responses to stress are both helpful and normal. Please try and remember this if you find yourself feeling nervous.

Jamieson evaluated his scientific article's impact with two different groups of students in two different papers. One was composed of Harvard juniors and seniors who were studying for the Graduate Record Examinations (GRE), the exam you must pass to be admitted to graduate school. These bright students felt threatened by a high-stakes test. The other group consisted of older adults taking remedial (high school) math at a community college in Cuyahoga County, Ohio. These low-achieving students experienced confidence issues. They often reported having "math scar tissue" from decades of feeling like they're "dumb at math" or have a "bad math brain." To these adults, remedial math presented a demand that far exceeded their perceived coping resources. But what happened when Jamieson convinced both groups that their visceral stress responses were actually assets, not liabilities?

Jamieson's results proved astounding. For the Harvard students, the stress-can-be-enhancing article boosted math GRE scores from an average of 705 in the control group (on a scale of 800) to 770 in the treatment group. That's the difference between being admitted to a mediocre graduate program versus a top-flight graduate program. In the community college experiments, which were replicated three times, Jamieson gave the treatment right before the second (of three) major in-class exams. He found that students in the treatment group performed better on the final two exams, compared to the control students, who spiraled into worse and worse performance. Jamieson also analyzed students' saliva for cortisol. He found that the stress-can-be-enhancing treatment reduced cortisol (and increased testosterone) for the rest of the semester—but cortisol remained elevated in the control.

Jamieson's study shows that the Cuyahoga students would have been stuck in a cycle of worsening performance, spiking cortisol, and spiraling threat. But his treatment caused students to view their stress and anxiety as a resource, not a deficit. It slowed or even reversed the threat cycle. Putting the two studies together, Jamieson showed how a stress-can-be-enhancing appraisal of our body's stress physiology can powerfully benefit both high achievers and struggling students.

Jamieson's brief interventions took about five minutes to complete. How could such a short exercise have made such a difference? The reason comes from the power of appraisals. When people face a stressful event, their appraisals determine their responses (figure 7.2). One can therefore target someone's appraisals and break the link between a demanding stressor and their threat-type response. In the case of unavoidable stressors (like hard exams), the appraisal approach unlocks a powerful class of possible interventions.

The benefits of targeting appraisals, however, tend to be narrow. For example, in Jamieson's studies he found that his intervention helped people think differently about test anxiety. But that same message wouldn't necessarily work as well for other kinds of stressors, like giving a presentation at work or feeling lonely at college. Our culture constantly bombards us with negative, stress-is-debilitating beliefs, and so people will fall back into that belief eventually. The challenge of overriding our culturally inherited belief system is called the *transfer problem*.

Recently, I teamed up with Jamieson and other scientists to try and overcome the transfer problem in stress. To do so, we developed what we call the *synergistic-mindsets* intervention.

Synergistic Mindsets

In 2018, I got a call from Danielle Krettek Cobb, a creative designer at Google. A few years earlier, she started a small upstart group within Google's machine-intelligence unit, called Empathy Lab. Empathy Lab brought together philosophy, art, literature, and technology with Krettek Cobb's infectious energy. Cobb had an impressive track record in tech. She was a designer at Google X, Google's "moonshot factory." Before that, she worked under Jony Ive and Steve Jobs at Apple, helping to launch iconic products such as the iPad. And prior to that, she worked on the Air Jordan line under Phil Knight at Nike.

In 2018, Krettek Cobb saw the future, and the future was artificial intelligence (AI). (This was four years before the public release of ChatGPT and other generative-AI language technology). Krettek Cobb worried that the rush to create machines that could do the work of humans would fail to account for what makes us human. She thought AI could function as a supportive friend to help us become better humans, not replace our humanity. Empathy Lab's sweatshirts proclaimed, THE FUTURE IS FEELING, and touted being on TEAM HUMAN. (Snarky Google engineers retorted they were on "team robot.") To elevate the team-human agenda within Google's machine-intelligence group, Krettek Cobb picked a demonstration case study. She decided that Empathy Lab would design AI systems that could help people anticipate and deal with stress. Krettek Cobb wondered: What if someone's ecosystem of devices—smartwatches, phones, and apps— could detect negative stress and say something in response to help us deal with our stress before it spiraled out of control? If she could bring this possibility to life, Krettek Cobb reasoned, she could create a powerful case study of how to integrate machine intelligence with human empathy.

Krettek Cobb called me because she had a problem. Suppose your personal AI could detect negative, threat-type stress responses. What should it say to you to help you cope with stress better? Should it tell you to stop being stressed? Give you directions to the closest yoga studio? Remind you to breathe, as though your brain stem wasn't already taking care of that? Krettek Cobb rejected these obvious, superficial ideas. She understood that our culture's stress-is-debilitating belief system was likely to generate all kinds of nonsense advice about stress, but she needed help identifying a viable alternative. I didn't know how to answer her question either. And so, we created a team with affective scientists Jeremy Jamieson and James Gross, and leading social psychologist Christopher Bryan, to generate the basic scientific breakthroughs.

Together, we developed the theory of synergistic mindsets. Not only has this theory yielded one of the most effective treatments we have ever developed, but it's also turned out to be a key practice of mentor-mindset teachers, parents, and managers.

When we looked at the literature, we saw two kinds of messages that could help people thrive during stressful situations. One was a growth mindset: the idea, growing out of Carol Dweck's research, that abilities are not fixed but can be developed with effort and coaching. The growth mindset causes people to view difficulty as a positive challenge—a chance to learn, grow, and improve—rather than as a threat. Crum's stress-can-be-enhancing belief gave us the second idea. As we saw in the Jamieson experiment, the stress-can-be-enhancing belief causes people to view their own bodily stress responses as assets—resources that help them deal with stressful demands—thereby promoting challenge-type stress responses. Krettek Cobb wanted to know which of these two ideas we should consider.

One day it dawned on us: the answer was *both*! The two beliefs go together. They're synergistic. Together, these ideas can help people overcome two different terrifying barriers to their development. The first barrier is, *Oh no, I can't do this*, and the second is, *Even if I did do it, I would be so stressed and overwhelmed that I would fail.* The growth mindset helps people positively engage with a challenge that will cause stress. The stress-can-be-enhancing belief helps people channel the inevitable negative feelings that stress causes.

Imagine you were a college student taking hard classes, or a young employee preparing a presentation for a senior vice president. Suppose you had a growth-mindset belief and embraced intellectual challenges, but still had a stress-is-debilitating belief. As your growth mindset led you to labor at the edges of your abilities, your stressful demands would increase. If you thought that demanding stress was a bad thing—a sign that you're doing something wrong—then you might cope poorly. Maybe you would procrastinate; maybe you would self-handicap or just avoid the situation altogether. The stress-is-debilitating belief could undermine your growth-mindset belief.

Now imagine the opposite. Suppose you had a stress-can-be-enhancing belief and a fixed-mindset belief. In this scenario you would believe that your stress could serve as an asset for performance, but you wouldn't bother trying hard because you believed you couldn't improve your areas of weakness. A fixed mindset prevented you from putting your stress-can-be-enhancing beliefs into practice. See table 7.1.

The synergistic mindsets was a scientific breakthrough because it showed how complementary these two ideas were (as shown in table 7.1). But before we would be ready to spread the word (or bake it into a product), we needed hard evidence that it worked. We got the proof from one of the most immersive experimental methods in social psychology.

Table 7.1. The Synergistic-Mindsets Framework

	STRESS BELIEFS	
	Stress-is-debilitating beliefs	Stress-can-be-enhancing beliefs
Ability beliefs Growth-mindset beliefs	I could grow from this challenge if I could handle it, but the stress is going to make me fail.	**Synergistic Mindsets** I could grow from this challenge by using my stress responses as a resource for learning and performance.
Fixed-mindset beliefs	This challenge is hard because I lack ability, and my stress response is making me perform even worse.	I might be able to my use my stress responses as a resource, but they can't help me grow because ability is fixed.

In 1993, biopsychologist Clemens Kirschbaum published an ingenious way to study social stress. Social stress refers to stressors that threaten our feelings of status or respect by making us feel like our social selves are being judged and evaluated. Kirschbaum created the Trier Social Stress Test (or TSST for short). At the time, researchers had designed far more methods for studying *physical* stress than for *social* stress. In the *cold pressor test*, participants submerge their hands in an ice-cold bucket for a minute or longer. In the *carbon dioxide (CO₂) challenge*, participants use an inhaler to fill their lungs with CO_2, temporarily creating a sensation of suffocating. But how could researchers study the *social* stressors that regular people experience in their modern social lives? To find an answer, Kirschbaum came up with his uniquely socially painful (but ultimately harmless) TSST procedure.

Here's how the TSST works (see figure 7.4). Researchers bring participants into a psychology laboratory. (In our studies they're usually aged eighteen to twenty-three.) Researchers connect them to devices that monitor their blood flow, their breathing rate, the electrical activity in the sweat on their skin, and their blood pressure, among other things. These provide the stress measurements. The participants rest a bit to get stable measures (the baseline period). Then researchers take them through any intervention (or control) materials (the treatment period). In our studies they complete the synergistic-mindsets intervention. Then the social stress begins. Surprise! Participants have to give a speech in front of two evaluators. The topic is what makes someone popular and likable at your age. The evaluators, participants are told, will judge their speeches based on whether they know what they're talking about. The participants don't know that the evaluators have been trained by us, the researchers, to be impossible to impress. Participants then have three minutes to prepare their remarks (the prep period) and five minutes to speak (the speech period). While participants give their speeches, two stone-faced evaluators sit in front of them with clipboards, judging their every move. The speech period is a double social stressor. Most people find extemporaneous public speaking to be highly demanding. In addition, the topic creates a strong implication that if you give a poor speech, you must not be popular or likable. The unimpressed evaluators therefore seem to confirm your low social status.

After the speech, we spring another surprise: It's time to do mental math! You must count backward from 968 in increments of seventeen as fast as you can. If you make a mistake, the two evaluators stop you and make you retry each number. Again, they are unrelenting and unforgiving. This is a potent social stressor because most people in Western countries such as the United States dislike doing mental math in front of others. After five minutes of math, participants take a break and recover.

Figure 7.4. The Trier Social Stress Test (TSST) and the corresponding biopsychological measurements.

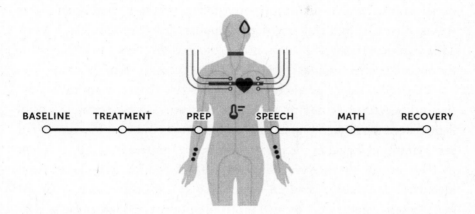

Kirschbaum designed the TSST to simulate real-life social-emotional stress in its most concentrated form. Suppose you're in a meeting and your boss's boss puts you on the spot. They ask you to provide an analysis of a complicated problem in front of a room filled with senior managers. Failure could mean you're no longer in line for a promotion. That's a lot like the TSST. So is the experience of being in a college calculus class. The professor cold-calls you to answer a challenging question in front of the whole class, seemingly outing you as someone who doesn't belong. These scenarios, like the TSST, frighten us because they carry the risk of humiliation. But they're also great ways to study positive, challenge-type stress versus negative, threat-type stress. If you think about these situations in the right way—with a positive appraisal—they present opportunities to make positive impressions on people whose opinions really matter.

A healthy response to the TSST (and the situations it is meant to represent) is a challenge-type stress response. In a challenge-type response, participants embrace the stressful experience. They engage with the speech and do their best on the math. By contrast, in a threat-type response, participants withdraw. They avoid. To figure out which of these two responses people are showing, the researchers look at differences in how constricted the participants' blood vessels are, which, as noted, is a telltale sign of whether people are showing challenge- or threat-type responses. Specifically, researchers are looking at total peripheral resistance, or TPR. TPR is the amount of pressure on the blood vessels in your periphery—when blood vessels constrict (as in a threat-type response), pressure rises; when blood vessels dilate (as in a challenge-type response), pressure falls. Thus, lower TPR indicates that you possessed the resources to meet the demands of the speech and the mental math—you had a challenge-type response.

The TSST was a great way to evaluate the synergistic-mindsets intervention (i.e., growth-mindset beliefs plus stress-can-be-enhancing beliefs) before recommending it for Google's stress products. Therefore, in a 2022 study published in the journal *Nature*, we ran several hundred young people through our intervention and the TSST. Half of participants completed the synergistic-mindsets materials (see excerpts in box 7.3) and half of them completed a control protocol prior to completing the TSST's speech and mental math tasks.

Box 7.3. Excerpts from the Synergistic-Mindsets Intervention

The synergistic-mindsets intervention included two kinds of messaging: growth mindset and stress-can-be-enhancing. (Chris Bryan and I were the lead authors; Danielle Krettek Cobb, Jeremy Jamieson, James Gross, and Meghann Johnson contributed key ideas.)

Growth-Mindset Messaging
When you're faced with difficult challenges and you keep trying until you get better, your brain grows new connections and becomes better at taking on new challenges in the future. . . . When something does feel really difficult, your brain learns how to respond more effectively to that challenge. It's a lot like the way rigorous exercise makes your muscles really sore at first but, with training, your muscles don't just get stronger, they also recover more quickly when you push them to their limit.

Stress-Can-Be-Enhancing Messaging
People often mistake their body's stress response for a sign that they're in a situation they can't handle. It's easy to do—racing heart, fast breathing, sweating—these are also ways our bodies respond in emergencies, when

we're in real trouble. This is a mistake that actually can cause you to perform worse because, if you think your stress response is a problem, you're more likely to be worried about it and get distracted from performing. . . . You can use your body's stress response effectively next time you feel it kicking in while you're trying to perform or master something difficult. When you start to feel anxious, try to remind yourself that this is your body's way of helping you to rise and meet the challenge you're facing. That should help you to spend less time worrying about the fact that you feel anxious. Then you can focus on what you're doing and let your body's stress response give you the extra boost you need.

Our study's results were clear. Among young people in the control group who didn't get the synergistic-mindsets intervention, we saw a striking increase in TPR. That was a threat-type response. Some felt so threatened that they just stopped talking halfway through the speech, as though they'd rather say nothing than risk saying something dumb. Among participants in the synergistic-mindsets group, however, we saw a strikingly different pattern of results. They showed much lower TPR reactivity. That meant more blood could be pumped through their blood vessels (see figure 7.5), bringing more oxygenated blood to their brains and muscles, powering better performance. These results were important because they showed that the treatment didn't *remove* stress. Those participants were still sweating; their hearts were racing. They looked stressed from a nonscientific perspective. But this stress was positive; it was fuel for optimal performance. This happened because the synergy of the growth mindset and the stress-can-be-enhancing mindset allowed participants to make a challenge appraisal. The growth-mindset belief helped participants to see the speech and the math less as something terrifying to escape and more as an opportunity to challenge themselves and perhaps develop new skills. From there, the stress-can-be-enhancing belief helped participants to recognize their bodies' stress responses as sources of extra resources that they could channel to meet the challenge before them.

Our synergistic-mindsets treatment helped participants to see the daunting speech they were being asked to give as something they had the

resources to handle. That prevented their minds and bodies from thinking they would fail. Instead, they were directing their attention toward the
prospect of success (see box 7.3).

A follow-up experiment showed that both beliefs were important.
When we removed either the growth-mindset or the stress-can-be-enhancing content, we didn't see the same benefits for stress responses as the
synergistic treatment that put both mindsets together. Thus, it was truly
the complementary nature of the two mindsets that made the difference.
(Note that each solitary mindset on its own yielded benefits in other studies; it was just the response to the extreme social stress of the TSST that
required both.)

Did the synergistic-mindsets intervention overcome the transfer problem and show effects that lasted over time? In another experiment, we
gave the intervention (or a control) to ninth- and tenth-grade students at
a public school in the Rochester, New York, area that almost exclusively
served Black and Latinx students who lived in a poor community. The
students experienced many physical and social stressors, including threats
of violence, food insecurity, and cultural stereotyping. Could a short online
intervention focused only on academic stressors help them cope with their
everyday stressors? It did. We measured emotional well-being and collected

*Figure 7.5. The effect of the synergistic-mindsets treatment on threat-type stress
responses during the Trier Social Stress Test (TSST) (y axis is TPR reactivity).*

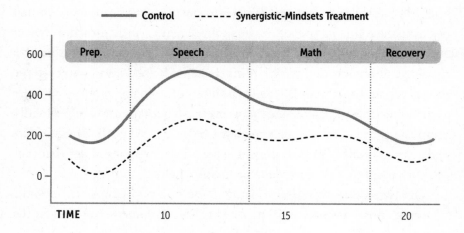

saliva samples (to analyze for cortisol levels) three times per day, over five days after the intervention. We found higher well-being and lower cortisol levels, consistent with reductions in threat-type stress responses. We also found that students passed their classes at higher rates—especially their most challenging science and math classes—a year later. Thus, when we targeted overall beliefs about stressors and stress responses, the students transferred their synergistic mindsets to new situations far into the future.

Language that Supports Synergistic Mindsets

Our studies showed that synergistic mindsets had great potential, even from a short intervention (see box 7.3) lasting only twenty or thirty minutes. A problem remained, however. We needed to know: Can you say something shorter to support a young person's mindsets?

We next examined the natural language that could help young people deal with stress. Dr. Cameron Hecht, a postdoctoral fellow at my research institute, led a research study on the supportive language that helps echo the synergistic mindsets. He showed that a short online synergistic-mindsets treatment proved twice as effective when it was accompanied with a supportive statement from the professor. What was the supportive statement? The professor explained that they had designed hard timed quizzes to help students build their skills and learn to cope with stress, in a low-stakes setting that didn't count for much of their grade. When students received this mindset-supportive message, they felt like they could truly grow and learn in the class, even if stressed. That match between their personal beliefs and the ideas in the classroom culture doubled the benefits of the synergistic mindsets. When professors didn't do this, students saw a mismatch between their synergistic mindsets and the classroom culture. The intervention was half as potent.

Hecht's study also gave us a window into the best things for students to say to themselves before a hard quiz. The results were illuminating. Examples from the most successful students—those who used the synergistic mindsets effectively for the rest of the semester and coped better with stress—appear in box 7.4. They tended to focus on embracing stress, not shying away from it. The least successful students in the synergistic-mindsets experiment didn't do that. They suppressed their stress, telling themselves to fake like they aren't stressed, or saying to themselves that they shouldn't feel stressed. When people retained the old view that stress is debilitating—and should be suppressed—then participants didn't profit from the intervention.

Box 7.4. What the Most Successful Students Said to Themselves About Stress Before Taking a Hard Timed Quiz

- "Before I take each quiz, I remind myself that nerves are normal and that I am prepared. I tell myself, 'You did the reading, and any nerves/increased heart rate is your body's way of helping you. Try your best and the results are not a reflection of you as a person.' "

- "Instead of spiraling into a frenzy over my increased heart rate, I begin to think of that feeling as my body pumping the adrenaline needed to pull through a challenge. I used to get so hung up on the jitters leading up to/ during tests and quizzes, but I am slowly starting to recognize that feeling as a learning experience that I can grow from."

- "As I start to feel my stress or anxiety increase during a quiz, I remember that these are meant to challenge me. Through this challenge, it will reinforce my studying and note-taking habits. My results will continue to improve."

- "Before every quiz, my body starts to panic. I wonder if I studied efficiently enough or if I retained any of the important information. However, I know now that that feeling is actually beneficial for me. That feeling is going to help me grow. It's going to strengthen my brain and set me up for learning in the future. And that thought, it's comforting for me. It almost helps me relax while I am taking the quiz. It used to be when I panicked, I would read as fast as I could in hopes of getting the question over with. But that would then lead to me failing to comprehend it, wasting my time. That doesn't happen to me anymore."

Hecht's study showed that leaders need to align their language with the synergistic-mindsets message, and that young people need to echo it when they talk to themselves before a stressful situation. What does synergistic-mindsets language look like in the real world, when a leader speaks freely to a young person? To get to the bottom of this question, we examined one of the most stress-inducing rites of passage in modern society: the college-application process.

The Sergio Trifecta

Every year, millions of high school students apply to college. And every year, millions confront the stress of finding out where they will get in. Why? Because college admissions is often presented to kids as a referendum on their ability and potential. To parents, it can feel like the final verdict on whether they've done a good job. If young people feel overwhelmed by this pressure, they could struggle or give up during the application process. That could dash their dreams and underutilize their potential. What can adults say to help students overcome the stressful demands of college applications?

That's the question we asked ourselves when we launched into the next phase of synergistic-mindsets research. We studied thousands of text messages that stressed-out high school seniors sent to an app that uses AI to give college-application advice. An AI-powered app for college students could be a godsend, if it worked. For example, youth who are the first in their families to apply to college can't rely on college-educated family members to guide them through the daunting process. If AI could address even a fraction of the concerns applicants have, it could benefit thousands or even millions of people hoping to climb the socioeconomic ladder. If the AI-powered advice doesn't help, however, then they wouldn't see this benefit.

College applicants normally ask mundane questions, such as, *What's the deadline to pick a major?* AI can answer those types of questions easily because it responds by parroting what public websites already say, or humans can prewrite answers to a set of common questions. Interestingly, applicants often raise profoundly personal questions that the Internet can't readily answer. The app escalates these questions to human advisers, not AI. Examples include:

- "What if I am not good enough for college?"
- "I'm a first-gen college student. My parents both dropped out of high school. I feel so alone in all this."
- "I recently lost someone, and it has been hard to find motivation to continue my work."

How would you reply to these? Hopefully you would do a better job than the advisers in our dataset. For instance, in response to the third text above, an adviser wrote:

Hi ------, you are connected to a college adviser, and a live person here. I'm so sorry to hear this. We want to make sure you get the support you need. If you need to, you can contact The Crisis Text Hotline by texting HELLO to 741741. They are available 24/7 to respond to any kind of crisis. I understand how you are feeling—it can sometimes be difficult to focus, especially during a time like this, but it's extremely important that you continue to put your best foot forward. Here are a few tips [website] on how to stay motivated. Please let me know if you have any follow-up questions. Thank you!

In general, the human advisers followed this outline:

1. Sympathizing in a way that downplays the applicant's feelings
2. Offering a laundry list of advice without specific guidance
3. Sending the student off to go take care of things themselves

These responses didn't address the applicants' underlying fears and beliefs. The applicants worried that (1) their struggles—their lack of confidence, support, or motivation—would continue indefinitely even after they turned in their applications (i.e., a fixed-mindset belief), and (2) that their intense negative feelings—self-doubt, loneliness, or grief—meant that they would be overwhelmed and fail in college (i.e., a stress-is-debilitating belief).

What should the text message responders have said instead? To find out, we asked our most reliable source of mentor-mindset wisdom, Sergio Estrada, to answer the texts. I call his response the Sergio Trifecta. As shown in box 7.5, it has three parts: (1) validate and reframe, (2) seek to understand, and (3) offer to collaborate.

Box 7.5. The Sergio Trifecta: Language for Synergistic Mindsets

1. **Validate and reframe:** Sergio always validates where a person is coming from, why the source of their stress is legitimate. He never minimizes, he never diminishes, he never asks you to hide it away. Usually, he comes up with an external reason for your stress—for example, something that society or culture has put on you. He does that to avoid insulting young people. It also makes them open to reframing their stress. He wants them to see that the cause of their stress is not permanent and fixed. In addition, he finds a way to compliment young people so that they see the fact that they're stressed as a good sign—for example, as a sign that they care.

2. **Seek to understand:** Sergio never gives young people the fire hose—spraying advice from a high-pressure hose in a way that's impossible to digest. Instead, he asks questions. He tries to figure out what they've already tried, what's not working, and what's the next step. He does that to avoid telling them to try something that already hasn't worked.

3. **Offer to collaborate:** Last, Sergio doesn't tell young people to go it alone. He offers to collaboratively troubleshoot, just like he does in his classroom on a physics problem.

Once we had Sergio's responses in hand, we worked with psychologists to make them even more rooted in synergistic-mindsets ideas. Together with Carol Dweck—who developed the growth-mindset concept—and Chris Bryan, Jeremy Jamieson, Danielle Krettek Cobb, Meghann Johnson, and James Gross—who codeveloped synergistic mindsets—we came up with replies like those shown in box 7.6. It shows the Sergio Trifecta in action.

> **Box 7.6. Responding to a College Applicant's Question with a Synergistic Mindset**
>
> **Applicant:** Am I enough for college?
>
> **Sergio/Dweck/Bryan/Gross/Yeager:** I'm really glad you brought this question to me. It's a profound question, and I think it's really important that we think about it in the right way. This is a question that many students probably ask themselves at this stage, but not everyone is brave enough to ask someone else [validate]. I think the main reason so many people worry about this is because people in society talk too much about who got into which colleges as if getting into college is a test of how good or smart you are. College isn't about judging or measuring how good or smart you are. It's about giving you opportunities to grow and develop your knowledge and your mind [reframe: growth mindset]. Don't get me wrong. Those feelings of worry are very real, and they can be overwhelming at times. But from my perspective the fact that you're worrying about this says something very important: it shows you care a lot about this and you want to do well at it—and that's a key ingredient for success. I wonder if you could even try to think of your worries as a reminder that you care, and then use that caring to focus on becoming as prepared as you can for the exciting opportunities to learn and grow in college [reframe: stress can be enhancing]. Can I ask you to share a bit more of your own thinking with me? What are the main things you think about when you start to doubt that you're enough for college [seek to understand]? Let's see if we can help you focus on things that make you feel more confident [collaborate].

In a study led by Michaela Jones and Mac Clapper, we shared the original adviser responses and our Sergio Trifecta responses with one thousand young people. They rated the Sergio Trifecta responses to be superior. That study gave us hard evidence that the Sergio Trifecta proved more effective than the alternative.

I wanted to hear from young people who have experienced stress and grief, so I caught up with Hawi. I asked her what she thought of the Sergio Trifecta responses. Specifically, I asked her how they compared to what people said to her in the weeks and months after her mother died. "I think Sergio's approach is amazing," Hawi told me. She loved how he made people feel validated and heard, while suggesting better and more optimistic ways to think about stress. Hawi thinks that Sergio's questioning—his desire to understand—helps young people mired in stress or depression hear how their thinking sounds out loud, so that they can correct it if they sound too hopeless. Hawi called the Sergio Trifecta "realistic empathy." She meant that Sergio didn't try to fool young people into thinking that everything would be fine. He spoke honestly about their challenges. He legitimized where they came from. But he also used his honesty to get the young people to a more hopeful, optimistic place.

I asked Hawi if she had received any unhelpful responses when her mother first died. She had. Classmates and professors had offered her hollow advice like the human responders to the college-applicant text messages. They spent their time giving Hawi platitudes and false optimism. She hated the catchphrases *It will get better*, *It takes time*, and *Everything happens for a reason*. She thinks people say these platitudes when they want to convince themselves that they're being an empathic friend. In fact such words don't help. She wanted honesty and bluntness, not catchphrases. "Realistic comfort," she said.

Last, I asked her if her professor from the beginning of this chapter had sent the right response, now that she'd had a year to reflect on it. I was motivated to know that, in part, because Hawi was my student. I wanted to know if I had done the right thing. At the time, I was guessing. I wondered if my strategy of rigorous intellectual demand but logistical flexibility was the right philosophy.

"It helped me a lot," she said, "and it sent the message that 'I understand what you're going through, but I still want you to get something meaningful out of the class.'" The final project gave her something to work toward. "As much as it was work, it was *meaningful* work to me, and it was also a bit of distraction from the trauma of my mother dying."

Hawi is an inspiration. After all she's been through, she's thriving in the fast-track financial services program and traveling the world. Her heart still aches for her mother, but she knows her mother would be proud of what she's accomplished. Hawi also takes comfort in the idea that her story might help future mentor-mindset leaders learn to talk about stress more effectively.

Chapter 8

Purpose

A [person] who becomes conscious of the responsibility [they] bear toward a human being who affectionately waits for [them], or to an unfinished work . . . knows the "why" for [their] existence and will be able to bear almost any "how."

— Viktor Frankl, *Man's Search for Meaning* (1946)

The Purpose Problem

Damon Munchus is now a leader in J.P. Morgan's machine-intelligence unit, but earlier in his career he worked as a manager in J.P. Morgan's home-mortgage division. Munchus's team analyzed market trends to help the bank set the right price for a mortgage. It's detail-oriented work, mostly carried out by twenty-two- to twenty-five-year-old analysts, right out of college. "People were cranking hard-core on spreadsheets, grinding, working long hours," Munchus told me. The stakes were high: Imagine a family sitting down to close on a house thinking they would pay 4 percent interest and instead being told they have to pay 6 percent. That interest-rate jump would significantly raise monthly payments, and people plan their entire financial situations around their rates. Munchus's fact-checkers for home-purchase loan applications had to be 100 percent accurate. How could he motivate his employees to take every single application seriously, without coming across as an authoritarian jerk?

Parents (me included) often face a version of this problem. We sit at the dinner table, trying to get our kids to do *any* of their homework—let alone dedicate themselves to perfecting their English essays or social studies projects. Teenagers have a way of looking fiercely into our eyes and saying, *What's the point of this?* They turn us into babbling, unconvincing idiots who come up with lame rationales like, *Because I said so*, or *Because your teacher said so*. Can we do better?

If you applied all the lessons in the book so far, the young people in your life would know that they could meet high standards with the right support. But they still might ask, *Why should I meet your high standards?* After all, growth is hard. As we've seen, it can be stressful. If we don't help them discover a satisfying answer to this question, they could say the stress or discomfort of growth aren't worth it. They could end up disengaged or disillusioned. Can we develop mentor-mindset practices that give young people a deeper, more meaningful reason to grow and learn from our mentorship?

Pearla faces this challenge in her math classroom. She teaches eighth-grade Algebra I in a small town in northeast Texas, population forty-two hundred, located halfway between Tyler, Texas, and Shreveport, Louisiana. I met her six weeks before the state's Algebra I test. She had six weeks left to prove to her principal, her community, and herself that this year's students would perform even better than the last year's.

Though she wears large pink glasses and decorates her classroom with pink-patterned curtains, no one would call Pearla soft. "I'm a military wife. If you ever ask me a question, you better be prepared to hear the truth," she told me. She knew that too much of her self-worth was wrapped up in how a few dozen eighth graders would score on the state test, but she couldn't help it. She loved her students and knew the stakes; her community was socioeconomically challenged, with just 14 percent of adults receiving four-year college degrees.

Success in her Algebra I class represented a critical fork in the road for students. If they didn't do well in Algebra I, they wouldn't get admitted to rigorous high school courses (e.g., advanced sciences or math tracks ending in precalculus or calculus). A rigorous high school curriculum, in turn, predicts who will go on to earn college degrees. Unfortunately, in her community, only about 10 percent of eighth graders pass state tests at or above grade level. The test served as more than an assessment—it determined whether she had created a future rich in opportunity for the thirteen- and fourteen-year-olds in her classes. And she didn't know how it would turn out.

Pearla hoped that she could sustain the gains she had made the previous year, when her working-class students, especially those learning English as a second language, had performed the best they had in years. She attributed the previous year's success in part to the transformation in her classroom culture that came from her participation in the inaugural cohort of our program, called FUSE (Fellowship Using the Science of Engagement). This was a program we developed to scale the mentor-mindset practices from expert teachers like Sergio Estrada. She loved the program because it helped her change kids' minds about hating math. "I'm not a touchy-feely person by nature," she told me, but the mentor-mindset program emboldened her to start valuing her students' perspectives. She let them talk about their confusion and mistakes in class. That's something she never would have done before because she was afraid of ceding the floor to a gaggle of eighth graders. Pearla even asked for students' opinions on how the class was going and how she could support them to meet her high standards. These changes represented small but important steps for someone like her who was previously disinclined to take them. They contributed to her best classroom culture ever.

But as the test date approached for her second cohort of students, a problem remained. Students seemed to be forgetting concepts they were taught earlier in the year—proportions, ratios, exponential functions, polynomials. She suspected that the kids had sometimes memorized a set of algorithms for solving problems on autopilot and then forgotten them after each unit test. Pearla needed to motivate students to master the deeper meaning behind the math concepts, not just plug and play.

Why were Pearla's students stuck at the surface level? They "don't see the purpose of math," she told me. Although her mentor-mindset culture had succeeded in convincing her students that they *could* learn, they still didn't know why they *should* learn. Pearla had tried everything she could think of. She told them how valuable the tests were for her, for the school, and for their future. She hosted her own career day, inviting local adults to explain how they use math at work. And, like most teachers, she generously distributed candy. She could motivate students to turn in homework, but not to deepen their learning. Time was running out. Exasperated, Pearla asked me for my advice as a developmental psychologist: "How do you create the idea that math is meaningful?" She exhaled, on the verge of tears. "They just don't see a use for math at all." And the kids at her school weren't alone. "I've taught in ten schools in ten states. It's the same thing everywhere."

Even exceptional teachers struggle to support students who haven't identified their purposes for learning yet. Recall the bright-spot teachers that we located (the group from which we identified Sergio Estrada). When we surveyed their students, we saw a strong mentor-mindset culture. Fully 83 percent of students agreed that "it's okay for us to make mistakes and get confused," and 76 percent agreed that their teachers "motivate me to keep persisting and trying hard even when I'm confused or discouraged." But when we asked about a deeper purpose for learning and remembering the hardest content, not just the easy stuff, the numbers dropped. They ranged from just 51 percent to 57 percent. In even the best classrooms, just under half of students failed to see the purpose of learning.

As adults, we recognize that learning Algebra I taught us logical reasoning, which became important in realizing our ultimate career goals. But making that connection takes a cognitively sophisticated leap of abstraction. A person has to jump from factoring polynomials to logical reasoning. That's a big leap. Do young people naturally make that leap?

In another study, we asked students in each year from fifth to tenth grade, in both poor and affluent schools, to explain why it's important to learn *and retain* the concepts taught in their core classes (English, social studies, math, and science). Not a single student volunteered a link between the specific content they were being taught and the abstract skill they wanted to have in the future. Instead, we heard students say things like, "I don't know why I'm learning English," or "My science class is pointless and boring." Students had a very concrete view of what it meant for something to be *relevant*. When we asked a student why a math word problem about proportions and rates involving clowns getting in and out of cars might be relevant for their future, the student said, "I won't be working at a circus, so it's not relevant."

When students occasionally offered reasons for working hard in school, they talked about the exchange value of their success, but not the actual skills they were gaining. Their reasons for trying hard were things like, "To get good grades," or "To show my little brother that I can be a success." Students don't necessarily need to learn and retain information to achieve those goals. In fact, a decent strategy to get good grades is often to do the minimum possible to please each teacher so you have more time to spend on the other teachers' assignments.

In Western culture, adults tend to present young people with two sorts of rationales for learning: short-term self-interest and long-term self-interest. Short-term self-interest can take the form of an enticement, such as, *What you're learning is fun and interesting because it's related to something you enjoy,* or a threat, such as, *If you don't do this, then I'm going to yell at you or embarrass you or punish you.* Long-term self-interest typically follows a pattern like this one: *memorize this material, then earn a good grade on the test, then do well in school, then get into a good college, and then lead a happier life when you're an adult.*

Curriculum and instruction designers who seek to gamify the classroom embrace the short-term self-interest enticement strategy. These technocrats tend to think of relevance like marketers think of favorite colors. If marketers know you like blue, then they show you ads for blue shirts. I recently attended the ASU+GSV Summit, a conference for educational technology executives and investors. One designer proudly told me that his product uses AI to change the content of math word problems according to students' interests. If a baseball fan had to solve for X, the computer could turn X into a player's batting average. If a student liked TikTok, X might be how much money their favorite star makes in a year, or how many followers they need to increase ad revenue. This device is unlikely to be effective. Relevance isn't contagious. You can't manufacture enjoyment just because a task is *adjacent* to something enjoyable. Playing baseball is a blast. Calculating statistics about baseball isn't—unless you already love math. The weak intrinsic interest generated by superficial relevance simply can't compete with the alternatives: giving up, playing with friends, or even tuning in to the sports channel.

Appealing to long-term self-interest is perhaps even less effective, due to the well-known phenomenon of *temporal discounting*. Temporal discounting refers to the fact that rewards/punishments in the future tend to have less value than rewards/punishments in the present. Would you rather have five dollars now or ten dollars in a year? Many people would rather have five dollars now. Economists would say this means that you're willing to pay five dollars for the right to have your money now—that is, that the value of ten dollars is *discounted* by five dollars in a year. Different people can adopt different levels of discounting. Would you rather have five dollars now or fifty dollars in a year? Some people would say five dollars now, and others would say fifty dollars in a year. Researchers repeat this line of questioning with many combinations of now and later, until they can draw a line that pinpoints the exact ratio at which someone is willing to take a reward now versus in the future. That is the individual's temporal discount rate.

Economists recognize that some amount of discounting is rational because there's value in being able to use money now rather than later. For example, you could invest money now in capital that appreciates over time, while inflation decreases the value of money in the future. However, participants in economic studies tend to discount the value of future dollars far more than could be justified by such calculations. Researchers have furthermore found that young people in particular have a more "hyperbolic" rate of temporal discounting compared to older adults—that is, they depreciate the value of future rewards even more. Thus, young people think in a way that is considered more irrational by economic models, as it pertains to the trade-offs between the present and future value of rewards/punishments.

In light of temporal-discounting research, one can see why the conventional, long-term self-interest rationale won't work for young people. An adult is asking them to forgo certain pleasures now for the sake of uncertain pleasures in the distant future. *Don't play with friends, goof off online, or try to impress someone you're attracted to now, so that in your midthirties you can have a job that barely allows you to make your mortgage payment and only gives you two weeks of vacation per year*, the argument goes. Don't eat the marshmallow now, so that in twenty years you will get two marshmallows. I find it hard to imagine that even the most self-controlled and trusting teenager would think you're offering a good bargain.

But wait. Doesn't this temporal-discounting evidence mean that teen-agers' brains are flawed, shortsighted, or irrational? That they're wholly in-capable of making rational decisions? That excessive testosterone turns them into impulsive pleasure-seekers? Not exactly. The long-term rewards of learning in school (e.g., college, career, salary) may simply be too abstract for young people to understand. If these rewards were more concrete, then young people might be able to delay gratification in a way that appears more rational. Researchers have made this kind of mistake before. For decades, biologists thought that nonhuman animals (such as rhesus ma-caques) were impulsive and only focused on immediate rewards. But once they gave a version of the temporal-discounting task that was more rel-evant to the macaques' daily lives—foraging for food—then the macaques proved willing to give up modest immediate rewards for more rewards later.

Likewise, developmental scientists now believe that it's possible to overcome young people's seeming shortsightedness by presenting them with rewards and punishments that are common in their daily social lives. If young people's brains seek social rewards—status, respect, prestige—and hope to avoid social failures—shame, humiliation, rejection—then we can turn these motivations into assets, not liabilities, for healthy de-velopment. Young people's social sensitivities fuel an engine of learning that can help them fit into—or even change—their social surroundings. Evidence for this comes in part from the success of the EL (Expeditionary Learning) Education model.

The Purpose Solution

At Polaris Charter Academy, a kindergarten-to-eighth-grade public school in Chicago, Illinois, students don't ask, *Why should I have to do this?* Their ambition stems from the school's mantra—"We work together to get smart for a purpose"—and how it comes to life in students' classroom projects.

When Ameera Rollins was in seventh grade at Polaris, her social stud-ies class covered the US Constitution. They didn't just memorize the Bill of Rights. They examined what the document meant for active contempo-rary citizenship. After discussing how *they* were the citizens the document talked about, Ameera's class decided to exercise their rights to improve their community. Gun violence was, and remains, a tragic regularity in her area of Chicago—96 percent of her class knew a victim. Ameera's class launched a series of coordinated projects, interviewing community heroes dedicated to peace, recording their stories, and publishing them in an edited volume. Then the seventh-grade class wrote, directed, and produced anti-violence public service announcements that were shown on local television stations. Next, they organized a day of peace, asking people in Chicago to put down their guns for one day and volunteer. Ameera's class of middle schoolers succeeded in stopping gun violence in her large area of the city for that day.

Along the way, Ameera and her peers didn't complain about getting critical feedback on how to make their prose sharper or more compelling. They actively enjoyed digging into the records to identify local leaders, preparing meticulous notes for the interviews, rewriting and editing their drafts, and calculating budgets and cost projections for the public service announcements. They wanted to get smarter at history, writing, speaking, and math because each subject had a purpose.

Polaris is just one school in the larger EL Education network, which serves more than 450,000 students in one thousand schools across thirty-two states. A Mathematica evaluation study published in 2019 found that EL students learn about ten months' more math than peers in comparable public schools over three years. But what really stands out about EL is how much their students love learning the hardest material. EL doesn't motivate kids through threats of failure, bribes of candy, or turning homework into a video game. Instead, in EL schools students complete meaningful, real-world projects that are held to exceptional standards, in the service of a deeper purpose, such as contributing to the community.

In an Oakland EL school, teenage students used math and science to test the water quality in Lake Merritt, survey the public, and inform city council members about a proposed $198 million bond issue on the ballot. In Vermont, students used math and interviews to calculate the carbon footprint of the school and propose alternative energy sources (e.g., wind, solar, biomass) as part of a report delivered to the school board. In San Diego, middle school math students wrote a novel to help struggling students apply math, with each chapter explaining a different core concept to the protagonist. In Asheville, middle schoolers mastered the concepts of proportions and ratios to create a scale map of the world using a metric other than landmass, illustrating the magnitude of social issues such as electricity usage, HIV/AIDS deaths, or economic development. Sixth-grade students at Genesee Community Charter School in New York led the Reshaping Rochester project. They designed, fielded, analyzed, and reported on the public's opinions about the city's plans to rewater the Erie Canal waterway. Students interviewed more than one thousand citizens and produced complex statistical analyses in a final report that they presented to the mayor. Within a few years, the city adopted many of their recommendations and committed millions to the urban revitalization project. Like in Chicago, the EL students didn't say, *Why should I compute these statistics using algebra?* or *Why are you critiquing my work?* They knew exactly why they needed to learn hard, new concepts and why they needed to receive relentless critical feedback. Their community—and their earned prestige—depended on it. The teens in EL schools are not purely altruistic. These projects are also full of social interactions that grant status and respect. Yes, when they're out testing the waters the work is meaningful, but they're also laughing and flirting and trying to impress one another by looking smart and competent. Those immediate social rewards can motivate them to endure the rigors of giving their brains new skills for long-run success.

Ron Berger is one of the architects behind EL Education's approach of giving deeper learning a purpose. During his twenty-eight years of teaching, he was a mentor-mindset legend. He would occasionally bring students to tears in class because the work was so hard and the standards so high. But he would form such a deep bond with his students that, to this day, when he sees them on the street, they always greet him with a joyful hug or handshake, even normally stoic guys in their fifties. Berger has spent the last twenty years articulating and spreading EL's philosophy.

"It's not about *interest*, it's about *meaning*," Berger told me. He thinks curriculum designers are far too reliant on short-term interest, and long-term delay of gratification as ways to motivate kids. Neither is quite right, in Berger's view. "As a society we often say, 'Study now, get a good job later.' We're telling fifty million kids in the U.S. every year to wait for the second marshmallow." Berger thinks that it's far more effective to give young people meaning and purpose *right now* by asking them to learn skills to achieve something that has a direct impact on the community and on their social reputations. Because those skills are also what students need for success later in secondary school or college, it's also good for their long-run self-interest—even though that's not how it's framed. When this is done, students take their work seriously, Berger explains:

> If you tell kids to study World War II history because it's important to their lives someday, or because it's on a test, the kids who are people pleasers will do it, but the kids who don't care will say, *No way.* However, if you tell the kids that they're going to interview a WWII veteran in three weeks, and this person has never been interviewed before, and you'll be able to honor them by being the first to uncover their stories, then there is an incredible pressure to learn— and the threat of an awful shame if you fail to honor the veteran because you were unprepared. That's powerful. Kids will read and read, they'll ask for feedback, they'll work in groups, they'll do the grueling work, not because it's interesting, but because it's meaningful. It's immediate gratification, but for a sense of self-respect and accomplishment, not candy or points.

The EL Education network of schools grew out of the popular Outward Bound program, which takes young people on survival expeditions in the wilderness. A core tenet of Outward Bound's philosophy is that young people are capable of far more than we give them credit for. Furthermore, when we treat young people like they can make meaningful contributions, they will become highly motivated. Outward Bound was founded by Kurt Hahn, who like Viktor Frankl, author of *Man's Search for Meaning*, was a Jewish man captured by the Nazis during WWII. He later escaped to the UK, where he cofounded many successful schools. Berger thinks the success of EL's approach can be summed up in Hahn's famous quotation:

> There are three ways of trying to win the young. There is persuasion, there is compulsion, and there is attraction. You can preach at

them: that is a hook without a worm. You can say, *You must volunteer*, and that is of the devil. You can tell them, *You are needed*. That appeal hardly ever fails.

You are needed. When we communicate that, we say to young people, *Your skills, your energy, your talents, your contributions are all essential. They matter.* In Frankl's terms, this gives young people a *why* for their existence, and it helps them bear almost any *how*.

The EL Education story suggests a simple solution to the challenge of motivating young people. In general, we adults tend to tap into the wholly wrong sources of motivation for young people. We appeal to frivolous or pragmatic motives, such as immediate enjoyment or long-term self-interest, likely because of our society's collective focus on their neurobiological incompetence. Yet this cultural worldview blinds us to the fact that young people will forgo many pleasures on their quests for meaning, significance, or contribution because these offer routes to status and respect. Berger often cites the example of older adults who visit the shopping mall and complain about the immature, lazy, unruly teenagers loitering about. Then moments later they sit down at a restaurant and are waited on perfectly by a polite, competent, and prompt teenage server—but hardly notice. In general, Berger thinks we have the wrong cultural belief about young people, which traps us in the wrong approaches. That flawed cultural belief system is called the *norm of self-interest*.

The Norm of Self-Interest

Dale Miller, a psychology professor at the Stanford Graduate School of Business, coined the term *norm of self-interest*. At least since Enlightenment-era philosopher Thomas Hobbes wrote his treatise *Leviathan*, Western society has believed people to be selfish by nature. But Miller proposed another perspective. What if people only *seem* to behave in self-interested ways because they think *everyone else* is self-interested? People tend to conform to what they perceive to be the norm, Miller argued, so a perception of self-interest spurs a cycle of copycat self-interest.

This distinction matters. If people are by nature purely selfish, then the only way to motivate them is to appeal to their self-interest (readers of chapter 4 will recognize this as Theory X). But if people only *appear* to be selfish because they *perform self-interest* to match what they believe to be the norm, then it's possible to offer other, more beyond-the-self rationales that might engage them.

As one illustration of the norm of self-interest, Miller cites a study of blood bank donations he conducted in the 1990s. While canvassing for potential blood donors, Miller's team asked half the participants if they would sign up to donate their blood for free. They asked another half if they would donate blood for a payment of fifteen dollars (about thirty dollars today). Miller also asked all the participants whether they thought offering payment would make other people more likely to donate blood. The offer of money—that is, the appeal to material self-interest—didn't affect people's likelihood of agreeing to donate blood. However, the participants thought that *everyone else* would be *twice as likely* to donate if they were paid. On the basis of this study and others like it, Miller concluded that in the U.S. people often think the motivational impact of self-interest is greater than it truly is.

To the extent that many adults—teachers, parents, coaches, managers, and more—also conform to the norm of self-interest, they may have a narrow and imperfect view of what motivates young people. For instance, teachers who think that students are fundamentally self-interested could invoke self-interested rationales to entice them to learn. Students who privately care a great deal about social justice and contributing to their communities in turn learn that *teachers* only care about self-interest, which discourages students from ever discussing their purposes. Therefore, teachers may not say anything about more meaningful reasons for learning. The norm of self-interest limits the scope of rationales teachers draw from when they try to motivate young people.

In addition, students may look around at their peers and see that they never talk about justice or contribution—at least not in school. They may feel even more out of step with others' rational, self-interested motives. These ineffective rationales may not motivate students. Next, the frustrated teachers may try to increase the pressure with offers of more rewards or more threats of punishment. That could strengthen the negative feedback loop. And so it goes until we end up with a school that is more or less bereft of more profound motivations for learning.

This cycle can be stopped. The EL Education example showed this. Also showing this is a set of scientific experiments we conducted to promote a sense of purpose in young people. These experiments provided direct evidence that teenagers' temporal-discounting brains are not inevitably short-sighted. They can be influenced in powerful and long-lasting ways when adults appeal to deeper, more meaningful, and self-transcendent purposes.

Purpose and Healthy Eating

Youth obesity has been increasing for decades, with drastic consequences: diabetes, heart disease, and even premature death. A person's diet has five times more impact on obesity than physical inactivity. Ultraprocessed, high-calorie junk food (e.g., Cheetos, Oreos, Twinkies, Lunchables, soda, and energy drinks) account for an outsize proportion of the problem. According to some calculations, even a 1 percent reduction in hypercaloric food intake, if it could be sustained, would stop or reverse the United States' obesity crisis. Therefore, public health experts have spent millions developing a wide array of programs to change teenagers' food and drink choices.

Unfortunately, the programs don't work. Dr. Eric Stice, a scientist at the Oregon Research Institute, examined the effects of all past programs and found that they don't show any benefits, on average. In fact, teenagers who participate in these programs tend to *gain more weight* than those who don't. Healthy-eating interventions, similar to anti-smoking programs (chapter 1), are another black eye on the face of the conventional public health approach.

Many conventional anti-obesity programs have the same flaws as a middle school health class. They include lectures about the long-term health impact of today's dietary choices, coupled with half-hearted attempts to incentivize healthy eating (e.g., points, prizes, games, and competitions). These pragmatic, self-oriented arguments are doomed to fail. The future risk of becoming overweight or developing diabetes in twenty or thirty years is simply too abstract to motivate young people. Frivolous trinkets can't compete with the billions spent by food companies on making junk food addictive.

I saw this firsthand during my time as a middle school teacher. A skinny and tall seventh grader named Elizabeth had the same thing for lunch every day: Flamin' Hot Cheetos and a root beer. I told her that such unhealthy snacks could come back to hurt her when she grows up. "Yeah, but I'm skinny right now," she retorted. "And it's delicious." Argument over.

In 2012, Chris Bryan, Cintia Hinojosa, and I ventured into this problem space. We asked: If the conventional, pragmatic argument wouldn't work, what would? This problem interested us because it offers such a good example of the behavior-change challenges discussed throughout this book. Food scientists in laboratories engineer ultraprocessed foods to be addictive. Consuming them awards a clear and immediate payoff to kids while abstaining from them extracts a hedonic cost.

Eating healthy also has a social cost. Imagine a thirteen-year-old plopping their tray down at the lunch table with a salad and a glass of water. In many schools, they're asking to get teased by friends eating Nutella and Frito pies and drinking Red Bull or Prime. And for what? Is that healthy thirteen-year-old supposed to say, *I'm having salad so I don't get diabetes in my fifties*? That explanation would go over like a lead balloon.

Bryan, Hinojosa, and I reasoned that if we could solve this challenge, then we might be able to apply our approach to a broad category of adolescent-behavior-change problems.

Our first foray into changing eating behaviors came from consulting work Bryan and I conducted to design an attraction to promote healthy habits in Disney World's Epcot theme park. At the time, Epcot had just suffered a failed launch of their Habit Heroes attraction, which had been designed with the support of conventional public health researchers. In the original Habit Heroes exhibit, the visitor was an overweight child who was guided through three rooms by fit and attractive trainers (Will Power and Callie Stenics) as they fought the bad guys, who were all overweight. The Snacker was a round, heavy fairy who spewed tasty treats, and Leadbottom was a heavy man who broke every couch he sat on. Kids who went through the Disney attraction defeated these bad guys by, for example, shooting them in the head with a broccoli gun to make them drop their cupcakes. In the end, the avatar got skinnier. The Montreal *Gazette* ran the headline, "Disney anti-fat attraction called 'horrifying.' " Epcot promptly shut the exhibit down.

Soon after, they brought in Bryan and me as experts to retool the attraction, using insights from behavioral science. That's how we ended up living at Epcot for a few weeks at a time, working with the Imagineers to create an improved attraction.

Bryan and I decided to flip the script. Rather than make an argument about long-term health, we wouldn't talk about health at all. Instead, we would try to increase the social-status appeal of healthy eating. We would rebrand healthy eating. It should no longer be a sacrifice you had to make because grown-ups said so. Instead healthy eating should be an impressive undertaking that would earn admiration in peers' eyes. If we could do that, we reasoned, we could give adolescents an immediate, concrete social reward for eating healthy.

We changed the exhibit to focus solely on healthy behavior (eating right), not on consequences (weight). Then we depicted the protagonists with all different body shapes, all striving to be healthy. Next, we turned the antagonists into evil ghouls who prevented citizens from achieving their healthy inclinations. The blocker, for example, stole the healthy and wholesome foods that you really wanted to eat and replaced them with addictive, ultraprocessed foods. Unlike the old Habit Heroes, which had depicted teens who wanted cupcakes but had to resist and use self-control to eat fruits or veggies, we depicted citizens diving toward healthy food, with ghouls like the blocker trying to bar their way. We sought to convey the idea that people who ate unhealthy food had been robbed of their freedom to choose an alternative. Healthy eaters, meanwhile, demonstrated autonomy and independence.

The retooled attraction was a success. Newspapers praised the attraction's "kinder, gentler" approach. Millions of families over the next four years visited Habit Heroes.

Even so, Chris Bryan and I thought it would have been better to depict the ghouls, such as the blocker, as the junk food companies themselves. After all, these were the real-world culprits who lured kids away from their natural inclination to eat nutritious foods and toward unhealthy diets. As detailed in extensive journalistic reports such as Michael Moss's *Salt Sugar Fat: How the Food Giants Hooked Us*, companies spend a lot of money to make food addictive to children, and then they market it to them at a young age, especially in poorer communities. Bryan and I knew about the success of Bogusky's "Truth" campaign, which worked so well with teen smoking in the early 2000s (chapter 1). Building on those ideas, we thought that we could infuse healthy eating with a broader purpose—namely, that of fighting for social justice and making the world a better place. At Disney World we couldn't portray real companies, probably because the negative depiction would anger advertisers. Therefore, Bryan and I joined up with Hinojosa, at the time a senior in college working on her honors thesis. We spun the idea out to test in contexts where we had the freedom to draw on what we thought would be an even more powerful source of motivation.

Our post-Disney intervention program took the form of an exposé of the food companies' manipulative marketing practices. Students read and responded to the exposé on a computer during their health or physical education classes. Our exposé article, titled "Food in America: The True Story," explained "what food companies do behind our backs and how teens can take a stand to make the world a better place." It described, for example, how food scientists create snacks like Flamin' Hot Cheetos to have the most addictive possible combination of cheesiness, meltiness, crunchiness, and spiciness, bypassing your brain's natural satiety mechanisms. The article further reported how food companies use cartoons and mascots to sell junk food to young children, such as Chester Cheetah or Tony the Tiger. In addition, the article revealed that top executives at Kraft and Yum! Brands—many of whom used to work at tobacco companies—knew full well how unhealthy their products were and often forbade their own children and grandchildren from eating them. This conveyed the hypocrisy of the food companies, which would hopefully draw the ire of the teens. The content of the article was factual and based on meticulous reporting. An overview appears in figure 8.1.

Our exposé had two rhetorical goals. First, it framed healthy eating as a way to "stick it to the man." Eating healthy became a way to take a stand and stop the executives at food companies from controlling their choices

Figure 8.1. An excerpt from the exposé values-alignment intervention.

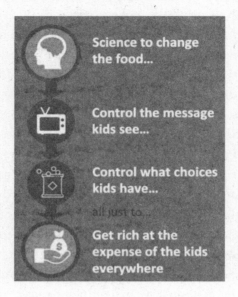

through lies. Second, it emphasized the social justice consequences of food marketing. The intervention framed healthy eating as a way to stand up for people in need. Because autonomy and social justice are both core values for young people, we suspected that this new framing would increase the social-status appeal of healthy eating—and therefore motivate the desired change in behavior. In summary, our exposé aimed to shift the identity of a healthy eater. Instead of healthy eaters being *lame nerds who do what adults tell them to do*, they were *independent-minded people who fight to make the world a fairer place.*

Our exposé intervention had three key elements to drive the message home. First, we presented quotes from high school students, which we had gathered during our pilot testing, and which explained how to turn their anger into action. For example, the kids in our study read this:

Those guys are such hypocrites. I can't believe the executives get money by making addictive junk food and they don't even eat or drink it themselves! They get rich while poor people and little kids get unhealthy food. . . . My friends and I are going to take a stand right away: No more money to companies that manipulate poor people and little kids into eating and drinking junk that makes them sick. —Jennifer H., ninth-grade volleyball player.

Second, we allowed kids to write their own suggestions for fighting back against the food companies. They described how somebody else their age could figure out how to respond. We call this a *saying-is-believing* exercise: by writing an argument to convince somebody else of an idea, you end up convincing yourself.

Third, we gave kids an activity called *make it true*. This involved seeing deceptive food advertisements and writing graffiti on them to turn the lies into true statements. This activity captured the subversive thrill of rebelling against the establishment but channeled it into healthy behavior. An example of a kid's graffiti appears in figure 8.2.

We call this a *values-alignment* approach to interventions. The exposé aligned the healthy, long-term behavior (eating right) with a short-term value that has motivational immediacy (status and respect). The logic underlying this approach is that it's usually easier to change behavior by

Figure 8.2. A teenager's graffiti on a food advertisement to make it true.

aligning the behavior with something people already care about than by trying to get them to care about something different. In this case, rather than attempting to stop eighth graders from being rebellious and independent, we showed them how healthy choices could be aligned with their existing values of rebelliousness and independence.

In our experiments we compared the values-alignment intervention with a control group that also focused on healthy eating but applied a conventional approach. The control group content came from middle school health-class textbooks and from government campaigns to promote public health through healthier eating.

Our first experiment evaluated the values-aligned exposé intervention with 536 eighth graders in Texas. We looked for effects on food choices a day later. We did so by having the principal of the school make an announcement (several weeks before our experiment) that he would give the eighth graders a snack pack to reward them for working hard to prepare for the state tests. On the morning after students read the exposé, teachers handed out snack-pack forms, on which the kids indicated whether they wanted their rewards to be ultraprocessed junk food (e.g., Flamin' Hot Cheetos, Doritos, Oreos, Sprite, or Coke) or healthy food (fruit cup, nuts, baby carrots, or water). Once kids made their choices, then our team spent the day packing the snacks. Kids got them at the end of the day. Critically, the kids didn't know that the snack pack was connected to the exposé they had read the previous day. After students read the article, they made healthier choices in the treatment group relative to the control group.

In our second experiment, we tracked what kids bought in the lunchroom for the rest of the year. We found that kids, especially boys, who completed the values-aligned exposé intervention bought less junk food, and more healthy food. Strikingly, the effects held up for the entire three-month period that we tracked them. Youth in the intervention group proved more willing to show up at the lunch table with a salad or a fruit cup rather than Flamin' Hot Cheetos and a root beer. The reason why, our analyses showed, was because we increased the social-status appeal of healthy eating. Eating healthy didn't look lame. It looked awesome.

The most interesting findings came from our analyses of testosterone levels. Prior to the study, we collected testosterone samples from the eighth graders' saliva (if their parents had given us written consent). We found that when adolescents read the control article, which simply presented diet and health information that was typical for a middle school health class, their testosterone predicted more junk food purchases, especially among boys. But when participants read the values-aligned exposé, the opposite was true. The high-testosterone boys—the ones who typically seem the most impulsive and shortsighted—made the healthiest choices.

This result confirms a major flaw in the neurobiological-incompetence model. Instead of thinking of the adolescent brain as fundamentally flawed due to puberty's hormones, we can think of it as *ready to change* in response to the prospect of status and respect. We harnessed that readiness by reframing healthy behavior in line with adolescent values.

Boring but Important

Twenty years ago, I was an okay (not great) middle school English teacher. But one of the few things I got right was the project my seventh-grade class did after reading *The Outsiders*, a tragic young adult novel that ends in conflict and death. I challenged my class to use the lessons of the book to come up with conflict-resolution workshops for the younger grades. They conducted a thematic analysis, analyzing each character and their motivations, and used that analysis to write and perform skits loaded with life lessons. Like the students in the EL Education schools, my students conducted extensive research, sought out critical feedback, persevered, and met a high standard. That experience stayed in the back of my mind throughout graduate school, working under the mentorship of Dr. William Damon, the author of *The Path to Purpose*. I wanted to know: Could connecting learning tasks to a beyond-the-self purpose spur a motivation for deeper learning? In 2014, we published a paper showing that it could.

Our 2014 experiment started with a simple observation. Many of the tasks that help us learn and master important skills are tedious. We called them *boring-but-important* tasks. Examples include showing your work in math, proofing and editing an essay, taking careful notes for a historical analysis, or double-checking data in a spreadsheet. These are the kinds of tasks they would have to do if they worked one day in Damon Munchus's mortgage division at J.P. Morgan. When young people don't have a good reason to work hard on these kinds of tasks, the effort can feel like an unfair imposition on their time, so they don't pay close attention to the details. But, we hypothesized, when young people see a purpose behind their attention to detail, then they may be motivated to work hard to get it right, even if the task isn't fun. Our purpose intervention, therefore, sought to instill the latter perspective.

The purpose intervention took the form of a short (about twenty minutes) self-administered online survey, similar to the growth-mindset, stress-mindset, and values-alignment interventions. It communicated three messages: (1) deeply learning skills now can be useful for many careers or roles in the future, (2) you can use those skills to make a difference for something in the world beyond your own self-interest, and (3) the reason why teachers give you boring-but-important assignments is because they think you can develop the skills that will help you make a difference. The

Figure 8.3. An infographic presented in the purpose intervention.

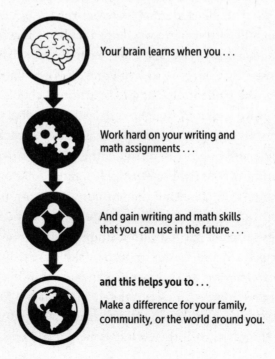

Your brain learns when you . . .

Work hard on your writing and math assignments . . .

And gain writing and math skills that you can use in the future . . .

and this helps you to . . .

Make a difference for your family, community, or the world around you.

infographic in figure 8.3 summarizes the purpose intervention's main argument.

How did we communicate these messages? We took several steps. First, our intervention asked the students to reflect on a social or community issue that mattered to them—something that made them mad when they thought about it, like poverty or violence or political division. Furthermore, they reflected on how having a stronger brain could help them do something about it. Next, we needed to overcome the norm of self-interest. To do so we presented true statistics from a survey we conducted on other students' reasons for learning. We informed kids that "making money in the future was hardly ever the only reason—or even the main reason" why students worked hard in school. Instead, we said, most students said they also work hard for personal reasons such as becoming an educated person who has something intelligent to say about what's going on in the world, wanting to learn so they can make a positive contribution to the world, or having the freedom to pick the life they want to live. These statistics were true, but they were news to students because the norm of self-interest had masked them.

We followed the survey statistics with some quotations from former students. Upper-year students gave statements such as, "Doing well in school is all about preparing myself to do something that matters, something that I care about," or "I want to be an educated person, because educated people get more respect and more freedom to live the way they want to." Note that we didn't deny that people have some self-interest— that would have undermined our credibility. But we did say that people have a mix of both self-oriented and beyond-the-self-oriented motives, and that doing something hard but meaningful is a route to status and respect. Finally, to drive the messages home, we asked students to write their own persuasive essays about why working hard and learning in school could be related to a "positive impact you want to have on the people around you or society in general."

Did the purpose intervention work? First, we found that just about every student in our studies dug into the material and wrote something profound, whether they attended an elite college or an underfunded middle school or anything in between. These results showed us that the intervention had tapped into something meaningful that students didn't get asked to think about very often.

Next, we looked at whether the purpose intervention motivated students to work harder on boring-but-important tasks. In our experiment we gave the purpose intervention (or a control activity) to 429 undergraduate participants. Right after that, we asked them to complete the Academic Diligence Task (ADT), which measures people's likelihood of persisting in the face of temptation. The ADT presented participants with a choice: you can either "do math" (single-digit subtraction) or "play game or watch movie" (i.e., goof off on the Internet). The ADT's computer program secretly tracked how long people do math versus goof off. (It's like a computer-based marshmallow test.) See figure 8.4. Our experiment found that in the control group, the longer people worked on the task, the less math they did, and the more online goofing off they did. But when participants first completed the purpose intervention, they delayed gratification. As time went on, they did more math and played 50 percent fewer videos or games. Purpose solved the temporal-discounting problem.

Did the benefits of purpose last over time? In another experiment we conducted with 338 ninth-grade students, we found the purpose intervention improved grade point average (GPA) months later, at the end of the

Figure 8.4. The Academic Diligence Task.

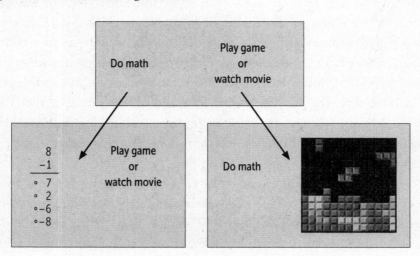

school year. The benefits proved the strongest for students who started out with low grades—the ones who were most disengaged also needed the intervention the most.

Our purpose experiment showed that if you encourage a meaningful purpose for learning—one that involves both contribution to others and the status and respect one can gain from having stronger skills—then you can motivate young people to show the discipline and hard work that adults usually fail to see when they follow a conventional approach.

Solving Damon Munchus's Purpose Problem

On the floor of the mortgage division at J.P. Morgan, how did Damon Munchus motivate his early-twenties employees to pay excessive attention to detail—that is, to do the boring-but-important work with integrity?

If Munchus was an enforcer, he would emphasize short-term self-interest. He would remind his employees that he owns their time from nine to five, so they better work hard for every penny he's paying them. In an enforcer mindset, work is transactional, not meaningful.

Instead, Munchus used the mentor mindset. He emphasized to his employees the broader *purpose* of the work. "They have to make a connection to the broader narrative of 'our customers depend on us to get it right.' They must see that the work they do can help a customer and that their piece matters." He would explain to his team that if they didn't help the mortgage lenders understand how their business is going, then the lenders can't set fair and stable rates, which are essential to allowing people to buy their homes—and for many people a home is their most important purchase. His team understood what their work meant to a family, to a first-time homebuyer. Munchus also emphasized what would happen if the team slipped up and made an oversight. The bank's competitors would love nothing more than for J.P. Morgan to seem untrustworthy because they could steal their business. Munchus helped his team understand how their work affected the reputation of the bank's entire ecosystem of financial services. He needed to be extra transparent on this front. Many of his employees had freshly graduated from economics or finance programs where the norm of self-interest dominated. He needed to make it clear that they could have a beyond-the-self purpose to help the customer even in the financial-services industry. By making his team of junior analysts customer obsessed, Munchus motivated them to be detail obsessed. Finally, Munchus didn't just scare them into working hard. He created a culture where he actively supported everyone's growth and development as they tried to meet his exceptionally high standards. Not only did his team overperform, but he ended up being one of J.P. Morgan's top mentors to diverse, young talent.

Purpose Pro Tips

How can we apply the science of purpose to the mentor mindset? Here are some pro tips I've learned from observing teachers, parents, and managers over the years.

Purpose Isn't Just a Gen Z Thing

These days, supposed experts on the next generation are everywhere. They all seem to echo a similar refrain: young people today want to have a sense of purpose in school and at work. Sometimes you hear complaints about this from members of older generations. To hear them tell it, they never cared about such nonsense. They showed up every day, gritted through their boring-but-important tasks, and collected a paycheck. But this is mostly nonsense—a fairy tale inspired by the norm of self-interest. Viktor Frankl and Kurt Hahn were writing about meaning and purpose before most baby boomers were born. What we're seeing with the new generation isn't a shift in young people's nature. It's a shift in awareness of what has motivated people throughout human history, and an erosion of the norm of self-interest in their generation. Young people today are more self-aware about their search for meaning.

Make Broad, Not Narrow, Arguments

Adults often make very specific arguments about careers that require a given course or skill. For example, Pearla brought in local professionals who described how they used math in their sales or accounting jobs. However, getting into a specific career is a low-probability event. Not all students will take inspiration from these concrete examples. *I won't ever be in sales or accounting,* students could easily say, *so I guess I don't need to pay attention to this.* Broader arguments typically prove more effective. For example, in our purpose intervention we argued that algebra or writing can teach you logical-reasoning skills that make your brain stronger, then you can use your stronger brain to solve problems in the world (and get good feelings of prestige from making a difference in your community). We didn't argue that they needed algebra to be a certified public accountant.

It's a Mix of Motives

In the early days of our purpose research, we learned that the most stable and meaningful sense of purpose had a *mix* of motives. Young people both wanted to contribute to the world around them *and* have meaningful and respected futures. They weren't martyrs, sacrificing all enjoyment in life for others' benefit. To the contrary, they had a clear sense of how both they and the world around them could benefit from their stronger skills. And the source of beyond-the-self purpose that helps motivate them doesn't have to just be community service—Frankl noted that a commitment to art or science or beauty can work as well.

Don't Cause Anxiety

The most serious mistake that I often see is invoking purpose in a way that causes anxiety. It can backfire to tell a young person that the whole world is counting on them learning and growing, and that if they fail they'll disappoint everyone and make people suffer. In fact, researchers who study how anxiety interferes with the brain's functioning often say something like that to make people freak out in a lab setting. So don't make purpose an all-or-nothing proposition. Instead, take a page from the mentor-mindset playbook. Emphasize your support for young people's learning. We don't want to stoke anxiety-ridden threat-type stress. We want to evoke challenge-type stress that fuels better learning and performance.

Chapter 9

Belonging

To sustain school success one must be identified with school achievement.... For such an identification to form, one must perceive good prospects in the domain, that is, that one has the interests, skills, resources, and opportunities to prosper there, as well as that one belongs there, in the sense of being accepted and valued.

—Claude Steele, Stanford University social psychologist

Two Dilemmas

Christina, a college physics instructor, knows that most students don't want to take her course. It's complex, it involves a lot of work, and many students struggle. Because medical schools require physics credits, the stakes are high, creating an additional layer of stress. Christina wanted her students to feel like they belonged in physics. Nothing she tried worked. She was friendly, and she offered extra office hours, but nobody came to meet with her. And like the rest of the physics department, she saw an alarming disparity in her data. Her students from poor families or low-quality high schools performed far worse than their peers. She wanted to know: What could she do differently?

Ingeboerg is a brilliant professional who's read every parenting book and article. Not long ago, she told me about how her seventh-grade daughter, Nora, was being bullied and excluded at her school in Norway. Nora's longtime group of four friends from elementary and early middle school wouldn't have anything to do with her. They wouldn't invite her to sleepovers, the movies, or birthday parties, and they excluded her from group texts. Who knows what they might be saying about Nora behind her back? One minute, she had a core group of popular friends who accepted her, and the next she's socially dead, a pariah. Her daughter felt crushed, crying on her mother's shoulder every night, asking, "What's wrong with me?" and "Why doesn't anybody like me?" and "Am I going to be a loser forever?" Even with all the books she'd read, Ingeboerg was at a loss for words. She wanted to know: What could she say to help Nora deal with this?

Different as these two problems may seem, they have very similar solutions. Both solutions draw on the new science of *belonging*. Over the last decade and a half, a series of scientific breakthroughs, many of them led by Stanford University social psychologist Greg Walton, have ushered in a new era in the science of belonging. Walton and his collaborators have overturned misconceptions of belonging as new age, feel-good puffery while yielding some of the best-validated strategies for promoting achievement and well-being, especially for people from groups who are marginalized, stereotyped, or left out.

The Need to Belong

From birth, human beings have a basic need to belong and to be accepted. Newborn infants, for example, prefer to stare at faces and listen to human voices rather than nonfaces or nonhuman sounds. Even in the womb, babies can recognize the difference between their mother's voice reading *The Cat in the Hat* versus a stranger's voice reading the same book. In 2017, the psychologist Carol Dweck published an influential theory arguing that this primal sociality comes from infants preparing for *accepting* interactions—those with a give-and-take synchrony. Accepting interactions help babies survive by bringing them closer to caretakers who will feed them and keep them safe.

As humans develop, we transition from dyadic interactions with caregivers to interactions with larger groups, especially in adolescence. Our parents may offer us unconditional acceptance, but our peers usually want us to bring something to the table. Thus, our need to be accepted becomes tied to our need to feel competent. After all, proving our competence to others is the basis of earned prestige in a peer group. See figure 9.1.

This basic idea extends beyond the peer group and applies to any institutional context. A teenager failing advanced math might say, *I don't belong in this class.* Their incompetence determines their unbelonging. On the other hand, a teenager who's an exceptional figure skater might say of the championship competition, *I belong here.* Their competence determines their belonging.

According to Dweck's theory, this mutually influencing tornado of needs—to be competent and to belong—morphs into the adolescent need for status and respect (see figure 9.1). When young people have something of value to contribute to a group—when they're competent and accepted—then they're accorded status and respect. That's earned prestige. By the same token, belonging threats spill over into our feelings of competence. Then they jeopardize the testosterone-sensitized drive for status and respect.

Unbelonging can be as serious to adolescents as a threat to maternal attachment is to a baby. Thus, even seemingly minor experiences that make a young person feel like they're a poor *social* fit for a group or setting can make them feel like a poor *intellectual* fit and scare them off.

This connection between feelings of intellectual fit and social fit was a breakthrough discovery made by Greg Walton when he was a graduate student at Yale University. Walton saw that the complexities of belonging

Figure 9.1. Dweck's (2017) developmental theory of needs.

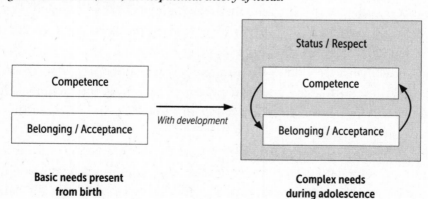

could help explain adolescent behaviors that seem perplexing to older generations. Why do some young people fight tooth and nail to get into a particular college, or land a specific job, but then drop out or quit when it starts getting tough? Walton surmised, and studies have later confirmed, that the biggest factor, in many studies, is *uncertainty* about whether they belong. Such uncertainties prompt people to look out for experiences that could signal that we lack the competence required to truly belong. Examples include receiving harsh criticism from a professor, needing to ask a clarifying question in class, or feeling confused during office hours. People may not ask for help to do better if they are worried that any struggles could reveal a lack of intellectual ability to succeed, and therefore a lack of belonging. Not taking steps to do better, people might then perform worse, intensifying doubts about belonging and competence. This process appears in figure 9.2, which shows how initial uncertainty about belonging and competence, over time, can transform into *Get me out of here!*

Walton's insights were important because society tends to downplay the need to belong. For an obvious example, nations around the world underestimated the psychological and educational impact of isolated learning during COVID-19 school closures. When people believe that young people's perspectives are not legitimate (i.e., neurobiological incompetence), they fail to recognize that belonging plays a vital role in their well-being or even survival. Some skeptics may even interpret the utterance *I want to belong* as meaning, *I want to be held to low intellectual standards.*

Figure 9.2. How a cycle of uncertainty about one's belonging and/or competence can lead to worse performance over time.

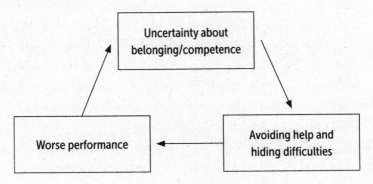

A good example of this mistaken thinking appeared in the 2022 culture war that emerged when New York University (NYU) fired Dr. Maitland Jones Jr., an old-school organic chemistry professor, a few years after he retired from Princeton University. Firsthand accounts from students make clear that Jones was an enforcer-mindset teacher. He designed his class to be exceptionally demanding. He touted his philosophy that "teachers must have the courage to assign low grades when students do poorly without fear of punishment." According to his criteria, he was exceptionally courageous. Compared to other teachers, Jones Jr. gave out significantly lower grades. Because organic chemistry is a required course for medical school, that meant many more students wouldn't become doctors, a fact that Jones Jr. didn't regret. "Unless you appreciate these [organic chemistry] transformations at the molecular level," he told the *New York Times*, "I don't think you can be a good physician, and I don't want you treating patients." Jones's students started a petition against his class, and the administration subsequently fired him. Jones's defenders, and Jones himself, blamed his firing on *young people these days* failing to live up to his lofty standards. They accused the university of pandering to a woke and feeble student body who wanted participation-trophy A's, not authentic achievement. Jones Jr.'s critics, meanwhile, argued that he set excessively high standards, that young people these days shouldn't be asked to memorize outdated formulas. Both sides missed the point, however. The point was this: Jones Jr. was outrageously, epically, historically bad at addressing belonging.

Laura Janda, now a globally recognized professor of linguistics, took Jones Jr.'s organic chemistry class at Princeton in the 1970s. She wrote about a time she asked a question in class. Jones Jr. mocked her, imitating her with a girlish, naive voice. He then asked the rest of the class to join him in laughing at her. "It still hurts 50 years later," she wrote. She was glad that he was fired because "all students deserve to be treated with respect." At NYU, when students asked Jones Jr. for assistance, they were met with "dismissiveness, unresponsiveness, condescension, and opacity about grading," according to the administration's report.

The reason for Jones Jr.'s behavior was his adherence to the neurobiological-incompetence model. His go-to response to student confusion was *shame*. When asked why so many students did poorly, he blamed their inconsistent attendance, their weak work ethic, and their addiction to screens, not his inability to respect them or connect with them. In his mind, he had supported students by posting online videos that clarified concepts he had explained poorly during class. The fact that students didn't learn meant, to him, that they didn't care enough—or weren't smart enough—to succeed. Jones Jr. didn't consider that his lectures often had nothing to do with his exams, that his videos were boring or discursive, and students hated feeling belittled in his class, so they stopped showing up. He had a classic enforcer mindset: blaming, shaming, telling, yelling, but rarely listening or validating or adapting.

None of the newspaper articles I read about the Maitland Jones Jr. saga deviated from the basic narrative that the high standards were the problem—when in reality, his failures as a teacher stemmed from his lack of support. Jones's impossible-to-reach standards, with little support, caused large proportions of students to question their competence and, in turn, their belonging—not just in his class, but in the field of medicine overall. The all-standards, low-support approach might not flummox students who already have every advantage and support from their families. A handful of top students at Princeton—which, according to large datasets of American's tax returns, is home to some of the most advantaged people in the world—liked Jones Jr., for example. If the only students who can benefit from a professor's teaching are the ones who can substitute their own resources to make up for his many flaws, then that's exclusive excellence, not inclusive excellence.

Social psychologist Mary Murphy, author of the book *Cultures of Growth*, has conducted surveys with hundreds of university professors. She finds that professors who have an enforcer mindset like that of Maitland Jones Jr. tend to create what Murphy calls a "culture of genius." This culture of genius tends to create achievement disparities between students from minority groups and their peers from majority groups. Their gaps are twice the size of the disparities seen in classrooms where teachers support everyone. These achievement disparities can start a corrosive cycle that confirms the professors' negative stereotypes about minority groups. If professors like Jones Jr. start out believing that minority students can't succeed and treat them dismissively, their disrespect will produce disengagement and low performance that will fulfill their prophecy.

The flawed media coverage of the Maitland Jones Jr. story—which focused solely on the standards, not his lack of support—convinced me that many gatekeepers are ill prepared to support belonging. Our society doesn't even understand that belonging is a problem we need to solve.

Even when leaders and organizations appreciate the importance of belonging, their commonsense approaches miss the mark. I'm often sent examples of belonging campaigns designed by enthusiastic college administrators. The execution of these well-intended campaigns reveals a fundamental misunderstanding. Messages of belonging frequently have an image of a college mascot or a lonely youth jumping for joy emblazoned with the words YOU BELONG! However, belonging isn't achieved by fiat. To the contrary, we secure our sense of belonging through experiences of looking competent in front of the people whose opinions we care about—earned prestige.

A student who comes to college feeling nervous about their ability to succeed and who immediately struggles in their large introductory classes won't suddenly believe that they belong just because a student services office gave them a YOU BELONG sticker for their laptop. With a protector mindset, people are generally sympathetic to belonging concerns, but they try to downplay them through the power of positive thinking. Unfortunately, that doesn't work.

To really understand belonging, and overcome these ineffective enforcer- and protector-mindset approaches, we need to turn to a rigorous scientific investigation of belonging. As we will see, science points to a key element that can help young people feel a sense of belonging: *beliefs about the possibility of change and improvement.*

Consider a lovely study led by the London Business School social psychologist Aneeta Rattan, who was trained by Carol Dweck. Rattan's study examined the well-known "It Gets Better" campaign. This campaign was created in response to a rash of suicides and suicide attempts among LGBTQ+ youth in 2010. In the campaign, celebrities and civilians posted impassioned videos encouraging queer youth to stay hopeful and optimistic for the future because "it gets better." This campaign offered a beautiful example of the public's compassion and empathy for young people. It also served as a natural experiment that revealed our culture's difficulty in knowing what to say to help them.

When Rattan coded the viral videos for the content of their messages, she found that 76 percent of the videos argued something like the following: *People who are mean to you now because of your sexual identity could never change and will always look down on you. But you can find different people who might accept you; for example, if you moved away from your hometown.* Such videos promise an oddly pessimistic vision. They're essentially telling queer youth that the people they're around now, whose opinions they care about, including their family, will never accept them. One day, however, they might be able to abandon the home and family and friends they have now for the chance to find at least one person somewhere else who might accept them. In experiments where Rattan showed those typical "It Gets Better" videos to queer youth, the participants said the messages weren't comforting. (See left column in table 9.1.)

In a minority of cases (just 22 percent of the time) Rattan found that the "It Gets Better" videos made a different argument: *people can change.* (See right column in table 9.1.) These videos argued that people's prejudiced attitudes toward queer youth could evolve over time, that society's norms could change, or that your family members could realize that they love you unconditionally even if they don't understand your gender or sexual identity. In Rattan's experiments, participants rated the latter people-can-change videos as far more comforting. The Rattan study provides another example, like the failed compliment-sandwich approach (introduction), to remind us that we can't trust many of our instincts about communicating with young people—especially when it concerns their belonging.

Table 9.1. "It Gets Better" Messages That Weren't Comforting (Left) and Were Comforting (Right)

"IT GETS BETTER" *WITHOUT* EXPLAINING HOW PEOPLE CAN CHANGE	"IT GETS BETTER" *WITH* EXPLAINING HOW PEOPLE CAN CHANGE
You can't let all the criticism and negative comments get you down. It truly doesn't matter what people think of you if you are happy with who you are. There is nothing wrong with being yourself, so don't let anyone tell you differently. If you can learn who you are and accept yourself now, you will make your life much easier because it only gets better as you move through life. It may seem like a struggle now, but by knowing that everything *will* get better, you can remain hopeful and enthusiastic for the future.	The bullying and getting made fun of that you may face in your youth or in high school will soon go away. As people grow up, they care less about differences such as sexual orientation and more about individual people's personalities because they no longer feel the need to put someone else down to make themselves feel better. Once people grow up and feel comfortable in their own shoes, they will let you feel comfortable in yours. Just get through these difficult teen years. It will get better.

Why are adults' instincts about belonging so untrustworthy? One answer looks to the Golden Rule. This is the idea that we should want for others what we want for ourselves. When I was in graduate school, the late Stanford social psychologist Lee Ross used to tell us that the Golden Rule was a great rule to live by but a terrible rule to design by. It can lead us astray because others don't necessarily want or need what we want, especially if we're more comfortable and secure than they are.

Suppose you lived in New York City and somebody who had never been to NYC was coming to visit you, so you needed to explain how to navigate public transportation. If you gave them the advice the way that *you'd* want to hear it, you might give them lots of details about which subway lines to take, which stops to get off and on at, whether to catch a cab and where to just walk, and how many blocks away this or that attraction is. You'd like that because you have a mental map of the city. It wouldn't work for *them*, however, because they don't. They would need to grasp basic concepts, like how a subway works or when it's safe to ride versus walk. In general, designing directions for someone who's very secure in their mastery of the public transportation system is very different from designing for someone who's new to the system.

Similarly, the Golden Rule fails us when adults who generally take their belonging for granted try to give advice to younger people who are in a more precarious position. We get ourselves in trouble again and again, on both the enforcer and protector side.

It's easy for an enforcer professor like Maitland Jones Jr. to design an organic chemistry class the way he would want to learn the content. But he wrote the textbook! And he has a pension from Princeton! He feels secure in his competence and his belonging. He's forgotten that his students don't. His Golden Rule design ended up crushing half the class or more, and he couldn't understand why, except to blame the students for not being him.

Likewise, it's easy for protector-mindset college administrators to say, *You belong*, without addressing the underlying threats to belonging. They're insiders! They went to college, and they work at one! People often downplay the importance of fears about belonging when they aren't threatened by such fears themselves.

If as a society we can't trust our instincts about belonging, then what can we do? Instead of using the Golden Rule, we can use the mentor mindset. Recall that in a mentor mindset we don't start with a presumption that young people's perspectives are illegitimate. Therefore we don't think that our own instincts should be trusted more. Instead, in a mentor mindset we have a neurobiological-*competence* belief. We think *it's normal and good for young people to be concerned about belonging, status, and respect*. A mentor's role is therefore to figure out which threats to status and respect could get in the way of young people feeling like they could belong, and then work toward alleviating those threats so that they can meet high standards. When we see young people encountering setbacks—whether it's confusion in chemistry class or bullying in the hallways—then with a mentor mindset we recognize that we haven't given them sufficient support yet. We then say and do what we can to support them through their difficulties, without telling them to give up and without doing things for them that they can do themselves.

As it turns out, one of the most powerful ways to use a mentor mindset to support belonging is through *storytelling*. Storytelling is a powerful tool to help young people see the possibility for change and improvement when they face problems of belonging. The "It Gets Better" campaign tried to harness the power of stories but executed the idea poorly. Luckily, there's a four-step process for storytelling that comes from large randomized experiments. These experiments harnessed the power of stories to help young people belong in college.

Storytelling 1: College Success

In 2011, Greg Walton published one of the most remarkable and influential papers I had ever read. In it, he described a belonging intervention that he had given to students in the spring of their first year of college. The belonging intervention consisted of reading survey statistics and stories from upper-year students, writing a short speech, and recording yourself delivering that speech (a *saying-is-believing* activity; chapter 8). These statistics and stories conveyed the potential for change by providing two messages: (1) the struggle to belong is normal (and therefore not a sign that there's something permanently wrong with you), and (2) those concerns tend to improve (but not just on their own—usually when people take active steps to become academically and socially integrated on campus). Participants needed about half an hour to complete the intervention. Shockingly, Walton and his coauthor, Geoffrey Cohen, found that three and a half years later, at the end of college, the grades of Black students in particular had improved. The intervention had eliminated approximately half of the Black-white disparity in grades.

Even more amazing was the follow-up analysis (conducted with Dr. Shannon Brady). By the time students were in their late twenties, those who got the belonging intervention showed greater well-being and job satisfaction. Belonging was the gift that kept on giving. Walton had somehow managed to bottle my great-grandmother Leona Sumners (introduction) into a half-hour survey that could be scaled to hundreds of thousands of students per year.

I had so many questions. For starters, how could a short activity have an impact even a few hours later, let alone years later? After all, most college professors think their students forget most, if not all, of what they say right after class. Next, how could changing someone's mind have an effect on their actual behavior and outcomes far into the future? Indeed, addressing inequality between groups feels so intractable. It wasn't clear to me how a purely psychological treatment could have an impact. And last, were Walton's results even trustworthy? Although the study was rigorously conducted and analyzed, the sample size was small. It was at least possible that the results benefited from a bit of luck.

I approached Walton with a proposition. I wanted to replicate his findings in larger and larger samples. I also wanted to study the steps between the short activity and the long-run outcomes, to understand why it worked. Lastly, I wanted to figure out how he crafted those stories that students read. I saw tremendous potential for the belonging intervention to help educators, managers, and parents, but in order for it to have that impact we'd need to unpack it. Walton was game. That began one of the most fruitful and energizing collaborations of my career. The end result was a set of practical tools for people to craft belonging stories that they can use in their contexts.

First, we replicated. We ran three experiments simultaneously in the spring of 2012, with the entire incoming class at Stanford (where Walton worked), the entire incoming class at the University of Texas at Austin (where I worked), and the entire outgoing class of seniors at several large urban charter school networks (who were working with us). The total sample was greater than ninety-five hundred students. Roughly three-fourths the students (randomly assigned) completed the belonging intervention via an online survey before college, and a fourth completed a control exercise. The belonging intervention improved first-year achievement, especially among students who were the first in their families to go to college (regardless of their race or ethnicity) and students who came from racial/ethnic minority groups (regardless of their parents' education levels).

Soon after, independent scholars replicated the effects, showing that the belonging intervention worked for middle schoolers as well. Recently, we formed a large consortium with social psychologists Mary Murphy, Christine Logel, and Shannon Brady and replicated the belonging intervention with over twenty-six thousand incoming students at twenty-two institutions. (We have since made Walton's belonging intervention available for free.)

Second, we discovered why the belonging-intervention effect lasted over time. It was due to a kind of snowball effect (which psychologists call a *recursive process*). See figure 9.3. Students who got the short belonging intervention, and who therefore felt less worried about their belonging, were more likely to get their hooks into the system. They visited office hours more, they joined extracurriculars, they chose to live on campus, they said they had mentors, and more. Why did this happen? When students recognized that their worries about belonging didn't mean anything bigger—that is, that they shouldn't be in college at all—then they were more likely to take the microrisks of meeting peers and talking to professors. Those reasonable microrisks then paid off because they *created* belonging, in the form of having more friends or professors who knew their names.

Overall, our study revealed that students—especially students from groups who are made to question their belonging and have a greater likelihood of dropping out—have far more agency and ability to belong than society gives them credit for. They needed to alleviate constant threats to their belonging. In our studies, students were able to get that from the short intervention that taught them how to think about belonging in a more useful way. The belonging intervention was, as Geoffrey Cohen likes to say, "the final straw lifted from the camel's back."

Third, Walton (with me and many others) articulated the key aspects behind the belonging stories that made them work. We wanted to identify the ingredients that underpinned successful storytelling so that people could write new stories suited for their purposes, rather than simply borrowing our stories and expecting them to work in any context. Although the intervention seemed like a magic trick (i.e., untrustworthy) before we replicated, I suspected that once we had replicated it, it would seem like a magic bullet (i.e., a universal solution). As it turns out, teachers and parents have tried to hand out a magic worksheet of stories to evaporate belonging concerns and inequity. As we've already established, because of

Figure 9.3. The positive snowball effect started by the belonging intervention.

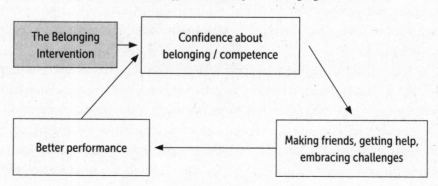

the Golden Rule problem, different audiences need different stories—storytelling isn't a one-size-fits-all solution.

What makes a good belonging story? Let's take a look at one from my UT Austin experiment conducted with Walton, shown in figure 9.4.

The story has four elements. The first block of highlighted text explains that struggle is normal. This reassurance is meant to dispel the idea that students are alone in their struggles and therefore uniquely unsuited for college. The second block of highlighted text provides an example of how change was possible. We don't want to say, *Everybody struggles*, but then imply that the struggles will be endless. The third block of highlighted text explains what actions students could take once they realized that change was possible. We've found students don't always know the behaviors that can lead them to develop belonging; they think it just happens. The action steps help students be intentional. The fourth block of highlighted text explains how those realizations and steps start a snowball effect. This is important because the story needs a happy ending, while also not overpromising that belonging concerns will evaporate overnight. In our studies, students tend to read anywhere from three to eight stories like this. (Note that we source the stories from former-student interviews, and then we edit them to make sure they have the key themes in the right order.)

Suppose you were a professor trying to tell a belonging story to help a wayward college student. Or a manager trying to tell a story to a new employee who's questioning their belonging. What would you say?

We asked this question to a group of faculty in a fellowship program we conducted during the 2020–2021 school year for instructors teaching large entry-level math and science. We had two professors from physics, two from chemistry, two from biology, and two from calculus. Collectively, our fellows would teach almost every premed and pre-engineering student at the university. They were accomplished and rigorous professors, but they wanted to add belonging stories to their repertoires. They were the anti–Maitland Joneses. Together with the fellowship codirector, Kristin Patterson, we led our fellows through a belonging-story writing exercise.

One of the fellows that first year was Dr. Christina Markert, whom you met in the introduction to this chapter. She's an accomplished,

Figure 9.4. An annotated example of a belonging story.

Coming to UT felt like a whirlwind—exciting and confusing, all at the same time. Going to my first math and science courses, I felt pretty overwhelmed. My high school classes weren't that good, so there were certain things I didn't know how to do yet. Like I was embarrassed to admit that I'd never looked through a microscope before, so I didn't know how to use one. At first, I didn't speak up in my classes because I worried what other students might think. It seemed like they knew more than me. But then I decided, I'm paying for this class so I should get the most out of it. So I asked my lab mate to show me how to work the microscope and asked a friend how she took notes. I also went to my professor's office hours to get tips about how to learn and succeed in class. What I know now is that college is something you learn how to do over time. If you open up and let people know what you don't understand yet, they will help you. Putting myself out there felt risky, but it really paid off in the long run.	**Struggle is normal** **Change is possible** **Action steps** **Snowball effect**

detail-oriented, tenured physicist. She was trained in Germany and still speaks with an accent that sometimes intimidated her mostly Texas-born students. She surprised her class in the fall of 2020 by telling them a story of her struggles. Early in her career, she told them, she failed an important physics exam. At the time, she cried about her failure, thinking it was the end of her career (*normalize*). Then, she realized that her preparation was the issue, not her ability, and so she took the failure as a starting point to improve her study strategies (*change is possible*). She talked to the students who did well and asked them for advice and tried adjusting her learning strategies (*action steps*). Finally, she improved her grade and realized that she could succeed. Then she took off on her new trajectory toward professional physics (*snowball*).

Christina could also offer them concrete support connected to her story. She told them that since she needed to learn at a different pace from the exam schedule, she wouldn't judge them for needing to do the same. Therefore, students could either retake exams later or correct missed problems later. Her logistical flexibility (and intellectual rigor) gave struggling students even more reason to believe that their worries about belonging could change because she presented them with a legitimate prospect of becoming more competent over time.

The results of her storytelling amazed Christina. Students came to office hours more, but not to gripe about their grades like they normally did. Instead, they came because they were curious and wanted to understand the concepts. Their enthusiasm energized Christina. She even renamed these periods *drop-in hours* to signal that she wanted students to drop in to chat because *office hours* made many students feel like they were being sent to the office. Although Christina gave her class the same hard tests as she always did, more students passed than ever—especially the final exam—with smaller racial, ethnic, and gender disparities. Perhaps most importantly, students loved the course.

Below are some excerpts of what Christina's students said the year she was in our mindset fellowship program. As you read them, keep in mind that these are eighteen-to-twenty-year-old premed students in a hard class that could derail their entire career aspirations if it went poorly. (That is, they were disinclined to be positive.)

- "I was resenting having to take physics as it has always been a hard subject for me. Dr. Markert was so intentional about sharing her own experiences and encouraging everyone to feel confident in themselves. That did so much to boost my confidence and make me feel prepared to handle the material. I have truly never had a professor thus far who is as attuned to student needs as Dr. Markert. She made physics an amazing experience!"
- "I have always struggled with physics as a subject. It has always been a source of anxiety and discomfort for me. . . . Thank you, Dr. Markert, for the first time in my life making me feel as if there is a place for me in STEM and that my questions and attempts at learning are valid!"
- "She reminds me of the good in the world and all the reasons I wanted to come to college in the first place."

The impact this experience had on Christina herself was perhaps even more amazing. The mentor mindset proved a win-win for her. On the last day of our fellowship, she provided a testimonial of her own personal snowball. By the end, there wasn't a dry eye in the house.

It was a revelation that students' confidence about their belonging could have such an impact on their engagement, Christina said. Once the students were more engaged, Christina enjoyed her teaching much more. She started looking forward to class in a new way because students were sharing their opinions about the content much more. In a fascinating parallel to her students' reactions, her experience with belonging reminded her of why she went into physics in the first place.

This first year (and subsequent replications) of our faculty fellowship convinced us that the guidelines in figure 9.4—and a little bit of coaching—could help overcome the Golden Rule problem. By and large, the faculty crafted meaningful stories. You can do the same.

Interestingly, years before I extended Walton's research to the professors' stories, Carol Dweck and I brought it to an entirely different problem space: coping with high school bullying.

Storytelling 2: Bullying, Stress, and Revenge

Think back on Ingeboerg's problem at the beginning of this chapter. Her daughter Nora was getting bullied and excluded by her friends, and her sadness broke Ingeboerg's heart. Like most of us, Ingeboerg wanted to stop Nora's suffering by solving her social problems for her. If we're being honest, most parents also worry how other parents will judge us if we don't intervene (or if we intervene too much). These dual pressures create a powerful temptation to go into protector mode. They give parents a strong sense of urgency to take shortcuts, circumventing the mentor-mindset response.

Experiencing bullying or exclusion can obviously make children feel they're bad (e.g., a loser or worthless). To counteract these feelings, we often tell our children that *they* are great but that the *other* people—the mean bullies—are the bad ones. They must have had bad things happen to them that made them mean (they come from bad homes, etc.). Bullies with a capital *B*, straight out of 1980s popular culture. If our children are being victimized by demon children who lack empathy, then the next steps are obvious: harass the school or the other children's parents (because they clearly don't punish bullying severely enough), tell your child to avoid the sociopaths (because they'll never stop their assaults), and let every other parent know that (1) those bullies are horrible, and (2) you did everything you could to save your child.

Decades of careful scientific studies on bullying's causes and solutions tell us that bullying is more complicated than being a bad person. Furthermore, this fixed worldview harms young people—both bullies and victims.

Picture a stereotypical bully in your mind. If you're like most millennials or millennial-adjacent people, you think of Moe, the bully who terrorized Calvin from the *Calvin and Hobbes* comic strip that appeared in the 1980s and '90s. Moe is drawn with a Cro-Magnon forehead, implying low intelligence. He lacks social or emotional skills, so he uses violence to solve all his problems.

How accurate is this stereotype? Not very. In 2015, my collaborators and I published a paper that reviewed past studies purporting to show what causes and prevents bullying. We analyzed data from hundreds of thousands of kids who were questioned around the world. The truth we discovered is so different from the Moe stereotype that it makes me want to cry.

From kindergarten until about sixth grade, Moe-like behaviors that we call bullying have a clear cause: poor self-control and executive function, which refers to the suite of skills children use to manage their impulses. Children who struggle to control their impulses—for example, who have a hard time not hitting others when they're mad or insulting others if they're offended—are more likely to be nominated by peers as the bullies of the crowd. Usually, however, these kids don't conform to our image of the autocratic *Lord of the Flies* bully who rules with an iron fist. Instead, the students who can't control their impulses may come across as bullies to peers, but mainly they just annoy the other kids in class, usually due to disabilities or learning differences (ADHD, Tourette's, emotion-regulation problems, etc.). They are affected by disorders that make impulse control a challenge. They're often in special education for behavioral, not cognitive, reasons. The last thing most of these children need is to be told they are unempathetic, Moe-like monsters. What they really need are better skills for making friends—for finding acceptance, status, and respect in a peer group. Most would be perfectly happy to trade bullying for a friend or two.

Starting in seventh grade and continuing to twelfth grade, the science tells a different story about bullying among older kids. When we analyzed the data from hundreds of thousands of students from around the world, we found that the bully who punches a peer to get lunch money was more or less extinct. Instead, the data showed that the *stronger* a student's social and emotional skills, the *more* likely they were to be seen as a bully in school. What could explain such a reversal? Here, too, the reason was fascinating.

Our data, and the data collected by independent scholars, showed that adolescents' *social goals* played a role. The more adolescents said their main goal was to be at the top of the social hierarchy, the more they tended to bully others. For example, in one study we conducted, the more a teenager said it was their main goal to look more popular than others, the more they wanted to exclude a low-status peer in the lunchroom. Importantly, by the high school years, the concept of bullying changes dramatically, becoming more social and indirect in nature. Rather than Moe stealing Calvin's lunch money, teenagers plotted *Succession*-esque sabotage to destroy the reputations of their status competitors.

University of California, Davis, sociologist Robert Faris led a beautiful study that directly showed this phenomenon (see figure 9.5). He found that kids who had secured top status didn't engage in bullying. Nor did the high school kids with very low status—they couldn't get to the top anyway. Instead, the high schoolers who came near the very top level but stopped just shy of reaching it were the ones who bullied others the most. They had plenty of status and respect *but not enough*. They felt insecure about keeping their mediocre place. And so they were willing to use bullying to finally get to the top.

These data challenge many of the popular stereotypes about bullying, and they should influence how people tend to respond. Bullying in the post-elementary-school age range mostly stems from a desire for status and respect—which is healthy and developmentally appropriate—combined with very shortsighted and harmful strategies for gaining status and

Figure 9.5. Semipopular kids bully more to get more status.

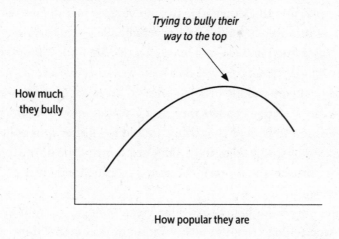

Trying to bully their
way to the top

How much
they bully

How popular they are

respect. Notice what I'm not saying. I'm not saying adolescents who bully need more social skills (in contrast to younger children). As Faris's study shows (see figure 9.5), the semipopular kids already have social skills. Instead, the problem is they often use these skills to strike the right balance of meanness and plausible deniability. Youth need to learn different routes to gain status and respect—leadership or kindness or contribution to the community. They need a different way to feel awesome.

Would an enforcer approach give that to them? Probably not. Young people need a mentoring approach that helps them learn how to attain social success without causing unjust suffering to others. Indeed, some of the most promising antibullying programs for high school and late middle school have done away with assemblies and swag and slogans. Instead they look more like leadership-development programs.

With this understanding, let's return to Ingeboerg's problem. What should she say to seventh grader Nora to help her when she's bullied and excluded by friends? Carol Dweck and I set out to answer that question, building in part on Walton's insights about belonging stories.

Carol Dweck is most well-known for her work on the growth mindset of intelligence—the idea that you can get smarter over time. But people can also adopt a growth mindset about personality—the idea that people can change how they treat others.

Early in my graduate career I pitched an idea to Carol: How about we apply this people-can-change idea to help victims of bullying? We thought that a fixed mindset—"bullies can never change"—caused people to lose hope for the future, just like the least-effective "It Gets Better" videos. On the other hand, if young people had a growth mindset about people's potential to change—the idea that bullies could learn to stop what they're doing and seek status another way—then young people would have a legitimate reason to believe that things would get better. Our collaboration led to a series of studies that to this day are some of the only experimental treatments proven to improve the stress, coping, and mental health of victimized youth.

To give youth the belief that people can change, we built on Walton's work on storytelling. In our growth mindset of personality intervention, we told high schoolers a story about an adult who ran into someone who used to bully them back in high school. The former bully had changed, regretted their actions, admitted that they think about it a lot, and asked the former victim to understand that they had done it out of a misguided attempt to gain status. (We interviewed many adults who felt this way about what they had done in high school, so we were summarizing true stories.) We explained how this chance encounter helped the adult realize something important, which is that people can change. Further, this realization helped the adult process the powerful emotions they had felt—the hatred and shame—and start changing them into emotions like pity, which didn't consume them.

We used this story as a launching-off point into the science of how people can change. We explained how adolescence is a time of seeking out status and respect, how that drive can lead some young people to do harmful things, and how kids who bully need to learn different ways of behaving. We further explained that as the brain matures, young people learn how to change their behaviors; for example, by seeking out more productive outlets for their appetite for status, such as leadership. Last, we argued that people who are shy and have few friends can also change. They can learn to be more social once they feel comfortable. Thus, even if they are excluded by some peers, they can still have a good social life in the future.

These people-can-change messages had two purposes. First, they aimed to reduce hatred. Hatred is a destructive and corrosive emotion that grows out of the belief that another person's or group's essence is fundamentally horrid and rotten to the core. For instance, social psychologist Eran Halperin found that when Israelis and Palestinians thought the other group was bad and could never change, they endorsed aggressive counterterrorism measures. If they thought the other group could change, they felt angry, but they were open to the peace process. In the high school context, when young people believe bullies can't change, they enter a cyclone of hatred. They show a seething desire for revenge. We wanted to reduce that outcome by conveying the possibility of change. Notably, we didn't guarantee that change would happen or happen quickly. Nor did we say that a victim of bullying needs to change their tormentors. Instead, we just made an argument that change is possible. That proved enough to take the edge off the hatred.

Second, the people-can-change message targeted the victims, not the bullies. We were trying to give victims hope that they could find greater acceptance and belonging in the future. Here, too, we took care not to imply something simplistic or misleading. We didn't say, *If only you changed, then people would like you.* Instead we explained that it's possible to overcome shyness or loneliness by learning communication skills, or even just by making friends. In fact, many high school friendships blossom through extracurriculars, and idiosyncratic interests drive which extracurriculars students join. Therefore, young people change their friend groups over time as they figure out what kinds of activities they want to be doing. Again, we didn't promise that change happens overnight. But we said it's always possible.

The people-can-change intervention next shared a few stories. They were collected from upper-year students and highlighted the same elements as the belonging stories. For instance, the intervention told the story about a student whose middle school best friends abandoned her at the start of high school, saying, "They walked by me without a smile or a hello." She felt like a nobody, ashamed and alone. She even wondered if she would have no friends for all of high school (normalize struggle). However, she started to realize that her friends had probably excluded her because they're insecure and caved to peer pressure to hang out with new people, so their motives aren't about her (change is possible). With this in mind, she decides that although her old friends might come around in the future, she's going to start finding new friends in the meantime. She also reminds herself that it's just the first week of school, so she has plenty of time (action steps). Last, the girl talks about how she made new friends who expanded her horizons. In addition, one of her old friends came back and regretted excluding her. Now she has a better group of friends that she can really depend on, and she feels like she belongs in her school (snowball effect). After students read a few stories like this, we had them write their own story like it to drive the information home.

This people-can-change intervention is easy to scale up. It's pretty short (around twenty-five minutes). It can be delivered as an assignment on a computer for individual students. Over the years, we've tested this intervention with thousands of students. The results have been remarkable.

In one experiment we published in 2013, we gave high school students either the people-can-change intervention or a control intervention that taught them social problem-solving skills. A third group received no intervention. Then, all the students completed a task in which they (temporarily) experienced exclusion by peers in an online game, and then had a chance to take revenge on the peers who excluded them. The group who got skills training were just as vengeful as the group who got nothing. Skills training didn't work. But the group who received the people-can-change intervention showed 40 percent less revenge. These results suggested that the message about change could stop the cycles of aggression and violence so often seen in schools.

In another experiment we published in 2016, the people-can-change intervention improved coping with stress. When we put high schoolers through the Trier Social Stress Test (see chapter 7), we found that the short intervention prevented harmful threat-type cardiovascular reactivity and promoted helpful challenge-type responses. When participants thought people could change, they seemed energized. They wanted to do something useful about their social difficulties. When they thought people could never change, they wallowed in damage and defeat. We found similar results in a new study with more than a thousand ninth-grade students who received the intervention in the first month of starting high school. On days when their belonging and status were under threat, students who learned people can change were more optimistic and resilient, in their minds and in their bodies.

Believing people can change can start a snowball effect that improves long-run mental health. In studies published by us and by independent scholars such as Dr. Jessica Schleider, the people-can-change treatment, given just one time, has reduced symptoms of depression and chronic stress. Our findings surprised the clinical psychology community. Therapists are used to long, multisession treatments. In some cases this was appropriate. Now, with the advent of our so-called single-session treatments, there are new doors being opened to scalable, universal support for youth mental health. For young people who are coping with mental health crises—in the midst of a shortage of therapists—the possibilities are exciting.

How did these messages help Ingeboerg's daughter Nora?

Nora hated being excluded. For the most part, Ingeboerg resisted the temptation to be a protector. She didn't harass the school. She did call one of the other girls' moms because they were (supposedly) friends. The other mom said, "I'm very sorry for Nora," but she wouldn't intervene. The other mom explained that she had been miserably bullied when she was a kid and said, "I'm very happy that my daughter is being included with the popular girls." She wouldn't tell her daughter to include Nora because "I don't want to mess that up for her." Ingeboerg was stunned. The other mother was so very clearly projecting her own insecurities onto the situation. Nora would suffer. That was unacceptable.

This nevertheless gave Ingeboerg a plan of what to say to Nora.

Ingeboerg explained to Nora that her friends are insecure and chasing higher popularity. They're popular but not yet at the top. (Like the bullies in Faris's study.) Excluding Nora was part of their strategy. She told Nora that their actions are unfair, but they're going to have to realize that for themselves. In the meantime, Nora needed to put herself out there in different classes and activities. She should make some new friends when she's ready. Ingeboerg conveyed that (1) Nora's struggles were normal and valid, (2) it's possible things could change but not immediately, (3) she could take steps right away to start improving the situation, and (4) her efforts could snowball into something better down the road.

A year later, Nora had new friends. She didn't hate her old friends and she didn't want revenge, even though she was angry. That hurt didn't own her anymore, however, so she could move on. What's more, Nora now had direct experience with a new, more hopeful story in her mind that she could tell herself. Nora now believed it gets better and that she belonged. It wasn't because her mom told her to believe in her belonging, but because she had taken actions to experience it firsthand. That's the power of the mentor mindset.

Section III

Building a Better Future

Chapter 10

Inclusive Excellence

How do we retain and nurture these people who have come to us wanting to participate in the excitement of scientific discovery?
—Keivan Stassun, award-winning astrophysicist

Inclusion by Design

Bang! Bang! Bang!

"Uh . . . Keivan," Josh Pepper said to his professor, "Dan's going to need another laptop."

Dr. Keivan Stassun is an award-winning, world-renowned astrophysics professor at Vanderbilt University. Dr. Josh Pepper, at the time, was a postdoctoral fellow in Stassun's laboratory. Dan was a brilliant programmer and master's student who was also working in Stassun's laboratory. Dan was in the midst of coding a new software platform that would let astrophysicists examine massive datasets of telescope observations for patterns, such as the location of new planets. Dan is also autistic. A side effect of Dan's neurodiversity was that he had little tolerance for frustration. Unfortunately, frustration was inevitable when he was inventing complex software for space exploration. Every so often, Dan's frustration would get the best of him. He would bang his laptop on the hard metal table, destroying it in the process.

After Dan's third broken laptop, what did Pepper and Stassun do? They didn't let Dan go. That would have been the enforcer move.

Instead, they bought him a hardened construction-site laptop. It could fall off a tall building and keep ticking. Problem solved! Dan's work could continue without interruption. Within a few years, Dan's software was the cornerstone of a major scientific publication in the journal *Nature*, the world's most venerated outlet for publishing scientific experiments. Dan's software was also licensed to NASA, which used it to find planets that might one day save the human race.

Stassun knows that his way of working is not normal in the dog-eat-dog world of professional science. Lab resources are tight. Spots in graduate programs are limited. Stassun is usually busy launching probes to mine minerals on asteroids or supervising telescopes on satellites, activities that put him among the world's most successful scientists. (To put Stassun's record into perspective, most scientists work their entire lives to have one paper published in *Nature*. Stassun has thirteen *Nature* papers.) Researchers at Stassun's level rarely spend time mentoring even the most prepared and easy-to-work-with students, let alone students needing accommodations.

Stassun is different. He's committed to *inclusive excellence.* He thinks all young people with passion and purpose should have opportunities to earn places in their fields of interest, not through unearned handouts, but by making genuine scientific contributions.

Stassun is currently focused on neurodiversity. His Frist Center for Autism and Innovation is the first of its kind to be dedicated to inclusive excellence for autistic students. Three autistic students (and counting) have completed their PhDs in physics through the center, with one to two more expected each year. More than eighteen autistic students have interned.

The Frist Center's mission is personal. You see, Stassun's son is rather severely autistic. "I'm trying to bend the world just a little bit so that the one my son grows up into will be more like the world that I need it to be for him," he told me. As the parent of a special-needs child, I cried when Stassun said this.

Approximately 1 percent of the world's population has autism spectrum disorder (ASD) in some form. ASD does not discriminate across race, ethnicity, nationality, or social class. ASD has two core features: impairments in social communication and restricted, repetitive behaviors.

Claire Barnett, who has ASD and works as the communications director for Stassun's center, describes ASD this way: You make minimal eye
contact, you're bad at small talk, your body language conveys disinterest,
you have difficulty interpreting the implied meanings of words, and you
come across as too straightforward. Barnett is also quick to point out that
ASD is a normal part of human diversity. This means that ASD frequently
co-occurs with important personal strengths. For example, people with
ASD often have an ability to see novel patterns in data or hyperfocus at
work. These skills, which Dan has in spades, formed the basis of a real
scientific contribution. Even so, it's hard for people with ASD to carry out
the more subtle social aspects of science that are important to the collective scientific enterprise, such as meetings with colleagues, contentious
debates about theory or data, or casual conversations in the break room.

For the past decade, Stassun's lab has sought to identify and troubleshoot around those subtle challenges—and do so without lowering the
lab's high standard for scientific productivity in the world's top journals.
They also have their eyes set on a bigger vision. In Claire Barnett's words,
their mission is "giving autistic people the respect they deserve, by recog-
nizing strengths, supporting them in areas of challenge, celebrating what
makes them unique, and simply giving them the space to be themselves."

Here's an example. The center allowed people to virtually attend
the weekly laboratory meeting, the lifeblood of most scientific-research
groups, well before the COVID-19 pandemic made Zoom meetings ubiq-
uitous. Usually this meeting is held in an actual lab, which is not so much
a meeting space as it is an echoing room with flickering artificial lights
surrounded by heavy machinery, not to mention boisterous students and
faculty. The lab environment proves distracting, or even triggering, for
scholars on the ASD spectrum, who often have sensory disorders. Stassun could have enforced an iron law of in-person attendance. Instead, he
fired up the webcam and allowed anyone to join virtually. That way, his
neurodiverse students had total control over their space, the volume, and
the lighting, so they could pay attention and contribute to lab meetings.
Interestingly, the accommodation for autistic students ended up benefiting neurotypical individuals who couldn't always attend in person.

In another accommodation for autistic students, Stassun set extremely high expectations for professional communication in his lab. "I didn't know how to properly communicate," Stassun's postdoctoral fellow Pepper told me about working with Dan in the early days. "That was my first experience working so directly and closely with someone with that severity of autism symptoms." The lab, like most workplaces, had a communication style filled with jokey double entendres or plays on words. "People tend to have a nudge-nudge, wink-wink way of talking," Stassun told me. Take for example, the comment, *Are you working hard or hardly workin'?* A neurotypical person can read the context—the half smile, the affable tone of voice—and infer that the speaker is making a half-hearted attempt to be clever. Dan, like many people with ASD, responds differently. He might take the question seriously and answer, *Well, I'm working hard but not as hard as I was yesterday, and I hope to work harder later this afternoon, but right now I can't get anything done because you're asking me questions.* A throwaway phrase could escalate into a thirty-minute debate, ending in Dan screaming or melting down.

What did Pepper and Stassun do? They didn't let their discomfort with Dan's meltdowns prevent them from including Dan in research meetings. Instead, everyone in the lab adopted a direct, literal communication style. No jokes. Just the facts, among all researchers, autistic or not. "We only discuss what we need to do to get the work done together," Stassun said. Pepper also learned to save his debates with Dan over technical or theoretical matters for email rather than the hallway. The new accommodations precluded the miscommunication and screaming and allowed Dan to gather his thoughts, which were far more coherent with the extra time. When Stassun's lab made that change, Dan shined. "Everyone in the lab saw his valuable contributions to the team," Pepper told me.

Strassun's approach is the mentor mindset in action. He focuses on everyone meeting high standards for genuine scientific contributions, while accommodating any differences that could create roadblocks for some students. It's his version of maintaining intellectual rigor while allowing logistical flexibility.

Perhaps most fascinating is how all trainees, autistic or not, tended to benefit when Stassun designed his lab to be more inclusive. Everyone benefited when they were obliged to communicate with precision. "Often, in conversations with neurotypical colleagues, our ideas are not fully formed, and we allow our sentences to trail off. We end with a laugh, expecting everyone to infer our meaning," Stassun explained. You can't do that with an autistic listener. These days in Stassun's lab, you have to complete your thoughts and say what you mean. If you don't, then Stassun or his colleagues prompt you to do so before it frustrates Dan or the other autistic trainees. The new protocol helps *everyone* sharpen their thinking.

Stassun's work with the Frist Center is even spilling over into his parenting. Now, when Stassun helps his autistic son do his ninth-grade math homework, he doesn't offer him a pat on the back or try to form a buddy-buddy rapport. He sticks to the facts. His disciplined approach avoids a meltdown and helps his son stay focused.

It's worth considering how Stassun's mindset differs from the battleground in our culture war over concepts like inclusion, accommodations, or equity. On the one side, the enforcer-mindset crowd claims that accommodating differences means caving in to the demands of woke wimps. On the other side, the protector-mindset types fight to remove any obstacle that causes discomfort, even when the obstacle is the extremely high standard for scientific productivity. Everybody loses in this war.

Stassun promotes a third way. He doesn't take an enforcer-like view that if only Dan were tough or dedicated enough, he could learn to not overreact. Nor does he create a different, lower set of "autistic standards" for contribution. He doesn't want anyone to do that for his son, and he doesn't do it in his lab, which has a real mission of scientific discovery. But Stassun also provides many specific supports, such as allowing Dan to attend lab meetings virtually or asking other trainees to hone their communication styles. Ultimately, Stassun and the rest of the lab members directly benefited from those accommodations for diversity, in terms of their own scientific reasoning and also in terms of Dan's new, more efficient data visualization software.

Most people aren't professional astrophysicists. Nonetheless, the example of Stassun's lab is informative. It surfaces serious misunderstandings that fuel our culture's debate over diversity, equity, and inclusion. People often fall into a debate about principles—what's morally right—not about pragmatic means for achieving better outcomes for all. Is it morally better to maintain rigorous standards, inclusion be damned, or to prioritize only inclusion while abandoning standards of excellence? Stassun's mentor mindset helps us realize that any of us can hold on to our value of maintaining standards while also valuing inclusion by providing necessary supports.

Why is it important to focus on *inclusive excellence*? There are a lot of popular books out there on optimal leadership and performance. They tell the story of what made one outlier CEO the best, how one company produced the perfect products, or why one musician or athlete was more of a genius than all the rest. When I read those books, I've often thought, *This story doesn't help me solve my problems*. The elite 0.1 percent of performers usually already have every resource in place before any psychological trick put them over the top. It's not very useful to know why 99.9 percent of people don't perform well. Most of us would rather learn how to help anyone achieve excellence regardless of their background.

Think about it. A teacher like Sergio doesn't get to pick the students in his class. He needs to know how to get *all* of them to succeed, not just the two or three who would have passed regardless of what he did. Parents don't get to choose their kids' individualities. They must figure out how to support their children, however they come out of the womb. And managers know that if they can successfully retain a large pool of high-level talent, they won't need to hire expensive outside talent with less insider knowledge.

In general, I think most parents, teachers, managers, and other leaders want to promote *inclusive excellence*—enabling anyone with a desire to excel, regardless of their background, to reach a high standard—rather than *exclusive excellence*—allowing only a tiny, well-resourced few to reach a high standard. We'll explore how the mentor mindset can advance inclusive (rather than exclusive) excellence in physics, a field that's so demanding that it's surprising anyone's thinking about inclusive excellence at all.

Really? Physics?

It's a bit ironic that a subfield of *physics*, of all disciplines, is teaching us a lesson about inclusion. If you ranked all the scientific disciplines by conventional metrics for inclusion—the percentage of PhDs that go to women, to Latino/as, to African Americans—then you would find that physics is among the most exclusive and unequitable disciplines in all the sciences. (One can't do a similar analysis of neurodivergent inclusion because the data aren't available.) Studies show that professional physicists have generally convinced themselves that this inequity is the unavoidable consequence of a cold, hard fact: members of underrepresented groups simply aren't qualified. It wouldn't make any sense to water down an entire branch of essential human knowledge just to make room for people who can't meet a standard, the logic goes.

Culturally, physicists are obsessed with measurement. This obsession with measurement spills over into their graduate admissions processes. For decades, graduate programs in physics relied more or less exclusively on a *single number*, a candidate's score on the GRE math test, as a universal screening tool for determining whether applicants could meet the rigorous standards in top graduate-level physics programs. Programs typically set a hard cutoff point—say, 700 out of 800—and refuse to interview anyone below the threshold. If that narrow range excludes more than 95 percent of African American applicants, so be it. If the test could be believed—and they believed the test—then those applicants couldn't cut it in top-level physics anyway. Physicists didn't even try to hide this perspective. It was like a law of the universe. Feeling embarrassed by it would be like regretting the speed of a falling object. It wouldn't make any sense.

Given this history, it's surprising that a rebellion against the GRE started in physics. Yet over the last two decades, a small spark of interest in promoting inclusive excellence by challenging the GRE's dominance in admissions has grown into a blaze that has spread across the sciences and, increasingly, the humanities.

Surprisingly, Dr. Keivan Stassun lit this fire. You see, his work on neurodiverse inclusion at the Frist Center for Autism and Innovation is a second career of sorts. He made his first contribution by revolutionizing physics admissions and graduate-student training programs to make the field more racially, ethnically, and socioeconomically inclusive.

I met Stassun when we both spoke on a panel moderated by Dr. Beverly Daniel Tatum, who was then the president of Spelman College, an

HBCU (historically black colleges and universities). The panel was being held on behalf of the KIPP (Knowledge is Power Program) charter school network, and the topic was *college persistence*. KIPP wanted to understand why many of their graduates, who came almost exclusively from low-income families, didn't finish college. Stassun had a place on the panel because he was one of the rare leaders who didn't just *talk* about inclusion in higher education, he actually *created* it.

Stassun's graduate program at Vanderbilt has graduated 150 students from underrepresented backgrounds with master's degrees or PhDs in physics; it is the top producer of Black master's students in physics, and his lab has awarded more PhDs in astrophysics to Black scholars than any other lab. Stassun's student Fabienne Bastien made a major discovery about how we understand the galaxy, and when she published it in *Nature* she became the first-ever Black lead author of an astrophysics paper in the journal's 154-year history. Another student became the first Black woman to receive NASA's top postdoctoral fellowship. Graduates of Stassun's program are now professors, scientists, and mentors, and they're changing the field for the better.

Before Stassun could accomplish this, he had to persuade physics graduate-admissions offices to stop caring exclusively about the GRE. To do so, Stassun didn't challenge the validity of the GRE scores, per se, although there are grounds for such challenges. Instead, he pointed out a flaw in the *interpretation* of the GRE scores. Physicists were assuming something that they hadn't proved. They assumed that the GRE math score was a measure of readiness to make professional, PhD-level contributions to the future of physics. But that's not what the test measured. The GRE math test mostly measured applicants' recollection of high school algebra and geometry. Stassun thought that a better alternative was painfully obvious. If you wanted to measure a student's readiness for professional physics, *then you should see how they actually did in professional physics.* Before people apply to PhD programs, get them in a lab. Let them find hard questions that interest them. Watch as they try to answer those questions with the tools of the field and publish their findings in journals. If you already know a student can do what professional physicists do, Stassun argued, then why would you keep them out of your program due to some other number that *isn't* a direct measure of their possible contribution to physics? If they've already shown they can cut it, then let them in already!

Stassun suspected that his competence-and-contribution-focused approach to graduate admissions would prove far more equitable than a GRE-only approach. The GRE tends to quantify how good your high school math teacher was, yet the quality of high school math teachers isn't evenly distributed. Due to historical factors such as residential zoning, real estate, and property tax policies that go back a century or more, Black or Latinx families are far more likely to attend poorer schools with lower-quality math teachers. While students from minority groups were often exceptionally bright and well prepared for graduate-level physics work, in part because of success in undergraduate courses or in research labs, they tended to earn math GRE scores outside the top range. Stassun looked at this state of affairs and said, "Wow, I want to admit those students who mastered college physics while also having to reteach themselves the relevant high school math concepts. They must have the grit they need to succeed!" Meanwhile, other physicists shrugged and said, "They're not qualified." Stassun thought this dismissive attitude led to an idiotic waste of talent.

Stassun's mission to reduce or eliminate the use of the GRE in physics admissions maps onto our culture's toxic debates. The old guard, enforcer-mindset physicists said, *Stassun is trying to get rid of the GRE so he can lower standards and let anybody in regardless of qualifications.* These faculty feared a world in which they might spend years and hundreds of thousands of dollars training incapable students who never graduated. Their worry was founded, partially, in the reality that protector-mindset activists often *do* want to lower the standards for entry in the name of equity. Stassun argues that both sides have it wrong. The GRE was never the correct standard to begin with, so advocates for standards need not defend it. Applicants must meet the real high standard: readiness to make contributions. This requirement is still rigorous, it still requires excellence, but it relies less on your family background or which high school you went to. "It's like the old adage about the marine corps," Stassun told me. "They don't care where you come from, but you will get to the end, and when you do, *you will measure up.*"

To really win his argument, Stassun had to produce data. After all, even Albert Einstein didn't win his Nobel Prize in Physics until Robert Millikan's experiments validated his theoretical predictions. Over the last twenty years, Stassun has built a new model for graduate training, the Fisk-Vanderbilt Bridge Program. By taking a closer look at how the program works, we can uncover common mentor-mindset principles that any of us can emulate as we work with young people—whether it's internship programs, summer intensives for sports or the arts, or any other youth-serving program outside of professional physics.

Laura Vega's Story

When Laura Vega was a little girl, her father used to drive her family south from San Antonio, Texas, where she lived, to Mexico to visit her extended family. Because he preferred driving at night, they'd stop for gas around 3:00 a.m. somewhere in the vast, unpopulated desert near the border. There was always a clear, dark sky. She'd walk a few dozen yards away from the mini-mart to escape the light pollution. Then she'd turn her eyes up toward the stars, shining like glitter. She distinctly remembers feeling overwhelmed by the stars' majesty, making her feel so small in a vast universe. Vega was always interested in science. She watched television shows like *Bill Nye the Science Guy* and *The Magic School Bus* whenever she could. She regularly went to the library to check out astronomy books about nebulae and learned a simple principle: physics governs everything that we see. But it was these brief moments alone in the desert that gave Vega clarity about her purpose. She would be an astrophysicist.

Vega has now earned a PhD in astrophysics from Stassun's Fisk-Vanderbilt program. She works at NASA's Goddard Space Flight Center in Washington, DC, where many of NASA's outer space research instruments are controlled. She studies the high-energy radiation that small stars called red dwarfs give off when they flare (i.e., have massive explosions on their surfaces). This research forms a critical part of NASA's search for habitable planets in other solar systems. Red dwarf flares give off so much radiation that they strip off a nearby planet's atmosphere, which would make the planet inhospitable for humans. At the same time, planets need radiation to start biogenesis—that is, for life to evolve. Vega's team analyzes space-telescope data to come up with better and better measures of red dwarf radiation, to find out where the flares have destroyed atmospheres versus where planets might be capable of supporting life. Said differently, *there's a chance her research could one day save humanity.*

Vega's work offers a good example of why so many people advocate for inclusive excellence. It simply empowers more great people to do more great work, maybe for the betterment of humanity. Interestingly, despite Vega's impressive talents, her contributions to astrophysics almost didn't happen.

Vega attended Thomas Jefferson High School, on the West Side of San Antonio. Achievement at Jefferson was generally low—the school gets a three out of ten on the data-aggregation site GreatSchools—and opportunities to learn were few. Jefferson didn't offer AP Physics or Calculus, courses which are usually minimum requirements for majoring in physics in college. The physics class that Jefferson High did offer was an elective, and it only required easier precollege math. The teacher used a droning memorization style of instruction that didn't engage the class, so students turned disruptive. "I was probably the only student who wanted to take physics," Vega told me, but the teacher "killed a little bit of the excitement" she had for the field. Vega set aside her astrophysics aspirations for the rest of high school. She focused instead on other areas of growth and learning. She worked on overcoming her fear of public speaking, tied to lingering doubts about her English-language abilities. (Vega spoke only Spanish until she was in kindergarten.) She courageously got into theater and played in a mariachi band.

During Vega's sophomore year at the University of Texas at San Antonio (UTSA), she tried physics again. She enrolled in a huge, impersonal introductory college-level class—the kind that often weeds students out. She loved it, despite its difficulty. As Vega took more advanced college physics and astronomy courses, she didn't struggle much with the content, although increasingly she was the only woman or the only Latina in the class. Vega eventually earned a spot working in the laboratory of UTSA astrophysicist Dr. Eric Schlegel. Schlegel specialized in analyzing the data collected by one of NASA's floating X-ray observatories that circle the Earth in high orbit. Vega made valuable contributions in Schlegel's UTSA

lab by working with the X-ray data on a galaxy called Messier 51, described
by NASA as a "grand spiral staircase sweeping through space," located 31
million light-years away from Earth. Vega's work with Schlegel on M51 was
eventually published in her field's top journal, the *Astrophysical Journal*.
Vega's mentors encouraged her to apply to PhD programs and fulfill her
dream of becoming an astrophysicist at long last. Her high school hadn't
provided her with a solid foundation in math, so she wasn't confident
about her chances. She feared disappointing herself or her mentors. In the
end, she didn't apply. For the second time in a decade, she gave up on her
dream.

Giving up didn't take. In her last semester, Schlegel's lab paid for Vega
to attend a professional conference called SACNAS (Society for Advancement of Chicanos/Hispanics and Native Americans in Science). It was
so obvious that she "was dying to do research," Schlegel said. Vega was
thrilled by the all-expenses-paid trip for her to present her research and
build her network. Serendipitously, at SACNAS Vega talked for a long time
with Dr. David Ernst, who cofounded the Fisk-Vanderbilt Bridge Program
with Stassun. That little bit of luck changed her life.

Ernst explained to Vega how Fisk-Vanderbilt operated differently from
a conventional PhD program. For instance, the Fisk-Vanderbilt program
didn't take GRE scores. Instead, applicants submit coursework and transcripts and undergo a lengthy interview to assess the strengths they would
bring to the program. Vega's stories of grit and resilience, such as joining
mariachi and a theater program to overcome her fears of public speaking,
would count for something, unlike at other top programs. In addition,
she'd start in a master's program at Fisk University, a historically Black college in Nashville, while working in cutting-edge research labs like Stassun's
at Vanderbilt. She'd have two years to learn the tools of the trade—the
programming languages, the software, the statistical methods, and more—
at Fisk, a school that excels at preparing students from minority groups
for professional careers in science. Students who do well enough in Fisk's
courses and in the lab at Vanderbilt are then automatically admitted to
Vanderbilt's PhD program, where they start on equal footing with every
other student. This plan sounded pretty good to Vega. She had worried
about how she would measure up to people who had far more coursework

and high-level research experience in college. In the spring of 2013, she applied to the Fisk-Vanderbilt program and was admitted. That fall, she moved to Nashville, Tennessee, still trepidatious but eager to start living her dream.

Much has been written about more inclusive admissions policies. However, the real work of inclusive excellence happens well after admission, once students arrive on campus. Vega still had to cope with many psychological challenges, such as being a Latina in a field of predominantly white and Asian men, and competing with peers who went to private college-prep high schools or elite universities. Stassun's program was carefully crafted to help students like Vega build a bridge that linked her background and identity to her future in astrophysics, through a sophisticated combination of *high standards* and *high support*. These are two essential elements for promoting inclusive excellence.

The Mentor Mindset and Inclusive Excellence

Think back on the wise-feedback Post-it Note study from the introduction. Geoffrey Cohen invented wise feedback with his adviser, social psychologist Claude Steele, who is a leader in the psychology of stereotypes and how they influence motivation. Cohen and Steele and I weren't trying to study motivation in general. We specifically wanted to understand motivation *across the identity-group divide*—for example, when white teachers give critical feedback to students from underrepresented minority groups, or when men critique the work of women. Our studies showed that although all students profited from wise feedback, students whose identity groups experienced marginalization or exclusion benefited even more. The wise-feedback research was why, over a quarter of a decade ago, Steele wrote:

> [Students from underrepresented groups] should have challenging work and high standards, instead of remedial work and low standards. . . . Demand more, rather than less. A lot of what's wrong is the presumption that they can't do the work. . . . [Furthermore], at the heart of the drive to retain students must be mechanisms to convince students that their instructors are on their side.

Steele offers a great description of the mentor-mindset philosophy and its application to inclusive excellence. As it happens, data from researchers working in many different disciplines beyond psychology over the last sixty years—anthropology, education, sociology, and more—have supported Steele's conclusions and the idea that the mentor mindset is a powerful tool for inclusive excellence.

Dr. Franita Ware was a PhD student at Emory University when she picked up an article written by her professor Dr. Jacqueline Irvine titled "Warm Demanders." In that article, Irvine described the work of the anthropologist Dr. Judith Kleinfeld. Kleinfeld had reviewed Rosalie Wax's study of teachers on the reservation (chapter 2). She also conducted her own ethnography of teachers of Inuit students. Kleinfeld labeled Wax's effective teachers *warm demanders*—they were high on warmth (supports) and demand (standards). Kleinfeld's term had a profound influence on Irvine, Ware, and much subsequent research.

When Ware read about warm demanders, she wanted to understand how the label might apply to highly effective Black educators. Ware had just observed teachers in Atlanta public schools. One fifth-grade teacher stood out. "When I saw her, I said, 'This is it.' This is a warm demander," Ware told me. Ware spent the rest of her graduate career conducting an influential ethnography of highly effective equity-promoting Black teachers of Black students.

One day, Ware saw something surprising. The effective teacher commanded an entire class of ten- and eleven-year-olds. She was "fussing at them" because only half of them had turned in their homework. What would an enforcer do in this situation? They would yell, tell, blame, shame, and disrespect the students. What would a protector do? They might ask nicely for students to do their work, but the students would ignore them. Ware didn't see either of these approaches. Instead, the teacher demanded that students live up to her expectations, but respectfully. Here's how Ware's 2006 article described the students' responses (emphases added):

> The students were *absolutely quiet* and *looked at her with respect* while she spoke. No one moved. . . . Yet, all students seemed to respond by listening and showing facial gestures that indicated remorse. . . .

When she concluded, the students pleasantly and quietly followed the procedure she outlined as they fulfilled their tasks.

Ware captured the essence of the mentor-mindset approach to inclusive excellence in this passage. Teachers, parents, and managers using the mentor mindset lay a foundation of respectful relationships. They take young people seriously and expect them to live up to their potential, while providing the necessary supports. With these structures, young people find the motivation to do the right thing.

Today, Ware is a prominent trainer of educators, and she has made a new discovery. While Black educators commonly used warm-demander pedagogy with their Black students, educators of any race or ethnicity can learn the pedagogy and apply it to any group of young people. Anyone, regardless of their background, can learn to promote inclusive excellence with a combination of high standards and high support.

In the mid-1990s, the sociologist Roger Shouse analyzed data from the High School and Beyond (HS&B) study. The federal government's National Center for Educational Statistics commissioned the study, and famed sociologist James Coleman directed it. HS&B included more than one thousand high schools and fifty-eight thousand students randomly selected from across the country. This national study could test whether the stories captured in Wax's and Ware's ethnographies applied more broadly.

Shouse used the HS&B data to find the ingredients of inclusive excellence. He sought to find schools with high overall performance but also *equitable* performance—schools where all students, regardless of race, ethnicity, or social class, did well. Shouse found that these schools scored high on two dimensions: academic expectations and social support. *They were mentor-mindset schools.*

Shouse's analysis shows that Ware's findings were not just interesting anecdotes. They held up on a national level. The mentor mindset transformed the lives of all young people and especially those who were marginalized by their race, ethnicity, or socioeconomic status.

This science can help us notice key elements that make Stassun's Fisk-Vanderbilt Bridge Program an especially good example of the mentor mindset. It can help us answer questions such as: How does the program effectively combine high standards and high support?

Keivan Stassun, Mentor-Mindset Exemplar

"It all starts with my mom," Stassun said when I asked him about the origins of his inclusive-excellence work. Keivan Stassun's mother is from a small village in Mexico. She came to the United States across the southern Arizona desert facing peril, armed with courage and a thirst to participate in the American dream. Although Stassun is a natural-born citizen, he still remembers his mother's pride the day she became a U.S. citizen. She raised him with a patriotism rooted in the American dream and a belief in upward mobility. "She would literally say to me," Stassun told me, "that she had gotten me to base camp, and my job was to reach the summit, and when I got there, I had to make sure that other people had an easier way up."

Nobody in Stassun's low-income neighborhood in LA talked about becoming an astrophysicist. He was admitted to the University of California, Berkeley, on a full scholarship, with a catch—it was called an *affirmative action* scholarship. His label was widely known. Other freshmen looked at him like he didn't belong, like he was an admissions mistake. "I experienced impostor syndrome as much as anybody," he said. Doubt didn't knock him off track. "Rather than ask whether I deserved the opportunity, instead I would ask, 'What should I do to be worthy of it?' " Stassun told me.

Years later, Stassun took that lesson with him into his mentoring. He would deliver a speech to bridge students like Laura Vega on the first day of the Fisk-Vanderbilt program. Most students come into the program grateful and nervous. "They're grateful for the chance," Stassun thinks, "but nervous that somebody made a mistake and they didn't deserve it." These fears about belonging are often called *impostor syndrome*: the persistent worry that you were only admitted because someone misjudged you, and soon will discover the fraud you are. To address this anxiety, Stassun assures students that they were judged accurately to be the most well equipped to succeed in this rigorous program. Then he challenges them to focus on their future contributions—not their prior test scores. "You came into a bridge program, and you may think of it as a second chance.

Or you may think of it as somebody taking a chance on you because you couldn't get in the regular way. Let's immediately get out of the space of whether you are good enough to be there or whether you deserve it. You are. Instead, let's focus on what you're going to do to make good on that investment."

Back in Berkeley's undergraduate physics program, Stassun was excelling. He soon earned his PhD from the University of Wisconsin–Madison.

Stassun's PhD commencement was a turning point. His mother flew to Wisconsin for the ceremony. She was so proud that she insisted that he wear the entire regalia, with the gold tassels and all. At dinner, she asked a question: "*¿Y ahora que?*" [Translation: *And now what?*] Stassun gave a very literal and academic answer, focusing on writing this or that paper, or winning this or that grant. Stassun's mother gave him a look of such deep disappointment. She had clearly expected a different kind of answer, because in Spanish the connotation of *¿Y ahora que?* was *You've been given so much, so now what are you going to do with it?* "I realized I had forgotten myself," he told me. Stassun came to his senses and told her he would use his degree to become a professor. Once he was a professor he would use his influence to help others climb the mountain too. Stassun's mother liked that answer much better.

I love how this story compares to Leona and Pete's story from eighty years earlier (see the introduction). Stassun's mother, like my great-grandmother Leona, held her son to high standards for making a contribution. She didn't let him off the hook. But she also loved him unconditionally. Stassun, like Pete Sumners, took his mother's mentor mindset and applied it to his work, ultimately benefiting the lives of hundreds of students, such as Laura Vega. This is a beautiful example of how the mentor mindset operates as a kind of intergenerational inclusive-excellence engine.

In the spring of 2022, Stassun visited my lab at UT Austin to teach us about the particulars of his program. Here's what we learned.

Stassun's program maintains exceptionally high standards for legitimate contributions to physics. They expect students to master software-programming tools, generate complex images from data, author papers, present them at professional conferences, and publish them in journals. Many labs trying to be equitable or inclusive don't do this. They fall into a protector mindset with lots of pats on the back but little real-world contribution.

In Stassun's lab, before a student gives their first real scientific talk at a professional conference, the lab devotes an entire meeting to a practice run. This is often needed. Giving a technical talk about physics terrifies students who have a fear of public speaking or who struggle with impostor syndrome. Nevertheless, Vega (and eventually all other students in the lab) had to stand up and hold court for an hour, while the lab gave specific and direct feedback on every aspect of the talk—how well she set up the research question, how clear her graphs and figures were, whether she highlighted the key findings sufficiently, and so on. "By the time we're done giving the feedback," Stassun explained, "I'm able to say authentically and credibly that you've heard all the criticism you'd hear at the conference. So you're basically ready in terms of content and knowledge." He believes it's far better to get this feedback in a supportive group of people who want you to succeed, rather than to receive critique onstage in front of future employers. He also believes that sugarcoating and withholding feedback doesn't help anybody.

Stassun also upholds high expectations for writing. "I'm a real dictator when it comes to publishing," he told me. His mantra is "the only thing that matters is the paper we write." It doesn't count if a student writes a clever bit of code or makes a fancy data graph. You must take it all the way to the finish line and turn it into a published paper that contributes to the field, with your name on it. His students start writing papers with Stassun on day one. "There comes a point where you go from being a student to being a scientist and having the feeling that you have generated science," Stassun told me. At the weekly lab meetings, they exclusively talk about their papers in progress (unless someone is practicing a conference presentation). A student projects their paper on the screen, and the nitpicking begins. For the next hour, a dozen or more scientists comment on what the story is in the data, whether the figures are right, whether the results make sense, and how the study contributes to the field. Laura Vega recalls feeling nervous and exposed during critiques of her scientific article, but the experience proved essential to her development as a scientist.

I can confirm that Stassun's approach to writing is not standard practice. Many advisers try to protect their trainees from potential stress or embarrassment. Some even go so far as to question the academic "rat race" of publishing, characterizing it as foolish or trivial or pointless, preferring instead to celebrate a student's brilliant ideas rather than their work products. Those people perform equity but don't create it. That's not Stassun. "I really believe that it's kind of hollow to give people intellectual pats on the back and not push them to the point where they can feel the fruit of scientific labor, which is that their ideas appear in a peer-reviewed journal."

Stassun's students do not always feel *comfortable* with the high standards. They're often stressed or even afraid. Yet those high standards are a crucial part of preparing young people to belong in high-performing spaces. When you leave Stassun's bridge program you don't take the mentor with you. Vega can't call up Stassun and put him on speakerphone to testify to her interrogators, *Vega's really smart! She belongs!* You take your record of accomplishments with you. The publications on your curriculum vitae. If we don't empower young people to own any authentic accomplishments, then they leave our care just as vulnerable as they were when they entered.

Laura Vega drove this point home when she told me that the other PhD students at Vanderbilt sometimes act like the bridge-program graduates came in through the back door, as though it was easier to get in. Then she thinks about how, in the bridge program, you actually have to publish your work. She has papers where she is the lead author, and in better journals than the "front door" students. She didn't come through the back door. She deserved her spot.

"It's pretty clear that if you get first-authored papers into top journals then you've earned your voice," Vega told me. Stassun's emphasis on publishing goes back to his solution to feeling like an impostor at Berkeley. He's arming young people from underrepresented groups with infinitely transferable, lifetime-guaranteed trump cards that say *I belong.* It's earned prestige.

Protector-mindset leaders don't do this. They try to take the shortcut to inclusive excellence. They puff underrepresented groups up with false praise and low standards.

Importantly, Stassun doesn't throw people into the fire and say, *I have high expectations!* That's the enforcer mindset. To promote inclusive excellence, a mentor-mindset leader must match those high expectations with equally high supports.

Supportive programming takes place every day in Stassun's bridge program. Monday: writing hour. Tuesday: outside speaker. Wednesday: lab meeting. Thursday: "astro coffee" conversations about new papers. Friday: *vino de vida*, a wine-and-social gathering after a long week of work.

These activities are designed to link students with peers in their cohort, senior peers who are about to graduate, and postdoctoral fellows who advise on professional development. Every quarter, students meet with their mentoring committees, which are webs of mentors that Stassun helps them create, strategically chosen to help them acquire access to data, technical equipment, or skills they need to meet their ambitious goals. The committees allow students to forge important professional connections beyond Stassun himself, a network of possible letter writers and employers.

Earned Prestige, Belonging, and Competence

Deep down, Vega knew she belonged in physics because she was producing high-quality work that she felt proud of. She nevertheless experienced moments of self-doubt. A few years into the program, she bombed an important qualifying exam. She knew the content, but her brain locked up under the pressure, leading her to say the sun was nearly five hundred billion years old when she meant five billion. Feeling stupid, she started packing her things to move back to San Antonio. Stassun intervened. He said to her as directly as possible, *You are doing well. You can do this.* After all, the metric of whether students can do good science is whether they can do good science, not how well they can take a test. And Vega was doing good science. It was Stassun's Leona moment! Vega got back to work.

Stassun knew it could be unnerving to have impostor fears improve but never completely fade away. He told a personal story to Vega and the rest of her cohort in the bridge program. As a child, Stassun had a noticeable speech disfluency—a lisp. A speech pathologist taught him a trick for positioning his tongue on the roof his mouth before he said certain words, and that helped. His lisp never went away, however. To this day, he does the trick before he speaks. But over time he's learned to feel comfortable with his lisp and the tongue trick, and it doesn't stop Stassun from public speaking. Stassun thinks that's a lot like becoming an insider in an elite space that has historically underrepresented your group. "Feeling like an impostor declines gradually and incompletely," Stassun tells them, but it doesn't have to derail their success. They shouldn't interpret a persistent worry about belonging as a sign that they can't ever belong. It's a hassle but it doesn't get to determine their future.

A few years later, Laura Vega finished her PhD with a slew of publications in the top journals in astrophysics. She started her postdoctoral fellowship working at NASA's Goddard Center. When we spoke, she had been working there for a few months.

Just the day before, Vega had given a nerve-racking, important research talk to the science directorate. It was attended by senior scientists, engineers, and staff members from all the different science divisions. "There's so much suffering, at least for me, with public speaking," she told me. The night before her talk, Vega had an anxiety nightmare that she was about to perform at a mariachi concert but didn't have a mouthpiece that would let her instrument work—essentially, that she would lose her voice, let everyone down and ruin the performance. Then she thought back to Stassun's story about his lisp. She had been trying to do something similar by joining Toastmasters and using biofeedback technology to feel more comfortable speaking publicly. Most of all, she reminded herself of her accomplishments. They meant she belonged.

Giving the talk was mostly a blur. Then something unexpected happened. She started getting questions—curious questions. People got really excited about the topic. She had a kind of out-of-body experience. Vega saw herself in that seminar room, as someone who used to stare at the stars in the desert between Texas and Mexico and dream of astrophysics, now engaging a room of senior NASA scientists, proud of what she had done. "I was like, 'Yeah, I did that.' " Those moments fuel her ambition to stay in the field and keep making contributions, despite her anxieties. That's the power of earned prestige to confer status and respect.

Vega's story offers a powerful reminder of what inclusive excellence is. It's not the enforcer's impossible, arbitrary standard that kicks minds like Vega's out of the field or prevents them from ever entering in the first place. That's exclusive excellence.

Nor is it the protector's soft, wishy-washy, watered-down standard with "lots of love." That's inclusion for inclusion's sake, without the excellence. That wouldn't get someone who went to a high school like Vega's to the point where they can present to a room of top NASA scientists.

Inclusive excellence grows out of the belief that someone's potential to contribute isn't reduced to a single number on a test like the GRE. Nor is the chance to make a contribution limited to those who fear nothing and have every advantage. No. Every young person has the potential to contribute. When we respect, honor, and support that potential through a combination of high standards and high support, then we motivate and inspire young people from all groups to reach higher, accomplish more, and make our society stronger.

One day Stassun stepped into the elevator and at the last second held the door for his colleague, another physics professor. As they chatted casually about the bridge-program students, the colleague said Stassun was lucky. Why? After some clarification, Stassun understood the colleague to be saying that Stassun's background—poor family, immigrant mother, member of a minority group—gave him the good fortune of being a strong mentor for the bridge-program students. The colleague—a white man—felt like he didn't have that background. He decided he wasn't going to work with the bridge students.

Stassun agreed that he probably had an instinct for empathizing with the bridge students, but then he thought about it more deeply and he started to disagree. He's not autistic, and nevertheless he created the most inclusive lab for autistic students in all of science. When Stassun started out, he had no instinct for how to support students like Dan or his son. In fact, his instincts for helping the bridge students—which focused on thinking abstractly about social narratives like stereotypes or impostor syndrome—were completely wrong when it came to inclusion for autistic students. His ability to promote inclusive excellence for such different groups had more to do with his mindset than anything else. He believed any motivated student could be held to a high standard and supported as they worked to meet it.

Stassun's story shows us that there's nothing stopping any leader from adopting a mentor mindset and using it to include more people in their field's standards of excellence.

Chapter 11

Future Growth, Part One

Justice, justice you shall pursue.

—Deuteronomy 16:20

Status, Respect, and Mentoring for Future Growth

Ralph Cornell

Most people living outside Los Angeles have never heard of Ralph Cornell. But every day millions of people living in LA are affected by his contributions.

Cornell, born in 1890, was California's most influential landscape architect of the twentieth century. He has been called the Olmsted of Los Angeles because he was as respected and prolific in LA as was Olmsted, the designer of Central Park, in New York City. Over his fifty-year career, Cornell became the master architect for Pomona College and the University of California, Los Angeles; he developed Torrey Pines' first-ever "dry ground park" in San Diego that used California-native plants; and he's responsible for many of LA's most beloved public spaces, including Beverly Gardens Park, Griffith Park, and the Franklin D. Murphy Sculpture Garden. Trees that he planted a century ago—often over objections from clients who wanted quick-growing trees that wouldn't last—still stand to this day. I interviewed several of LA's leading landscape architects. All of them still consult his work. Interestingly, Cornell would not have made these contributions if he hadn't found the right mentor at the right time: Professor Charles Baker.

Cornell came from a poor family that lost everything soon after they moved to California. In 1909 he ended up at Pomona College, about thirty-five miles east of LA, because it was cheap. He happened to take a class taught by Baker, a biologist. At the time, landscape architecture wasn't much of a field at all—and certainly not on the West Coast. In the early 1900s, the dominant approach could be described as *plant whatever looks good right now, water it a ton, and hope for the best.* Baker sensed that Cornell might have something new to add to a growing movement, originating from Olmsted's firm on the East Coast, that sought to professionalize landscape architecture. Baker designed a series of increasingly difficult tasks for Cornell to complete—creating detailed drawings of different California-native plant species, photographing families of plants in their native habitats, and so on. Often, Baker himself couldn't do these tasks, but he could uphold critical and demanding standards. Cornell would have run through a brick wall for him. Baker was transparent about where his standards came from: he thought Cornell's work was good enough to be published. Cornell worked hard to meet this standard, and eventually they published their art, accompanied by Baker's biological commentary, in academic journals. Some of Cornell's drawings of California-native plants are still definitive today. (I once met a tattoo artist for rock stars at a bar and I was surprised to learn that he exclusively uses Cornell's century-old drawings for tattoos involving flora.) Baker next encouraged Cornell to apply to Harvard's landscape architecture program, where he was admitted. He then received formal training that served as the foundation for his long and prolific career. Reading hundreds of pages of Cornell's oral history transcripts, recorded shortly before his death in 1972, one gets the sense that the most vivid memories in his life come from that time when he worked so hard to meet the demanding expectations of Baker, a mentor who respected him and whose respect Cornell craved. "Professor Baker shaped my destiny.... He had the knack of inspiring young [people]," Cornell said in his oral history sixty years later. "This youth business is rather important," he concluded.

In midlife, Cornell became a mentor himself. "He was trying to establish the professionalism of landscape architecture in this outpost in the West," Brian Tichenor, one of today's leading LA architects, told me. Cornell, like his mentor, had exceptionally high standards. He critiqued gardeners who would throw a European tree somewhere and think that watering it would fix any problem. But he wasn't an elitist. He wanted more people in the profession to meet the field's standard. Ruth Shellhorn was one of the only female landscape architects working in LA in the mid-century. She credits Cornell's mentorship with helping her secure a place in the field. Shellhorn would go on to design the streets and plazas at Disneyland, including the iconic Sleeping Beauty Castle. The trees she selected for Disneyland remain seventy years later. The Cornell-and-Shellhorn story supports a simple truth. "We're . . . building for the future," Cornell said of his landscaping philosophy. "We're putting things in now which we envision as they will appear fifty years hence." His words turned out to be both literally and metaphorically true.

Daniel Lapsley

Dr. Daniel Lapsley is a professor of adolescent psychology at the University of Notre Dame. He grew up in Pittsburgh, where his father was a coal miner while his mother was a homemaker. He never thought about college because nobody in his family had ever been. One summer day in 1965, just before he started seventh grade, Lapsley and his friends were hanging out at a gas station after playing basketball. Lapsley struck up a conversation with a college-aged guy who was waiting for his car to get fixed. Soon the topic turned to the Vietnam War. Lapsley was a reader, and he precociously defended President Johnson's domino theory of communism in the region and the United States' role in the war. The college guy argued the other side in earnest, a little surprised that Lapsley had done his research, but also encouraging him. He gave no hint of ridicule, sarcasm, or belittlement. When his car was ready, he turned to Lapsley and said, "You are an extraordinarily bright kid. Have you thought about going to college?" Then, for reasons Lapsley still doesn't understand, he asked if Lapsley had read Dante's *The Divine Comedy* and said how much he would enjoy it—implying that Lapsley would be up for the challenging read. Lapsley was twelve. He can still remember the exhilarating pride—the earned prestige. "I walked home as if striding mountains. Imagine this stranger urging me to go to college, wondering if I've read Dante." This interaction offers a good example of what I mean when I say that earned prestige is motivating. Eventually Lapsley did indeed go to college, just like the stranger had recommended. And he never left. He earned his PhD and spent his entire adult life as a college professor; he now serves as a lead mentor in the university's program to support first-generation college students. Of this fateful day, Lapsley wrote:

> When I reflect on the course of events that have led to my present station in life, the encounter with the stranger at the gas station looms larger than any teacher, larger than anything that happened in any school. The stranger at the gas station planted an idea, raised a possibility that had not occurred to me. He gave me information about myself that was opaque to me. It made me feel special, talented. . . . This clear, vivid memory I have never shaken. And I credit this encounter, this stranger, with setting me on the path that was unusual for kids in the steel town of my birth.

I think about Lapsley's story quite often, for a few reasons. Mostly, it offers a reminder to be careful what we say to young people. We never know if our words might start a snowball that affects them—and others— far into the future. Nor do we know if glib dismissiveness of them will be resented for decades.

Lapsley's story also resonates with something I haven't told you yet about the wise-feedback experiments (in the introduction). In those studies, we didn't just track whether students revised their essays for a couple of weeks. We also tracked them for six years after they got the Post-it Note. In a paper we published in 2017, we found that students in the treatment group, especially students in the minority in the school, benefited from the onetime note a whole year later, showing fewer discipline incidents. Furthermore, they were more likely to attend college six years after the experiment. Although our study was small, its results were fully consistent with Lapsley's story. This suggests that the right display of respect for young people's abilities, at the right time, coupled with emotional support, can make a meaningful, lasting difference.

Finally, I love Lapsley's story because he did something similar for me. I took Lapsley's course—my first class in psychology—while I was completing a master's in education during the summer before my second year as a teacher. His class was both practical and philosophical. It thrilled me. I overdid it on my term paper, writing far more than he asked for. A typical professor would have given it back to me and said, *This didn't meet the requirements for the assignment. Do it over.* Or they might have pointed out that I, having no training in psychology, had no idea what I was talking about. But Lapsley treated me like the guy at the gas station had treated him—not looking down on me, taking me seriously, encouraging me to do even more. Lapsley spent a long time walking me through his feedback. He wasn't effusive, but he said, "I do think there's something to what you are trying to argue." He even said that my paper might be publishable in a journal, and he'd be willing to help me rework it. It was the first time anyone had treated me like a scholar. I loved it. Lapsley was like Baker, helping Ralph Cornell prepare his work for publication when Cornell was my age. A few weeks later, I scrapped my plan to go to law school. I prepared my application to do graduate work in Lapsley's field, and he was my only credible letter writer. Thus, he was responsible for my admission. It's not an exaggeration to say that the research I conducted for this book would not have happened if not for Lapsley treating me with dignity and respect—with a mentor mindset—at a time when I was deeply uncertain of my abilities and goals in life.

Mentoring for Future Growth

Both Cornell's and Lapsley's mentorship speak to something I call the *therapist's problem*. This is a vexing challenge that confounds even the most astute and conscientious mentors.

The therapist's problem refers to the fact that it's hard to at once help young people when they're under our care and prepare them to apply their skills effectively after they leave our care. A therapy session typically only lasts an hour, but people's problems are with them the other twenty-three hours of that day—not to mention the twenty-four hours of every nonsession day. If a therapist can help a patient only during the hour, they're not adding value. The patient might as well distract themselves more cheaply; for example, by watching a movie. A good therapist adds value beyond simple distraction. They help patients apply better thinking skills after the session ends. The therapist's problem applies by analogy to anyone who's able to mentor a young person.

For many parents, most of the time they will spend with their children in their lifetimes will be over when their child turns eighteen. Have they spent that time wisely, in a way that will stay with their children for the next seventy or eighty years of their lives?

Secondary and postsecondary teachers get even less time, roughly four to five hours per week for nine or ten months. Have we given our students content knowledge and learning strategies that will help them in the next year's class—let alone throughout their academic careers?

Managers might have a direct report for six to eighteen months because their direct reports will get promotions. Have we encouraged work habits and an organizational culture that will help our employees add value as they move up the ladder?

Youth-serving organizations face a similar problem. Its name in the scientific literature is *fade-out*. This refers to well-intentioned programs that have a short-term impact but don't help in the long run. Consider the after-school volunteer mentoring program with fun and games but no lasting benefits for youth; the overprotective, elite private school that insufficiently prepares students for failure in the real world; the summer program where a camp high wears off the moment kids get back to school; or the weeklong professional conference at the company's expense that's fun to attend but changes nothing about employees' work processes upon return. Because of fade-out, the therapist's problem leads to a tragic waste of organizational time and resources.

How can one solve the therapist's problem? Status, respect, and the chance to earn prestige are preconditions for influencing young people long after they leave our care.

A great example came from Chip Engelland, the NBA's best shooting coach (see the introduction). His summer campers took over leading all the drills by Tuesday of the second week. He gave them a "coach in the head." They improved a lot in those two weeks, but they also were prepared to coach themselves for the next fifty weeks of the year. In the NBA, Kawhi Leonard and the host of other players Engelland coached didn't suddenly lose their shots when they didn't have Chip in their ears. He gave them a "coach in the head." Why would a coach in the cutthroat, win-now-obsessed world of professional basketball take the long view? Because the team gets better when players are improving outside of their few hours with Chip.

Chip Engelland's methods illusrate what I call *mentoring for future growth*. This solves the therapist's problem. Mentoring for future growth happens when the *processes* we use with young people instill skills or ways of thinking that continue to help them after they leave our care.

Sergio Estrada wasn't teaching his students little tricks to solve physics problems for next week's quiz; he was prepping them to major in science in college. Stef Okamoto wasn't only trying to pump productivity out of employees to meet a quarterly target; she wanted her mentees to become leaders in management excellence. Lorena didn't referee a fight between her kids to get the shouting to stop that instant; she could stop her kids from bickering with no more than a lift of an eyebrow once they knew what she expected. The mentor mindset pays off both now and in the future, if we do it right. Thus, leaders can use the mentor mindset even if they're under pressure for immediate outcomes.

Mentoring for future growth is undermined by the enforcer and protector mindsets. In the enforcer mindset, we believe that young people are not competent enough to do anything without the direct guidance and instruction of the leader. Therefore, we use short-term, compliance-based strategies that only last as long as we directly enforce them.

On the other hand, in the protector mindset we might think nothing can be done to change the young person for the long term. Protectors focus on getting the young person over a short-term hump, leaving them enfeebled going forward.

Neither of these mindsets mentor for future growth because they don't think young people can handle it. It's like a therapist saying, *There's no use in me teaching you better thinking skills for dealing with depression and anxiety because you'll never figure out how to use them anyway.* Making someone feel better for an hour, but incapacitated the rest of the week, is bad therapy.

Not only does mentoring for future growth solve the therapist's problem, it's also far more gratifying. The mentor-mindset exemplars I interviewed sprang to life talking about their mentees. A few of them even told me about their personal successes (I had to look them up or ask third parties), but all couldn't stop talking about their mentees' successes.

Mentoring for future growth can help any of us feel like our efforts to mentor young people are well placed and could positively affect a person's life in the long run. With the right mentor mindset, we can have an impact whether we interact with a young person for an hour, a week, a summer, or eighteen years. We can start snowball effects that follow young people wherever they go.

Let's turn our attention to two case studies that reveal how to more reliably influence young people in the long term. One (presented in this chapter) involves America's most influential freshman-calculus professor. The other (in chapter 12) involves perhaps the most remarkable experiment I've ever been involved with.

Uri Treisman's Mentor Mindset

Calculus class in freshman year of college has long suffered from a perverse version of the therapist's problem. Not only does the course often fail to help young people long after they take it, but it can actively *harm* their growth. A poor score in calculus discourages students from pursuing advanced technical careers in math, science, engineering, and computer science. The course is hard, fast-paced, and unforgiving. Students fall behind if they don't already know how to study or if they get lost making sense of a foreign language of computational tricks named after dead mathematicians whose surnames provide little useful information. (L'Hopital's rule has nothing to do with urgent medical care, it turns out.) Most universities simply accept that freshman calculus demands four months of suffering. It's the educational equivalent of passing a kidney stone. They also accept the deep inequities tied to the course. Students with fewer advantages are less likely to enroll in a rigorous freshman calculus class and less likely to pass if they do take the course. That makes it much harder for them to continue on a path to advanced technical careers.

In short, freshman calculus is a gatekeeper. Could it be a gateway instead? Imagine the possibilities for long-term growth if the course could have more equitable pass rates *and* prepare more students for futures of contributions to math, science, and related fields. Nobody has done more to make this dream a reality over the last fifty years than Uri Treisman.

"Let's serve them oysters." That's the first thing Treisman said to me, with a grin on his face, when I told him about an event we were planning for public school teachers.

Treisman is a math educator who won the MacArthur Genius Grant for his equity-promoting calculus workshops at Berkeley. In the five years before he launched his workshops, from 1973 to 1977, fully 33 percent of all Black students at Berkeley failed calculus, and very few went on to graduate in math or math-related technical fields. Again, these were Berkeley students—some of the highest achievers in the whole state. But once Treisman implemented his workshops, 97 percent of Black students passed calculus and almost twice as many as before, 65 percent, persisted on to math or math-related degrees.

From the latter result, we know that Treisman had prepared the students to succeed in future rigorous math courses. He's mentoring for future growth. According to one account, by the early 1990s, 40 percent of all Black PhDs in mathematics were graduates of Treisman's programs. You could say that Treisman is the Michael Jordan of solving the therapist's problem in freshman calculus.

For the last thirty years, Treisman has been a professor at UT Austin, where he continues to teach freshman calculus. On the day he made his comment about oysters, we were discussing a project in which we sought to identify educators who, like Treisman, excelled at creating inclusive excellence year after year. My team had conducted a statistical analysis of data from more than a thousand teachers, and we singled out twenty bright spots who might have Treisman-like qualities. We wanted to study their secrets. Among them was Sergio Estrada, whom I would meet for the first time in just a few weeks. Treisman was going to facilitate our meetings with these bright-spot teachers. His key concern at this point was that we honor and respect these teachers, while shaking them out of their routines so that they shared their wisdom with open minds. His proposed solution, blurted out that day, was to serve them oysters.

Several years before we launched our hidden-Treisman project (my term, not his), which identified Sergio Estrada, I spent two fall semesters watching Treisman teach freshman calculus (as noted in chapter 2). My reasoning was, *You have to watch Michael Jordan play before he retires.* I soon learned what Rosalie Wax (chapter 2) meant when she said that mentor-mindset teachers were "real characters." They're quirky in their own ways, but they maintain high standards and high support. Treisman treats a ceramic dog statue like a foreign dignitary in class (his students send it postcards when they travel abroad). He spends his weekends translating sections of the Old Testament from the original languages with his friend who works in the White House. While intensely focused on math equity, he's a broad thinker who could get interested in any idea. He's a real character.

Treisman's standards in his calculus class can seem harsh to an observer. On the first day of class, I heard him say, "Two-thirds of you will get As, but I'll work you so hard you'll want to cry." Moments later when he said, "After your first all-nighter . . ." stunned students turned to each other and said, "*First?* How many all-nighters will there be?" Was he trying to get students to drop the course? Or was he telling a joke about the high expectations? He didn't say. Students would, indeed, bond through many late-night study sessions in which they finished a problem set just in time to squint at the sunrise on their walk back to their dorms.

A few minutes later Treisman expressly clarified that his high standards were for everyone. "At some point in the course all of you will say, 'What the hell is that?' You may just differ in *when* you say it." He was informing the know-it-all students that he wasn't going to tolerate showing off in a way that would discourage the students seeing the material for the first time. And he was telling students who were new to calculus that they belonged.

In a focus group I conducted years ago, I once heard a young Latina student tell the following story. She said one day her freshman-calculus professor made two or three students who got 100 percent on the midterm stand up in front of the class. According to her, the professor apologized to them publicly and announced, "I have failed you by underestimating you. You surpassed my expectations, but I neglected to give you an exam that was truly worthy of your preparation. To make it up to you, we're going to take away your one hundred percent and give you a new, harder test. In addition, you'll need to complete extra proofs each week that are harder than the rest of the class." The story astonished the rest of the focus group. One participant, vicariously outraged, asked, "Weren't they furious? Did the class rebel?" The question surprised the student telling the story. "No, of course not!" she answered. "Why would we do that? We want to be doctors and engineers and mathematicians, and we want to compete with the best. Why would we want anything less than a professor who pushed us to our limits?"

I interjected, "Did your calculus professor's name happen to be Uri Treisman?" "Yes, how did you know that?" she replied. I said, "Because he told me this story, too, but until now I thought he was exaggerating." A few years later when I sat in on his class, I saw him do the same thing, with the same results. I routinely witnessed things in Treisman's class that I never thought I'd see in any academic setting.

Treisman gets away with challenging his students to such an extent because his level of support matches the height of his standards. He's a true mentor-mindset exemplar, through and through. At the top of his list is his deep respect for the humanity in each student. They reciprocate that respect with devotion. I have seen students email him years later to ask him for career advice, discuss their purpose in life, debate religion and politics and justice, and question how they can know whether they truly love their partner. He can push his students beyond their current limits because he is a walking, talking transparency statement who reminds them how much he cares about their welfare and future contributions every ten minutes.

Did Treisman's philosophy spring fully formed from his brain, like the goddess Athena, who sprung from Zeus's skull and disguised herself as the capital-*M* Mentor? If so, the rest of us couldn't hope to emulate him. Luckily, Treisman's methods have an origin story. By understanding this story, we can see how the rest of us mere mortals can make his unique style our own.

Uri Treisman was born in a mostly Jewish section of Brooklyn, New York, inhabited by remarkably intellectual working-class families. In middle school, he taught himself college algebra from a book he checked out from the library. When asked if he had any mentors growing up, he told me about Louis, the local kosher butcher. What lessons had Louis taught him? "How to give people gifts without them being indebted," Treisman told me, rather cryptically.

When Treisman was in the third grade, his father went to the hospital for an extended stay. Treisman was old enough to know that he needed to support his poor single mother and younger brother. Louis gave him a job bringing free organ meats to people who were poor in the community. When Treisman showed up for work, he'd first get an impromptu lesson on the Talmud from Louis. A favorite of Louis's was an exegesis on "Justice, justice you shall pursue," from the Old Testament book of Deuteronomy. Then Treisman would leave to make his rounds. Louis told Treisman very specifically and precisely to go to the house, ring the bell, and then say, "Someone asked me to deliver this to you, and they said it was yours, not theirs." I asked Treisman why that was an important lesson. He choked up. In fifteen years of knowing him, I'd never seen him so emotional. He was reflecting on his Lapsley moment, his spotlight memory of a mentor who changed his life. Treisman said that we have responsibilities that extend beyond ourselves. "Charity is wonderful," Treisman told me, "but your first concern is to do justice." Louis the butcher would harp on this if a delivery boy complained about not receiving a thank-you. "It's never good for people to owe you what should happen through justice," Louis told Treisman and the other delivery boys.

Years later, when Treisman was designing his calculus workshops, he drew on Louis's principle. He objected to Berkeley's practice at the time of putting racial- or ethnic-minority students in remedial programs while expecting them to thank the university for the extra support. In his view, the chance for their effort to translate into high performance belonged to minority students by justice, not charity. Treisman's style was designed to fix that injustice.

After a rocky middle school experience, Treisman went on to be an accomplished math student in high school, but his fire for justice burned strong. Rather than go to college, Treisman moved to Israel to work as a farmer on a kibbutz. A bite from a deadly pit viper in the field derailed that life and landed him in a hospital in LA to recover.

Treisman didn't have enough money to return to Brooklyn or Israel, so he stayed in LA, eventually putting his farming skills to use by working on a landscaping team. Around this time in his early twenties a chance encounter with a mentor changed Treisman's trajectory. It pulled him back into the intellectual life of his high school years.

Because of this mentor, Treisman started seeing how landscape architecture was connected to the philosophical ideas that invigorated him in his youth. That caused Treisman to thirst for deeper learning. His thirst led him back to math courses at a community college, and soon after that at UCLA. Two years later, he earned UCLA's top math award, and then started his PhD at UC Berkeley under the legendary mentor and mathematician Leon Henkin, whose training traced a direct lineage back to Leibniz, the codiscoverer of calculus in the 1600s. Treisman then started his famous calculus-workshop programs, launching his distinguished fifty-year career.

Who was this unexpected mentor who changed Treisman's life? It was the landscape architect Ralph D. Cornell.

Treisman, while gardening at the community college, was pursuing a horticulture certificate so he could get a raise. In the mid-1960s, Cornell was at the height of his power and influence, and he remained keen to spread the professionalism and rigor of landscape architecture in LA. Cornell delivered a series of free public lectures that Treisman happened to sign up for. "Cornell comes in dressed in fine attire," Treisman told me. "I was profoundly impressed by him." Treisman was surprised when Cornell spoke plainly—not arrogantly or condescendingly. Cornell wanted people to understand him, and then apply the rigorous principles of his field of landscape architecture. Treisman felt invited into Cornell's intellectual world, welcomed to play with the ideas. From Cornell, Treisman learned three powerful design principles that would later influence the foundations of his calculus workshop.

I'll admit that I was skeptical when Treisman first told me his Cornell story. What could landscape architecture possibly have to do with freshman calculus? Let alone mentoring? However, as I read Cornell's personal papers, stashed in the UCLA Library, I became convinced that landscape architecture made a perfect metaphor for mentoring. Cornell describes his field as the "architecture of the changing." The minute you finish planting a garden or a park, your work might seem done. However, the real growth has only just begun. You're dealing with nature, not brick and mortar. Cornell distinguished his work from construction, which he called the "architecture of the static." Cornell pointed to the example of planting redwood trees at Pomona College, which started three to four feet tall but, with appropriate care and patience, had now grown into towering and majestic landmarks. In human affairs, as in landscape architecture, we should act with an eye toward whom the person could become, rather than look for shortcuts to a finished product.

Principle #1: Watch Where People Walk

The first principle Treisman learned from Cornell was that it's unwise to build a park until you watch where people walk. Consider the example of the great grassy lawn in the heart of Pomona College's campus. The administration had imposed a large, rectangular, grid-like structure on the sidewalks. The problem was that students who walked from one end to the other liked to look at a beautiful mountain in the distance, and they had to walk diagonally to keep their eyes on it. This created a foot-worn path in the grass that looked ugly and cost money to continually fix. Landscape architects call this a *pathway of desire* because park visitors show designers what they want by voting with their feet. Ideally designers understand the pathways of desire before they build the park. Pomona's leadership didn't. How did they respond? By erecting one-to-two-foot barriers around the sidewalks to stop people from walking on the grass. Sure, the ugly, expensive barriers fixed the lawn-maintenance problem, but they prevented people from fully appreciating the natural assets of the landscape. Cornell believed the better approach would have been to watch where people walk before the shovel ever hit the dirt. When Cornell built Griffith Park in LA, he famously rode around the park on horseback for hundreds of acres. He looked at the land. What are the vistas? What are the native plant communities?

Where does the rain run off? If visitors would want to appreciate an asset such as a large rock or a mountain view, then how could he frame and accentuate it? How do you screen an eyesore so it doesn't detract from the overall experience? Griffith Park is now considered a masterpiece of highlighting a space's natural assets in a way that follows the pathway of desire.

At UC Berkeley in the mid-1970s, social programs to address achievement disparities were like Pomona's sidewalks—clunky, post hoc, and misaligned with minority students' pathways of desire. The university responded to low pass rates for Black and Latinx students by throwing them into stigmatizing remedial programs that highlighted their deficits rather than accentuating their assets. The programs drilled students on high school math concepts or explained how to study in college, rather than treating students with the respect they craved as serious college math students.

Treisman, inspired by Cornell's philosophy, disapproved of this approach. These supposedly remedial students were actually the top scholars in the state. In high school, they didn't get tutored; they tutored others. Being treated like they were deficient was humiliating. Treisman had personally tutored a handful of students the summer before they took calculus. He knew they were prepared. And yet they still did poorly in Berkeley's calculus class. Clearly, whomever had designed the student-support programs hadn't done a thorough analysis. They hadn't watched where people walked.

Like Cornell riding the grounds on horseback, Treisman ended up quasi dropping out of his math PhD program. He conducted an ethnography of calculus students at UC Berkeley. For eighteen months, Treisman followed students to their dorms and houses, to their late-night study groups and their pretest cram sessions. This process yielded insights that in the ensuing decades would revolutionize higher education student-success programs.

Treisman's ethnography followed twenty Black students and twenty Asian American students, mostly of Chinese descent. Both groups of students came from relatively poor working-class backgrounds. Treisman noticed that Black students tended to study alone, not in groups. The Asian students, by contrast, tended to study in groups, occasionally pulling all-nighters as a team. They would troubleshoot problems together, check each other's work, and share tips they gathered from meetings with the professor or TAs. Sometimes they'd call in an older sibling or cousin who had taken the course to quiz them. This communal approach proved far more efficient than studying alone, where the only way to get unstuck was to look for clues in a similar problem in the book.

Treisman realized that two key beliefs led Black students to study alone rather than in groups. First, they believed in a strong separation between their social and academic lives. Many Black students succeeded in high school by shielding themselves from peer pressure, which meant studying with fewer friends. This strategic isolation became a liability in college because it discouraged them from studying in the most effective way. Second, Black students believed Asian students were simply smarter at math. They didn't realize that Asian students tended to study together fourteen hours per week. That was much more than the recommended eight hours a week that Black students studied alone. Thus, Asian students studied more fruitfully for more hours—they weren't simply more talented by virtue of their race or ethnicity.

Treisman's insights might seem obvious in retrospect, but they were revolutionary at the time. Student-success offices at universities were so deeply entrenched in a deficit-oriented way of thinking that they almost exclusively resorted to protector-mindset practices. They lowered standards and mandated study-skills classes. But Black (and Latinx) students didn't need that. They needed to study *differently*; for example, by doing the hardest problems together in a group, like the most successful Asian students were doing.

Professors, for their part, often resorted to an enforcer mindset. They explained the content and left it up to students to learn it. Professors told themselves it wasn't their fault that no more than two Black students ever got above a B- in any semester that decade. Yet Treisman believed students from all groups, with the right support, could meet the course's high standards.

After walking the metaphorical grounds, in 1978 Treisman got to work designing his Berkeley calculus workshop. He created a vibrant and rigorous support program in which students would collaboratively troubleshoot the hardest problems. It was the opposite of remedial. Whereas students in the normal calculus class would memorize theorems and computational tricks, Treisman's workshop students would *prove* them. Thus, the group study sessions became synonymous with taking your academic progress seriously, rather than waving the white flag. In that way, Treisman's workshops solved the pathway-of-desire problem. He found out how students naturally wanted to be perceived while studying—as high-status overachievers—and he aligned his program according to that desire. The enforcer and protector mindsets would never have landed on this solution because they wouldn't have thought that Black students had legitimate reasons for studying alone or too infrequently.

Not only did Treisman's workshops help Black students learn more effectively, they also disabused students of false beliefs about the origins of success. In Treisman's workshop, everyone struggled because the work was at such a high level. Treisman was transparent about giving students serious work at the level required of future professional mathematicians. He was taking them seriously. Struggling didn't prove that they *couldn't* learn; it proved that they *were learning*.

Eventually, Black students in the workshop started to match the performance of their Asian peers. Suddenly, old stereotypes about who could succeed at math started to fade away, replaced by a confidence that, with the right learning strategies, all students could have futures in advanced, technical careers that require high-level math. (Decades later, Treisman's successes were influential in shaping both Claude Steele's stereotype-threat theory and Carol Dweck's growth-mindset interventions.)

Here's a key lesson from this story for those of us who aren't calculus professors. When we mentor for future growth, it's far better to give young people *experiences* that show them they are capable of meeting the high standard with the appropriate support, rather than offering them unfounded assurances of their abilities—or, worse, hiding the standards from them altogether.

As Treisman worked out how to engage calculus students in collaboratively troubleshooting hard problems, he drew on a second key insight from Cornell's lectures.

Principle #2: Pay Attention to Entrances

Most public parks are designed to give people a sense of refuge from the hustle and bustle of daily urban living. Once inside, you're invited to explore. However, visitors need to pass through a clear entry point to the garden. If it's not clear that they're in a different place, they would remain in their previous state of mind and never be affected by the park. Cornell, therefore, obsessed over how people entered the garden. "The garden entrance is a portal to the land of heart's desire," he wrote. For instance, in the southwest corner of UCLA's famous sculpture garden, Cornell literally makes visitors cross a bridge. That's a clear signal that it's time to think differently—about art, your life, or your future.

Treisman reflected on the principle of entrances as he realized that the transition from high school math to advanced college-level calculus can be jarring. It's like they're entering a new social world. Indeed, many students have accumulated a kind of "math trauma" from years of being evaluated as smart or not smart, mostly on the basis of how rapidly they got a problem right. In Treisman's calculus workshop, he planned to give students problems that might take thirty minutes to solve. He wanted students to tinker with the problems and see what happened if they attempted something different. In effect, he wanted them to act like insider mathematicians who belonged. Treisman suspected that the half hour of struggle could pose a problem if it simply inflamed students' psychological math scar tissue of thinking that fast equals smart at math and slow equals dumb at math. Treisman obsessed over how to open students' minds to experiencing things differently. He decided he would need clear signposts at the start of his course to convey his message: this space is different, old beliefs don't apply here, prepare for new assumptions, prepare to be changed.

Thus, Treisman thought carefully about how students would enter his calculus workshop. He needed a clean break from the remedial protector philosophy of the post–civil rights era. He also needed a transparent signal that his culture would be the opposite of the toxic enforcer-mindset culture that only rewards quick right answers in math.

Treisman's solution was clever and a bit odd: He invited students to *tea*. Black and Latinx math students at Berkeley received a letter from the university administration telling them that they had been identified as having potential to become faculty members one day. They were invited to an orientation for an honors program *over tea*. Most students had never been to tea. (To this day I haven't!) The experience was just strange enough to shake them out of their prior expectations. Once students arrived, the orientation focused solely on the skills and assets they brought to the class, not the deficits they would need to remediate. The facilitators explained that they would challenge the students because they respected the students' potential. The students heard not a whiff of disrespect. They were in a new space, free to explore and grow.

Principle #3: Plan for Future Growth

The most influential lesson from Cornell's lectures is this: a well-designed garden plans for future growth. A designer needs to imagine what a tree or a shrub will look like fully grown, not what it looks like on the day it's planted, or else they might end up with quick fixes that cause new problems down the road. Consider a tree that grows into a power line, or one whose roots get so big that they crack the sidewalk. "The required skill," Cornell said, is to be able to "visualize something which isn't too bad when you finish with it, but which is going to get better" as it grows.

The math equivalent of failing to plan for future growth is something I've heard public school superintendents complain about. Teachers give students math tricks that help them pass a quiz or worksheet that week but fail to help them when the surface features of the problems change. For instance, fifth-grade teachers have said of fractions that you should just put the big number on top. That's bad advice because it backfires later when students get to fractions that are smaller than one. In calculus, a teacher might say to memorize L'Hopital's rule to find the limit of a function. Treisman does the opposite. Usually, he teaches students how math tricks *don't* work. In one lecture I witnessed, Treisman put up four functions, three of which L'Hopital's rule *didn't* work for. Students spent forty-five minutes figuring out why. Treisman wants his students to understand the deeper principles so they can think like mathematicians in the future.

A corollary of this third principle is to be patient when a garden doesn't look perfect on the day it's planted. At first, the trees are small. The shrubs haven't grown together. The flowers are buds. It often takes five to ten years for things to grow properly. "It is never fair to judge anything in an incomplete stage," Cornell lamented, "and that is the human tendency."

In many college math classes, professors demand that all students master a given concept by a certain point in the semester; for example, by giving a rigid, all-or-nothing midterm with no opportunity for future improvement. Treisman thinks that approach punishes students who are taking a course for the first time or who had a lower-quality high school education. Such students could still figure the concept out in mid-November. But if they were punished based on the early returns they would never grow. Therefore, Treisman offers an optional final exam that could replace the midterm. His policies allow for future growth. That makes his course far more equitable.

Treisman's future-growth exam policy had a powerful impact on Ivonne Martinez, a student who took the class the year I observed it. (Ivonne is beautifully profiled in Paul Tough's book *The Inequality Machine*, which also examines Treisman's teaching.) Ivonne was a talented salutatorian from her high school, but she nevertheless bombed her first few midterms in Treisman's class. "My high school wasn't challenging enough," Ivonne told me, and Treisman's class presented a whole new level of challenge. "I was stressed to the point where I would cry." But because Treisman's grading scheme allowed for future growth, she didn't give up hope. "I redirected my stress back into my studying," she told me. The light bulb finally turned on in the last few weeks. She aced the final, and that replaced her failed midterms. She ended up with a good grade in Treisman's course.

When I talked with Ivonne during her senior year in college, she told me that the Treisman experience changed her life. She finished a degree in mathematics—one of the only Latina scholars at UT to do so. Then she earned a full scholarship to a data-science program at Harvard University and a prestigious fellowship in Amazon's machine-learning group. Stated differently, she didn't just memorize math for Treisman's test and forget it. Eight years later, she's still building on the math she learned her freshman year and making valuable contributions to her field as a result. That's the fruit of Treisman's planning for future growth.

Is Treisman Replicable?

Treisman is, indeed, a "real character." In part two (chapter 12), I want to show you that his practices can be built into programs that transcend any single individual. His practices can be summarized in terms of two broad concepts: promoting *tenacity* and building *purpose*. (See the practical section at the end of this book for more elaboration.) Allow me to tell you the story of how we took Treisman's insights about tenacity and purpose—which were the culmination of his fifty years trying to use the mentor mindset—and applied them in an entirely different setting: summer camp.

Chapter 12

Future Growth, Part Two

We are all better than we know. If only we can be brought to realise this
we may never again be prepared to settle for anything less.

—Kurt Hahn

The Summer Camp Study

About ten years ago, an energetic camp owner named Steve Baskin came
to my office and wouldn't leave until I talked to him. At the time he was in
his late forties, intense, fun loving, and kid centered. His mind raced a mile
a minute with new ideas for adventures. He's exactly how you'd picture a
summer camp owner to be.

Baskin came with a version of the therapist's problem faced by an
urban charter school network he was working with, KIPP, which mostly
serves students from low-income families and from Black, Latinx, or Asian
backgrounds. Having worked with KIPP on a few projects, I have found
their teachers to be rigorous and well trained and usually quite supportive.
The whole school might be characterized as having a mentor mindset. That
could explain their remarkable track record of getting students to graduate from high school and admitted to college. Indeed, I would say they are
among the most successful social experiments in poverty reduction over
the last two decades. That's why it was so surprising that although KIPP
students were getting admitted to college, they weren't graduating. Dropping out kept many young adults from eventually earning living wages

and breaking the poverty cycle, despite receiving a high-quality secondary education.

I once conducted a study with Angela Duckworth and Greg Walton in which we tracked all graduating seniors at four KIPP high schools. We found that just 16 percent earned a bachelor's degree in four years; looking at six years, that number was 31 percent. (We found similar results for four other charter networks in our study and even worse results for comparable district schools; thus, this was not a KIPP-specific problem.) It seemed that the network's mentor mindset was optimized for success *in* KIPP, not *after* KIPP. They suffered from the classic therapist's problem.

Baskin and his KIPP school partner hatched a zany idea for solving this problem. *We should send the kids to summer camp.*

Most people wouldn't think that summer camp has much to do with charter schools or college persistence. Most might think of it the way my daughter, Scarlett, described camp to me the first time she went: "Dad! It's a bunch of kids, walking around, like a huge block party, no grown-ups telling you what to do, just having fun nonstop for a whole week. It's awesome!"

She's not wrong, but as a developmental psychologist I also believe camp is serious business. Think about it. At camp, you struggle at first to do hard, scary things (e.g., climb a ropes course, learn to water-ski, make friends with strangers) in the care of supportive adults. Then you get lauded with status and respect for overcoming your fears. At Steve Baskin's Camp Champions, kids are celebrated multiple times per day for taking such reasonable risks and surviving. Having seen this in action, my scientific opinion is that camp creates a struggle-success-status positive feedback loop. Each day at camp could, in theory, teach a kid a miniature version of a belonging story that just might help them persist in college.

Some preliminary evidence for Baskin's camp idea came from an analysis conducted by Donald Kamentz. At the time, Kamentz oversaw college-going initiatives for a similar urban charter network. His analysis showed that the charter school students who persisted in college tended to be disproportionately those who had been to an intensive weeklong summer backpacking trip in the wilderness with classmates and new friends, such as Outward Bound.

It was as though they experienced in a week or two, by analogy, all the fears of freshman year that Treisman tried so hard to help them with—fear of making friends, of surviving on your own, of overcoming obstacles you previously thought impossible—and, inevitably, *it all turned out alright in the end*. The participants seemed to acquire a personal Freytag's Pyramids in their minds, letting them know how the hero's journey would end. That personal story might solve the therapist's problem and help them thrive even after they left the care of their high-quality charter high school. Thinking of this analysis, I realized that maybe Baskin's camp idea wasn't so crazy after all. But I saw one big problem that could threaten the whole project.

Do kids tend to believe that the adversities in camp settings have anything to do with the adversities they face in high school or college? Perhaps not. Psychologists have found that many young people tend to think in a limited, concrete way about their experiences. For instance, they may not see how overcoming their fear of waterskiing would be related to overcoming their fear of factoring trinomials in algebra. What's the way to help young people see this connection?

A partial answer comes from fascinating research conducted in the 1990s by psychologists James Youniss and Miranda Yates, which powerfully influenced my thinking. They wanted to know how and whether participation in community service (e.g., volunteering to help the homeless) influenced adult civic engagement (e.g., voting and volunteering). The Youniss-and-Yates study showed that a deciding factor was whether the volunteers *reflected*. When youth reflected on how volunteering was aligned with their values and identity—their broader qualities—then they transferred their high school volunteering experiences to adult civic engagement. It solved the therapist's problem. A 2014 meta-analysis of the same phenomenon, involving more than twenty-four thousand youth volunteers, further showed that the number of hours of volunteering didn't mean anything in the absence of reflection. The more youth reflected—and therefore consolidated their experience into an identity—the better the long-term results.

The Youniss-and-Yates research suggested to me that our goal shouldn't just be for kids at camp to overcome adversity. If we want camp to carry over into their real lives, far into the future, they also need to reflect on how the lessons form a part of their identities.

Baskin and I resolved to overhaul the camp experience to provide continuous opportunities for reflection. What did we want campers to learn from those reflections? We needed a few abstract concepts that would apply both in camp and later in school. Informed by my observations of Treisman's class, we settled on the identities of having *tenacity* and *purpose* because we suspected these two identities could help students persist in college. (For a detailed review of what these two themes looked like in Treisman's class, see the "Putting It into Practice" section for chapter 11 at the end of this book.) In addition, we suspected tenacity and purpose were hidden strengths that many KIPP students already had but that they hadn't learned to generalize to the college experience. We wanted to take a strength-based, not a deficit-based, perspective. I had worked closely with KIPP students before; several had interned in my research lab. I knew that many already showed tenacity on a daily basis, especially by dealing with the adversity that accompanies poverty. I knew that many had a deep sense of purpose—to contribute to community, improve society, and make a better life for their families.

Baskin and I added reflections on how kids' behaviors at camp displayed tenacity and purpose. First, we trained counselors to call out campers' behaviors, like riding a scary zip line or climbing a tall rock wall, as evidence of tenacity (e.g., overcoming fears) and purpose (e.g., by showing the younger campers how to embrace a reasonable risk). They did this both in the moment and during the nightly reflections in the cabin. This tactic was inspired, in part, by Treisman's approach of putting a nearly impossible problem on the board, letting students struggle, and then zooming out to praise them for having the courage to embrace a challenge that prepares them to be leaders in their fields. Next, we asked counselors to write letters to the KIPP campers on the last day of camp, calling out the tenacity and purpose each camper showed that week. These letters worked a bit like the belonging stories from upper-year students in the Walton belonging studies. They gave the campers a template for how to view their daily behaviors as a part of their identities. Furthermore, the campers themselves wrote reflections on the last day of camp, just like at the end of the Walton belonging studies. They wrote about a time when they had to do something hard and scary, but it turned out well. This exercise gave students a chance to practice seeing their identities as ones that had tenacity and purpose. Finally, we followed up with the campers back in school. In October, we asked them to reflect on how the challenges they overcame during the summer—their reasonable risks—compared to the fears and difficulties they were currently facing in their freshman year of high school. What they wrote about might sound mundane, but the reflection proved meaningful. Students wrote things like, "When I was afraid of the ropes course this summer, it taught me that I could overcome my fear of asking a question in math class." Although they could readily make this link when prompted, they didn't do it without the reflection prompt. They had strengths, gained through experience, but no adult had ever asked them to carry these strengths over into the classroom. In our study, we didn't leave it up to chance that campers would discover how to link their tenacity and purpose from one setting (camp) to another (school). Instead, we ensured they would make that link through these guided reflection exercises.

In summary, we took elements from Treisman—helping students adopt identities as both tenacious and purposeful—and infused them into a summer camp that already had demanding and supportive camp counselors. This way we could test whether the insights from Treisman's mentor mindset would apply in a totally different setting. Did this mixture help solve KIPP's version of the therapist's problem?

Baskin sponsored roughly one hundred campers on a full scholarship per summer, and so for two summers in a row Baskin and the KIPP school essentially flipped a coin to decide which half of the two hundred students would get a free week of reflection-infused camp (a treatment group) and which half of the two hundred would get a week of extra academic enrichment (a control group). We picked students who were rising ninth graders, about to make the transition to high school, a challenging time during which most students would need to apply tenacity and purpose. All of the 403 students in the study were Black or Latinx and/or came from poor families. Then, we waited five years to examine students' college enrollment data.

KIPP's college data showed us that students who had attended Baskin's summer camp were more than ten percentage points more likely to be at a four-year college (versus being at a two-year college or not in college at all).

That result was astonishing. It's very hard to get students to persist in college, even with very expensive programs. Most available treatments don't work, probably because most programs come from a deficit, neurobi-ological-incompetence model. In the camp study, by contrast, we took the mentor-mindset approach of accentuating strengths like tenacity and pur-pose—in the context of a supportive relationship with a counselor. When we did that, we witnessed a solution to the therapist's problem: enduring benefits, years after a program ended.

Young people have many one-week experiences that don't seem to change their lives in the slightest. What explains camp's snowball effect years later? We can never be completely certain, but I interviewed campers eight years after camp to try to find out. Because I had their essays and their letters, I could corroborate their memories with evidence. What I learned shocked me.

Eight Years of a Rolling Snowball

My interviews showed me that the former campers showed impressive lev-els of tenacity and purpose throughout their educational careers, in part because Camp Champions helped them tell themselves better and more optimistic stories about early adversities in college. (Note that I didn't share anything about my involvement with the camp, or my hypotheses, until the end of the interviews. Everything shared here comes from their unvarnished memories.)

Emmanuel's Story

When Emmanuel showed up at Texas A&M, a university with a pre-dominantly white student body and a notoriously outrageous freshman-orientation program called Fish Camp, everything he saw screamed (metaphorically), *You are a minority! You don't belong here!* Soon, however, he realized that he *could* fit in—he just had to discover what he had in common with people. "It was the same experience as at Camp Champions," he told me. What did he mean by that? Emmanuel vividly remembers the feeling of showing up at camp and not knowing anybody. "It was scary, and I was thinking, *Am I going to get along with them? Are they going to judge me?*" On his first day at Camp Champions, he got off to a poor start. He failed the swim test, and for the rest of the week he was one of only four kids forced to wear a life vest in the pool. His initial worries about belonging were exacerbated by an evening ritual at Camp Champions called Torchlight. The ceremony appears very strange to an observer, full of inside jokes and cheers. "On the first night, I was like, 'Oh this is weird,'" he told me. Prior to each ceremony, the camp's staff select one camper who showed tenacity and purpose that day to be the Torchlighter. This individual literally lights the torch that starts the evening assembly. Soon Emmanuel wanted to earn the honor of lighting the torch. The next day he decided to try the Jet Ski, even though he couldn't swim. He was terrified of his face crashing into the water. To this day he remembers the experience. "It was more fun than scary." That's a challenge appraisal, most likely spurred by the support of his counselors. That achievement started a snowball. He later tried waterskiing, trail riding, and archery. "I had never done that kind of thing before." Importantly, he faced these new challenges with the support of his counselors. "They were very encouraging. They would try to push you, but if you didn't want to do something they didn't force you." On one of the last nights, Emmanuel was selected as the Torchlighter among several hundred campers for his tenacity and purpose. He still remembers how proud he felt lighting the torch that night—a clear illustration of the unforgettable power of status, respect, and earned prestige. Along the way, he made friends and stopped feeling like an outsider.

Four years later, Emmanuel had this story in his head as he made the transition to Texas A&M. Despite his initial worries about belonging, he "ended up finding out that it really is a community. I just had to put in the effort to go to events." Emmanuel started attending community service events, where he bonded with other students who also had a sense of purpose for contributing to others, even though they came from very different backgrounds. That realization started a snowball that bled over into his academic work. He had been struggling with motivation in his

first major, construction science, because it focused on the mundane aspects of managing a construction site. He felt called to be an architect and
change communities for the better. Emmanuel wasn't daunted by the challenge of switching to the architecture program. He took summer courses
in drawing and software and started thriving. He even graduated on time,
unlike 85 percent of his KIPP-graduate peers. Now he has an important
job working for the city, where he reviews blueprints before construction
of major new initiatives is launched, as the only person in his family to
have a stable and well-paying white-collar career.

Karime's Story

As a little girl, Karime was painfully shy and lacked confidence. She had
few friends or hobbies. Her family was also financially insecure. Her father,
who immigrated to the United States from Mexico, worked a low-wage job
from 9:00 a.m. to midnight seven days a week. These days, Karime is a
senior at the University of Texas at Austin, majoring in philosophy and mi-
noring in business, with a certificate in computer science. She's interned
at top public relations firms in Washington, DC, and she's heading to a
top law school this fall, which she hopes will power a career working for
social justice causes. Karime has purpose in spades. She's also a counselor
for Austin Sunshine Camp, whose mission is to "provid[e] the magic of
overnight camp without the barrier of cost." In addition to practicing the
law, "one of my goals in life is to start a free summer camp," she told me.

Karime credits Camp Champions for helping spark this passion. "I
was really, really shy," she told me, but "I remember looking up to my counselor, thinking, *She's so outgoing. I want to be like her.*" Each night, her cabin
had to go up in front of the whole camp at the Torchlight ceremony and
perform a chant or a skit. The performances felt terrifying at first, but the
counselors helped her get out of her comfort zone. As she gained confidence, Karime became a reasonable-risk-taking machine. By the end of
camp, she'd bonded closely with two girls, one of whom is her best friend to
this day and was her biggest confidant through the tumultuous high school
years. She overcame her fears and jumped on the blob—a huge floating
bag of air in the lake—and learned how to wakeboard, even though she

failed at first. She learned how to paint for the first time and was hooked. A few months later, "my wall at home was filled with paintings." To this day, her first art project from camp hangs in her room. During her distinguished high school career, Karime overcame her shyness and led multiple student organizations. When she got to UT Austin, she struggled, like many of Treisman's students who were the first in their families to go to college. Unlike most students, however, she had a positive story about her belonging. "I never doubted myself, and I knew I belonged here," she told me. "It was just confusing why I was doing bad." She didn't conclude she wasn't cut out for college. A key reason why was her sense of purpose. "Seeing my parents struggle always made me ensure that I went to college," she said. After camp, she became interested in policy debates and current events, which drove her to philosophy—a notoriously difficult major—and the law. Now she's on track for a bright future of contribution to society.

At the end of our interview, I shared the results of our study with Karime. I asked her if she thought it was plausible that camp had set in motion a snowball that helped KIPP students in the long run. As she looked over the roster of her cabin from eight years prior, she said, "I actually agree with that. I don't see any names of people who are not in college anymore." What did camp teach her? "It showed me that even when I don't have friends there, I could still find activities that I enjoyed, like painting. And even with my shyness, I can still put myself out there and do things that are out of my comfort zone. I learned a lot that I still use to this day."

Kevin's Story

In middle school, Kevin struggled so much in his classes that he didn't see himself going to college. His mom, like most of his uncles and cousins, worked the night shift in the stockroom at Walmart. "I never thought I would graduate high school," he told me. "I was not a good student." Walmart could give him a job if nothing else worked out. Now, eight years later, he's the first college graduate in his family, and he has a clear purpose in life: to be a music teacher by day and a professional jazz musician by night. Of all the KIPP campers I interviewed, Kevin's life was perhaps most strongly influenced by his camp experiences.

Kevin was apprehensive when he arrived at Camp Champions. He didn't know the other kids in his cabin, the counselors played "privileged-kid" sports he had never seen (like lacrosse), he couldn't swim (like Emmanuel), and he too was baffled by the evening Torchlight. "We were all like, 'What the hell is this?'" Soon, the possibility of getting recognized at Torchlight for having tenacity and purpose—the chance to earn prestige—encouraged him to take reasonable risks.

By the end of camp, he had become best friends with the other campers, and he remains in touch with them. Just the week before our interview, Kevin had talked with them about their one week of camp eight years earlier. Kevin is naturally shy, but when he started college he thought back to making friends at camp. Those memories inspired him to join a fraternity, which became a valuable source of social support throughout college. At camp, Kevin also overcame his fear of water. On the exit letter he wrote to himself when he was thirteen, he said that his favorite part of camp was:

> When I was scared about trying to wakeboard. At first, I didn't know how to wakeboard. When I got on the boat with my friends and we drove out to the middle of the lake, I decided that I wanted to try it first. Come to find out that I failed. I tried it a second time and I got better at it.

Kevin also internalized the notion of having a purpose. He told me a story from his sophomore year in high school, when he got a call from a girl in his class who was reaching out for help and didn't know whom to turn to. She told him she had no purpose in life, that her existence felt meaningless. She sounded suicidal. Kevin went into summer-camp-counselor mode. He told her that he was here for her. He assured her that it's hard to figure out what your purpose is, and it takes time. Everybody has something to contribute, he told her, but people are at different spots in their journeys of discovering what that is. That better, more optimistic story about purpose seemed to talk her off the metaphorical ledge. After that night, they stayed friends, but he didn't think much about it again. Then a year later she called him again. She told him she had been contemplating suicide on that night when they talked but hadn't since.

Summary: Camp Champions Study

Our KIPP camp study had only a modest sample size. We can't guarantee that the same benefits would occur every time. I would love to see it replicated in another eight-year study.

Yet Emmanuel, Karime, and Kevin all reported experiences that so closely aligned with our driving hypotheses that they suggest something important. Camp, like Treisman's class, seemed to give young people personal stories—conflict, rising action, climax, falling action, resolution—that they could tell themselves in the midst of early-college difficulties. The powerful narratives unlocked the grit, resilience, and purpose that the campers already possessed and allowed these qualities to shine through. They carried those hopeful stories with them as they faced future adversity, providing a vivid example of how to mentor for future growth. That's the legacy of the mentor mindset.

Coda

This book has revealed how much of the common sense about young people we were told by our culture is actually nonsense. What seems like neurobiological incompetence to adults is often the result of a young person's healthy pursuit of status and respect. When we honor that need, by using a mentor mindset rather than an enforcer or protector mindset, we can support young people's healthy development and unlock their potential to shape the world for the better.

Importantly, you don't have to be born with a mentor mindset to use it. You too can adopt a mentor mindset that rejects a protector and enforcer mindset, just like Stef and Sergio did. You're now armed with a suite of practices—transparency, questioning, and more—that means you don't have to start from scratch. You now have tools that the exemplars in this book had to discover for themselves. "I'm jealous of your readers," Treisman told me. "I wish I could have read this book fifty years ago."

As you embark on your mentor-mindset journey, I encourage you to think about the story you will tell yourself about your own tenacity and purpose. Just like the freshman-calculus students and the campers learning to water-ski, you will face adversity as you try to implement the ideas in this book. You may find that ideas that started out clear to you in your mind become muddled when you try them with a real-life teenager or Gen Z employee. That's normal. It doesn't mean that a mentor mindset doesn't work or that you can't be a mentor. Usually, it means that you're on your way to becoming a mentor. I encourage you to keep in mind Lorena Seidel's advice that you can almost always get a do-over if you make a mistake. I've found that young people are far more forgiving of us than we realize when we apologize in earnest and spend time respecting their perspectives. In summary, moments of struggle here or there in implementing the advice in this book will be normal; you can take steps to overcome those struggles (e.g., rereading sections and asking for do-overs), and eventually you will start to see changes in how young people interact with you, including less defensiveness and more collaboration.

In short, this book has been a call to action—a plea for you to discover your purpose for adopting a mentor mindset. I made this plea not just because of the urgency for our young people, although global inequality, mental health, and political division make it urgent. Not just because our economy needs a well-trained technical workforce that's unafraid to grow, learn, and develop as technology changes, although it does. Not just because our political system needs the next generation to be engaged citizens who fight to protect the cherished institutions that safeguard our most important freedoms. I made this plea because all of us—every teacher, parent, manager, or anyone else who interacts with a young person—can become the kind of people we truly aspire to be when our mentoring, both official and unofficial, improves the lives of young people long after they leave our care. Think of Ralph Cornell's pride in the growth of trees he planted fifty years earlier, except our pride will be even greater when we, like Treisman, have left behind a legacy of young people whose accomplishments surpass our own.

Anyone can contribute to this future reality. You could wield enormous influence with a brief encounter, like Lapsley's college student at the gas station. Or you could make a more intensive commitment like Stef Okamoto, whose mentees skyrocket up the corporate ladder, or like Sergio Estrada, whose students are diversifying the future of science. No matter our role, we can help make the world into the kind of place we need it to be for our young people, like Stassun said. I encourage you to go forth like Louis the butcher, who sent free meats to the poor in 1950s Brooklyn. Your gift will be the status, respect, and opportunities to earn prestige that you afford to the next generation. As you do this, remember Louis's greeting: *Someone asked me to deliver this to you, and they said it was yours, not theirs. You deserve it because it is just.*

Putting It into Practice

Overview

Here are activities and pieces of advice for putting the key ideas from each chapter into practice. You can complete these right after reading a given chapter, or you can wait until you finish the book to digest and apply what you've read. The content of this section draws from the actual intervention activities and workshops I use in my work. Thus, I've seen much of this content have an impact on readers like you.

I codeveloped the material below with Rosalind Wiseman, an expert in young people who authored *Queen Bees and Wannabes* (which was the basis for the film *Mean Girls*), among other notable books about young people. In the twenty years since the publication of her first book, Wiseman has become one of the leading consultants to help parents, teachers, and anyone who cares about young people create a culture of dignity and respect. In particular, Wiseman has a knack for saying the right thing at the right time to young people. I'm grateful that Wiseman has added her substantial practical wisdom to this final section of the book.

As you read this section, I recommend having a journal handy to take notes. If you'd like to get a copy of the activities or protocols I describe below, or if you want to read more of the research, then you can find that information linked in the notes section.

Introduction

Here are a few reflection questions to get the ideas flowing.

1. What challenges or frustrations bring you to this book, and in what domain? For instance, it could be something in your role as a boss, teacher, parent, coach, or something else. What's the biggest frustration or pain point that you'd like to improve, using the insights in this book?

_____

_____

_____

_____

_____

2. Has there ever been a time when someone older than you treated you in a way that made you feel respected and motivated, like Chip Engelland, Pete or Leona Sumners, or in the wise-feedback study? What was the experience like and how did it make you feel? If it was motivating, why? (Usually, these are some of our most profound memories.)

_____

_____

_____

_____

_____

Your answers to these questions can be your motivation for getting the most out of this book. Revisit them (and update them) throughout the book. Your answers can remind you (1) how you want to use the insights in your life, and (2) how your own actions could give young people meaningful experiences that mirror your own.

Chapter 1

1. Think about the young people you interact with in the role that's most relevant to you (manager, parent, teacher, etc.). What's a behavior that seems irrational, like a transplant patient not taking their immunosuppressants? For instance, at work it could be young employees who pass up opportunities to impress their boss. At home it could be a risky behavior such as trying illegal substances. At school it could be giving up on an important assignment. *Choose a behavior that matters to you because we'll have some follow-up questions next.*

In my role as _____, *a frustrating behavior of a young person I interact with is . . .*

_____

_____

_____

_____

_____

_____

2. The parenting expert Dr. Becky Kennedy talks about the importance of making the "most generous interpretation" of a young person's behavior. This is the interpretation that doesn't assume young people are completely incompetent or ill-natured, but instead assumes they were acting in good faith but had some reason for their behavior that made sense to them at the time. As you think about the frustrating young-person behavior you wrote in the box above, what is the most generous interpretation of their behavior? Try to think about how the behavior could be motivated by a desire to escape the adolescent predicament and gain status or respect—even if to us it seems misguided.

The most generous interpretation of their behavior is that they were trying to meet their need for status and respect by . . .

---

3. Often, if young people can address their needs for status and respect in other ways, then they become less likely to engage in irrational or frustrating behaviors. What's another way that you, in your role as a leader, could help the young person meet their need for status and respect?

I could use my position to help them meet their need for status and respect in a different way by . . .

---

4. Take a look back at figure 1.3 (page 50) which showed the language in the Vegemite study. It highlights four key principles of respectful language: (1) ask, don't tell; (2) honor their status, don't invoke yours; (3) validate and explain, don't diminish; and (4) presume agency. Now try to adapt the language to your own problem. Imagine having a conversation with the young person whose behavior you've been writing about so far. What are two to three disrespectful things to say that you'd definitely want to avoid? What are two to three respectful things to say that you'd definitely want to say? For instance, a disrespectful thing for a boss to say would be *I'm older and wiser than you, and you have to listen to me.* That *tells, invokes your higher status*, and *takes agency*. A more respectful thing to say would be *I think I understand what's driving [behavior], but I'm not certain, so could you*

tell me a little bit more about what's underlying it? Because maybe we could find another way to address any concerns so that you can continue advancing your career. That *asks, grants them status, explains* your reasoning, and *presumes agency.*

Some disrespectful *phrases I would definitely not want to use are . . .*

_____

_____

_____

_____

_____

_____

Some respectful *phrases I would definitely want to use are . . .*

_____

_____

_____

_____

_____

_____

Chapter 2

Now is a good time to do a self-assessment of our own mindsets. Below are a few survey items that we've asked in scientific studies of the enforcer, protector, and mentor mindsets. They're edited slightly to be relevant across different roles (managers, parents, and educators). Remember to be honest. After you answer each, we recommend reflecting on why you gave your answers.

Group One

Read each statement, and then circle the answer in the box below it that matches your opinion.

1. One of the main reasons why young people fail or perform poorly in school or at work is because they've been too lazy to listen to what they were supposed to do.

1. Strongly agree	2. Agree	3. Mostly agree	4. Mostly disagree	5. Disagree	6. Strongly disagree

2. Young people who struggle to do well at school or work usually lack the work ethic to do well.

1. Strongly agree	2. Agree	3. Mostly agree	4. Mostly disagree	5. Disagree	6. Strongly disagree

3. The most important values that young people should learn are obedience to adults and respect for authority.

1. Strongly agree	2. Agree	3. Mostly agree	4. Mostly disagree	5. Disagree	6. Strongly disagree

Reflection. Take a look at your answers to the Group One questions above. Why did you provide the answers that you did? Write a few sentences explaining your thinking below.

The reason for my answers was ...

_____

_____

_____

_____

_____

Group Two

Read each statement, and then circle the answer in the box below it that matches your opinion.

1. Most young people are so fragile that they would lose their confidence and give up if they struggled or were stressed out.

1. Strongly agree	2. Agree	3. Mostly agree	4. Mostly disagree	5. Disagree	6. Strongly disagree

2. When young people experience failure, it debilitates their performance and productivity.

1. Strongly agree	2. Agree	3. Mostly agree	4. Mostly disagree	5. Disagree	6. Strongly disagree

3. In a large meeting or in a classroom, it's better to let only young people who know all the answers speak up, so that nobody has to worry about looking dumb in front of their peers.

1. Strongly agree	2. Agree	3. Mostly agree	4. Mostly disagree	5. Disagree	6. Strongly disagree

Reflection. Take a look at your answers to the Group Two questions above. Why did you provide the answers that you did? Write a few sentences explaining your thinking below.

The reason for my answers was . . .

_____

_____

_____

_____

_____

Interpretation of Scores

Scoring Group One. As you may have guessed, the items in Group One measure aspects of the *enforcer* mindset. If your total score was under ten, then you ended up on more of the enforcer side. Notice the emphasis in the items on the incompetence and lack of character among young people as a main explanation for poor behavior (questions 1 and 2). That interpretation leads to the recommended behavior of having the adults do the thinking—and the young people do the complying (question 3). In general, our data show that people who agree with questions 1 and 2 are far more likely to also agree with question 3.

What should you do if your score was under ten for Group One? Don't worry! It means that you're concerned with (and probably maintaining) high standards for performance. That's great! It means you're halfway to the mentor mindset. You just need to add support. But it also means that you might want to pay close attention throughout the book to the ways that mentor-mindset exemplars support young people. You can add that support to your high standards.

Scoring Group Two. Group Two measures the protector mindset. If your total score was under ten for Group Two, then you're on the protector side. Note that it's possible for people to both be enforcers and protectors on these items. The reason why is that many enforcers become protectors when they want to seem nice, and many protectors become enforcers when young people get out of control. This just goes to show that nobody is stuck in one mindset or another forever.

Notice that the items in Group Two focus on protecting young people from stress, frustration, and failure. It comes from a belief that failure or stress are debilitating (questions 1 and 2), and that belief in turn leads to behaviors that can deprive young people of opportunities to grow or learn (question 3). If that's you, don't despair. It's great that you care about young people's feelings and want to help them. Now you just need to add more rigorous standards to that concern.

Next Steps. If you had high scores on both, that's great! Assuming you answered honestly, that means you're not inclined to use an enforcer or protector mindset. There's more to a mentor mindset though. It's not just an absence of enforcer/protector mindsets. We need to back up our beliefs with action. That's why the rest of this book is so heavily focused on practical solutions.

Chapter 3

Here is a key consideration for using the mentor mindset to bridge the generational divide.

Emphasize Learning and Growth, Not Labels

When people are accused of being an -ist (e.g., sexist, racist, etc.) they immediately want to disprove the allegation. While that reaction makes sense, we need to look beyond the all-or-nothing world of prejudiced versus unprejudiced people.

For example, people accused of racism might argue, *I don't have a racist bone in my body*, or *But I have Black friends!* That defense is nonsense because it implies racism is an immutable physical characteristic that would prevent you from making any cross-race friends. The better way to look at this issue is that everyone is on a journey of learning. Everyone, no matter what their background, grew up in a society that sometimes divides people and perpetuates stereotypes. Given that, we're all learning how to be less influenced by isms. We can all get better at living ethically in a complex multicultural society. When we keep that in mind, we can use better language during a conflict across the generational divide. That calmer language can reduce the temperature and help us collaboratively troubleshoot—rather than be at each other's throats.

A Scenario for Parents

A few years ago I witnessed a conversation between a young white woman in her early twenties and her mom, a baby boomer. The mom said something potentially biased about people of color that set her daughter off. It was clear to me, at least, that the mom wanted to be inclusive and equitable toward people of color, but she hadn't gotten around to questioning the ideas she learned about race (or gender or sexuality) in Wisconsin in the 1970s. The daughter jumped all over her mom, shaming and blaming her, giving her a lecture. Shocked, the mom said, "I don't have a racist bone in my body." After all, most baby boomers spent their adolescence explaining the civil rights movement to their parents in the 1960s and '70s. They tend to view themselves as having done a lot already to make our society more equitable. In the end, neither changed their mind.

The daughter needed to learn how to correct older folks with more grace. Meanwhile, the mother needed to signal that she was open to learning.

For example, the mother could have said:

You have thought about these issues in a different way than I have, and we were raised in really different times. And I really want to listen and learn how you see things. I can't promise that I will completely agree with you, but I promise that I'll do my best to understand. What I ask from you is your patience and belief that I am doing my best and we both believe that we have the same goal: treating everyone with dignity and making our society fairer and more equitable.

Such a statement would have sent a clear signal to the daughter that this dialogue was a troubleshooting zone, not a shame-and-blame zone. Instead of both women digging in their heels and focusing on whether they were right to defend their honor as non-ists it allows both of them to possibly change their minds. Why? Because when the mom says she can learn from the young person's perspective, she's respecting her daughter. A respectful response can be hard to manage when someone yells at you, but the alternative is worse. The mom requests that her daughter show her respect as well. With a foundation of mutual dignity, it's possible to form a treaty. Real learning can happen.

Reflect on this scenario on the lines below. Which parts stand out? If something similar happened to you, how would you adapt these ideas for your context?

Something that stood out to me about this scenario was . . .

_____

_____

_____

_____

If something similar happened to me, what I would do or say would be . . .

_____

_____

_____

_____

_____

A Scenario for Bosses

Bosses can take the journey-of-learning approach to bridging the generational divide as well. Dr. Melissa Thomas-Hunt saw this work well at Airbnb. When customers complained about bias in the company's rental bookings, the company took it seriously. One powerful step was to empower and elevate nineteen different "employee resource groups," such as Black@Airbnb, which aims to improve the experience of Black employees in tech. A company with an enforcer-mindset culture wouldn't have done that—they might have even said that it's biased to have these kinds of affinity groups. Airbnb's mentor mindset, however, started with the presumption that different groups have different things to teach senior management, owing to unique experiences and backgrounds, and the company as a whole might be better if managers learned those wide-ranging lessons. This assumption was validated when the Black@Airbnb group released a manual for an effective employee resource group. Their recommendations didn't just improve the experience of minority groups—they made *everyone* at the company feel more included and respected. By taking a learning stance rather than a defensive stance, Airbnb transformed itself from a company with a major public relations crisis on its hands into one of the top destinations for talented workers from diverse groups.

Reflect on this scenario on the lines below. Which parts stand out? If something similar happened to you, how would you adapt these ideas for your context?

Something that stood out to me about this scenario was ...

_____

_____

_____

_____

_____

If something similar happened to me, what I would do or say would be ...

_____

_____

_____

_____

Summary

The enforcer mindset makes the generational divide worse. When we demand compliance without compassion, then young people feel like their perspectives are disrespected, which in turn causes many of the frustrating behaviors we complained about in the first place. The protector mindset fully concedes power and control to the next generation, and that isn't right either. Young people may have valuable perspectives, but they're often far narrower than the broad lens we develop with age, experience, and wisdom. A mentor mindset, however, can resolve the generational divide by learning from young people's perspectives, while also aligning their ideas with what we already know is best for everyone's long-term interests.

Chapter 4

What are some times where we've been pulled into enforcer or protector mindsets, despite our good intentions? These questions will help you reflect on how the lessons from Stef's and Sergio's stories could apply to your own life. *Remember, nobody is 100 percent enforcer or 100 percent protector. We're all a mix of both.* Our standards and supports can go up or down. The trick to using the mentor mindset is to notice which relationships and situations trigger us to drop supports or standards, and then adjust.

Getting in Touch with Your Enforcer Mindset

1. In which relationship in your life are you most likely to use an enforcer mindset?

_____

_____

_____

_____

_____

_____

2. Have you had any experiences in your past that might have led you to endorse Theory X and associated beliefs, such as the myth of the demanding leader? (At Microsoft, Theory X came from the lore around Jack Welch and other top CEOs; Sergio learned Theory X through film, through false role models like Oscar, and from a faulty recollection of his former teacher.)

_____

_____

_____

_____

_____

3. In moments where you're using an enforcer mindset, remember that you're half-right: you have *high standards*. How could you remember to add the other half: the *supports* that young people need? (For Sergio, he realized that he had to have a better plan for support structures, well in advance of a moment when he's holding someone to high standards.)

Getting in Touch with Your Protector Mindset

1. In which relationship in your life are you most likely to use a protector mindset?

---

2. In what way, if at all, might your protector mindset be influenced by a misunderstanding of Theory Y? (For Stef, it was her extreme dislike of the flipping-tables culture of Microsoft that caused her to overcorrect against Theory X and adopt a distorted view of Theory Y.)

---

3. In moments where you're using a protector mindset, remember that you're half-right: you have *supports*. How could you remember to add the other half: the *high standards* that young people need? (For Stef, she realized that she was harming people she cared about by withholding honest feedback from them or by rushing to solve their problems without permission.)

_____

_____

_____

_____

_____

_____

Chapter 5

Transparency and the Three Mindsets

Let's think about the transparency practice in terms of the three mindsets. In both the enforcer and protector mindsets, we tend to start with pejorative beliefs about young people. Then those beliefs lead us to think that transparency is unnecessary (enforcer) or debilitating (protector). The mentor mindset starts with a different, more respectful worldview, and therefore leads us to understand why transparency is needed and effective. See table 5.1 below.

Table 5.1. Transparency and the Three-Mindsets Framework

	ENFORCER MINDSET	PROTECTOR MINDSET	MENTOR MINDSET
Worldview	I shouldn't have to explain myself. The young people who expect me to be transparent are overly sensitive and entitled.	I can't say what I'm really thinking about young people's incompetence because I want to be nice. They can't handle the truth.	I need to accompany my high standards and support with an explanation because a power disparity (and a barrier of mistrust) can make the meaning of my behavior ambiguous.
Actions	Charge ahead without explaining our intentions. Demand compliance.	Withhold uncomfortable information or give bland praise, even if it makes them feel weak or helpless.	Explain that your high expectations and high support come from your belief in their high potential to be successful.

Using Transparency Statements

Let's see how we can use the transparency mentor-mindset practice. Recall that a transparency statement is needed when there's a power disparity (causing a barrier of mistrust), especially early in an interaction. It involves a statement of your benevolent intent. To be convincing it needs to be about *your intent specifically*, not *people like you*. Transparency statements can emphasize both messages (what something means) and opportunities (chances to act). And a little repetition can't hurt! In general the goal is to move what young people hear closer to what we intend to communicate (see table 5.2).

Table 5.2. Why a Transparency Statement Is Needed Across Different Roles

ROLE	WHAT WE SAY OR DO	WHAT WE INTEND TO COMMUNICATE	HOW YOUNG PEOPLE HEAR IT
Parents	"How was your day?"	"I love you, and I care about you, so I want to know if there are any issues I should be aware of."	"My caregiver is intrusive because they don't trust my ability to handle things myself."
Bosses	"Here are the things you need to fix about your work before your next performance review."	"I care enough about you that I'm giving you clear, direct, and useful feedback so you can get a raise."	"My boss thinks I'm terrible at my job."

Parents

Scenario. You've picked up your child from school or an activity. You're excited to hear about their day. As they get in the car, you can tell that they're not happy. You want to know what the issue is, so you ask them. How do they respond? "I'm fine," they say. No information. Then silence.

This common scenario frustrates parents because driving in the car is a great opportunity to be a mentor to your child, but the chance is wasted when the conversation hits a dead end.

It's easy to think the low-quality conversation results from your child's surliness or standoffishness. However, you could also look at it as a miscommunication. You, as the parent, want to share your concern (see table 5.2, row 1). The child, however, interprets your questioning as a sign of distrust or contempt. *They're asking me these questions because they don't think I can handle things myself,* young people are apt to think. Where does that come from? Not out of thin air. It comes from most parents' habits of responding to any update besides *fine* by going into red alert problem-solving mode. It's far easier, young people may think, to simply avoid the conversation than it would be to put up with thirty minutes of follow-up questions and plans for fixing any and every problem they're facing.

This miscommunication comes, in part, from the spiking levels of testosterone (and other pubertal hormones), which cause young people to read between the lines as they try to interpret our words and actions. In this case, they're likely to interpret our attempts to help as a sign that we think they're not competent enough to solve their own problems. When we realize this, then it's obvious that if we transparently address the elephant in the room—the disrespect they feel from the intrusion—then they might be more willing to have the conversation.

Recommendations. When your child gets in the car, say hello and that you're happy to see them. Maybe pay them a compliment but don't make a big deal of it or some such. Then stop talking—give them a moment of silence. (We could all use more silence in our lives.) If they respond to your well-meaning silence with, *What's going on? Why aren't you asking me a ton of questions?* you can say, *I've thought about how I usually interact with you when I see you at the end of the day, and I've realized that I ask you too many questions and I can come across as interrogating you. That's not my intention. I care about you, and I'm interested in what's going on/it's fun to know what's going on with you.*

If they are clearly in a bad mood when you see them, just take a pause before you ask them anything. When it seems like the right time, you can say, *It looks like you had a really bad day. I'm pointing that out because I'd like to be a resource to talk it through with you, if that helps. I'm offering because I know it's usually really hard for anyone to solve problems on their own. If you don't want to talk about it, however, I respect your privacy. If you do want to talk about it at any point, I'm here. I promise to just listen and not jump to conclusions.* This statement is important because it transparently signals that your main goal is to help them in the long term, not intrusively take over their personal lives; thus it reduces a key threatening concern they have.

As your child starts talking, you can also signal to them that you're not going to turn the unsolicited-problem-solving dial up to eleven. One way is to use Stef's management tip of saying, *Can you tell me whether this is just a venting session or if you want something to change? I'm asking so that I don't respond in a way that could make it worse.* That's a way to transparently signal that you're trying to collaboratively troubleshoot it, not solve their problems for them.

Reflect on this scenario below. Which parts of this script stand out? What would you change?

_____

_____

_____

_____

_____

Bosses

Scenario. You're a manager, and you're scheduled to give performance feedback to a young person you supervise. Although their work overall is of high quality, they're still new to their job, and they will need to fix some things in order to maintain promotional velocity. How can you give critical feedback in a way that makes your mentor mindset transparent to them?

Recommendations. As you adapt the transparency practice from the examples above (and in chapter 5), try to avoid a few key mistakes, such as: Don't send group emails with criticism that could come across as public accusations about what the young person has done wrong. Don't use the compliment sandwich because young people really want the truth. Don't compare them to other employees who are doing a better job. And try not to be vague with your criticism (e.g., "your attitude") because that's not concrete enough for them to fix.

Recall that a transparency statement works best at the beginning of a possibly threatening conversation. A performance review is potentially threatening because it could be a precursor to a lower bonus or being managed off the team. Therefore I recommend saying something up front that frames the review as a routine action, such as, *This is a regular performance review where we go over your work and identify what is going well and what we need to work on. It's also an opportunity for you to share with me about your experience working here, so that I can help you get unstuck if there are any places where something is getting in the way.* This can also be a good time to use a version of wise feedback: *Although we're going to cover some areas where you can grow, remember that my reason for doing this is to help you stay on a path with promotional velocity by exceeding expectations.*

Then, as you review the standards and expectations and the young person's performance relative to them, it's important to call out places where they have earned prestige with strong work. The performance review is a kind of adolescent predicament, and the way to assuage it is to grant the young person the status and respect they've earned.

When a young person has fallen short of expectations, it's important to talk about it, but a transparency statement can help here as well. You can say, *There are a few areas where I'm seeing mistakes/underperformance. I'm going to ask you a number of questions about these areas, but before I do I want to be clear that my goal is to understand your perspective. I'm not trying to belabor the point or embarrass you. Therefore, if it seems like I'm asking too many questions, please just know that it's coming from a place of not wanting to make unwarranted assumptions about you. After all, if I misunderstand things, then my advice would be unhelpful.*

Note that in an enforcer mindset, it's tempting to think, *I shouldn't have to say all this stuff; they should be tough enough to just take the feedback.* In theory, yes, it would be nice to be able to speak our minds and move on. But that's ignoring the power of the adolescent predicament. When we do that, not only do young people react negatively to performance feedback, but we waste our time giving feedback that's never put to use—or managing hurt feelings. In the end, everyone is happier if we are more transparent about our benevolent intentions than we think we need to be.

Educators

Scenario. You're a teacher giving feedback to a student who has been struggling in your class. They feel that they have tried but they are continuing to make the same mistakes. You want to give them feedback, but you don't want to further frustrate them. In the past you have tried to give them feedback, but they have gotten defensive.

Reflect on this scenario below in light of the advice for parents and managers. Which parts of this script could be lifted and used again? What would you change?

_____

_____

_____

_____

_____

Chapter 6

Questioning and the Three Mindsets

Let's think about the questioning practice in terms of the three mindsets. The pejorative beliefs underlying the enforcer and protector mindsets cause us to think that transparency is a waste of time (enforcer) or too stressful (protector). The mentor mindset starts with the presumption that young people have legitimate perspectives that lead to their behaviors. Thus, when we understand their perspectives by asking questions, we can better align our actions with young people's long-term well-being. See this in table 6.2 below.

Table 6.2. Questioning and the Three-Mindsets Framework

	ENFORCER MINDSET	PROTECTOR MINDSET	MENTOR MINDSET
Worldview	Young people's behaviors come from faulty perspectives (shortsightedness, selfishness, entitlement), and so there is no point to asking questions to understand them.	Young people would find it uncomfortable or stressful to have to answer questions or explain themselves, so it's better not to ask probing questions that challenge their thinking.	Young people's behaviors make sense to them from their perspectives, usually driven by their views of gaining status and respect. We need to ask questions to understand that.
Actions	Tell, don't ask.	Don't tell, don't ask.	Ask, don't tell.

Using Questioning

The *questioning* mentor-mindset practice lays the foundation for *collaborative troubleshooting*, which you saw Stef and Sergio put into practice in chapters 2 and 4. Here, we'll examine how to embed questions in your collaborative-troubleshooting routine as a parent, boss, or educator. We have to *ask* before we can collaborate on a solution.

Why Ask Questions When Collaboratively Troubleshooting?

Collaborative troubleshooting helps young people overcome their fear of making embarrassing mistakes. Recall that the surge in testosterone during the adolescent years makes students attuned to being looked down on. When we troubleshoot, we show young people that we're not judging them for mistakes, but instead we genuinely want to understand why they might be struggling and how an issue might be fixed. Therefore, collaborative troubleshooting comes across as a respectful thing to do, which makes it motivating to young people.

Stef and Sergio and other mentor-mindset leaders ask questions as a part of their collaborative troubleshooting because it helps them get smarter. The more we ask questions that help us see problems the way young people see them, the better we can explain the solutions to them in the future. After all, we don't know how to prevent a misconception if we never find out why a young person was confused in the first place. Thus, asking questions while collaborative troubleshooting makes us more effective leaders over time.

Overview of Collaborative-Troubleshooting Routine

Collaborative troubleshooting is a three-step routine to help leaders get the most out of their one-on-one conversations with young people about mistakes, frustrations, or confusion. The three steps are:

1. Surface young people's thinking.
2. Validate what they already got right.
3. Bridge to a better understanding.

Think about the metaphor of mining mistakes to find the good in them. When mining for precious gems, we have to surface the jewel, identify its strengths, and then polish and refine it to reveal the treasure. That process is similar to the three steps of collaborative troubleshooting.

How to Collaboratively Troubleshoot

It's easy to miscommunicate with young people, even if we're trying to use mentor-mindset practices. That's why we have to pay attention to the nuances of asking questions and troubleshooting with young people. Look at table 6.3 below. It shows each of the three steps of collaborative troubleshooting. Read the second column as though you were a young person, undergoing the adolescent predicament, testosterone coursing through your body. Ask yourself: Will young people hear our words in the ways we intended to communicate?

What, if any, reflections do you have on the information in the table below?

_____

_____

_____

_____

_____

_____

Table 6.3. How Collaborative Troubleshooting Could Be Miscommunicated to Young People

COLLABORATIVE TROUBLESHOOTING STEP	WHAT WE SAY OR DO	WHAT WE INTEND TO COMMUNICATE	HOW YOUNG PEOPLE HEAR IT
1. Surfacing thinking	"What were you thinking?"	"I want to understand your reasoning so I can explain it a different way."	"You weren't thinking."
2. Validating what they got right	"Don't you remember that I already told you how to do this?"	"I know you have this knowledge in you, and I believe that if you retrieved it, you could do it right."	"You don't remember this because you weren't paying attention or you don't care."
3. Bridging to a better understanding	"This is an easy problem. Just do [simple algorithm]."	"You already have a lot of the pieces you need, we just need to help you put them together."	"You are so dumb that you don't even know how to do the easiest stuff."

Next, let's look at some sample scripts and advice for each of the three steps. These can help make *what young people hear* more similar to *what we intend* to communicate.

1. Surfacing thinking

The first step is to ask authentic questions with uptake. These questions build on young people's thinking and have a genuine curiosity behind them. This step is important because we can't always guess exactly what young people were thinking when they made a decision. If we make incorrect assumptions, young people can feel disrespected and shut down. Therefore the best approach is to *ask, not assume*.

Example scripts:

- *Could you show me what you've tried already, so I can understand your reasoning? Then we can try to troubleshoot it together.*
- *I'm not going to tell you things you already know because that's not respectful of your time. That's why I'm going to ask you a few questions to understand what you were thinking, so we can try to solve the problem together.*

2. Validating what they got right

Say something concrete and transparent about what the young person did correctly, even if they made a mistake overall. This step matters because the brain tends to focus only on the negative, which can make young people take an all-or-nothing perspective on a mistake. They may think the leader believes they have nothing of value, which feels disrespectful. Also, if we don't acknowledge the parts they got right, they might discard those parts as also wrong. Therefore it's important to make a clear and authentic statement of what young people got right.

Example scripts:

- *I love the thinking that you showed when you [describe what they got right].*

- *I'm impressed that you already knew how to set this up. Now we just need to figure out how to do the final piece.*
- *The parts you already got right will come in handy later on when we do things that are more advanced.*

3. Bridging to a better understanding

Leading questions, of the sort that Plato had Socrates ask in *Meno*, can help young people bridge to a better understanding. These questions build on what they already know and help them see a connection to what they need to learn. Leading questions are a way to impart knowledge while also having young people own their thinking. In the examples below, pay attention to the second half of each question. These leading questions ("How might they . . ." or "What would happen if . . .") are a clear signal to troubleshoot and tinker.

Example scripts:

- *Let's build on the thinking you already did. What would happen if you _____?*
- *So if you know this part already, then what can you tell me about _____?*
- *You already understood two tricky pieces [name them]. How might they now apply to _____?*

Reflect on these scripts below. Which parts of these scripts stand out? If you were going to apply them to the young people in your life, what would you change?

_____

_____

_____

_____

_____

_____

Chapter 7

Stress and the Three Mindsets

Let's think about the meaning of stress in terms of the three mindsets. People with an enforcer mindset think that stress must be the result of an individual's character flaws, and so they unhelpfully advise stressed-out young people to suck it up. However, unalleviated chronic stress will eventually take a toll on mental health. People with a protector mindset view stress as a destructive force that young people can't deal with, and so they try to minimize the stress in young people's lives. However, no one can grow without challenges. In a mentor mindset, we view the stress response for what it is: the part of our minds and bodies that mobilizes resources to keep us alive. See this in table 7.2 below.

Table 7.2. Talking About Stress and the Three-Mindsets Framework

	ENFORCER MINDSET	PROTECTOR MINDSET	MENTOR MINDSET
Worldview	Stress is a nuisance that comes from weakness or poor planning.	Stress can crush young people and derail them from their goals, so they must be protected from it at all costs.	Stress is a natural by-product of young people choosing to challenge themselves, and it is a resource that can fuel better performance
Actions	Tell young people that if they want to be responsible and successful they need to suppress and overcome their stress.	Tell young people to reduce their stressful demands and avoid stressful situations in the future, and/or solve their problems for them.	Remind young people that their stress is usually a sign that they're doing something impressive, and encourage them to embrace those feelings to power their performance.

Using-the-Stress Practice

Let's look at the ways to talk about stress from a mentor-mindset perspective. A useful start is the synergistic-mindsets message (i.e., positively evaluating the challenge and embracing the stress response). But that's not enough. Recall Hecht's study, which showed that when leaders echoed the synergistic mindsets, they doubled the benefits of the synergistic mindsets. The way to echo the synergistic-mindsets message is to use the *Sergio Trifecta*: validate, seek to understand, and offer to collaborate. Let's see what this looks like for parents and bosses (because I showed examples for educators in the chapter).

Parents

Scenario. Your child has a major assignment due in one of their advanced classes the next day. They feel stressed and overwhelmed because they've been paying more attention to their extracurriculars than to this particular class, so they've fallen behind. You see them starting to get anxious and tense and overreacting to everything. You offer to help. They get mad and say they want to just drop the class and take something easier.

As parents we are torn between different goals. On the one hand, we want to teach our children responsibility and accountability, so in this case we're inclined to put our foot down and tell the child they have to finish the class and just deal with the stress. On the other hand, we want to protect them from anguish, so we're inclined to tell them that the advanced class isn't that important and they can drop down a level. The Sergio Trifecta can accomplish both goals. We can help them meet a high standard, keeping them on track for better opportunities in education and the workforce in the future, while also supporting them so that they're not at risk for a mental health crisis.

Example scripts:

- Validate: Don't judge or blame them for getting into this situation. It's not the time for that. Instead, validate their feelings. You can say, *I understand why you're really stressed right now, and I think it's legitimate. You're doing a lot, from your advanced classes to your extracurriculars, and that's really impressive. I think anyone who's chosen to challenge themselves like you have would feel similarly. So you shouldn't feel bad about being stressed because it's normal.*

- Seek to understand: Next, don't jump into a mode of trying to solve their problems for them—either by telling them to deal with it or by telling them to quit. Instead, you can be curious about what the issues are and where they're stuck. You can say, *I don't want to give you any advice without first understanding what you've tried so far. What isn't working yet for you?*

- Offer to collaborate: Once you have asked authentic questions with uptake (chapter 6), and figured out what they need, then you can offer to collaborate. You shouldn't simply delegate responsibility and tell them to go figure it out. Nor is it a good idea to try to intervene on their behalf (e.g., by complaining to their instructor). Instead, it's more helpful to use your unique position to get them unstuck by helping them solve the specific challenges they raised in response to your questions. For instance, if they're mostly worried about the specific assignment that's due, you can say, *Let's take a look at what you've done so far and see what we need to do differently. Although you understand the assignment more than I do, sometimes it can help to have a second person walk through the plan for how to tackle it. That can make it seem a lot more manageable. Remember: sometimes the stress of a deadline can help us focus our attention and do better, so long as we have some help with planning out a line of attack. I'm here to be a sounding board for as long as you need to get a handle on the assignment.*

Reflect on this scenario below. Which parts of this script stand out? What would you change?

_____

_____

_____

_____

_____

_____

Bosses

Scenario. Suppose that instead of a major school assignment, your young direct report is prepping a major presentation for senior management. They're so stressed that they can't even make progress. What is a mentor-mindset way to help them deal with their stress and knock the presentation out of the park?

Example scripts:

- Validate: Your first goal is to reduce the pressure to be perfect by complimenting them on how far they've gotten to this point. *I'm noticing that the magnitude of this presentation is really stressing you out. I want to start by saying that's normal. You're presenting to senior management. You've got a great opportunity to impress them in front of you, but it's also normal; it's a sign that you've chosen to do something impressive that not everybody has the courage to do.*
- Seek to understand: Next, your goal is to understand what's blocking them so that you don't solve the wrong problem. *Just so we can make sure that this goes as well as possible, I'd like to hear from you about how far you've gotten, what you've tried so far, and what's not working for you. I want to know that before I give you any advice because it's not a good use of your time to hear a bunch of suggestions that you've already tried out. Where are you in the process now, and where are you getting stuck right now?*
- Offer to collaborate: Last, your goal is to offer to collaborate specifically on the parts that they will have a hard time doing well at their career stage. Usually, we do that by offering to walk through drafts, hear a practice talk, or connect them with other experts in the company who give good presentations or who give great feedback. *Okay, now that I think I understand the issue, I'd like to suggest a few things.* At this point you're aiming to give very concrete guidance specifically on the issues that are holding them back the most—and therefore causing them to think that the demands are exceeding their coping resources. *First, I*

think I can be helpful in solving some of the organizational issues, so I'd like to work with you on that. These are issues I faced a lot when I was starting out, so I know they're fixable, but they're hard to fix without an outside perspective. Second, I want to introduce you to X, who tends to give really great feedback. X knows a lot about how the senior management team tends to view presentations like this, so they're going to be a good resource. If you do a practice talk with X, then I'm confident you will have caught any of the issues that would come up in the real thing. That's important because one reason this can feel so stressful is the uncertainty about what the senior management will say, so we never feel prepared enough. X can help fix that.

Reflect on this scenario below. Which parts of this script stand out? What would you change?

_____

_____

_____

_____

_____

Educators

Read through the first parenting scenario above. Now imagine that instead you're addressing a student who's struggling in your class.

Which parts of the parenting script stand out to you as an educator? What would you keep? What would you change?

_____

_____

_____

_____

_____

Chapter 8

Purpose and the Three Mindsets

A mentor mindset grows out of the belief that young people have the potential to reshape our society for the better, provided we offer them the proper motivation and support. We can appeal to their senses of obligation and responsibility for improving culture and society. See table 8.1. This can help us to answer young people's *why* questions.

Table 8.1. Purpose and the Three-Mindsets Framework

	ENFORCER MINDSET	PROTECTOR MINDSET	MENTOR MINDSET
Worldview	Young people are shortsighted and selfish.	Young people would wither and crumble if they tried to pursue ambitious goals that could change their communities or the world.	Young people are capable of making a broader contribution to society, with the right support, and would be motivated to do so because it confers social status.
Actions	Attempt to motivate with appeals to narrow, immediate self-interest.	Attempt to motivate with appeals to narrow, immediate self-interest.	Attempt to motivate with appeals to long-term, beyond-the-self contribution.

Using Purpose

How can leaders support young people's purposes for learning in their daily conversations? Consider these scenarios:

- A teacher wants her students to be motivated to prepare for the state test by doing their best on a practice worksheet.
- A mother wants her child to do some extra assignments at home so they can do better in their advanced math classes.
- A boss wants his young direct report to learn a new

management skill at an off-site workshop so that they can make the team more efficient (and get in line for a promotion).

We've conducted experiments that compared specific and concrete phrases that invoke a purpose for learning. These experiments have uncovered phrases that work and phrases that don't.

The Purpose-Note Study

We conducted an experiment in which teachers gave students a boring but important assignment, and like in the wise-feedback study, we appended different handwritten notes from teachers on the tops of the assignments (randomly assigned). The note that had the biggest impact on young people's scores on the assignment read, *I'm giving you this assignment because I think you have the potential to get an interesting job and make people's lives better one day, if you develop your skills on assignments like this one.* We asked students how they would react if they got such a note. They said things like, "This is an awesome note. . . . It makes students think about their future life and makes them do it more confidently," or "I could do this if it means having a good job and helping people one day. Besides, having a teacher believe in you feels pretty good."

The winning note had three essential elements. First, it emphasized that this activity would enable students to learn a skill that they could use in many different settings in the future. This emphasis was important because students tend to assume that most activities don't matter and have no long-term value apart from a letter grade. Second, those skills could benefit the student in the future. It says that the skills could lead to an interesting job, which they might enjoy. Third, the activity taught skills that could empower the student to help others, giving the assignment prosocial, beyond-the-self value.

Our experiment showed that all three elements were important. When we removed any of the three elements, the note proved less effective.

One note just emphasized the skills students would get: *I'm giving you this worksheet because I think it can help you practice your skills.* This message sounds innocuous or positive, but in fact it came across as an insult that offended students. When we asked students how they might feel if they got this kind of note, they said, "I'm pretty sure that a student will feel kind of dumb, like they don't know how to use writing skills." Students interpreted a note that gave no purpose but to develop skills as implying, *I think you lack skills and need to fix that.*

Other notes emphasized the student's immediate short-term interests. When the note said, *I'm giving you this worksheet because it might be interesting to you*, then students were incredulous. They said, "That's what teachers say when something is definitely *not* going to be interesting." When the note said that the teacher was giving the worksheet *because it will be useful for you*, then students wanted to debate, saying, "It might be useful for a grade, but will it be useful in the real world?" Only when we had all three elements (skills, long-term self-interest, and beyond-the-self impact) did students think that most of their peers would be motivated by the note.

Parenting

Let's adapt the purpose note for the parenting example of motivating your child to do the extra practice problems.

- Skill development: Don't portray the problems as pointless busy work to please a teacher. That's not a good reason to do it, especially if the child doesn't respect (or feel respected by) the teacher. Instead, portray it as a learning opportunity. You can use growth-mindset language here: *This is a chance to grow your mental muscles even further. You're going to be able to use that better and stronger brain in the future to do lots of different things.*
- Personal benefits: Don't overpromise that one assignment can change their lives in the future. Instead, emphasize how mastering the content sets them up for having the freedom to choose the career options that matter most to them: *If you understand this subject on a deep level, it's going to open a lot of doors for you because this is something that a lot of colleges value and that you*

can use in many different majors. That means that you'll have an easier time picking a major and eventually a job that you're the most interested in.

- Beyond-the-self benefits: Don't imply that students are solely self-oriented; for example, by talking about how much money students will make in the future. Students already know that better jobs pay more. Instead, emphasize that you see them as people who have a lot to bring to a better future, which they can accomplish with their stronger brains: *You can also think of your hard work on this assignment as you doing your part to help others. Why? Because the more you build your skills and strengthen your brain, the more prepared you're going to be to tackle the social issues that are most important to you in the future. After all, the problems that society hasn't solved yet are also the hardest ones, and we're going to need all the strong brains we can get if we're going to solve them.*

Bosses

These same steps and scripts can be adapted to the workplace as well. Bosses rarely talk to their employees in terms of their growth, but they could. In fact, Ole, the top manager from the Obs supermarket in Norway, routinely talked to his young direct reports in this way; for example, when he sent them to off-site trainings to level up their management skills.

Reflect on the purpose-note study below. Which parts of the script above could you apply to a direct report that you've sent to get trained on a new skill? What would you change?

_____

_____

_____

_____

_____

Chapter 9

Belonging and the Three Mindsets

The three mindsets lead to different perspectives on belonging. In an enforcer mindset, belonging is a choice. If someone doesn't fit in, then they didn't care enough or weren't brave enough to make friends or become integrated. Therefore they should accept whatever consequences come from that choice. In a protector mindset, belonging is all that matters, and it's easily compromised. Therefore, the goal is to safeguard belonging by removing anything that could threaten it—whether by reducing intellectual standards or attempting to artificially boost a sense of belonging ("YOU BELONG"). In a mentor mindset, however, belonging is a narrative that young people construct for themselves. When they experience threats to belonging, they might need help telling themselves a new story. Other times, they might need the mentor to intervene and manage the threat. Or they might need actual opportunities to belong, such as more inclusive peer or affinity groups, as at Airbnb (chapter 3). With support, the young person can create their belonging; for example, by seeking out the relationships and growth opportunities that appeal to them the most. See table 9.2.

Table 9.2. Belonging and the Three-Mindsets Framework

	ENFORCER MINDSET	PROTECTOR MINDSET	MENTOR MINDSET
Worldview	When young people feel like they don't belong, they're usually right. It's a sign that they don't have the talent or don't care enough to come to belong.	When young people feel like they don't belong, they are helpless and debilitated. They have to be protected from any belonging threat, such as failing to meet high expectations.	Young people's uncertainty about belonging is important and legitimate, but it could change; for example, through the agentic steps young people take to create their belonging.
Actions	Act as though belonging is irrelevant.	Take any action possible to protect young people from questioning their belonging.	Give young people a better narrative, through both words and deeds, so they can cope with and overcome possible threats to belonging.

Using Belonging

I'm often asked by managers, coaches, professors, and other educators how to deploy the science of belonging for groups, classes, or teams. Some of the problems they ask about are:

- Secondary school students are working on a project in a small group in class, and some of the girls laugh and make fun of the other girls who make a mistake.
- College students are working on a group presentation, and one young man dominates the conversation and doesn't let anyone else contribute.
- A diverse team at a tech company is working on a new product, and nobody wants to rock the boat or offend anybody else. They withhold their honest opinions, so the product doesn't get the criticism it needs and ends up being mediocre.

All these problems are either rooted in, or contribute to, concerns about belonging. Below are my recommendations for practices that prevent or address them. Only some of these ideas have been tested directly in experiments. Others have been developed with expert practitioners. All of them, however, are what I personally use to promote belonging with classes or teams. Artifacts for each practice are linked in the notes at the end of this book.

Overview of Belonging Practices for Groups and Teams

Figure 9.6 overviews the practices and the best timing to use them. Some are key to launching a group or team well, so they should be done first thing. Others are crucial for making sense of a major challenge or setback because those are times that could evoke uncertainty about belonging and competence. A third set of practices work best at milestones, such as the end of a term or the launch of a product. What they all have in common is that they're designed to set up better, more optimistic storytelling in a young person's mind.

Smarter getting-to-know-you activities. We've all experienced icebreaker activities for groups out there. Unfortunately, most prove as ineffective as the compliment sandwich. For instance, members of a group will commonly share some superficial information (e.g., their favorite cereal

Figure 9.6. An example timeline for activities to promote belonging in a group.

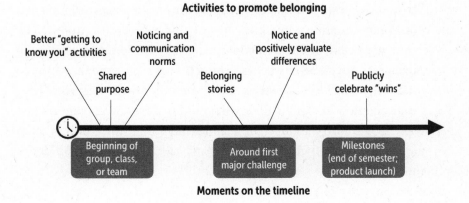

or a TV show they watch). This exercise doesn't do anything to resolve un-certainties about belonging. People worry about belonging because they worry that others may not value them as a person or may view them as incompetent, not because they don't know somebody's breakfast routine. What works instead?

I recommend—and frequently use—the fast-friends protocol, devel-oped by the brilliant social psychologist Arthur Aron. (The protocol is freely available online.) In the fast-friends exercise, pairs of people take turns asking and answering questions that gradually increase in intimacy. For five minutes, they answer questions in set one, which require only a little bit of self-disclosure (e.g., "What would constitute a 'perfect' day for you?"). For the next five minutes they answer questions in set two, which require more self-disclosure (e.g., "What is your most treasured mem-ory?"). In the final five minutes they answer questions in set three, which are quite intimate (e.g., "Complete this sentence: 'I wish I had someone with whom I could share . . .' "). Aron's experiments have found that pairs of people who complete this fifteen-minute protocol end up being more vulnerable and honest with a stranger than they've been with some of their closest friends. The University of California, Berkeley, social psy-chologist Rodolfo Mendoza-Denton found that the fast-friends protocol was especially effective for people who are in a minority group if it's used to help them make friends with others in the majority group. Whenever I teach, students tell me they are shocked by how much the fast-friends protocol made them feel heard, valued, and included, despite anything potentially embarrassing they've revealed in this brief period of time.

Fast friends works to address belonging uncertainty because it targets the root of what holds people back from being effective in groups. The adolescent predicament causes people, especially those facing threats to their social standing (such as negative stereotypes or marginalization), to worry that others will look down on them when they make mistakes. They worry that people will exploit their vulnerability. Fast friends doesn't just *tell* people not to worry about that; it *shows* them that this group or team is a safe place to be vulnerable. It's an *experience* that justifies confidence in belonging.

Shared purpose. A second activity that I use every time is a shared-purpose activity. During this exercise, members of a team all say what they hope to get out of the group, class, or team and how it fits into their personal or professional goals. Furthermore, they explain how they see the hard work of the group or team contributing to something beyond themselves. The shared purpose doesn't have to be grandiose. For instance, in a psychology class, students describe how they plan on using the knowledge to improve their own performance, how they want to complete an impressive final project that they can talk about in a job interview, and how they want to use the tips in the class to help family members (e.g., younger siblings) succeed.

What's the value in this shared-purpose activity? I've often found that higher-status groups (e.g., students whose parents have college degrees) tend to mistakenly assume that lower-status groups (e.g., students whose parents don't have college degrees) aren't motivated by the same kinds of goals as they are because of the norm of self-interest (see chapter 8). Then, looking down on their lower-status peers, they don't treat them with as much respect. But when groups surface their shared purposes—including their goals of helping others—then it tends to a sense of mutual respect.

Noticing routines and communication norms. One of the biggest killers of team cohesion is a sense among some members—especially those from groups who are marginalized or underrepresented—that their work doesn't matter. They don't feel like they need to come to meetings or speak up because the group or team will do fine without them. When they don't show up, the other group members think that the absent ones just don't care and/or aren't reliable. That judgment erodes trust that everyone can contribute. For example, I often hear about students in community college classes who arrive late, hide in the back of the class, and eventually stop coming, assuming that nobody cares whether or not they show up. Unfortunately, slogans like "You Matter" don't solve this problem. Young people need to *experience* mattering, in the actions of their group or teammates.

I recommend two activities to address this. The first is a *noticing routine*. After a group forms, everyone takes the time to share their preferred means of communication (e.g., text, email, Slack, etc.) and their contact information. Next, everyone in the group agrees to message others in the group if an important meeting begins and somebody is missing, using their preferred means of communication. Members agree to say something like, *Hey, we're getting started. Just reaching out because we'd really love to have you and your contributions be a part of this.* The goal isn't to blame and shame, but to make people feel like their contributions matter and would be missed. College classes that use this tend to get very high attendance rates (>90 percent).

A second activity sets *communication norms*. It involves explicitly discussing high expectations for collaborative communication in the group. Again, this is best done during one of the first group meetings. I like to use the well-known *constructive-and-destructive-group-behaviors* protocol. In this protocol, the members of a group or team each select *one* constructive group behavior that they see themselves bringing to the group (cooperating, clarifying, inspiring, harmonizing, risk-taking, process checking), and they ask groupmates to help bring that out of them. Next each member selects *one* destructive behavior that, if they're being honest, they're at risk of bringing to the group (dominating, rushing, withdrawing, discounting, digressing, blocking). They ask that groupmates try to help them not bring that behavior to the group. This protocol works because it licenses everyone in the group to be proactive in helping each other be the best version of a groupmate. Without this activity, it might seem rude for one person to say *You're dominating the conversation. Stop!* to another. But after this activity, anyone can request a change in behavior without seeming like they're policing everyone else.

First Major Challenge

Belonging stories. Before or during a challenging period (such as a crunch to meet a deadline at work or a major exam in class), it's useful to present belonging stories to the group (see figure 9.4, page 242, for the template). These stories can help young people who are struggling to see that their difficulties are neither permanent nor abnormal or help those who *aren't* struggling to have more compassion for their peers.

One way to present belonging stories is through the reading and writing exercises that Walton and I used in our experiments, but that's not the only way. For example, a panel of former members of the group or team could address the current members in a short Q and A. Each member of the panel can be coached to follow the template in figure 9.4. Similarly, leaders can record interviews with the former members and play them for the group. We call this a *peer-modeled mindset*. Dr. Cameron Hecht and I (with colleagues) experimentally evaluated the peer-modeled-mindset approach in rigorous undergraduate biology courses. We found that it improved performance especially for students from underrepresented groups.

Notice and positively evaluate differences. A person's sense of belonging becomes threatened when they worry that their team won't value or include "people like me." One way to overcome this is to *notice and positively evaluate* the characteristics that make them and their group different. It's important to notice differences (rather than gloss over them) because they are meaningful parts of people's backgrounds. We can't pretend as if something essential about us doesn't exist—at least not for long—and others shouldn't pretend to be blind to it. It's useful to positively evaluate differences; for example, by saying how the group overall can benefit from new and varied perspectives.

Northwestern University business school professor Dr. Nicole Stephens evaluated an intervention that's similar to the peer-modeled-mindset activity described above. She convened a panel of college students from different family backgrounds—some were first-generation college students, and some had parents with college degrees. The former group described how college was more difficult for them because they had to navigate the complex system on their own, without guidance, and usually with less family wealth than their peers. Then, they described how their background gave them a valuable perspective on college; for example, that they would make sure to take advantage of every opportunity that their parents sacrificed for (e.g., clubs, extracurriculars, labs, meeting with professors). Stephens found that this panel improved the grades of students who were the first in their families to go to college.

Milestones

Publicly celebrate wins. Young people like to hear recognition for their hard work on a team or in a group. After all, if they've done something to earn prestige, then they'd like to receive it—or else they may feel like suckers for toiling away without recognition. This problem has only increased in importance as more work has moved online, with less face-to-face communication. For many young people, weeks or months of work can feel like a tree that fell in the woods, with nobody around to appreciate it. This issue can contribute to a lack of belonging on a team because it can make people feel like their work doesn't matter.

My final recommendation is to plan celebration rituals to publicly name the respect-and-status-worthy accomplishments of young people at regular intervals. These celebrations can happen at team retreats, at presentations to celebrate a major milestone achieved, or at all-staff meetings. Newsletters can offer a celebratory platform, but my recommendation is that live verbal descriptions of employees' impressive work, delivered in front of colleagues, tend to have the most impact.

With an enforcer mindset we might say: Isn't this ritual just puffing up self-esteem? After all, weren't employees simply doing their jobs and meeting expectations? Puffing up people's self-esteem is when you praise them for fulfilling rudimentary requirements like showing up for work on time. Doing high-quality work to meet or exceed our high expectations is genuinely impressive. If we ask employees to do something advanced and difficult and they actually pull it off, then we should celebrate it.

Bosses

Reflect on this practice below. Which parts could you use with a team that you're leading? Which parts would you change? If you can, draw out your own timeline for the practices in your journal.

_____

_____

_____

_____

_____

_____

Educators

Reflect on this practice below. Which parts could you use with a class that you're teaching? Which parts would you change? If you can, draw out your own timeline for the practices in your journal.

_____

_____

_____

_____

_____

_____

Chapter 10

How can mentors emulate Stassun's culture of inclusive excellence? One powerful concrete strategy is to create what he calls the *mentoring committee*, in the workplace (e.g., for employees whom you wish to elevate) or in academia (e.g., graduate students, as in Stassun's case). It can prove especially important for young people who may not come from backgrounds that gave them many high-level contacts in their chosen professional fields (or in highly selective settings in general). The point of the committee, then, is to turn the mentor's network of connections into resources for the mentee's growth.

Overview of the Mentoring Committee

The mentoring committee is a constellation of experts who have been strategically chosen to include people who can provide relevant training experiences or job opportunities. Some experts belong to the mentee's home organization. Others are external, in other organizations. Usually, the mentors have access to some tool, such as a telescope or dataset, or they have some unique skill, such as a rare data-analysis method or experience in a given labor market, that would supercharge a mentee's progress. Mentees form a committee of these experts, both internal and external, each of whom provides access to at least one unique resource (e.g., a tool or skill).

Why Form a Mentoring Committee?

Stassun finds that having a mentoring committee is more effective than having a single Mentor with a capital *M* to take care of a student's academic, social, and emotional needs. A main reason is bandwidth. There are a limited number of mentors available, and none can do everything. Even Stassun, if he's asked *Will you be my mentor?*, finds himself asking, "To what end?" In the bridge program, Stassun coaches students to say something more like this: *My aspiration is to work on exciting question X. I've done a self-assessment and planning exercise, and I determined that one of the things I'm going to really need some mentoring around is method Y. I've heard that you know that method better than anyone. I'm wondering if you could be on my mentoring committee and meet with me for an hour every three months to make sure I'm on track with that method.* That statement outlines a very specific ask. Most mentors will say yes because the student seems organized and motivated. The mentoring committee solves the problem that busy people don't have time to be a mentor. It also means that the student will have impressed multiple future employers, like the bridge student who added a mentor from Yale University to her committee and later became the first Black woman to earn a PhD in physics there.

How Do You Form a Mentoring Committee?

Stassun recommends that mentees first think about the kind of work they want to be doing and the kind of impact they want to have on the field. Then mentees meet with Stassun or another senior scientist to lay out the skills they already have, the skills they will learn from their existing mentors, and the skills they'll need to learn elsewhere. "They're building a bridge from where they are now to where they want to be," Stassun explained to me. See figure 10.1.

Once mentees have identified the missing resources in their bridge, then they work with the mentor to identify experts who could be a link to

Figure 10.1. Mentors' resources build a bridge to the mentee's desired skills.

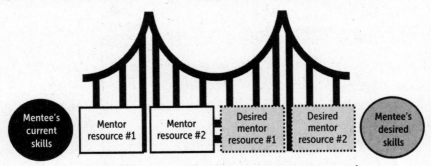

those resources. At that point, it's Stassun's job (or the job of other mentors in the Fisk-Vanderbilt program) to search the Rolodex for people who might be able to mentor for that specific resource—maybe someone who went to graduate school with him, or who served on a national panel with him. Stassun uses his personal network and social capital to link mentees with desired mentors. Then he brokers an introduction (and assures the mentor that it won't be a massive time commitment). Once students have filled in their mentoring-network map (figure 10.2), then they meet a few times per year with their committee. Stassun's team also reviews the network periodically to see which other planks need to be added to the bridge. In summary, the mentoring committee is a way of collaboratively troubleshooting the problem of how mentees can prepare for their desired careers.

Figure 10.2. A simplified mentoring-committee network. Note: Dark lines are established links; dashed lines are desired links.

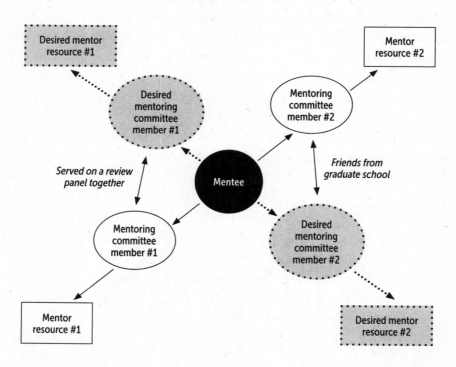

Bosses

Reflect on the mentoring network. Which could you apply to a direct report that you're mentoring in your organization? How would it have to be adapted for your organization?

_____

_____

_____

_____

_____

_____

Parents

Parents often have a hard time using their networks to help their children. Many children reject their parents' connections with others, either because they devalue their parents' expertise or because they don't want an unfair advantage. Many parents, meanwhile, want to avoid doing everything for their children; for example, by having their friends and associates give their children jobs. For parents, I recommend a far more youth-led version of the network. Using open-ended, authentic questions with uptake, parents can ask questions of young people as they fill out their own networks. Parents: try not to fill in the circles and boxes with your friends and associates. Instead, ask leading questions.

Start with the young person's goals: *What are some things you'd like to accomplish with your career [in high school, in college, in your summer internship].* Pick a grain size that feels manageable. Next, ask for an honest assessment: *What are the things you already know how to do that will get you there, and what are things that you're going to have to learn?* After understanding how they see their steps (and feel free to ask leading questions), then you can have them fill out the circles and boxes in figure 10.2 as they see fit. Who is already in their network, maybe at school or in their peer group? Who could they do an informational interview with? How could they find out which other nodes they'd need? The most important thing is that it needs to feel like (and actually be) something that's led by them.

As a parent, your stance should be one of curiosity, deep interest, and respect—for instance, by being impressed by their maturity and foresight. That stance is more likely to help the young person stick with their plan.

Chapter 11

The legendary Uri Treisman does many things that are uniquely indicative of a mentor mindset. For a long time, outsiders marveled at his approach and his results, but they didn't think they could be like him. The same might be true for parents or bosses who want to apply Treisman's insights in their situations. By this point in the book, hopefully you know that you can learn from his expertise, adapt it, and put it into practice. To help you do this I've created some reflection questions so that you can apply his insights to the organization or group you're leading—whether it's at home, in the workplace, at university, or on a sports team.

Insight #1: Watch Where People Walk

As parents, we often think we know best. We look at our children, we see where they need help, and we prescribe solutions. We form this habit from the moment our children are born, before they can talk. As they become adolescents, however, things change. Young people start developing their own pathways of desire, which may or may not map onto the paths we want them to walk. Unfortunately, we can't design a mentorship experience that prepares them for long-term growth unless we understand their paths.

As bosses, we commonly make the same mistake. We look at our young employees and see unfinished products. Many companies lay out a developmental path for those young employees, often rooted in the path that the senior management followed. But is that necessarily the right path for the next generation? John Mackey at Whole Foods should have examined that question. If you're a manager, what are some pathways of desire that you see in your young employees, or in the next generation in general, that could be powerful assets if harnessed?

As educators, when we look at students who are in need of help, we tend to view them primarily in terms of their weakness and deficiencies, not their strengths. Therefore, many educators tend to rely on remedial (and disrespectful) programs, like Berkeley did in the 1970s with Black math students. Chip Engelland, the NBA's best shooting coach, does the opposite. He doesn't see a player for the flaws in their shot; he sees their shot as fundamentally good but just in need of a tune-up, as he said to Kawhi Leonard (see introduction). For educators thinking about students who are struggling, what are the pathways of desire that could act as strengths to be amplified in the future?

Now take some time to reflect: What is a metaphorical pathway of desire that the young people you have in mind naturally walk and seem determined to walk, despite the very clear sidewalks we've laid out for them? Try to think of something that matters deeply to them, that their attention and energy naturally gravitates toward. Describe it on the lines below. To answer this, you might imagine yourself doing the equivalent of Ralph Cornell riding the grounds of the park on a horse, or Uri Treisman going undercover at the dorms for minority students at Berkeley. How could you discover a valuable pathway of desire to build on?

A valuable pathway of desire for the young people I have in mind is . . .

_____

_____

_____

_____

_____

One way I could "walk the grounds" to discover what this pathway looks like for young people is . . .

_____

_____

_____

_____

_____

One way I could build on this underappreciated asset (rather than focusing on deficits) is to . . .

_____

_____

_____

_____

_____

Insight #2: Pay Attention to Entrances

Parents, ask yourselves: What's the parenting equivalent of the entrance to a park, where your expectations get a refresh? We may find it hard to think about an entrance into new relationships with our children because we've been in ongoing relationships with them for their entire lives. But consider the opportunity of a change in the schedule, or any change in their status or roles—for example, the start of summer, the start of the school year, the transition from elementary to secondary school, or from secondary school to college, and so on. In those moments, we can mark the transition across the threshold by resetting expectations. We can say, *Now that you are [starting middle school/going into summer/coming home from college], you're a different, more mature person, and that means that our relationship has to evolve. Now is a good time to talk about what will be new, what you can expect from me, and what I expect of you.* To be like Treisman, you can mark this by doing something special—your version of inviting them to tea. You could take them to a new restaurant, or on a trip, or simply allow them to have dessert before dinner. Anything to shake them out of their routine and clearly communicate, *The baggage from our relationship from before is no longer relevant, can be set aside, or maybe discarded altogether; this is new.* You may be surprised how much significance you can convey with a small gesture that makes the entrance to a new era feel different.

Reflect a second. What's a time coming up that could serve as an entrance to a new era for your child, where you could reset some of your ways of interacting with each other?

_____

_____

_____

_____

_____

_____

    The most obvious entrance for bosses to pay attention to is new-employee onboarding. All too often, we simply throw new hires into the deep end and tell them to sink or swim. And all too often, the only ones who end up swimming are the ones who already walked in the door with great advantages (e.g., family members who were in that field). Thus, failing to pay attention to entrances makes the workplace, and our society, more unfair. Bosses also tend to think that orientation is primarily a job for HR. We think, *I'm not the expert on payroll and benefits, so I'll leave it to HR to tell new employees everything they need to know.* But when young people enter a new, intimidating setting that puts them in the adolescent predicament, they need more than *logistical* information; they need *existential* information. Thus, as we saw in chapter 9, it's important to cue up messages about belonging particularly as people start in a new role. Applying Treisman's insights and Stassun's example (chapter 10), those messages could be targeted to the baggage young people bring with them. How can we signal that their impostor fears don't apply? That previous struggles or failures don't have to be their destiny here? Or even that previous status or respect they might have taken for granted in their old setting needs to be re-earned in this new setting?

    Reflect a second. What's a way that your organization *fails to consider the entrances* for young people? What are some positive opportunities to consider it more in the future?

_____

_____

_____

_____

_____

_____

Educators can apply Treisman's insights by planning rituals around the start of a new semester or a major unit. We need to signal clearly that something new and different is possible. Students who have struggled with the subject in the past, and have "scar tissue" from the experience, need a clean break. Cultural rituals like Treisman's can send the message that *This is different, you can be a new and different student from this moment, you can accomplish more than you thought possible*. Treisman calls this *disequilibrating*: he's trying to knock students out of the equilibrium they've settled into. For example, he starts the class by playing music from a playlist developed by international students who were asked to share their culturally meaningful music. Treisman also tells students that one day they'll look back on their fears and insecurities and laugh. Further, he gives students bonus points on the first day for the best wrong answer—an answer that made him think.

One of the secondary math teachers in our hidden-Treisman project had a quirky way of getting students to leave behind their fear of mistakes in math. Next to the chalkboard, he hung a poster of a dancer in a ridiculous shark costume. On the first day, he showed a video of that shark dancer looking goofy in the background of Katy Perry's Super Bowl halftime musical performance. His point was that sometimes you look goofy when you try something outside your comfort zone, but it's better to try. Next he puts a hard math problem on the board, calls on a student, and says, "Be the shark!" He keeps it up all year. It's a weird yet effective way to signal that his class is different. Students don't have to carry their old fears of mistakes anymore.

I have my own way of disequilibrating students. I like to use the fast-friends protocol (chapter 9's "Putting It into Practice" section). It feels new and different. I host a former-student panel on the first or second day, in which the former students talk about how they used what they learned in my class in their current job or in a job interview. These testimonies signal that something new and different is happening because most classes simply tell students what to learn but never explain why. I also appoint the *party-planning committee* on the first day (a reference to *The Office*). I tell incredulous students that they're going to make so many friends in class that they'll want to celebrate. I also pull out my dad jokes. For example, I give imaginary bonus points to students who have the courage to raise their hand and talk in front of the class. Then I explain that imaginary bonus points can be redeemed for imaginary prizes.

The point isn't to encourage you to copy our quirks. These idiosyncratic habits fit our personalities. They only work because they're authentic to who we are. But you have the same overarching goal we do. You want to shake students out of their old expectations, as early in the class as possible, so that they can suspend any doubts about their abilities or belonging until later, after they've worked in earnest in the class. You want students to embrace your precociously high standards and take advantage of the supportive resources you offer them, and they're more likely to do that if they see how the class is different from ones in the past.

Reflect a second. How could your course disequilibrate students early in the semester to get them to discard any old fears or hang-ups and embrace the opportunity to learn in your class? What's something new and unexpected that could send the signal *this place is different*?

_____

_____

_____

_____

_____

_____

Insight #3: Plan for Future Growth

Parents can plan for future growth by finding ways to transfer responsibility to their children. One of the most frequent complaints I hear from parents is that they have to do everything for their children. But when you watch what parents actually do, they act like protectors, grabbing the metaphorical steering wheel the second their children veer off course. Such parents are like landscape architects who install flowering plants that die every winter and then complain about how much gardening they have to do each year. They're using short-term strategies, so don't be surprised if the benefits don't last!

The parenting coach Lorena Seidel is the epitome of planning for future growth. For example, she decided to never referee her children's fights.

Normally, when parents are embarrassed by their children yelling at each other, they rush in to solve the problem. They ask what the fight is about, and they tell their kids what the solution should be. Parental intervention can stop the fighting in the moment, but as soon as another fight breaks out, parents have to step in again.

Lorena simply refused to do that anymore. The next time her children fought, she demanded that they come up with a solution themselves. Her kids did the talking, not her. This approach took longer than when she solved the problem herself, but she waited patiently and prevented them from walking away. Soon enough, her children figured out how to resolve their own fights. An investment in time up front has saved her from having to put on the striped jersey and referee hundreds of fights in the future.

Reflect a second. How has your parenting failed to *plan for future growth*? What are some positive opportunities for you to do this better in the future?

_____

_____

_____

_____

_____

Bosses can plan for future growth by investing in employees' skill development over time. For instance, you could give employees time on the clock to take courses that teach skills outside their everyday job requirements. Or you could allow employees to work on projects that are in a different department or on a different team, so that they can develop new expertise in a low-stakes setting. It can be hard to commit to this approach in a culture that prizes short-term profits or quarterly stock prices because the payoff of planning for future growth might come months or years in the future. Those acquired skills, however, will prove useful in the future when the person or the organization has to pivot. Having somebody versatile on staff who already knows how to do a newly needed task can make the work go much faster, compared to going out and hiring for that specific skill. What's more, young people who feel like they're growing are more likely to stay with an employer because they're adding valuable human capital, while also feeling respected. Thus, planning for future growth in the workplace can be more efficient, in terms of saving HR costs and the ability to pivot (e.g., when technology changes), than a management strategy solely focused on short-term performance.

Reflect a second. What's a way that your organization fails to *plan for future growth*? What are some positive opportunities that managers have to do this better in the future?

_____

_____

_____

_____

_____

_____

Educators can plan for future growth by directly adapting Treisman's practices. The first step is to stop thinking that your job is to prepare your students to earn an A on a given exam that semester or year. Your main goal is to guide students to retain a deeper and more sophisticated understanding of your discipline long after they've left your class. For example, Sergio Estrada's main goal is to impart a working knowledge of the basic concepts in physics so that his students are equipped for strong postsecondary careers in science or mathematics. He doesn't care what score students earn on the AP exam, as long as he knows they've learned how to think like physicists. As it so happens, he also has the most students in the district who earn a score of 3 or above (a passing grade). Thus, Sergio plans for future growth, but his efforts help with short-term growth as well.

One practice that Sergio and Treisman have in common, and that almost any educator can emulate, is a very flexible policy on retaking exams. Sergio allows students to retake their exam and get back half the points they missed. If a student earned an 80 percent, then they can retake the test to earn another 10 percent back and raise their grade to a 90 percent. Treisman, as I mentioned in chapter 11, allows students' final exam scores to overwrite their scores on all the midterm exams. These exam policies have two major effects. They account for the fact that different students have different rates of learning, especially when so many students start the semester far behind their peers. In addition, these policies create an incentive for students to reexamine their mistakes and learn from them. When students revisit their misunderstandings, they build a better understanding that they can carry with them long into the future.

Reflect a second. How could your policies or procedures in class (e.g., your exam- or assignment-grading policies) be better aligned with your *plan for future growth*? What are some positive opportunities for you to do this better in the future?

_____

_____

_____

_____

_____

Storytelling and Anticipatory Socialization

While Treisman was living his double life as an ethnographer, he started reading the sociologist Robert Merton's 1940s classic theories of *anticipatory socialization*: the idea that mentors can help prepare a young person to live in a world that they do not yet belong to. This suggests that young people need to see how their previous experiences overcoming struggles prove they could overcome analogous struggles in the future. In two years observing Treisman, I saw that he had routines and rituals designed to impart two lessons to socialize young people into a future in the field: *tenacity* and *purpose*. He teaches these lessons day in and day out using his own brand of storytelling that mirrors what we learned in chapter 9. Treisman was the reason why we emphasized these two ideas in our Camp Champions study.

Tenacity

A few years ago I talked to a friend who was completing a PhD in mathematics. She told me a story about slinking into her adviser's office to apologize for having a "bad math week," which meant that despite lots of effort, she hadn't solved a certain proof because she made a logical error way up at the top. The adviser laughed knowingly and said, "That's it? Talk to me after you've had a bad math *year.*" My friend went on to explain that 99 percent of the daily experience of professional mathematicians working at the top of their fields is getting problems *wrong.* Most people have been socialized from a young age to think that the top math people can get every problem right without difficulty. In fact, struggle and confusion aren't just a *common* experience for the world's top mathematicians—they're *almost all* the experience. Most professional mathematicians are working on previously unsolved problems. *Of course* they struggle if millennia of talented math people couldn't solve them. The *tenacity to persist through struggle* is a key skill for professional mathematicians to master. Therefore, Treisman's students would learn it.

How do you instill the tenacity to persist through struggle? You follow the same steps as telling a belonging story (chapter 9). Treisman doesn't give a belonging story all at once. He does it continuously, throughout his teaching, in a process he calls *perspective giving.* With perspective giving, Treisman will introduce a hard problem, then take a step back and say something about what it means for students and their math identities, and then dive back into the math. It's natural and seamless—and effective at socializing students into the field of mathematics. In doing so he touches on the four main themes of a strong belonging story. Here are some perspectives I saw him give when I observed his teaching for two years:

Normalizing struggle. On the first day of class, Treisman says, "Everyone in this class will struggle, and that's by design." To prove it, he says, "You'll be doing problems that only ten percent of previous classes got right." Sometimes he'll tell students how many minutes people normally struggle on a given problem. He does this to stop students from expecting to solve a problem quickly or thinking that a lengthy grind means they're bad at math. Instead, he affirms to his students that he's asking them to do ambitious work because he respects their potential.

Evidence of change. Treisman doesn't discourage his students by implying that the difficulties are endless. Instead, he gives them a story about how their struggles will improve. Note that he never promises that the math will be *easy*. Instead, he emphasizes that problems that used to seem impossible will become doable, so the class can move on to the next hard problems. He says things like, "In this class you'll learn to struggle and like it," and "You might be asking yourself, 'Am I going to be completely confused?' The answer is no, you're going to be increasingly confident."

Action steps. Next, Treisman constantly refers to features of the course that are designed explicitly to support students as they learn to struggle and like it. He reminds them of action steps they can all take to achieve success, such as relying on their peers to help them learn the material—an insight that goes back to his days as an ethnographer at Berkeley. He clarifies that "your biggest resource is each other." To back that up, he sometimes calls on students to tell him the name of their neighbor, and if they don't know, they lose points. This tactic encourages students to introduce themselves to each other every period. Then during a lecture, he pauses every five or ten minutes, especially after a hard concept, and says, "Okay, let's make sure your neighbor understands that." Students have to explain the material to their neighbors. He tells his class that "many students did well in high school by being loners, but we've found that students did better if they studied half the time alone and half the time in groups." Ultimately, he's preparing them for engaging in mathematical discourse, not just during the class but going forward in the field.

Snowball. Treisman constantly talks about snowball effects. He emphasizes that steps that students take now to work through struggle and think mathematically with others can start a positive cycle that could take them to where they want to go in life. He often does this with sarcasm, saying, for example, "As juniors, you'll all laugh about the insecurities you had as freshmen." He drives home the point that their efforts now will be worth it.

Purpose. Last, Treisman encourages a sense of *purpose* for careers in math and related fields, in ways that go beyond (and add texture to) what

I shared in chapter 8. He instills a readiness to contribute to the field or to society, while also connecting to students' identities and backgrounds. He aims to make the struggle and suffering worth it, so that students stay in the field. His purpose-building activities might seem out of place in a typical calculus course, but they work.

Treisman starts a startlingly high proportion of his sentences in class with the phrase, "When you're leaders in your fields . . ." He finishes those sentences by explaining how students will use the lesson from the day's lecture when they're leading a report for the National Academy of Sciences or heading the research division at a major corporation and so on. At first this seemed like an odd thing to say to eighteen-year-olds who don't know if they can pass a single calculus class, let alone chair a national commission on cryptography. Then I realized why it works. It's a respectful thing to say because it implies they have value and will do impressive things. That respect makes it motivating. In addition, he's explaining that what he's teaching them has a point. Learning the day's lesson is not a hoop they're jumping through to get an A. It's a step they're taking toward a high-status professional life. In my own teaching, I've started saying, "When you're leaders in your fields . . ." any time I introduce something hard or confusing as a way of showing students that the difficult content is my way of taking them seriously. Note that it's not the magic phrase that matters here, it's the respectful connection to future status.

As another unusual exercise, Treisman asks students to skim reports coming out of the National Academy of Sciences. "Browse the reports, find two to three things that are stunning, and write a one-to-two-page essay," he says. Treisman tells the students that they're future scientists, and scientists like to browse the edges of their disciplines and get an impression of what's new. Of course, most of these technical reports are inscrutable to college freshmen. Treisman assures them that when *he* looks at these reports he only understands about 25 percent. Therefore, if students feel confused, they're becoming *more* like professionals in the field because he feels the same way. He wants students to adopt identities as professional scientists, and he breaks down what that means: constantly skimming the horizons of the field, despite your confusion.

Treisman's final purpose-supportive activity is his most powerful. It is his ritual for connecting students with their backgrounds—their high schools, hometowns, and teachers. Toward the end of the semester, he has students write letters to their high school math teachers, offering their thanks for getting them to where they are, but also explaining how much they learned in their college calculus class. Students write their letters after a full semester in which Treisman has mentioned the "high school way of doing things" as a foil for his more advanced "college way" of doing calculus. There's a lot to unpack in this sophisticated practice. Treisman critiques the "high school way of doing things" so that students don't feel bad or dumb for misunderstanding something. They can blame their high school education, not themselves. At the same time, Treisman knows that most students feel a deep sense of gratitude toward their high school teachers. He can't trash a student's hometown any more than Chip Engelland (see the introduction) can say to a player, *Your shot is terrible, and you have to change everything.* Their past experiences got them to where they are. Treisman, as we've seen, needs to understand people's strengths and assets before he critiques them. Thus, his letter-writing ritual honors students' teachers and backgrounds while also connecting them to a better future.

Chapter 12

If your organization wanted to plan for future growth, how could you emulate the Camp Champions method? This question is as relevant for bosses in summer internship programs as it is for leaders in outdoor programs, schools, or extracurriculars.

The Transfer Checklist

Here's a recipe to plan for transfer. Read each. Then check whether each element is present in your organization. The more checks you have, the more prepared you are for transfer.

Table 12.1

ELEMENT	EXPLANATION	CHECK?
Choose consistent themes	What are the high-level lessons you want people to take away from overcoming challenges? (At Camp Champions it was *tenacity* and *purpose*, but you can choose whichever terms you want to emphasize.)	
Legitimately challenging activities	What are the opportunities to earn prestige; for example, by taking on truly impressive challenges? These are critical for young people to gain meaningful senses of accomplishment rather than hollow self-esteem boosts.	
In-the-moment reflections	Are leaders present with young people in the midst of their challenges so that young people take away the right lessons from their challenges? It can be important to name a personal quality such as tenacity or purpose in the moment because they are often abstract.	
End-of-day/week reflections	Does the group have an opportunity to reflect at the end of the day or week to capture the times when they exemplified a given quality during the day/week? This is important to turning a momentary experience into a narrative story that the young person can tell themselves about the kind of person they are.	
Letters	Do the leaders write the young people letters after the group activity, reminding them of the impressive things they accomplished and the personal qualities they displayed? At Camp Champions, the counselors wrote to students a few weeks after camp, outlining the bravery of the campers and what it said about their tenacity and purpose. Those letters served as reminders of the life lessons even after they left the camp.	

ELEMENT	EXPLANATION	CHECK?
Long-term reflections that bridge settings and facilitate transfer	Are there opportunities months or even years later to reflect on how the young people have transferred the lessons to their daily lives or to next challenges? At Camp Champions, we followed up with a short writing exercise in which the former campers explained how they had to display tenacity and purpose once they were back in their KIPP schools. That served to help young people take the lessons from camp and tell themselves a story of how they applied to adversity at school.	

Acknowledgments

The ideas in this book began in 2014, when I was a fellow at Stanford University's Center for Advanced Study in the Behavioral Sciences (CASBS). While in residence, I hopped over to give a talk in the psychology department at UC Berkeley and met Ron Dahl (from chapter 1). A fabulous conversation ensued, and within a month or so the status-and-respect hypothesis was born. Eager to apply the new ideas, CASBS helped me host meetings with doctors from Stanford's medical school to talk about adolescent-behavior-change problems. Those meetings (and conversations with my wife, then an ICU nurse at a nearby hospital) taught me about the transplant crisis facing youth. I'm grateful to CASBS, Ron, and the Stanford doctors for helping to launch this journey.

A few years later I was introduced to my agent, Richard Pine, by Angela Duckworth. We talked through some of the key ideas. I sent him a prospectus and he turned it down. "This is not the best book about young people I've ever read," he told me. I was bummed but not crushed. It would be three more years before I had something readable back to Richard. On the second try, he loved the book, but he thought it was missing a signature vocabulary term. One day, it hit him: the *mentor mindset.* I talked it over with my former PhD advisor, Carol Dweck, author of *Mindset*, and she thought it might work. But it felt incomplete. It needed an opposite. "What's it like to not have the mentor mindset?" she asked. From there, we developed the *enforcer mindset* and the *protector mindset.* I'm grateful to Richard and Carol (and Angela) for their contributions. At the time, however, I didn't know how to turn those ideas into a work of narrative nonfiction.

My continuing education in nonfiction prose came from Paul Tough, the author of *How Children Succeed* and *The Inequality Machine.* On dozens of occasions, I relayed a detail from an interview to Paul as he patiently listened and then said, "Yeah, that's one way to tell the story—but it would be a better story if you said . . ." This always led me back to do more reporting. Every time, a much better (and more complete) story emerged. Paul also helped me reverse-outline chapter structures from Michael Lewis and Malcolm Gladwell and Robert Caro (and his own books), all of whom served as inspirations for my prose. Oh, and Paul edited multiple drafts. I'm not quite sure why he did this, because he had no obligation to. I suppose he's just a really, really awesome dude.

Rosalind Wiseman not only helped with the practical sections at the end of the book but she also edited multiple chapters and helped me to settle on a home for many of the stories in the book. Rosalind has great wisdom about young people, and she made many valuable contributions in the homestretch of writing.

I'm grateful to my publisher, Jofie Ferrari-Adler. Jofie's goal in life is to be a really great caddy, and he certainly walked alongside me, helping me figure out how far I had to go, and how to make the tough choices when it counted. I deeply appreciate the rest of Jofie's team at Avid Reader Press for bringing the book to life, especially Alex Primiani and Meredith Vilarello, from the cover to the design to the publicity and marketing.

The book benefited from the gift of time the many sources provided during interviews. They sat for interviews usually with no other benefit than a desire to contribute their experiences for the betterment of others' lives, and occasionally because I bought tacos. Many of them are named or cited in the book, but a few others to thank are Lisa Genecov, Tony Pace, Kevin Estrada, Mari Rege, all of the staff at Encircle, Javier Rios, Lorena Seidel's clients, and many more. Thank you for your generosity.

All of my studies that are described in the book were conducted with collaborators. There are too many to thank (and many are mentioned in the book), but I want to make sure to recognize Christopher Bryan, Meghann Johnson, Matthew Giani, Ethan Burris, Robert Josephs, Quinn Hirschi, Mary Murphy, Cameron Hecht, Fortunato (Nick) Medrano, Danielle Krettek Cobb, Dora Demszky, Ron Dahl, Adriana Galvan, Kyle Dobson, Andrea Dittmann, and Geoff Cohen.

Many mentors helped me develop the work described in this book: Carol Dweck, Greg Walton, Uri Treisman, Tony Bryk, Adam Gamoran, and Harrison Keller.

I would also like to thank the entire team at the Texas Behavioral Science and Policy Institute, especially my senior cofounders, Chandra Muller and Rob Crosnoe, both great mentors, for their many contributions to the work reported in this book. Thanks also to Jenny Buontempo, Rebecca Boylan, Pratik Mhatre, Shannon Green, Carolyn Sanchez, Megan Smith, and more.

The ideas in this book were refined by putting them into practice over the last four years through the Texas Mindset Initiative (TxMI), and later the Fellowship Using the Science of Engagement (FUSE). Many thanks to the OnRamps program (led by Jennifer Porter), and the UT Austin College of Natural Sciences, especially Melissa Taylor, David Vanden Bout, Kristin Patterson, Stacy Sparks, Ruth Buskirk, Anita Latham, Michael Marder, Christina Markert, and the other TxMI fellows.

I wrote much of the prospectus and the first half of the book as a scholar-in-residence at the Holdsworth Center's beautiful lakeside campus in Austin, Texas. Thank you to Pauline Dow and the rest of the Holdsworth team for making me feel at home.

Many funders supported the scientific papers described in this book. My first major funder was the Raikes Foundation, and I remain grateful for the support of Jeff and Tricia Raikes. Other generous funders include the National Science Foundation, the National Institutes of Health, the Bill & Melinda Gates Foundation, the William T. Grant Foundation, the Jacobs Foundation, the Yidan Prize Foundation, Schmidt Futures, the Thrive Foundation for Youth, the John Templeton Foundation, the Robert Wood Johnson Foundation, the Spencer Foundation, and the Bezos Family Foundation.

Paige Harden gave me excellent advice on how to outline a chapter before writing it. That helped me finish the book on time.

Several groups came together for book-club-like meetings to discuss early drafts. They profoundly shaped the final organization and text in the book: Vail Mountain School, the

Hun School, EL Education (Ron Berger and Scott Hartl), and UMass Amherst (Farshid Hajir).

Lastly, I'm grateful to my family. My wife, Margot, was an incredible supporter and thought partner. My four kids gave this book inspiration and also a sense of personal urgency, because I'm desperate to use the ideas to improve my own parenting. Thank you to Susan and Scott Yeager for all you did to raise me the right way. Any flaws that remain are my fault, not yours.

Notes

Introduction

1 *dark and despairing terms*: Adam M. Mastroianni, "The Illusion of Moral Decline," *Experimental History*, December 13, 2022, https://www.experimental-history.com/p /the-illusion-of-moral-decline; Adam M. Mastroianni and Daniel T. Gilbert, "The Illusion of Moral Decline," *Nature* 618, no. 7966 (June 2023): 782–89, https://doi .org/10.1038/s41586-023-06137-x; John Protzko and Jonathan W. Schooler, "Kids These Days: Why the Youth of Today Seem Lacking," *Science Advances* 5, no. 10 (October 2019): eaav5916, https://doi.org/10.1126/sciadv.aav5916; John Protzko and Jonathan W. Schooler, "Who Denigrates Today's Youth? The Role of Age, Implicit Theories, and Sharing the Same Negative Trait," *Frontiers in Psychology* 13 (May 2022): 723515.

2 *"Just Say No" campaign*: Peter G. Bourne, " 'Just Say No': Drug Abuse Policy in the Reagan Administration," in *Ronald Reagan and the 1980s: Perceptions, Policies, Legacies*, ed. Cheryl Hudson and Gareth Davies (New York: Palgrave Macmillan, 2008), 41–56, https://doi.org/10.1057/9780230616196_4.

2 increased *the appeal*: Zara Abrams, "More Teens than Ever Are Overdosing. Psychologists Are Leading New Approaches to Combat Youth Substance Misuse," *Monitor on Psychology*, March 1, 2024, https://www.apa.org/monitor/2024/03/new -approaches-youth-substance-misuse; Victor C. Strasburger, "Prevention of Adolescent Drug Abuse: Why 'Just Say No' Just Won't Work," *Journal of Pediatrics* 114, no. 4, part 1 (April 1989): 676–81, https://doi.org/10.1016/S0022-3476(89)80721-8.

2 *(D.A.R.E.) program*: S. T. Ennett et al., "How Effective Is Drug Abuse Resistance Education? A Meta-Analysis of Project DARE Outcome Evaluations," *American Journal of Public Health* 84, no. 9 (September 1994): 1394–1401, https://doi .org/10.2105/AJPH.84.9.1394; Donald R. Lynam et al., "Project DARE: No Effects at 10-Year Follow-Up," *Journal of Consulting and Clinical Psychology* 67, no. 4 (1999): 590–93; Christopher L. Ringwalt et al., *Past and Future Directions of the D.A.R.E.® Program: An Evaluation Review. Draft Final Report* (Washington, DC: US Department of Justice, 1994).

2 *75 percent of school districts*: Wikipedia, s.v. "Drug Abuse Resistance Education," last modified January 23, 2024, https://en.wikipedia.org/w/index.php?title=Drug _Abuse_Resistance_Education&oldid=1198239866.

2 more *likely to use drugs*: Michael A. Gottfried and Gilberto Q. Conchas, eds., *When School Policies Backfire: How Well-Intended Measures Can Harm Our Most Vulnerable*

Students (Cambridge, MA: Harvard Education Press, 2016); Dennis P. Rosenbaum and Gordon S. Hanson, "Assessing the Effects of School-Based Drug Education: A Six-Year Multilevel Analysis of Project D.A.R.E.," *Journal of Research in Crime and Delinquency* 35, no. 4 (November 1998): 381–412, https://doi.org/10.1177/002242 7898035004002.

2   *list of youth programs*: Scott O. Lilienfeld, "Psychological Treatments That Cause Harm," *Perspectives on Psychological Science* 2, no. 1 (March 2007): 53–70.

2   *reduce bullying*: David S. Yeager et al., "Declines in Efficacy of Anti-Bullying Programs among Older Adolescents: Theory and a Three-Level Meta-Analysis," *Journal of Applied Developmental Psychology* 37 (March–April 2015): 36–51, https://doi.org/10.1016/j.appdev.2014.11.005.

2   *teen obesity*: Eric Stice, Heather Shaw, and C. Nathan Marti, "A Meta-Analytic Review of Obesity Prevention Programs for Children and Adolescents: The Skinny on Interventions That Work," *Psychological Bulletin* 132, no. 5 (September 2006): 667–91, https://doi.org/10.1037/0033-2909.132.5.667.

2   *youth mental health*: Willem Kuyken et al., "Effectiveness and Cost-Effectiveness of Universal School-Based Mindfulness Training Compared with Normal School Provision in Reducing Risk of Mental Health Problems and Promoting Well-Being in Adolescence: The MYRIAD Cluster Randomised Controlled Trial," *Evidence-Based Mental Health* 25, no. 3 (July 2022): 99–109, https://doi.org/10.1136/ebmental-2021-300396; Eric Stice et al., "A Meta-Analytic Review of Depression Prevention Programs for Children and Adolescents: Factors That Predict Magnitude of Intervention Effects," *Journal of Consulting and Clinical Psychology* 77, no. 3 (June 2009): 486–503, https://doi.org/10.1037/a0015168.

2   *healthier social media use*: Janneke D. Schilder, Marjolein B. J. Brusselaers, and Stefan Bogaerts, "The Effectiveness of an Intervention to Promote Awareness and Reduce Online Risk Behavior in Early Adolescence," *Journal of Youth and Adolescence* 45, no. 2 (February 2016): 286–300, https://doi.org/10.1007/s10964-015-0401-2.

3   *"It's frustrating"*: Dr. Alex Sweeney, interview by the author, September 2019.

3   *I followed*: Manager, interview by the author, August 2022, November 2022, and August 2023; direct report, interview by the author, November 2022 and August 2023.

4   *The mentor's dilemma was first discovered*: Geoffrey L. Cohen, Claude M. Steele, and Lee D. Ross, "The Mentor's Dilemma: Providing Critical Feedback across the Racial Divide," *Personality and Social Psychology Bulletin* 25, no. 10 (October 1999): 1302–18, https://doi.org/10.1177/0146167299258011.

5   *view it as a personal attack*: Geoffrey L. Cohen and Claude M. Steele, "A Barrier of Mistrust: How Negative Stereotypes Affect Cross-Race Mentoring," in *Improving Academic Achievement: Impact of Psychological Factors on Education*, ed. Joshua M. Aronson (San Diego: Academic Press, 2002), 303–27.

5   *I published a scientific experiment*: D. S. Yeager et al., "Breaking the Cycle of Mistrust: Wise Interventions to Provide Critical Feedback across the Racial Divide," *Journal of Experimental Psychology: General* 143, no. 2 (2014): 804–24, https://doi.org/10.1037/a0033906.

7   *I shared the wise-feedback study*: Sweeney interview.

8   *outward signs of puberty*: Tom Hollenstein and Jessica P. Lougheed, "Beyond Storm and Stress: Typicality, Transactions, Timing, and Temperament to Account for Adolescent Change," *American Psychologist* 68, no. 6 (August 2013): 444–54, https://doi .org/10.1037/a0033586.

8   *hidden neurobiological and motivational similarities*: David S. Yeager, Ronald E. Dahl, and Carol S. Dweck, "Why Interventions to Influence Adolescent Behavior Often Fail but Could Succeed," *Perspectives on Psychological Science* 13, no. 1 (January 2018): 101–22, https://doi.org/10.1177/1745691617722620; Eveline A. Crone and Ronald E. Dahl, "Understanding Adolescence as a Period of Social-Affective Engagement and Goal Flexibility," *Nature Reviews Neuroscience* 13, no. 9 (September 2012): 636–50, https://doi.org/10.1038/nrn3313; "The Core Science of Adolescent Development," UCLA Center for the Developing Adolescent, 2020, https://develop ingadolescent.semel.ucla.edu/core-science-of-adolescence.

8   *affected by its surroundings*: Adriana Galván, "Insights about Adolescent Behavior, Plasticity, and Policy from Neuroscience Research," *Neuron* 83, no. 2 (July 2014): 262–65; Adriana Galván, "Adolescent Brain Development and Contextual Influences: A Decade in Review," *Journal of Research on Adolescence* 31, no. 4 (December 2021): 843–69; Elizabeth R. Sowell et al., "In Vivo Evidence for Post-Adolescent Brain Maturation in Frontal and Striatal Regions," *Nature Neuroscience* 2, no. 10 (October 1999): 859–61.

8   *ever-more-technical training*: David J. Deming, "The Growing Importance of Social Skills in the Labor Market" (working paper, National Bureau of Economic Research, August 2015), https://doi.org/10.3386/w21473; David H. Autor, "Skills, Education, and the Rise of Earnings Inequality among the 'Other 99 Percent,'" *Science* 344, no. 6186 (May 2014): 843–51; Daron Acemoglu and David Autor, "Skills, Tasks and Technologies: Implications for Employment and Earnings," in *Handbook of Labor Economics*, ed. David Card and Orley Ashenfelter, vol. 4B (New York: Elsevier, 2011), 1043–1171, https://doi.org/10.1016/S0169-7218(11)02410-5.

9   *feelings of status and respect*: Yeager, Dahl, and Dweck, "Why Interventions to Influence Adolescent Behavior Often Fail but Could Succeed"; Crone and Dahl, "Understanding Adolescence as a Period of Social-Affective Engagement and Goal Flexibility"; "The Core Science of Adolescent Development"; Lydia Denworth, "Adolescent Brains Are Wired to Want Status and Respect: That's an Opportunity for Teachers and Parents," *Scientific American*, May 1, 2021, https://www.scientificam erican.com/article/adolescent-brains-are-wired-to-want-status-and-respect-thats-an -opportunity-for-teachers-and-parents/.

9   *powerful effect*: Ronald E. Dahl et al., "Importance of Investing in Adolescence from a Developmental Science Perspective," *Nature* 554, no. 7693 (February 2018): 441–50, https://doi.org/10.1038/nature25770.

9   *as the cultural anthropologists call it,* earned prestige: Eldon E. Snyder, "High School Student Perceptions of Prestige Criteria," *Adolescence* 7, no. 25 (Spring 1972): 129–36; Joey T. Cheng et al., "Two Ways to the Top: Evidence That Dominance and

Prestige Are Distinct yet Viable Avenues to Social Rank and Influence," *Journal of Personality and Social Psychology* 104, no. 1 (2013): 103–25, https://doi.org/10.1037 /a0030398; Joseph Henrich and Francisco J. Gil-White, "The Evolution of Prestige: Freely Conferred Deference as a Mechanism for Enhancing the Benefits of Cultural Transmission," *Evolution and Human Behavior* 22, no. 3 (May 2001): 165–96.

9   *which I first proposed*: Yeager, Dahl, and Dweck, "Why Interventions to Influence Adolescent Behavior Often Fail but Could Succeed."

11   *"heart-stopping" and "terrifying"*: Joe Walsh, "Inside Doris Burke's 'Heart-Stopping, Terrifying' NBA Finals Interviews with the Spurs' Gregg Popovich," *ESPN Front Row* (blog), June 18, 2013, https://www.espnfrontrow.com/2013/06/inside-doris-burkes -heart-stopping-terrifying-nba-finals-interviews-with-the-spurs-gregg-popovich/.

11   *"genius"*: James D. Jackson, "Why Josh Giddey Is Excited to Have Chip Engelland as OKC Thunder Shooting Coach," *Oklahoman*, September 28, 2022, https:// www.oklahoman.com/story/sports/nba/thunder/2022/09/28/okc-thunder-josh -giddey-chip-engelland-nba-shooting-coach/69522942007/; Joe Mussatto, " 'He's a Genius': Shooting Coach Chip Engelland Already Impacting OKC Thunder," *Oklahoman*, October 16, 2022, https://www.oklahoman.com/story/sports/nba /thunder/2022/10/16/okc-thunder-already-seeing-results-from-shooting-coach -chip-engelland/69565401007/.

11   *"master at what he does"*: Fox Sports Australia, "Josh Giddey on His Partnership with SGA & the Influence of Engelland at OKC," posted on YouTube, September 26, 2022, https://www.youtube.com/watch?v=eM8jpg2hktM.

11   *"guru"*: Jeje Gomez, "With Chip Engelland Gone, the Spurs Move Closer to the Unknown," *Pounding the Rock* (blog), July 28, 2022, https://www.poundingtherock .com/2022/7/28/23281558/with-chip-engelland-gone-the-spurs-move-closer-to -the-unknown; Sean Deveney, "For Spurs Coach, Lessons with Hill Launched Success," *Sporting News*, June 14, 2014, https://www.sportingnews.com/us/nba /news/chip-engelland-grant-hill-shooting-nba-finals-san-antonio-spurs-miami-heat -duke/1cqsrnegnvfvr118dg5myqs01i.

11   *"shot doctor"*: Bill Barnwell, "The Shot Doctor," *Grantland* (blog), April 24, 2014, https://grantland.com/features/the-shot-doctor/.

11   *"legend"*: "NBA Stars Share Humbling Moments," *Philippine Star*, August 29, 2015, https://qa.philstar.com/sports/2015/08/29/1493921/nba-stars-share-humbling-mo ments.

11   *"recognizable by first name alone"*: Mussatto, " 'He's a Genius.' "

11   *shooting camps*: Here and throughout, facts regarding Chip Engelland, and his goals and mindset, come from an interview conducted with Engelland by the author, June 2023.

11   *and Shane Battier*: Shane Battier, interview by the author, May and September 2023.

12   *"He's the best"*: Deveney, "For Spurs Coach, Lessons with Hill Launched Success."

12   Moneyball *strategy*: Michael Lewis, *Moneyball: The Art of Winning an Unfair Game* (New York: W. W. Norton, 2004).

12   *one Thunder player*: Jackson, "Why Josh Giddey Is Excited."

12 *Chip helped him realize*: Barnwell, "The Shot Doctor."

12 *Chip said, "I felt his shot"*: Jeff McDonald, "How the Spurs Built Kawhi Leonard into a Monster," *San Antonio Express-News*, November 16, 2015, https://www.expressnews.com/sports/spurs/article/How-the-Spurs-built-Kawhi-Leonard-into-a-monster-6635560.php; Barnwell, "The Shot Doctor."

12 *explained to me what it's like*: All quotes and stories in this section are from the Battier interviews.

14 *"The mentor's dilemma resonated with me"*: All quotes in this paragraph from the Engelland interview.

15 *Around 150 people had gathered*: Observations made by the author in July 2019.

16 *Pete liked to tell stories*: Pete told the author these stories when the author was growing up.

16 *Pete's biggest contribution of all*: Interviews with Pete's employees and children conducted by the author at Pete's funeral in July 2019 and in phone calls in August and September 2022.

Chapter 1: What We Get Wrong

21 *parting advice of a woman, Terrie Hall*: "Terrie H.'s Story," Tips from Former Smokers®, Centers for Disease Control and Prevention, accessed February 2, 2024, https://www.cdc.gov/tobacco/campaign/tips/stories/terrie.html.

21 *Like 90 percent of adult smokers*: "Youth and Tobacco Use," Smoking & Tobacco Use, Centers for Disease Control and Prevention, November 2, 2023, accessed April 1, 2024, https://www.cdc.gov/tobacco/data_statistics/fact_sheets/youth_data/tobacco_use/index.htm.

21 *blockbuster report titled* Smoking and Health: US Department of Health, Education, and Welfare, *Smoking and Health: Report of the Advisory Committee to the Surgeon General of the Public Health Service* (Washington, DC: Government Printing Office, 1964).

21 *invested millions in making smoking look cool*: K. M. Cummings et al., "Marketing to America's Youth: Evidence from Corporate Documents," *Tobacco Control* 11, suppl. 1 (March 2002): i5–i17, https://doi.org/10.1136/tc.11.suppl_1.i5.

22 *landmark legal decision*: Walter J. Jones and Gerard A. Silvestri, "The Master Settlement Agreement and Its Impact on Tobacco Use 10 Years Later: Lessons for Physicians about Health Policy Making," *Chest* 137, no. 3 (March 2010): 692–700, https://doi.org/10.1378/chest.09-0982.

22 *charged with doing the opposite*: Matthew C. Farrelly et al., "Getting to the Truth: Evaluating National Tobacco Countermarketing Campaigns," *American Journal of Public Health* 92, no. 6 (June 2002): 901–7, https://doi.org/10.2105/AJPH.92.6.901.

22 *rigorous independent study*: Farrelly et al., "Getting to the Truth."

23 *effect of anti-obesity programs*: Eric Stice, Heather Shaw, and C. Nathan Marti, "A Meta-Analytic Review of Obesity Prevention Programs for Children and Adolescents: The Skinny on Interventions That Work," *Psychological Bulletin* 132, no. 5 (September 2006): 667–91, https://doi.org/10.1037/0033-2909.132.5.667.

23   *antibullying programs for late middle school and high school students*: David S. Yeager
     et al., "Declines in Efficacy of Anti-Bullying Programs among Older Adolescents:
     Theory and a Three-Level Meta-Analysis," *Journal of Applied Developmental Psychol-
     ogy* 37 (March–April 2015): 36–51, https://doi.org/10.1016/j.appdev.2014.11.005.

23   *backfire or prove useless*: David S. Yeager, Ronald E. Dahl, and Carol S. Dweck, "Why
     Interventions to Influence Adolescent Behavior Often Fail but Could Succeed,"
     Perspectives on Psychological Science 13, no. 1 (January 2018): 101–22, https://doi
     .org/10.1177/1745691617722620.

23   *number-one-ranked youth kidney transplant center*: Chronic Disease Research Group,
     Scientific Registry of Transplant Recipients, accessed March 18, 2024, https://www
     .srtr.org/.

23   *he told me about a fascinating set*: Dr. Steve Alexander, Stanford University Medicine
     Children's Health, interview by the author, August 2022. This interview provided all
     quotes and information from this source featured in this book.

23   *the chains of the dialysis machine*: BCRenal, "Non-Adherence and the Kidney Patient,"
     posted on YouTube, October 7, 2015, https://www.youtube.com/watch?v=tweuy2
     -z6W4; Phillippa K. Bailey et al., "Young Adults' Perspectives on Living with Kidney
     Failure: A Systematic Review and Thematic Synthesis of Qualitative Studies," *BMJ
     Open* 8, no. 1 (January 2018): e019926.

24   *fewer than 30 percent of children*: Priya S. Verghese, "Pediatric Kidney Transplan-
     tation: A Historical Review," *Pediatric Research* 81, no. 1 (January 2017): 259–64,
     https://doi.org/10.1038/pr.2016.207.

24   *closer to 95 percent*: Kyle J. Van Arendonk et al., "National Trends Over 25 Years in
     Pediatric Kidney Transplant Outcomes," *Pediatrics* 133, no. 4 (April 2014): 594–
     601, https://doi.org/10.1542/peds.2013-2775; Loes Oomen et al., "Pearls and Pit-
     falls in Pediatric Kidney Transplantation after 5 Decades," *Frontiers in Pediatrics* 10
     (April 8, 2022): 856630, https://doi.org/10.3389/fped.2022.856630.

24   *These drugs*: Verghese, "Pediatric Kidney Transplantation."

24   *"they're taking their pills completely wrong"*: Dr. David Rosenthal, Stanford Univer-
     sity Medicine Children's Health, interview by the author, August 2022.

24   *Alexander told me*: Alexander interview.

24   *once heard from a nurse*: Margot Yeager, RN, PNP, interview by the author, Novem-
     ber 2015 and August 2022.

25   *35 to 45 percent of all adolescents and young adults who receive transplants*: Sofia
     Feinstein et al., "Is Noncompliance among Adolescent Renal Transplant Recipi-
     ents Inevitable?," *Pediatrics* 115, no. 4 (April 2005): 969–73, https://doi.org/10.1542
     /peds.2004-0211; Oleh M. Akchurin et al., "Medication Adherence in the Transition
     of Adolescent Kidney Transplant Recipients to the Adult Care," *Pediatric Trans-
     plantation* 18, no. 5 (August 2014): 538–48, https://doi.org/10.1111/petr.12289;
     Jodi M. Smith, P. L. (M.) Ho, and Ruth A. McDonald, "Renal Transplant Outcomes
     in Adolescents: A Report of the North American Pediatric Renal Transplant Coop-
     erative Study," *Pediatric Transplantation* 6, no. 6 (December 2002): 493–99, https://
     doi.org/10.1034/j.1399-3046.2002.02042.x.

25 *reviewed the entire history*: Verghese, "Pediatric Kidney Transplantation."

25 *one experienced doctor told me*: Dr. Sharon Hymes, University of Texas MD Anderson Cancer Center, interview by the author, September 2022.

26 *gave a keynote*: BCRenal, "Non-Adherence and the Kidney Patient."

26 *one transplant recipient said*: BCRenal, "Non-Adherence and the Kidney Patient."

26 *another patient told me*: Kevin Estrada, interview by the author, January 2023.

26 *side effects of immunosuppressants*: Signe Hanghøj and Kirsten A. Boisen, "Self-Reported Barriers to Medication Adherence among Chronically Ill Adolescents: A Systematic Review," *Journal of Adolescent Health* 54, no. 2 (February 2014): 121–38, https://doi.org/10.1016/j.jadohealth.2013.08.009; P. Rianthavorn and R. B. Ettenger, "Medication Non-adherence in the Adolescent Renal Transplant Recipient: A Clinician's Viewpoint," *Pediatric Transplantation* 9, no. 3 (June 2005): 398–407, https://doi.org/10.1111/j.1399-3046.2005.00358.x.

26 *"One of them made me hairy"*: Estrada interview.

26 *Dr. David Rosenthal*: Rosenthal interview.

27 The Promise of Adolescence: Richard J. Bonnie and Emily P. Backes, eds., *The Promise of Adolescence: Realizing Opportunity for All Youth* (Washington, D.C.: National Academies Press, 2019), https://doi.org/10.17226/25388.

27 *more digestible summary*: "The Core Science of Adolescent Development," UCLA Center for the Developing Adolescent, 2020, accessed April 1, 2024, https://developingadolescent.semel.ucla.edu/core-science-of-adolescence.

27 status and respect from peers and mentors: Yeager, Dahl, and Dweck, "Why Interventions to Influence Adolescent Behavior Often Fail but Could Succeed."

28 *likes to tell a story*: Dr. Ron Dahl, University of California at Berkeley, interviews by the author, between November 2015 and January 2024.

28 *One day in the spring of 1998*: Alex Bogusky, interviews by the author, August and September 2023. Also see a description from the president of Crispin, Porter + Bogusky: Jeffrey J. Hicks, "The Strategy behind Florida's 'Truth' Campaign," *Tobacco Control* 10, no. 1 (April 2001): 3–5.

29 *a settlement to a class action lawsuit*: Paul A. Lebel, "Introduction to the Transcript of the Florida Tobacco Litigation Symposium—Putting the 1997 Settlement into Context," *Florida State University Law Review* 25, no. 4 (Summer 1998): 731–36; Hicks, "The Strategy behind Florida's 'Truth' Campaign."

30 *sent his young art directors undercover*: Hicks, "The Strategy behind Florida's 'Truth' Campaign."

30 *comes across as an affront to their autonomy and competence*: Martin D. Ruck, Rona Abramovitch, and Daniel P. Keating, "Children's and Adolescents' Understanding of Rights: Balancing Nurturance and Self-Determination," *Child Development* 69, no. 2 (April 1998): 404–17, https://doi.org/10.1111/j.1467-8624.1998.tb06198.x; Edward L. Deci and Richard M. Ryan, "The 'What' and 'Why' of Goal Pursuits: Human Needs and the Self-Determination of Behavior," *Psychological Inquiry* 11, no. 4 (2000): 227–68, https://doi.org/10.1207/S15327965PLI1104_01.

31 *needs to give them permission to buy them*: Dale T. Miller and Deborah A. Prentice,

"Psychological Levers of Behavior Change," in *The Behavioral Foundations of Public Policy*, ed. Eldar Shafir (New York: Russell Sage, 2012), 301–9.

31 *to get people to take health precautions*: R. F. Soames Job, "Effective and Ineffective Use of Fear in Health Promotion Campaigns," *American Journal of Public Health* 78, no. 2 (February 1988): 163–67, https://doi.org/10.2105/AJPH.78.2.163; Martin Fishbein et al., "Avoiding the Boomerang: Testing the Relative Effectiveness of Antidrug Public Service Announcements before a National Campaign," *American Journal of Public Health* 92, no. 2 (February 2002): 238–45.

32 *Anthropologists like to point out*: Arnold van Gennep, *The Rites of Passage* (Chicago: University of Chicago Press, 2019); Alice Schlegel and Herbert Barry III, *Adolescence: An Anthropological Inquiry* (New York: Free Press, 1991); Alice Schlegel and Herbert Barry, "Adolescent Initiation Ceremonies: A Cross-Cultural Code," *Ethnology* 18, no. 2 (April 1979): 199–210, https://doi.org/10.2307/3773291.

32 *modern society has lost the rite of passage ceremony*: Louise Carus Mahdi, Nancy Geyer Christopher, and Michael Meade, eds., *Crossroads: The Quest for Contemporary Rites of Passage* (Chicago: Open Court Publishing, 1996).

32 *wrote in a 2001 article*: Hicks, "The Strategy behind Florida's 'Truth' Campaign."

32 *The "Truth" campaign*: Hicks, "The Strategy behind Florida's 'Truth' Campaign"; Farrelly et al., "Getting to the Truth."

33 *first "Truth" commercials in Florida*: "Florida Tobacco Pilot Program: 'THANKING CUSTOMERS' Film by Crispin Porter + Bogusky USA," Ads Archive, AdsSpot, accessed March 18, 2024, https://adsspot.me/media/tv-commercials/florida-tobacco-pilot-program-thanking-customers-234460af6b49; "Florida Tobacco Pilot Program: 'SECRETS II' Film by Crispin Porter + Bogusky USA," Ads Archive, AdsSpot, accessed March 18, 2024, https://adsspot.me/media/tv-commercials/florida-tobacco-pilot-program-secrets-ii-59cd5535ec68.

33 *An initial evaluation found*: David Zucker et al., "Florida's 'Truth' Campaign: A Counter-Marketing, Anti-Tobacco Media Campaign," *Journal of Public Health Management and Practice* 6, no. 3 (May 2000): 1–6, https://doi.org/10.1097/00124784-200006030-00003.

33 *signed a master settlement agreement with the tobacco companies*: "The Master Settlement Agreement and Attorneys General," National Association of Attorneys General, accessed March 18, 2024, https://www.naag.org/our-work/naag-center-for-tobacco-and-public-health/the-master-settlement-agreement/.

33 *depicted twelve hundred young people*: BJaraPSU, "1200 PSA: Tobacco Kills (from the Truth)," posted on YouTube February 6, 2008, https://www.youtube.com/watch?v=Y_56BQmY_e8.

34 *a rebellious and autonomous person worthy of an adultlike status*: Christopher J. Bryan et al., "Harnessing Adolescent Values to Motivate Healthier Eating," *Proceedings of the National Academy of Sciences* 113, no. 39 (2016): 10830–35, https://doi.org/10.1073/pnas.1604586113; Christopher J. Bryan, David S. Yeager, and Cintia P. Hinojosa, "A Values-Alignment Intervention Protects Adolescents from

the Effects of Food Marketing," *Nature Human Behaviour* 3, no. 6 (June 2019): 596–603, https://doi.org/10.1038/s41562-019-0586-6.

34 *they found striking results*: Matthew C. Farrelly et al., "Evidence of a Dose–Response Relationship between 'Truth' Antismoking Ads and Youth Smoking Prevalence," *American Journal of Public Health* 95, no. 3 (March 2005): 425–31, https://doi.org/10.2105/AJPH.2004.049692; Matthew C. Farrelly et al., "The Influence of the National Truth® Campaign on Smoking Initiation," *American Journal of Preventive Medicine* 36, no. 5 (May 2009): 379–84, https://doi.org/10.1016/j.amepre.2009.01.019; Farrelly et al., "Getting to the Truth."

34 *teen smoking rates declined every year*: "Smoking Rates Decline Steeply in Teens in 2021," truth initiative, accessed March 18, 2024, https://truthinitiative.org/research-resources/traditional-tobacco-products/smoking-rates-decline-steeply-teens-2021.

34 *seat belt ads in the 1970s*: Wikipedia, s.v. "Seat Belt Use Rates in the United States," last modified November 13, 2023, https://en.wikipedia.org/w/index.php?title=Seat_belt_use_rates_in_the_United_States&oldid=1184983210; Mark G. Solomon, Richard P. Compton, and David F. Preusser, "Taking the *Click It or Ticket* Model Nationwide," *Journal of Safety Research* 35, no. 2 (February 2004): 197–201, https://doi.org/10.1016/j.jsr.2004.03.003.

34 *the current CEO of the "Truth" initiative told me*: Leadership team at the "Truth" initiative, interviews by the author, September and December 2022.

34 *the social rewards they already value*: Christopher J. Bryan, "Values-Alignment Interventions: An Alternative to Pragmatic Appeals for Behavior Change," in *Handbook of Wise Interventions: How Social Psychology Can Help People Change*, ed. Gregory M. Walton and Alia J. Crum (New York: Guilford Press, 2021), 259–85; Bryan, Yeager, and Hinojosa, "A Values-Alignment Intervention Protects Adolescents from the Effects of Food Marketing."

35 *experiences from his youth*: Dahl interviews.

36 *Plato wrote in the* Phaedrus: Plato, *Phaedrus*, trans. W. C. Helmbold and W. G. Rabinowitz (Cabin John, MD: Wildside Press, 1956).

36 *MacArthur Foundation Research Network on Adolescent Development and Juvenile Justice*: "Research Network on Adolescent Development & Juvenile Justice," MacArthur Foundation, accessed March 18, 2024, https://www.macfound.org/programs/pastwork/research-networks/research-network-on-adolescent-development-juvenil.

37 *MacArthur network argued*: Laurence Steinberg, "The Influence of Neuroscience on US Supreme Court Decisions about Adolescents' Criminal Culpability," *Nature Reviews Neuroscience* 14, no. 7 (July 2013): 513–18, https://doi.org/10.1038/nrn3509.

37 *A 2012 Supreme Court amicus curiae brief*: "Brief for the American Psychological Association, American Psychiatric Association, and National Association of Social Workers as Amici Curia in Support of Petitioners Evan Miller v. State of Alabama, Kuntrell Jackson v. Ray Hobbs, Nos. 10-9646, 10-9647" (2012), https://www.apa.org/about/offices/ogc/amicus/miller-hobbs.pdf.

37 *"would seem on present evidence to be wishful thinking"*: Franklin E. Zimring, "Penal Proportionality for the Young Offender: Notes on Immaturity, Capacity, and Diminished Responsibility," in *Youth on Trial: A Developmental Perspective on Juvenile Justice*, ed. Thomas Grisso and Robert G. Schwartz (Chicago: University of Chicago Press, 2000), 271–89.

37 Roper v. Simmons: Roper v. Simmons, 543 U.S. 551 (2005).

37 Graham v. Florida: Graham v. Florida, 560 U.S. 48 (2010).

37 Miller v. Alabama: Miller v. Alabama, 567 U.S. 460 (2012).

37 *One kidney transplant doctor I talked to*: Alexander interview.

37 *The same kidney doctor*: Alexander interview.

38 *Galván's well-known 2006 study*: Adriana Galván et al., "Earlier Development of the Accumbens Relative to Orbitofrontal Cortex Might Underlie Risk-Taking Behavior in Adolescents," *Journal of Neuroscience* 26, no. 25 (June 2006): 6885–92.

38 *Galván told me*: Adriana Galván, interview by the author, August 2022.

38 *young people often do* better *at goal-directed behavior than adults*: Linda Wilbrecht and Juliet Y. Davidow, "Goal-Directed Learning in Adolescence: Neurocognitive Development and Contextual Influences," *Nature Reviews Neuroscience* 25, no. 3 (March 2024): 176–94, https://doi.org/10.1038/s41583-023-00783-w; Maria K. Eckstein et al., "Reinforcement Learning and Bayesian Inference Provide Complementary Models for the Unique Advantage of Adolescents in Stochastic Reversal," *Developmental Cognitive Neuroscience* 55 (June 2022): 101106, https://doi.org/10.1016/j.dcn.2022.101106; Wan Chen Lin and Linda Wilbrecht, "Making Sense of Strengths and Weaknesses Observed in Adolescent Laboratory Rodents," *Current Opinion in Psychology* 45 (June 2022): 101297, https://doi.org/10.1016/j.copsyc.2021.12.009; Tobias U. Hauser et al., "Cognitive Flexibility in Adolescence: Neural and Behavioral Mechanisms of Reward Prediction Error Processing in Adaptive Decision Making during Development," *NeuroImage* 104 (January 2015): 347–54, https://doi.org/10.1016/j.neuroimage.2014.09.018.

39 *switch what they pay attention to more rapidly than adults*: Eckstein et al., "Reinforcement Learning and Bayesian Inference Provide Complementary Models for the Unique Advantage of Adolescents in Stochastic Reversal."

39 *including Galván's students*: Eva H. Telzer, "Dopaminergic Reward Sensitivity Can Promote Adolescent Health: A New Perspective on the Mechanism of Ventral Striatum Activation," *Developmental Cognitive Neuroscience* 17 (February 2016): 57–67.

39 *Kevin is in his early twenties*: Estrada interview.

39 *Ron Dahl published in 2014 with Jennifer Silk*: Kyung Hwa Lee et al., "Neural Responses to Maternal Criticism in Healthy Youth," *Social Cognitive and Affective Neuroscience* 10, no. 7 (July 2015): 902–12, https://doi.org/10.1093/scan/nsu133.

40 *Here's an example of what a teenager heard*: Lee et al., "Neural Responses to Maternal Criticism in Healthy Youth."

40 *Young people hate being made to feel like that*: Ruck, Abramovitch, and Keating, "Children's and Adolescents' Understanding of Rights"; Isabelle D. Cherney and Yee L.

Shing, "Children's Nurturance and Self-Determination Rights: A Cross-Cultural Perspective," *Journal of Social Issues* 64, no. 4 (December 2008): 835–56, https://doi .org/10.1111/j.1540-4560.2008.00591.x.

42 *able to use newly available technology*: Diane Goldenberg and Adriana Galván, "The Use of Functional and Effective Connectivity Techniques to Understand the De-veloping Brain," *Developmental Cognitive Neuroscience* 12 (April 2015): 155–64; B. J. Casey, Adriana Galván, and Leah H. Somerville, "Beyond Simple Models of Adolescence to an Integrated Circuit-Based Account: A Commentary," *Develop-mental Cognitive Neuroscience* 17 (February 2016): 128–30; Jennifer H. Pfeifer and Nicholas B. Allen, "Arrested Development? Reconsidering Dual-Systems Models of Brain Function in Adolescence and Disorders," *Trends in Cognitive Sciences* 16, no. 6 (May 2012): 322–29.

42 *first with animal brains*: Dylan G. Gee et al., "Early Developmental Emergence of Human Amygdala–Prefrontal Connectivity after Maternal Deprivation," *Proceed-ings of the National Academy of Sciences* 110, no. 39 (2013): 15638–43, https://doi .org/10.1073/pnas.1307893110.

42 *later with human brains*: Dominic S. Fareri et al., "Normative Development of Ven-tral Striatal Resting State Connectivity in Humans," *NeuroImage* 118 (September 2015): 422–37; Andrea Pelletier-Baldelli et al., "Brain Network Connectivity during Peer Evaluation in Adolescent Females: Associations with Age, Pubertal Hormones, Timing, and Status," *Developmental Cognitive Neuroscience* 66 (April 2024): 101357, https://doi.org/10.1016/j.dcn.2024.101357.

42 *talking to each other in exactly the opposite way*: Matthew Luke Dixon and Carol S. Dweck, "The Amygdala and the Prefrontal Cortex: The Co-construction of Intel-ligent Decision-Making," *Psychological Review* 129, no. 6 (2022): 1414–41, https:// doi.org/10.1037/rev0000339; Casey, Galván, and Somerville, "Beyond Simple Mod-els of Adolescence to an Integrated Circuit-Based Account."

43 *such as helping others or looking good in front of a peer*: Eva H. Telzer et al., "Neural Sensitivity to Eudaimonic and Hedonic Rewards Differentially Predict Adolescent Depressive Symptoms over Time," *Proceedings of the National Academy of Sciences* 111, no. 18 (2014): 6600–6605, https://doi.org/10.1073/pnas.1323014111; Eva H. Telzer et al., "Chapter Seven - Social Influence on Positive Youth Development: A Developmental Neuroscience Perspective," in *Advances in Child Development and Behavior*, ed. Janette B. Benson, vol. 54 (Cambridge, MA: Academic Press, 2018), 215–58, https://doi.org/10.1016/bs.acdb.2017.10.003; Telzer, "Dopaminergic Re-ward Sensitivity Can Promote Adolescent Health."

43 *Erik Erikson have argued for almost a century*: Erik H. Erikson, *Identity: Youth and Crisis* (New York: W. W. Norton, 1968).

43 *young people become highly attuned to social status and respect*: "The Core Science of Adolescent Development"; Yeager, Dahl, and Dweck, "Why Interventions to Influ-ence Adolescent Behavior Often Fail but Could Succeed."

43 *what this looked like in our evolutionary history*: Schlegel and Barry, *Adolescence*; Jane Goodall, *The Chimpanzees of Gombe: Patterns of Behavior* (Cambridge, MA:

Belknap Press, 1986); Rachna B. Reddy, Aaron A. Sandel, and Ronald E. Dahl, "Puberty Initiates a Unique Stage of Social Learning and Development Prior to Adulthood: Insights from Studies of Adolescence in Wild Chimpanzees," *Developmental Cognitive Neuroscience* 58 (December 2022): 101176, https://doi.org/10.1016/j.dcn.2022.101176.

43 *run the risk of being ostracized, which meant death*: Kipling D. Williams, "Chapter 6 Ostracism: A Temporal Need-Threat Model," in *Advances in Experimental Social Psychology*, ed. Mark P. Zanna, vol. 41 (Cambridge, MA: Academic Press, 2009), 275–314, http://www.sciencedirect.com/science/article/pii/S0065260108004061.

44 *pumps testosterone throughout your bloodstream, which affects many neural systems*: Eveline A. Crone and Ronald E. Dahl, "Understanding Adolescence as a Period of Social-Affective Engagement and Goal Flexibility," *Nature Reviews Neuroscience* 13, no. 9 (September 2012): 636–50, https://doi.org/10.1038/nrn3313; Ronald E. Dahl et al., "Importance of Investing in Adolescence from a Developmental Science Perspective," *Nature* 554, no. 7693 (February 2018): 441–50, https://doi.org/10.1038/nature25770; Cheryl L. Sisk and Julia L. Zehr, "Pubertal Hormones Organize the Adolescent Brain and Behavior," *Frontiers in Neuroendocrinology* 26, no. 3–4 (October 2005): 163–74, https://doi.org/10.1016/j.yfrne.2005.10.003; Wilbrecht and Davidow, "Goal-Directed Learning in Adolescence."

44 *In Shakespeare's play,* The Winter's Tale: William Shakespeare, *The Winter's Tale*, ed. J. H. P. Pafford., The Arden Edition of the Works of William Shakespeare (London: Methuen, 1963).

44 *Dahl points to studies of songbirds*: Beau A. Alward et al., "Testosterone Regulates Birdsong in an Anatomically Specific Manner," *Animal Behaviour* 124 (February 2017): 291–98; Beau A. Alward et al., "The Regulation of Birdsong by Testosterone: Multiple Time-Scales and Multiple Sites of Action," *Hormones and Behavior* 104 (August 2018): 32–40; Gregory F. Ball et al., "How Does Testosterone Act to Regulate a Multifaceted Adaptive Response? Lessons from Studies of the Avian Song System," *Journal of Neuroendocrinology* 32, no. 1 (2020): e12793.

46 *its ever-increasing demands for advanced, technical skills*: David H. Autor, "Skills, Education, and the Rise of Earnings Inequality among the 'Other 99 Percent,'" *Science* 344, no. 6186 (May 2014): 843–51; Daron Acemoglu and David Autor, "Skills, Tasks and Technologies: Implications for Employment and Earnings," in *Handbook of Labor Economics*, ed. David Card and Orley Ashenfelter, vol. 4B (New York: Elsevier, 2011), 1043–1171, https://doi.org/10.1016/S0169-7218(11)02410-5; David J. Deming, "The Growing Importance of Social Skills in the Labor Market" (working paper, National Bureau of Economic Research, August 2015), https://doi.org/10.3386/w21473.

46 *the brains of ten-year-olds and twenty-five-year-olds were similar*: "From 10 to 25: A Game of Adolescent Discovery," UCLA Center for the Developing Adolescent, 2021, accessed April 1, 2024, https://developingadolescent.semel.ucla.edu/core-science-of-adolescence/from-10-to-25-a-game-of-adolescent-discovery.

47 *an interruption in the Australian supply of Marmite*: "Vegemite," National Museum

of Australia, accessed March 19, 2024, https://www.nma.gov.au/exhibitions/defin ing-symbols-australia/vegemite; Robert White, "Vegemite," in *Symbols of Australia: Uncovering the Stories behind the Myths*, ed. Melissa Harper and Richard White (Sydney: University of New South Wales Press, 2010), 135–43; Wikipedia, s.v. "Vegemite," last modified February 21, 2024, https://en.wikipedia.org/w/index.ph p?title=Vegemite&oldid=1209364795; Paul Rozin and Michael Siegal, "Vegemite as a Marker of National Identity," *Gastronomica* 3, no. 4 (2003): 63–67, https://doi .org/10.1525/gfc.2003.3.4.63.

47 *the famous Stanford philosopher David Lewis*: David Lewis, *Papers in Metaphysics and Epistemology: Volume 2* (Cambridge, UK: Cambridge University Press, 1999).

48 *Our experiment used Vegemite*: Quinn Hirschi, David S. Yeager, and Eddie Brummel-man, "Testosterone Increases Behavioral Responsiveness to Respectful Language," *Open Science Framework*, July 11, 2016, https://osf.io/r5yv3/.

49 Should *is a key word*: Maarten Vansteenkiste et al., "Motivating Learning, Perfor-mance, and Persistence: The Synergistic Effects of Intrinsic Goal Contents and Autonomy-Supportive Contexts," *Journal of Personality and Social Psychology* 87, no. 2 (2004): 246–60, https://doi.org/10.1037/0022-3514.87.2.246; Maarten Vansteenkiste et al., "Identifying Configurations of Perceived Teacher Autonomy Support and Structure: Associations with Self-Regulated Learning, Motivation and Problem Behavior," *Learning and Instruction* 22, no. 6 (December 2012): 431–39, https://doi.org/10.1016/j.learninstruc.2012.04.002; Maarten Vansteenkiste et al., "Moving the Achievement Goal Approach One Step Forward: Toward a Systematic Examination of the Autonomous and Controlled Reasons Underlying Achievement Goals," *Educational Psychologist* 49, no. 3 (July 2014): 153–74; Maarten Vansteen-kiste et al., "Examining the Motivational Impact of Intrinsic versus Extrinsic Goal Framing and Autonomy-Supportive versus Internally Controlling Communication Style on Early Adolescents' Academic Achievement," *Child Development* 76, no. 2 (March 2005): 483–501, https://doi.org/10.1111/j.1467-8624.2005.00858.x.

49 *ask, don't tell*: See chapter 6 in this book.

49 *avoiding an I-know-better-than-you attitude*: Deci and Ryan, "The 'What' and 'Why' of Goal Pursuits"; Vansteenkiste et al., "Moving the Achievement Goal Approach One Step Forward."

49 *validate whatever negative experiences*: Renata K. Martins and Daniel W. McNeil, "Review of Motivational Interviewing in Promoting Health Behaviors," *Clinical Psychology Review* 29, no. 4 (June 2009): 283–93; Sune Rubak et al., "Motivational Interviewing: A Systematic Review and Meta-Analysis," *British Journal of General Practice* 55, no. 513 (April 2005): 305–12.

50 *Acknowledge that the young person can make up their own mind*: Deci and Ryan, "The 'What' and 'Why' of Goal Pursuits"; Vansteenkiste et al., "Moving the Achieve-ment Goal Approach One Step Forward."

50 *"doing your part" to help others*: Adam M. Grant, "Relational Job Design and the Motivation to Make a Prosocial Difference," *Academy of Management Review* 32, no. 2 (April 2007): 393–417, https://doi.org/10.5465/AMR.2007.24351328; David

S. Yeager et al., "Boring but Important: A Self-Transcendent Purpose for Learning Fosters Academic Self-Regulation," *Journal of Personality and Social Psychology* 107, no. 4 (October 2014): 559–80, https://doi.org/10.1037/a0037637.

51 *the Vegemite study was also designed*: Hirschi, Yeager, and Brummelman, "Testosterone Increases Behavioral Responsiveness to Respectful Language."

51 *got a dose of testosterone*: Robert Josephs and Craig Herman, Formulations of testosterone and methods of treatment therewith, US Patent US10258631B2, filed August 28, 2015, and issued April 16, 2019, https://patents.google.com/patent/US10258631B2/zh.

53 *They have one of the best teen organ-retention rates in the country*: Chronic Disease Research Group, "Scientific Registry of Transplant Recipients."

53 *Berquist acknowledged*: Dr. William Berquist, interview by the author, August 2022. Details in the chapter later confirmed with Berquist in February 2024.

54 *Like any great mentor*: National Academies of Sciences, Engineering, and Medicine, *The Science of Effective Mentorship in STEMM* (Washington, DC: National Academies Press, 2019), https://doi.org/10.17226/25568.

Chapter 2: The Mentor Mindset

55 The Right Stuff: Tom Wolfe, *The Right Stuff* (New York: Farrar, Straus and Giroux, 1979).

55 Top Gun: *Top Gun*, directed by Tony Scott (Hollywood: Paramount Pictures, 1986).

55 *On the sidelines of that square stood*: Rachna Reddy, interviews by the author, October to November 2022. Fact-checking with Reddy conducted in January 2024.

55 *status work as essential for survival*: Rachna B. Reddy, Aaron A. Sandel, and Ronald E. Dahl, "Puberty Initiates a Unique Stage of Social Learning and Development Prior to Adulthood: Insights from Studies of Adolescence in Wild Chimpanzees," *Developmental Cognitive Neuroscience* 58 (December 2022): 101176, https://doi.org/10.1016/j.dcn.2022.101176; Rachna B. Reddy and Aaron A. Sandel, "Social Relationships between Chimpanzee Sons and Mothers Endure but Change during Adolescence and Adulthood," *Behavioral Ecology and Sociobiology* 74, no. 150 (December 2020), https://doi.org/10.1007/s00265-020-02937-7.

56 *Michael Lewis's book* Liar's Poker: Michael Lewis, *Liar's Poker: Rising through the Wreckage on Wall Street* (New York: W. W. Norton, 1989).

56 *Reddy explained to me*: Reddy interviews.

57 *They live in Uganda*: Reddy, Sandel, and Dahl, "Puberty Initiates a Unique Stage of Social Learning and Development Prior to Adulthood."

57 *report from the U.S. National Academy of Sciences*: National Academies of Sciences, Engineering, and Medicine, *The Science of Effective Mentorship in STEMM* (Washington, DC: National Academies Press, 2019), https://doi.org/10.17226/25568.

57 *in Homer's* Odyssey *was an avatar for Athena*: Homer, *The Odyssey*, trans. Robert Fitzgerald (New York: Farrar, Straus and Giroux, 1998).

58 *a manager at ServiceNow*: Stef Okamoto, interviews by the author, July 2022 to February 2024.

58 *To her direct report Melanie Welch*: Melanie Welch, interview by the author, January 2024. Confirmation of details from Stef Okamoto via email in February 2024.

58 *Melanie was an honors student and an athlete*: "Melanie Welch," Lacrosse, Boston College Athletics, accessed March 20, 2024, https://bceagles.com/sports/womens-lacrosse/roster/melanie-welch/16229.

58 *one of the most successful dynasties in all of college athletics*: "DI Women's Lacrosse Championship History," NCAA, accessed March 20, 2024, https://www.ncaa.com/history/lacrosse-women/d1.

59 *With eleven minutes left in the fourth quarter*: NCAA Championships, "Boston College vs. Syracuse: 2023 NCAA DI Women's Lacrosse Semifinals | FULL REPLAY," posted on YouTube June 30, 2023, https://www.youtube.com/watch?v=sHCzyXSWbZo.

59 *sets up a mentor's dilemma*: Geoffrey L. Cohen, Claude M. Steele, and Lee D. Ross, "The Mentor's Dilemma: Providing Critical Feedback across the Racial Divide," *Personality and Social Psychology Bulletin* 25, no. 10 (October 1999): 1302–18, https://doi.org/10.1177/0146167299258011.

60 *Stef Okamoto doesn't believe in the incompetence model*: Okamoto interviews.

62 *our wise-feedback study in 2014*: D. S. Yeager et al., "Breaking the Cycle of Mistrust: Wise Interventions to Provide Critical Feedback across the Racial Divide," *Journal of Experimental Psychology: General* 143, no. 2 (2014): 804–24, https://doi.org/10.1037/a0033906

62 *Daniel Coyle, in his book* The Culture Code: Daniel Coyle, *The Culture Code: The Secrets of Highly Successful Groups* (New York: Bantam, 2018); "The Simple Phrase That Increases Effort 40%," Daniel Coyle, December 13, 2013, accessed March 20, 2024, https://danielcoyle.com/2013/12/13/the-simple-phrase-that-increases-effort-40/.

62 *soon after I wandered into Uri Treisman's calculus classroom*: Observations of Uri Treisman's teaching conducted by the author from August 2016 to December 2017. One of those semesters I sat with Paul Tough, who wrote about his observations in *The Inequality Machine*. Paul Tough, *The Inequality Machine: How College Divides Us* (New York: Mariner Books, 2021).

62 *Treisman was the walking, talking embodiment of the wise-feedback note*: Philip Uri Treisman, *Improving the Performance of Minority Students in College-Level Mathematics*, vol. 5 (Washington, DC: Distributed by ERIC Clearinghouse, 1983), n17; Uri Treisman, "Studying Students Studying Calculus: A Look at the Lives of Minority Mathematics Students in College," *College Mathematics Journal* 23, no. 5 (1992): 362–72, https://doi.org/10.2307/2686410; Claude M. Steele, "A Threat in the Air: How Stereotypes Shape Intellectual Identity and Performance," *American Psychologist* 52, no. 6 (June 1997): 613–29, https://doi.org/10.1037/0003-066X.52.6.613.

66 *more than eighty years of research*: Research on these styles goes back at least to Kurt Lewin's classic experiments in the 1930s. Kurt Lewin, Ronald Lippitt, and Ralph K. White, "Patterns of Aggressive Behavior in Experimentally Created 'Social Climates,'" *Journal of Social Psychology* 10, no. 2 (1939): 269–99, https://doi.org/10.1080/00224545.1939.9713366.

66 *Kurt Lewin was a Jewish scientist*: Wikipedia, s.v. "Kurt Lewin," last modified February 13, 2024, https://en.wikipedia.org/w/index.php?title=Kurt_Lewin&oldid=1206902406.

66 *Lewin published a revolutionary experiment*: Lewin, Lippitt, and White, "Patterns of Aggressive Behavior in Experimentally Created 'Social Climates.' "

67 *"dull, lifeless, submissive"*: Lewin, Lippitt, and White, "Patterns of Aggressive Behavior in Experimentally Created 'Social Climates,' " 283.

67 *"more spontaneous, more fact-minded, and friendly"*: Lewin, Lippitt, and White, "Patterns of Aggressive Behavior in Experimentally Created 'Social Climates' " 277.

67 *"chased each other around the room wildly"*: Lewin, Lippitt, and White, "Patterns of Aggressive Behavior in Experimentally Created 'Social Climates,'" 289.

68 *"he wasn't strict"*: Lewin, Lippitt, and White, "Patterns of Aggressive Behavior in Experimentally Created 'Social Climates,'" 284.

68 *"just the right combination"*: Lewin, Lippitt, and White, "Patterns of Aggressive Behavior in Experimentally Created 'Social Climates,'" 284.

68 *showed that Lewin's leadership styles applied to parenting as well*: Diana Baumrind, "Current Patterns of Parental Authority," *Developmental Psychology* 4, no. 1, part 2 (1971): 1–103; Diana Baumrind, "Authoritarian vs. Authoritative Parental Control," *Adolescence* 3, no. 11 (Fall 1968): 255–72; Diana Baumrind, "Effects of Authoritative Parental Control on Child Behavior," *Child Development* 37, no. 4 (December 1966): 887–907; Susie D. Lamborn et al., "Patterns of Competence and Adjustment among Adolescents from Authoritative, Authoritarian, Indulgent, and Neglectful Families," *Child Development* 62, no. 5 (October 1991): 1049–65; Laurence Steinberg et al., "Over-Time Changes in Adjustment and Competence among Adolescents from Authoritative, Authoritarian, Indulgent, and Neglectful Families," *Child Development* 65, no. 3 (1994): 754–70.

68 *Baumrind completed her PhD in 1955*: Nadia Sorkhabi and Robert E. Larzelere, "Diana Blumberg Baumrind (1927–2018)," *American Psychologist* 74, no. 7 (October 2019): 850, https://doi.org/10.1037/amp0000492.

68 *the psychologist Eleanor Maccoby later named*: Eleanor E. Maccoby and John A. Martin, "Socialization in the Context of the Family: Parent-Child Interaction," in *Handbook of Child Psychology*, ed. Paul Mussun and E. Mavis Heatherington, 4th ed., vol. 4 (New York: John Wiley & Sons, 1983).

68 *I recently conducted a small study*: This small study was conducted by David Yeager in partnership with Rosalind Wiseman. Students at four middle schools and high schools completed an anonymous survey administered via Qualtrics. The survey defined each of the three mindsets (protector, enforcer, and mentor). Next they answered a series of questions about each, such as: "In the box below, please tell us about a time when a teacher, parent, or another adult treated you with the [Enforcer / Protector / Mentor] mindset. Please describe the situation exactly the way it happened to you—where you were, what you were doing, what they said or did, what it made you think, and how it made you feel. Please write 4–5 sentences."

69 *Baumrind spent much of her later years clarifying*: Robert E. Larzelere, Amanda Sheffield Morris, and Amanda W. Harrist, *Authoritative Parenting: Synthesizing*

Nurturance and Discipline for Optimal Child Development (Washington, DC: American Psychological Association, 2013).

69   *in her book* Good Inside: Becky Kennedy, *Good Inside: A Guide to Becoming the Parent You Want to Be* (New York: HarperCollins, 2022).

70   *Dr. Rosalie Wax was a prominent cultural anthropologist*: Heather Fryer, " 'The Song of the Stitches': Factionalism and Feminism at Tule Lake," *Signs: Journal of Women in Culture and Society* 35, no. 3 (Spring 2010): 673–98.

70   *her brilliant career was derailed by sexism*: "Guide to the Rosalie Hankey Wax Papers 1967–1998," University of Chicago Library, 2008, https://www.lib.uchicago.edu/e/scrc/findingaids/view.php?eadid=ICU.SPCL.WAXRH; Murray L. Wax, "The School Classroom as Frontier," *Anthropology & Education Quarterly* 33, no. 1 (March 2002): 118–30, https://doi.org/10.1525/aeq.2002.33.1.118.

70   *because of a rule that said women could not be paid*: "Guide to the Rosalie Hankey Wax Papers 1967–1998."

70   *to a study of the dire educational conditions on the Pine Ridge Reservation*: Murray L. Wax, Rosalie H. Wax, and Robert V. Dumont Jr., *Formal Education in an American Indian Community: Peer Society and the Failure of Minority Education* (Long Grove, IL: Waveland Press, 1964).

71   *Later authors would label Wax's superteachers* warm demanders: Lisa Delpit, *Other People's Children: Cultural Conflict in the Classroom* (New York: New Press, 1995); Lisa Delpit, *"Multiplication Is for White People": Raising Expectations for Other People's Children* (New York: New Press, 2012); Franita Ware, "Warm Demander Pedagogy: Culturally Responsive Teaching That Supports a Culture of Achievement for African American Students," *Urban Education* 41, no. 4 (July 2006): 427–56, https://doi.org/10.1177/0042085906289710.

71   *The popular business author Kim Scott*: Kim Scott, *Radical Candor: Be a Kick-Ass Boss without Losing Your Humanity* (New York: St. Martin's Press, 2019).

71   *Sergio Estrada teaches at Riverside High School*: This statement was true at the time of the author's interviews with Sergio Estrada conducted between February 2020 and June 2022. Estrada has since moved on to other positions, according to interviews conducted by the author between June 2022 and January 2024.

71   *an analysis of the data from around 1,100 teachers*: Meghann Johnson et al., "Partnering with Expert Teachers to Develop Growth Mindset-Supportive Teacher-Training Materials" (conference presentation, 2023), Society for Research on Educational Effectiveness, Washington, DC.

72   *We called these teachers* bright spots: Chip Heath and Dan Heath, *Switch: How to Change Things When Change Is Hard*, 1st ed. (New York: Broadway Books, 2010); Ruth Baxter et al., "What Methods Are Used to Apply Positive Deviance within Healthcare Organisations? A Systematic Review," *BMJ Quality & Safety* 25, no. 3 (2016): 190–201; Willem Mertens et al., "A Framework for the Study of Positive Deviance in Organizations," *Deviant Behavior* 37, no. 11 (2016): 1288–1307.

72   *95 percent of Sergio's students pass college-level physics each year*: Sergio Estrada interviews.

73 *A Riverside student named Yvonne told me*: Jasmine Estrada called this the "pobre-cito" mindset, which is the idea that teachers think kids are poor and vulnerable and can't handle a high level of challenge. Yvonne (and Sergio Estrada), interview by the author, May 2022.

74 *My contribution to the literature*: David S. Yeager, Ronald E. Dahl, and Carol S. Dweck, "Why Interventions to Influence Adolescent Behavior Often Fail but Could Succeed," *Perspectives on Psychological Science* 13, no. 1 (January 2018): 101–22, https://doi.org/10.1177/1745691617722620; David S. Yeager, Hae-Yeon Lee, and Ronald E. Dahl, "Competence and Motivation during Adolescence," in *Handbook of Competence and Motivation: Theory and Application*, ed. Andrew J. Elliot, Carol S. Dweck, and David S. Yeager, 2nd ed. (New York: Guilford Press, 2017): 431–48.

75 *They get them by* earning prestige: Joseph Henrich and Francisco J. Gil-White, "The Evolution of Prestige: Freely Conferred Deference as a Mechanism for Enhancing the Benefits of Cultural Transmission," *Evolution and Human Behavior* 22, no. 3 (May 2001): 165–96; Eldon E. Snyder, "High School Student Perceptions of Prestige Criteria," *Adolescence* 7, no. 25 (Spring 1972): 129–36; Jerome H. Barkow, "Prestige and Culture: A Biosocial Interpretation," *Current Anthropology* 16, no. 4 (December 1975): 553–72; Joey T. Cheng et al., "Two Ways to the Top: Evidence That Dominance and Prestige Are Distinct yet Viable Avenues to Social Rank and Influence," *Journal of Personality and Social Psychology* 104, no. 1 (2013): 103–25, https://doi.org/10.1037/a0030398"; J. K. Maner and C. R. Case, "Dominance and Prestige," in *Advances in Experimental Social Psychology*, ed. James M. Olson and Mark P. Zanna, vol. 54 (New York: Elsevier, 2016), 129–80, https://doi.org/10.1016/bs.aesp.2016.02.001.

75 *To be respected, in the language of the Tsimane*: Christopher von Rueden, Michael Gurven, and Hillard Kaplan, "The Multiple Dimensions of Male Social Status in an Amazonian Society," *Evolution and Human Behavior* 29, no. 6 (November 2008): 402–15, https://doi.org/10.1016/j.evolhumbehav.2008.05.001.

75 *The Maori tribe in New Zealand has a beautiful term for it*: John C. Moorfield, "Whakamana," Te Aka Māori Dictionary, accessed March 23, 2024, https://www.maoridictionary.co.nz/; R. E. Paenga, "Whakamana Māori: Sociocultural Perspectives of Māori Education in Aotearoa" (master's thesis, University of Canterbury, 2017).

75 *Dr. Joseph Henrich explains that*: Cheng et al., "Two Ways to the Top"; Henrich and Gil-White, "The Evolution of Prestige"; Joseph Henrich, Maciej Chudek, and Robert Boyd, "The Big Man Mechanism: How Prestige Fosters Cooperation and Creates Prosocial Leaders," *Philosophical Transactions of the Royal Society B: Biological Sciences* 370, no. 1683 (December 2015): 20150013, https://doi.org/10.1098/rstb.2015.0013.

75 *Prestige offers a different route to status from dominance*: Cheng et al., "Two Ways to the Top."

76 *stop following as soon as the leader loosens their grip*: Lewin, Lippitt, and White, "Patterns of Aggressive Behavior in Experimentally Created 'Social Climates.' "

76 *Anyone can learn and develop the skills to contribute to their group in some way*: Bruce J. Ellis et al., "The Meaningful Roles Intervention: An Evolutionary Approach to Reducing Bullying and Increasing Prosocial Behavior," *Journal of Research on Adolescence* 26, no. 4 (December 2016): 622–37, https://doi.org/10.1111/jora.12243.

76 *satisfy their needs for status and respect*: Yeager, Dahl, and Dweck, "Why Interventions to Influence Adolescent Behavior Often Fail but Could Succeed."

76 *Read the sentence below and fill in the blanks*: The idea for this activity came from Ethan Burris, a professor of management at the University of Texas at Austin, who uses a version of it in his management and leadership courses.

77 *Research on the authoritarian personality*: Theodor Adorno, Else Frenkel-Brunswik, Daniel J. Levinson, and R. Nevitt Sanford, *The Authoritarian Personality* (New York: Harper & Brothers, 1950); John Levi Martin, "*The Authoritarian Personality*, 50 Years Later: What Questions Are There for Political Psychology?," *Political Psychology* 22, no. 1 (March 2001): 1–26.

77 *My research with my collaborator Carol Dweck*: David S. Yeager and Carol S. Dweck, "Mindsets That Promote Leadership: What We Believe about Young People Influences How We Treat Them" (working paper, University of Texas at Austin, 2024).

78 Dangerous Minds: *Dangerous Minds*, directed by John N. Smith (Hollywood: Hollywood Pictures, 1995).

78 Stand and Deliver: *Stand and Deliver*, directed Ramón Menéndez (Burbank: Warner Bros., 1988).

79 *Geoffrey Cohen's breakthrough research on wise feedback*: Cohen, Steele, and Ross, "The Mentor's Dilemma"; Geoffrey L. Cohen and Claude M. Steele, "A Barrier of Mistrust: How Negative Stereotypes Affect Cross-Race Mentoring," in *Improving Academic Achievement: Impact of Psychological Factors on Education*, ed. Joshua M. Aronson (San Diego: Academic Press, 2002), 303–27; Yeager et al., "Breaking the Cycle of Mistrust."

Chapter 3: The Generational Divide

82 *a grievance-airing tour*: John Mackey, "Whole Foods' John Mackey: 'I Feel Like Socialists Are Taking Over,'" interview by Nick Gillespie, *ReasonTV*, August 12, 2022, https://www.youtube.com/watch?v=3yLJi4hPNa4.

82 conscious capitalism: Isaac Chotiner, "The Whole Foods C.E.O. John Mackey's 'Conscious Capitalism,'" *The New Yorker*, February 22, 2021, https://www.newyorker.com/news/q-and-a/whole-foods-ceo-john-mackeys-conscious-capitalism.

82 *Mackey lamented*: John Mackey, "Whole Foods' John Mackey: 'I Feel Like Socialists Are Taking Over.'"

82 *interviews with Whole Foods employees*: Employees who worked in the Austin, Texas, Whole Foods office, interviews by the author, summer and fall of 2022.

82 *on the job-review site Indeed.com*: A search conducted by the author on Indeed for nationwide Whole Foods retail jobs yielded 13,860 total ratings, with 3,300 (or 24 percent) being a one or two. A search of the same category on the same day yielded just 10 percent for Wegmans grocery stores.

83   *in the Mackey worldview*: This statement is based on (a) the author's interpretations of Mackey's interviews; (b) publicly available profiles such as the previously cited *New Yorker* interview; and (c) confirmation of my opinions with one source who had personal conversations with Mackey on multiple occasions. The author reached out to Mackey's personal email for comment in 2023 and did not receive a reply.

83   *Roughly 68 percent of adults*: Analysis conducted with the Current Population Survey from 2022, using data publicly available at https://data.census.gov/.

85   *trashed the young in his work* Rhetoric: Aristotle, *The Rhetoric of Aristotle: Translated, with an Analysis and Critical Notes*, trans. James Edward Cowell Welldon (London: Macmillan, 1886).

85   *the prominent psychotherapist Anna Freud*: Anna Freud, *The Ego and the Mechanisms of Defence*, The International Psycho-Analytical Library, no. 30 (London: Hogarth Press, 1937).

85   *this generational moral decline is mostly a cognitive illusion*: Adam M. Mastroianni and Daniel T. Gilbert, "The Illusion of Moral Decline," *Nature* 618, no. 7966 (June 2023): 782–89, https://doi.org/10.1038/s41586-023-06137-x.

86   *Dr. Daniel Lapsley and Dr. Robert Enright compared*: Robert D. Enright et al., "Do Economic Conditions Influence How Theorists View Adolescents?," *Journal of Youth and Adolescence* 16, no. 6 (December 1987): 541–59, https://doi.org/10.1007/BF02138820; D. K. Lapsley, R. D. Enright, and R. C. Serlin, "Toward a Theoretical Perspective on the Legislation of Adolescence," *Journal of Early Adolescence* 5, no. 4 (Winter 1985): 441–66, https://doi.org/10.1177/0272431685054004.

86   *President Lyndon B. Johnson said*: Lyndon B. Johnson, "Special Message to the Congress: To Vote at Eighteen—Democracy Fulfilled and Enriched," June 27, 1968, American Presidency Project, https://www.presidency.ucsb.edu/documents/special-message-the-congress-vote-eighteen-democracy-fulfilled-and-enriched.

87   *"Human beings live in the realm of meanings"*: Alfred Adler, *What Life Should Mean to You* (London: Allen & Unwin, 1932).

87   *the* barrier of mistrust: Geoffrey L. Cohen and Claude M. Steele, "A Barrier of Mistrust: How Negative Stereotypes Affect Cross-Race Mentoring," in *Improving Academic Achievement: Impact of Psychological Factors on Education*, ed. Joshua M. Aronson (San Diego: Academic Press, 2002), 303–27

88   *the U.S. National Academy of Sciences defines* mentorship: National Academies of Sciences, Engineering, and Medicine, *The Science of Effective Mentorship in STEMM* (Washington, DC: National Academies Press, 2019), https://doi.org/10.17226/25568.

89   *Meet Ole*: Ole and five employees (two managers and three entry-level retail workers), interviews by the author, September and October 2022. Details about the working conditions and the success of Ole's branch were confirmed through discussions with faculty in the business school at the University of Stavanger.

91   *Wegmans, a grocery store chain on the East Coast*: In 2023, the magazine *Fortune* named Wegmans as number four on the list of the top one hundred companies to work for in the United States. Whole Foods is not on the list. "Fortune Media and Great Place To Work® Name Wegmans to 2023 *Fortune* 100 Best Companies

to Work For," Press Releases, Wegmans, April 4, 2023, accessed March 25, 2024, https://www.wegmans.com/news-media/press-releases/fortune-media-and-great -place-to-work-name-wegmans-to-2023-fortune-100-best-companies-to-work-for/.

91 *Wegmans has half the proportion of one- or two-star reviews*: Analysis of Indeed posts described above.

91 *Wegmans is number one on the* Forbes *list of best employers*: "*Fortune* Best Work- places in Retail™ 2023," Great Place To Work®, accessed March 23, 2024, https:// www.greatplacetowork.com/best-workplaces/retail/2023.

92 *Dr. Melissa Thomas-Hunt sees similar reluctance*: All quotations and stories from Dr. Thomas-Hunt, interview by the author, February 2023.

92 *the Stanford social psychologist Dr. Priyanka Carr*: Priyanka B. Carr, Carol S. Dweck, and Kristin Pauker, " 'Prejudiced' Behavior without Prejudice? Beliefs about the Malleability of Prejudice Affect Interracial Interactions," *Journal of Personality and Social Psychology* 103, no. 3 (2012): 452–71, https://doi.org/10.1037/a0028849.

94 *an after-school program and therapy provider: The Kelly Clarkson Show*, "Spirit Day Pt. 1: Utah Nonprofit Encircle Provides Lifesaving Resources For LGBTQ Youth & Families," posted on YouTube October 20, 2022, https://www.youtube.com /watch?v=X390kIfMNU4; "Encircle | An LGBTQ+ Youth & Family Resource," ac- cessed March 23, 2024, https://encircletogether.org/.

94 *suicide is the leading cause of death for young people*: "Complete Health Indicator Re- port of Suicide," Public Health Indicator-Based Information System, Utah Depart- ment of Health and Human Services, accessed March 23, 2024, https://ibis.health .utah.gov/ibisph-view/indicator/complete_profile/SuicDth.html.

94 *LGBTQ+ youth are three times more likely to contemplate killing themselves*: The Trevor Project, *2022 National Survey on LGBTQ Youth Mental Health—Utah*, 2023, https://www.thetrevorproject.org/wp-content/uploads/2022/12/The-Trevor-Project -2022-National-Survey-on-LGBTQ-Youth-Mental-Health-by-State-Utah.pdf.

94 *many more messages in the religious community about sex and sexuality*: "Stances of Faiths on LGBTQ+ Issues: Church of Jesus Christ of Latter-day Saints (Mormons)," Resources, Human Rights Campaign, accessed March 23, 2024, https://www.hrc .org/resources/stances-of-faiths-on-lgbt-issues-church-of-jesus-christ-of-latter-day -saint.

94 *the staff at Encircle told me*: Encircle founder (Stephanie Larsen), staff, and youth clients, interviews by the author, October 2021.

95 *haven't lost a single kid to suicide*: Larsen interviews.

95 *His research finds*: Dr. Stephen Russell, interview by the author, November 2022; Stephen T. Russell and Kara Joyner, "Adolescent Sexual Orientation and Suicide Risk: Evidence from a National Study," *American Journal of Public Health* 91, no. 8 (August 2001): 1276–81; Caitlin Ryan et al., "Family Acceptance in Adoles- cence and the Health of LGBT Young Adults," *Journal of Child and Adolescent Psy- chiatric Nursing* 23, no. 4 (November 2010): 205–13; Ann P. Haas et al., "Suicide and Suicide Risk in Lesbian, Gay, Bisexual, and Transgender Populations: Review and Recommendations," *Journal of Homosexuality* 58, no. 1 (2010): 10–51.

Chapter 4: Acquiring the Mentor Mindset

97 *Stef Okamoto was born in the late 1960s*: All details about Stef Okamoto, and all quotations, obtained from Okamoto, interviews by the author, August 2022–February 2024.

97 *Sergio Estrada was born in 1991*: Details about Sergio Estrada, and all quotations, obtained from interviews conducted by the author between February 2020 and February 2024. Key details were confirmed and supplemented by interviews with Jasmine Estrada (September 2022) and her mother (December 2023), and Kevin Estrada (December 2022). Details about Sergio Estrada's interactions with students were obtained from interviews with his former students conducted by the author between November 2022 and February 2024.

99 *CEO Steve Ballmer had created what many have described as a toxic corporate culture*: Kurt Eichenwald, "Microsoft's Lost Decade," *Vanity Fair*, August 2012, https://www.vanityfair.com/news/business/2012/08/microsoft-lost-mojo-steve-ballmer; Will Oremus, "The Poisonous Employee-Ranking System That Helps Explain Microsoft's Decline," *Slate*, August 23, 2013, https://slate.com/technology/2013/08/stack-ranking-steve-ballmer-s-employee-evaluation-system-and-microsoft-s-decline.html.

99 *Nadella recounted in his book* Hit Refresh: Satya Nadella, Greg Shaw, and Jill Tracie Nichols, *Hit Refresh: The Quest to Rediscover Microsoft's Soul and Imagine a Better Future for Everyone* (New York: HarperCollins, 2017).

100 *a veteran manager told me*: Interviews by the author, under condition of anonymity, June 2022–December 2023.

100 *I heard from another manager*: Interviews by the author, under condition of anonymity, June 2022–December 2023.

100 *Microsoft's culture during the Ballmer era harmed the bottom line*: Eichenwald, "Microsoft's Lost Decade"; Oremus, "The Poisonous Employee-Ranking System"; Nadella, Shaw, and Nichols, *Hit Refresh*.

100 *he promptly ushered in a "lost decade"*: Eichenwald, "Microsoft's Lost Decade"; Nicholas Thompson, "Why Steve Ballmer Failed," *The New Yorker*, August 23, 2013, https://www.newyorker.com/business/currency/why-steve-ballmer-failed.

100 *generated more revenue than all Microsoft's products*: Eichenwald, "Microsoft's Lost Decade."

100 *The company was losing*: Eichenwald, "Microsoft's Lost Decade"; Thompson, "Why Steve Ballmer Failed"; Oremus, "The Poisonous Employee-Ranking System."

101 *policy he implemented called* stack ranking: Oremus, "The Poisonous Employee-Ranking System"; Elizabeth G. Olson, "Microsoft, GE, and the Futility of Ranking Employees," *Fortune*, November 18, 2013, https://fortune.com/2013/11/18/microsoft-ge-and-the-futility-of-ranking-employees/; Stephen Miller, "'Stack Ranking' Ends at Microsoft, Generating Heated Debate," *SHRM*, November 20, 2013, https://www.shrm.org/topics-tools/news/benefits-compensation/stack-ranking-ends-microsoft-generating-heated-debate; Shira Ovide and Rachel Feintzeig, "Microsoft Abandons 'Stack Ranking' of Employees," *Wall Street Journal*,

November 12, 2023, https://www.wsj.com/articles/SB10001424052702303460004579193951987616572.

100 *managers ranked each employee's performance in one of three tiers*: Microsoft executive, interviews by the author, on condition of anonymity, fall 2022. Also see Miller, " 'Stack Ranking' Ends at Microsoft."

101 *10 percent or so had to be labeled low performers*: Microsoft executive interviews; "Stack Ranking."

101 Rank and yank *it was called*: Miller, " 'Stack Ranking' Ends at Microsoft"; Ovide and Feintzeig, "Microsoft Abandons 'Stack Ranking' of Employees"; Oremus, "The Poisonous Employee-Ranking System."

101 *one former Microsoft vice president told* Vanity Fair: Eichenwald, "Microsoft's Lost Decade."

101 mythology of the demanding leader: Author made this term up. Hence, no citation. Made you look!

101 *the demanding leader of lore was Jack Welch*: Jack Welch and John A Byrne, *Jack: Straight from the Gut* (Dublin: Business Plus, 2003).

101 *"sort the A, B, and C players"*: Welch and Byrne, *Jack.*

101 *"heavy on yelling and short on empathy"*: David Gelles, *The Man Who Broke Capitalism: How Jack Welch Gutted the Heartland and Crushed the Soul of Corporate America—and How to Undo His Legacy* (New York: Simon & Schuster, 2022); Kurt Andersen, "How Jack Welch Revolutionized the American Economy," *New York Times*, June 2, 2022, Books, https://www.nytimes.com/2022/06/02/books/review/the-man-who-broke-capitalism-david-gelles.html.

101 *GE was bloated and bleeding money*: Dr. Ethan Burris, interview by the author, September 2022. Also see Welch and Byrne, *Jack.*

102 *They needed to trim the head count*: Burris interview.

102 *fired more than one hundred thousand employees*: Gelles, *The Man Who Broke Capitalism.*

102 The Man Who Broke Capitalism: Gelles, *The Man Who Broke Capitalism.*

102 *GE recently split into three smaller companies*: Gelles, *The Man Who Broke Capitalism.*

102 *Adam Neumann, former CEO of the disgraced startup WeWork*: Dave Davies, "Short-Term Profits and Long-Term Consequences—Did Jack Welch Break Capitalism?," NPR, June 1, 2022, https://www.npr.org/2022/06/01/1101505691/short-term-profits-and-long-term-consequences-did-jack-welch-break-capitalism.

102 *Neumann's toxic work culture*: Davies, "Short-Term Profits and Long-Term Consequences"; Eliot Brown, "How Adam Neumann's Over-the-Top Style Built WeWork. 'This Is Not the Way Everybody Behaves,'" *Wall Street Journal*, September 18, 2019, https://www.wsj.com/articles/this-is-not-the-way-everybody-behaves-how-adam-neumanns-over-the-top-style-built-wework-11568823827?mod=rsswn.

102 *Calhoun announced that Boeing would return to stack ranking*: Dominic Gates, "Boeing to Slash about 2,000 White-Collar Jobs in Finance and HR," *Seattle Times*, February 6, 2023, https://www.seattletimes.com/business/boeing-aerospace/boeing-to-slash-about-2000-white-collar-jobs-in-finance-and-hr/.

102 *a sarcastic veteran of Ballmer's Microsoft quipped*: Posted on Facebook in February

2023. Kept anonymous to protect the identity of the senior employee who shared it with the author.

102 *Calhoun and his engineers were under fire*: Allison Morrow, "Dave Calhoun Was Hired to Fix Boeing. Instead, 'It's Become an Embarrassment,'" CNN, March 14, 2024, https://www.cnn.com/2024/03/14/business/boeing-ceo-dave-calhoun/index.html.

103 *Douglas McGregor famously called* Theory X: Douglas McGregor, "The Human Side of Enterprise," in *Adventure in Thought and Action*, Proceedings of the Fifth Anniversary Convocation of the School of Industrial Management (Cambridge, MA: Massachusetts Institute of Technology, 1957).

104 *motivated by what the psychologist Dr. Abraham Maslow called*: Abraham H. Maslow, *Motivation and Personality* (New York: Harper and Row, 1954); A. H. Maslow, "A Theory of Human Motivation," *Psychological Review* 50, no. 4 (1943): 370–96, https://doi.org/10.1037/h0054346.

105 *performance evaluation she shared with me*: Okamoto interviews.

108 *Their framework had three parts:* model, coach *and* care: Sherin Shibu and Shana Lebowitz, "Microsoft Is Rolling Out a New Management Framework to Its Leaders. It Centers around a Psychological Insight Called Growth Mindset," *Business Insider*, November 11, 2019, https://www.businessinsider.com/microsoft-is-using-growth-mindset-to-power-management-strategy-2019-11.

108 *Accolades soon followed*: Kathryn Mayer, "How the HR Executive of the Year Rebooted Microsoft's Culture," *Human Resource Executive*, October 6, 2021, https://hrexecutive.com/how-the-hr-executive-of-the-year-rebooted-microsofts-culture/; Kevin Okemwa, "Microsoft Is Officially the Best Company in the World, at Least According to TIME," Yahoo Finance, September 29, 2023, https://finance.yahoo.com/news/microsoft-officially-best-company-world-174543695.html.

108 *was ranked as the best company to work for in the world by Statista and* Time: Okemwa, "Microsoft Is Officially the Best Company in the World."

108 *When Sergio Estrada attended Riverside High School*: Interviews with Sergio Estrada, his family, his best friend, and his former students conducted by the author between February 2020 and February 2024.

113 *The principal directed Sergio to Oscar*: The names of all people connected to Sergio and described in this chapter have been changed to aliases except for Sergio, his family, and his calculus teacher.

116 *hero of the film* Stand and Deliver: *Stand and Deliver*, directed Ramón Menéndez (Burbank: Warner Bros., 1988).

116 *taught many of Escalante's former students*: Uri Treisman, email to the author, October 2022.

116 *"students will rise to the level of expectations"*: *Stand and Deliver*; Jaime Escalante and Jack Dirmann, "The Jaime Escalante Math Program," *Journal of Negro Education* 59, no. 3 (Summer 1990): 407–23.

116 *"barefoot, pregnant, and in the kitchen"*: *Stand and Deliver*.

117 *Michelle Pfeiffer's* Dangerous Minds: *Dangerous Minds*, directed by John N. Smith (Hollywood: Hollywood Pictures, 1995).

117 *Hilary Swank's* Freedom Writers: *Freedom Writers*, directed by Richard LaGravenese, widescreen (Hollywood: Paramount Pictures, 2007).

117 *Her essay titled "Please Stop Talking About* Stand and Deliver*"*: Adriana Heldiz, "Please Stop Talking about *Stand and Deliver*," *New America*, June 29, 2017, http://newamerica.org/weekly/please-stop-talking-about-stand-and-deliver/.

117 *Escalante didn't run his program alone*: Jerry Jesness, "*Stand and Deliver* Revisited," *Reason*, July 2002, https://reason.com/2002/07/01/stand-and-deliver-revisited-2/; Alicia Di Rado, "Math, Minus Escalante: Education: Fewer Students Are Passing a Calculus Placement Test since the Acclaimed Teacher Left Garfield High," *Los Angeles Times*, October 23, 1992, California, https://www.latimes.com/archives/la-xpm-1992-10-23-me-660-story.html; Elaine Woo, "Jaime Escalante Dies at 79; Math Teacher Who Challenged East L.A. Students to 'Stand and Deliver,'" *Los Angeles Times*, April 25, 2013, Obituaries, https://www.latimes.com/local/obituaries/la-me-jaime-escalante31-2010mar31-story.html.

117 *They lavished students with supports*: Escalante and Dirmann, "The Jaime Escalante Math Program."

118 *reality-distortion field of irrationally high standards from one insane man*: Walter Isaacson, *Steve Jobs* (New York: Simon & Schuster, 2011).

118 *in his influential 1956 book* The Presentation of Self in Everyday Life: Erving Goffman, *The Presentation of Self in Everyday Life* (New York: Knopf Doubleday, 2021).

119 *they dress up in backward baseball hats and drink out of red Solo cups*: Kristin Francis, "Red Solo Cups or American Party Cups? Surprising Souvenirs," *Souvenir Finder* (blog), March 21, 2014, https://souvenirfinder.com/red-solo-cups-beer-pong-souvenir-american-party-cups/.

120 *His school soon adopted a program called OnRamps*: OnRamps is currently directed by Jennifer Porter, whose work and dedication are greatly responsible for much of the research I conducted for this book, including finding Sergio Estrada. OnRamps, University of Texas at Austin, accessed March 23, 2024, https://onramps.utexas.edu/.

121 *in walked Santiago, a junior at Riverside in Sergio's class*: Sergio Estrada interview, fall 2021.

Chapter 5: Transparency

125 *"A lack of transparency results in distrust and a deep sense of insecurity"*: This is widely attributed to the Dalai Lama but I was unable to confirm the origin text or occasion.

125 *Andrew is a public school principal*: Andrew, interview by the author, Holdsworth Foundation in Austin, Texas, June 2022.

126 *Jane is a successful mid-career attorney at a large firm*: Jill (an alias), interview by the author, March 2023, as a follow-up to a story the author heard Jill tell at a wedding in fall 2022.

127 *he led a landmark study along with Andrea Dittmann*: Kyle Dobson, Andrea Dittmann, and David Yeager, "A Transparency Statement Transforms Community-Police Interactions" (forthcoming).

128 *When officers are engaged in community policing*: Wesley G. Skogan, *Police and Community in Chicago: A Tale of Three Cities* (New York: Oxford University Press, 2006).

128 *many experiments have evaluated community policing*: Charlotte Gill et al., "Community-Oriented Policing to Reduce Crime, Disorder and Fear and Increase Satisfaction and Legitimacy among Citizens: A Systematic Review," *Journal of Experimental Criminology* 10 (2014): 399–428.

128 *Dobson and Dittmann first decided to get to the bottom of the community policing conundrum*: Kyle Dobson and Andrea Dittman, interviews by the author, June 2021–February 2024.

129 *You can see this dysfunctional cycle in a transcript from a conversation in Dobson's experiment*: Dobson, Dittmann, and Yeager, "A Transparency Statement Transforms Community-Police Interactions."

130 *Dobson observed that a few officers had simply and elegantly solved the threat cycle*: See the qualitative study in Dobson, Dittmann, and Yeager, "A Transparency Statement Transforms Community-Police Interactions."

130 *Dobson called this solution a* transparency statement: See Dobson, Dittmann, and Yeager, "A Transparency Statement Transforms Community-Police Interactions."

132 *electrical signals from the sweat on people's skin*: I'm referring here to electrodermal activity, or EDA. In the supplement of the Dobson, Dittmann, and Yeager paper, we reported a laboratory experiment and a Bayesian analysis that was used to validate the EDA measures' interpretation with respect to positive versus negative stress during interpersonal interactions. For a background on EDA measurement, see Society for Psychophysiological Research Ad Hoc Committee on Electrodermal Measures, "Publication Recommendations for Electrodermal Measurements: Publication Standards for EDA," *Psychophysiology* 49, no. 8 (August 2012): 1017–34, https://doi.org/10.1111/j.1469-8986.2012.01384.x.

134 *Dobson and I got Officer Bohannon and Sergio Estrada together for a beer in Austin to find out*: This was in March 2022.

136 *public opinion surveys show that trust in the police has fallen to an all-time low*: Jeffrey M. Jones, "Confidence in U.S. Institutions Down; Average at New Low," Gallup, July 5, 2022, https://news.gallup.com/poll/394283/confidence-institutions-down-average-new-low.aspx.

136 *legitimate reason to suspect reputational or physical harm from a higher-power person*: Geoffrey L. Cohen and Claude M. Steele, "A Barrier of Mistrust: How Negative Stereotypes Affect Cross-Race Mentoring," in *Improving Academic Achievement: Impact of Psychological Factors on Education*, ed. Joshua M. Aronson (San Diego: Academic Press, 2002), 303–7; Alison V. Hall, Erika V. Hall, and Jamie L. Perry, "Black and Blue: Exploring Racial Bias and Law Enforcement in the Killings of Unarmed Black Male Civilians," *American Psychologist* 71, no. 3 (2016): 175–86.

137 *Dobson did an extra analysis of the officer-civilian transcripts*: Dobson, Dittmann,

and Yeager, "A Transparency Statement Transforms Community-Police Interactions."

137 *Mia Lagunas was a straight-A student*: Mia Lagunas, interview by the author, November 2022.

139 *Dr. Cameron Hecht is an award-winning scholar*: "Cameron A. Hecht," ResearchGate, 2024, https://www.researchgate.net/profile/Cameron_Hecht.

140 *Hecht identified the two critical pieces to this type of speech*: Cameron A. Hecht et al., "Efficiently Exploring the Causal Role of Contextual Moderators in Behavioral Science," *Proceedings of the National Academy of Sciences* 120, no. 1 (2022): e2216315120; Cameron A. Hecht et al., "Beliefs, Affordances, and Adolescent Development: Lessons from a Decade of Growth Mindset Interventions," in *Advances in Child Development and Behavior*, edited by Jeffrey J. Lockman, vol. 61 (Cambridge, MA: Academic Press, 2021), 169–97, https://doi.org/10.1016/bs.acdb.2021.04.004; Mary C. Murphy et al., "Global Mindset Initiative Working Paper 1: Growth Mindset Cultures and Teacher Practices," (working paper, Yidan Prize Foundation, 2021).

Chapter 6: Questioning

142 *"I shall only ask him"*: Plato, *Meno*, trans. Benjamin Jowett (New York: Liberal Arts Press, 1949).

142 *Kate is a mom of two and lives in Chicago*: Kate (an alias), interview by the author, October 2022. Also note three different parents told me a version of this story happening with their own children.

142 *Gary lived alone with his teenage daughter, Charlotte*: Story of Gary (an alias) reported during an interview with Lorena Seidel, conducted by the author, July 2022.

143 *Lorena was born in Brazil to an enforcer-mindset mother*: Lorena Seidel, interviews by the author, April 2022–January 2024. This chapter was sent to Seidel for fact-checking. Seidel interviews are the source of this and all other quotations from her.

146 *Stanford emotion scientist James Gross calls this strategy suppression*: James J. Gross and Oliver P. John, "Individual Differences in Two Emotion Regulation Processes: Implications for Affect, Relationships, and Well-Being," *Journal of Personality and Social Psychology* 85, no. 2 (August 2003): 348–62; James J. Gross, "Emotion Regulation: Current Status and Future Prospects," *Psychological Inquiry* 26, no. 1 (January 2015): 1–26, https://doi.org/10.1080/1047840X.2014.940781.

147 *Jen Wu is now one of Silicon Valley's most influential education-technology venture capitalists*: Jennifer Wu and I worked at Partners in School Innovation in San Francisco when I met her. Now she works for Reach Capital. "Jennifer Wu," LinkedIn, accessed April 1, 2024, https://www.linkedin.com/in/jencwu/.

149 *Elon Musk accused at-home employees of pretending to work*: Dominic Rushe, "Elon Musk Tells Employees to Return to Office or 'Pretend to Work' Elsewhere," The *Guardian*, June 1, 2022, Technology, https://www.theguardian.com/technology/2022/jun/01/elon-musk-return-to-office-pretend-to-work-somewhere-else.

149 *Individual psychology, Alfred Adler, 1927*: Alfred Adler, *Understanding Human Nature* (New York: Greenberg, 1927).

150   *Attachment theory, Mary Ainsworth, 1978*: Mary D. Salter Ainsworth et al., *Patterns of Attachment: A Psychological Study of the Strange Situation* (New York: Lawrence Erlbaum Associates, 1978).

150   *Positive discipline, Jane Nelsen, 1981*: Jane Nelsen, *Positive Discipline: Teaching Children Self-Discipline, Responsibility, Cooperation and Problem-Solving Skills* (Warren, OH: Empowering People, 1981).

150   *Positive psychology, Martin Seligman, 2000*: Martin E. P. Seligman and Mihaly Csikszentmihalyi, "Positive Psychology: An Introduction," *American Psychologist* 55, no. 1 (2000): 5–14.

155   *on display in Plato's famous work of philosophy* Meno: Plato, *Meno*.

155   *aretē in the Greek*: Wikipedia, s.v. "Arete," last modified March 21, 2024, https://en.wikipedia.org/w/index.php?title=Arete&oldid=1214870215.

155   *"There have always been true thoughts in him," Socrates says*: Plato, *Meno*.

156   *some brands of popular psychology tend to spread oversimplified, one-size-fits-all versions of practices like questioning*: Karen Huang et al., "It Doesn't Hurt to Ask: Question-Asking Increases Liking," *Journal of Personality and Social Psychology* 113, no. 3 (2017): 430–52.

156   *In an* authentic question: Sean Kelly et al., "Automatically Measuring Question Authenticity in Real-World Classrooms," *Educational Researcher* 47, no. 7 (October 2018): 451–64, https://doi.org/10.3102/0013189X18785613.

157   *A question* with uptake: Dorottya Demszky et al., "Measuring Conversational Uptake: A Case Study on Student-Teacher Interactions," in *Proceedings of the 59th Annual Meeting of the Association for Computational Linguistics and the 11th International Joint Conference on Natural Language Processing (Volume 1: Long Papers)*, ed. Chengqing Zong et al. (Stroudsburg, PA: Association for Computational Linguistics, 2021), 1638–53, https://doi.org/10.18653/v1/2021.acl-long.130; Dorottya Demszky et al., "Can Automated Feedback Improve Teachers' Uptake of Student Ideas? Evidence from a Randomized Controlled Trial in a Large-Scale Online Course," *Educational Evaluation and Policy Analysis* (2023): https://doi.org/10.3102/01623737231169270.

157   *Authentic questions with uptake are effective*: Demszky et al., "Can Automated Feedback Improve Teachers' Uptake of Student Ideas?"; Adam Gamoran and Martin Nystrand, "Background and Instructional Effects on Achievement in Eighth-Grade English and Social Studies," *Journal of Research on Adolescence* 1, no. 3 (1991): 277–300.

157   *Linguists such as Dora Demszky*: Demszky et al., "Measuring Conversational Uptake"; Demszky et al., "Can Automated Feedback Improve Teachers' Uptake of Student Ideas?"

157   *Authentic questions also have a beneficial effect on* cognition: Herbert H. Clark and Edward F. Schaefer, "Contributing to Discourse," *Cognitive Science* 13, no. 2 (April 1989): 259–94, https://doi.org/10.1207/s15516709cog1302_7; Demszky et al., "Measuring Conversational Uptake"; Sterling Alic et al., "Computationally Identifying Funneling and Focusing Questions in Classroom Discourse," in *Proceedings of the 17th Workshop on Innovative Use of NLP for Building Educational Applications*

(BEA 2022), ed. Ekaterina Kochmar et al. (Stroudsburg, PA: Association for Computational Linguistics, 2022), 224–33.

158   *considered the best hostage negotiator in the world*: Chris Voss and Tahl Raz, *Never Split the Difference: Negotiating as If Your Life Depended on It* (New York: Harper-Collins, 2016); "Chris Voss," The Black Swan Group, accessed April 1, 2024, https://www.blackswanltd.com/chris-voss.

158   Never Split the Difference *(and in his excellent MasterClass videos)*: Voss and Raz, *Never Split the Difference.*

158   *Voss's most interesting practice is* mirroring: Chris Voss, "Mirroring," Masterclass, accessed April 1, 2024, https://www.masterclass.com/classes/chris-voss-teaches-the-art-of-negotiation/chapters/mirroring.

158   *"I heard every word you said word for word"*: Voss, "Mirroring."

158   *described by sociolinguist Gail Jefferson in 1972*: Gail Jefferson, "Side Sequences," in *Studies in Social Interaction*, ed. David Sudnow (New York: Free Press, 1972), 294–338; Gail Jefferson, "Sequential Aspects of Storytelling in Conversation," in *Studies in the Organization of Conversational Interaction*, ed. Jim Schenkein (New York: Academic Press, 1978), 219–48.

159   *Consider this example from a negotiation between a mother and her teenage daughter*: Jefferson, "Side Sequences."

160   *Stanford psychologist Mark Lepper*: Mark R. Lepper and Maria Woolverton, "The Wisdom of Practice: Lessons Learned from the Study of Highly Effective Tutors," in *Improving Academic Achievement: Impact of Psychological Factors on Education*, ed. Joshua Aronson (San Diego: Academic Press, 2002), 135–58.

160   *University of Wisconsin–Madison researchers Martin Nystrand and Adam Gamoran*: Gamoran and Nystrand, "Background and Instructional Effects on Achievement in Eighth-Grade English and Social Studies."

161   *Dora Demszky and her team randomly assigned teachers*: Demszky et al., "Can Automated Feedback Improve Teachers' Uptake of Student Ideas?"

161   *I often saw Sergio question his students rather than tell them information*: The author first saw this on the day he met Estrada, which was during the "bright spots" meeting in Feburary 2020.

162   *Stef's former direct report Salonee Shah*: Salonee Shah, interview by the author, November 2022.

163   *Dr. Edgar Schein and Peter Schein*: Edgar H. Schein and Peter A. Schein, *Humble Inquiry: The Gentle Art of Asking Instead of Telling*, 2nd ed. (San Francisco: Berrett-Koehler, 2021).

163   *Others have called it* respectful inquiry: Niels Van Quaquebeke and Will Felps, "Respectful Inquiry: A Motivational Account of Leading through Asking Questions and Listening," *Academy of Management Review* 43, no. 1 (January 2018): 5–27.

163   *The Scheins define humble inquiry as*: Schein and Schein, *Humble Inquiry.*

163   *Lorena Seidel has a beautiful little routine*: Seidel interviews.

167   *One senior administrator at Encircle told me*: Encircle staff, interviews by the author, October 2022.

168   *Charlotte was staying up later and later to chat online with her Canadian boyfriend*:
      Seidel interviews.

Chapter 7: Stress

173   *Although stressful experiences feel unpleasant*: David S. Yeager et al., "A Synergis-
      tic Mindsets Intervention Protects Adolescents from Stress," *Nature* 607, no. 7919
      (2022).

173   *The last decade has ushered in a revolution in the science of stress*: Alia J. Crum, Peter
      Salovey, and Shawn Achor, "Rethinking Stress: The Role of Mindsets in Determin-
      ing the Stress Response," *Journal of Personality and Social Psychology* 104, no. 4
      (April 2013): 716–33, https://doi.org/10.1037/a0031201; Alia J. Crum, Jeremy P.
      Jamieson, and Modupe Akinola, "Optimizing Stress: An Integrated Intervention
      for Regulating Stress Responses," *Emotion* 20, no. 1 (February 2020): 120–25;
      Jeremy P. Jamieson et al., "Capitalizing on Appraisal Processes to Improve Affec-
      tive Responses to Social Stress," *Emotion Review* 10, no. 1 (January 2018): 30–39,
      https://doi.org/10.1177/1754073917693085; Wendy Berry Mendes and Jiyoung
      Park, "Neurobiological Concomitants of Motivational States," in *Advances in
      Motivation Science*, ed. Andrew J. Elliot, vol. 1 (New York: Academic Press, 2014),
      233–70, https://doi.org/10.1016/bs.adms.2014.09.001; Jim Blascovich and Wendy
      B. Mendes, "Social Psychophysiology and Embodiment," in *Handbook of Social Psy-
      chology*, ed. Susan T. Fiske, Daniel T. Gilbert, and Gardner Lindzey, 5th ed. (New
      York: John Wiley & Sons, 2010), 194–227.

173   *consider this message sent from an undergraduate student named Hawi*: Hawi (an
      alias), email to the author, April 5, 2022. Permission to reprint the email obtained
      by the author in March 2024.

174   *In the years since the fall of 2020*: In my informal count, prior to the pandemic I re-
      ceived one to three emails per semester about students' emotional well-being. Now,
      I typically receive ten to twenty. A survey across higher education institutions ap-
      pears here: Julian Roberts-Grmela, "Emotional Stress Remains a Top Challenge to
      Keeping Students Enrolled," *Chronicle of Higher Education*, March 23, 2023, https://
      www.chronicle.com/article/emotional-stress-remains-a-top-challenge-to-keeping
      -students-enrolled.

174   *Scientific surveys of mental health in the United States show that every year since
      2008*: Monitoring the Future | A Continuing Study of American Youth, accessed
      March 23, 2024, https://monitoringthefuture.org/.

174   *the rate of clinically significant anxiety rose another 300 percent*: Scott Keeter, "Many
      Americans Continue to Experience Mental Health Difficulties as Pandemic En-
      ters Second Year," Pew Research Center, March 16, 2021, https://www.pewresearch
      .org/fact-tank/2021/03/16/many-americans-continue-to-experience-mental
      -health-difficulties-as-pandemic-enters-second-year/; Katherine Schaeffer, "In
      CDC Survey, 37% of U.S. High School Students Report Regular Mental Health
      Struggles during COVID-19 Pandemic," Pew Research Center, April 25, 2022, ac-
      cessed October 6, 2022, https://www.pewresearch.org/fact-tank/2022/04/25/in-cdc

-survey-37-of-u-s-high-school-students-report-regular-mental-health-struggles-during-covid-19/; Scott Keeter, "A Third of Americans Experienced High Levels of Psychological Distress during the Coronavirus Outbreak," Pew Research Center, May 7, 2020, accessed December 27, 2020, https://www.pewresearch.org/fact-tank/2020/05/07/a-third-of-americans-experienced-high-levels-of-psychological-distress-during-the-coronavirus-outbreak/.

174 *An international survey sponsored by Salesforce*: "New Research: 76% of Students Identify Wellbeing as Top Challenge," Salesforce, June 23, 2021, accessed March 23, 2024, https://www.salesforce.com/news/stories/new-research-wellbeing-crisis/.

174 *in a survey from the American Council on Education*: Morgan Taylor et al., "College and University Presidents Respond to COVID-19: 2021 Spring Term Survey, Part II," American Council on Education, May 20, 2021, https://www.acenet.edu/Research-Insights/Pages/Senior-Leaders/Presidents-Respond-COVID-Spring-II.aspx.

174 *Stef Okamoto described the same concern among managers at Microsoft*: Stef Okamoto, interview by the author, fall 2023.

175 *I gave a talk to a large group of PhD-level social psychologists*: Talk in the Social and Personality Area Meeting at the University of Texas at Austin, January 2022.

175 *I interviewed Hawi a year later*: Hawi, interview by the author, May 2023.

175 *calls it the* stress-is-debilitating *belief*: Crum, Salovey, and Achor, "Rethinking Stress."

176 *Crum's work has shown*: Crum, Jamieson, and Akinola, "Optimizing Stress"; Alia J. Crum et al., "The Role of Stress Mindset in Shaping Cognitive, Emotional, and Physiological Responses to Challenging and Threatening Stress," *Anxiety, Stress, & Coping* 30, no. 4 (July 2017): 379–95, https://doi.org/10.1080/10615806.2016.1275585; Crum, Salovey, and Achor, "Rethinking Stress."

176 *We stress about being stressed*: Alia Crum and Thomas Crum, "Stress Can Be a Good Thing If You Know How to Use It," *Harvard Business Review*, September 3, 2015, https://hbr.org/2015/09/stress-can-be-a-good-thing-if-you-know-how-to-use-it; "Dr. Alia Crum: Science of Mindsets for Health & Performance," *Huberman Lab*, January 23, 2022, accessed March 23, 2024, https://www.hubermanlab.com/episode/dr-alia-crum-science-of-mindsets-for-health-performance.

176 *Crum has proposed a* stress-can-be-enhancing *belief*: Crum, Jamieson, and Akinola, "Optimizing Stress"; Crum, Salovey, and Achor, "Rethinking Stress"; Alia J. Crum, Isaac J. Handley-Miner, and Eric N. Smith, "The Stress-Mindset Intervention," in *Handbook of Wise Interventions: How Social Psychology Can Help People Change*, ed. Gregory M. Walton and Alia J. Crum (New York: Guilford Press, 2021), 217–38.

177 *many of young people's most potent stressors come from school*: This was a consistent finding in our large, NIH-supported study of adolescent stress. The data are publicly available at David S. Yeager, "Texas Longitudinal Study of Adolescent Stress Resilience and Health, 2016–2019" (Inter-university Consortium for Political and Social Research [distributor], 2022), https://doi.org/10.3886/ICPSR38180.v1.

178 *youth today are experiencing exceptional levels of stress and mental health problems*: U.S. Surgeon General, *Protecting Youth Mental Health: The U.S. Surgeon General's*

Advisory (Washington, DC: US Department of Health and Human Services, 2021), https://www.hhs.gov/sites/default/files/surgeon-general-youth-mental-health-advisory.pdf.

178 *resort to the language of self-care*: This can be readily seen in a Google Images search for the term *stress management*. (My search conducted on March 23, 2024, yielded only images related to self-care and a stress-is-debilitating mindset.)

179 *while offering* logistical *flexibility*: For a discussion of the distinction between intellectual and logistical rigor, and citations to scholars who first discussed this idea, see Katie Rose Guest Pryal, "When 'Rigor' Targets Disabled Students," *Chronicle of Higher Education*, October 6, 2022, The Review, https://www.chronicle.com/article/when-rigor-targets-disabled-students; Beckie Supiano, "The Redefinition of Rigor," *Chronicle of Higher Education*, March 29, 2022, News, https://www.chronicle.com/article/the-redefinition-of-rigor.

180 *over a year before most of the public knew about generative AI*: "Introducing ChatGPT," Open AI, November 2022, https://openai.com/blog/chatgpt.

180 *The graduation celebration was everything she could have asked for*: I base this statement on an email she sent me on the day she graduated and on a phone call during our interview in May 2023.

180 *the purpose of the human stress system is fundamentally good*: Crum, Jamieson, and Akinola, "Optimizing Stress"; Jeremy P. Jamieson and Emily J. Hangen, "Stress Reappraisal Interventions: Improving Acute Stress Responses in Motivated Performance Contexts," in Walton and Crum, *Handbook of Wise Interventions*, 239–58; Jeremy P. Jamieson, Wendy Berry Mendes, and Matthew K. Nock, "Improving Acute Stress Responses: The Power of Reappraisal," *Current Directions in Psychological Science* 22, no. 1 (February 2013): 51–56; Robert M. Sapolsky, *Why Zebras Don't Get Ulcers: The Acclaimed Guide to Stress, Stress-Related Diseases, and Coping* (New York: Henry Holt, 2004).

180 *To experience stress is to be fit for survival*: Sapolsky, *Why Zebras Don't Get Ulcers*.

180 *careful to distinguish a stressor from a stress response*: Richard S. Lazarus and Susan Folkman, *Stress, Appraisal, and Coping* (New York: Springer, 1984); Susan Folkman et al., "Appraisal, Coping, Health Status, and Psychological Symptoms," *Journal of Personality and Social Psychology* 50, no. 3 (March 1986): 571–79; Susan Folkman et al., "Dynamics of a Stressful Encounter: Cognitive Appraisal, Coping, and Encounter Outcomes," *Journal of Personality and Social Psychology* 50, no. 5 (May 1986): 992–1003.

181 *A* stress response *is how your body or mind reacts to a stressor*: Lazarus and Folkman, *Stress, Appraisal, and Coping*; Folkman et al., "Appraisal, Coping, Health Status, and Psychological Symptoms"; Folkman et al., "Dynamics of a Stressful Encounter."

181 *People's appraisals, or interpretations, of stressful situations*: Lazarus and Folkman, *Stress, Appraisal, and Coping*; James J. Gross, "Emotion Regulation: Current Status and Future Prospects," *Psychological Inquiry* 26, no. 1 (January 2015): 1–26, https://doi.org/10.1080/1047840X.2014.940781; Jamieson et al., "Capitalizing on Appraisal Processes to Improve Affective Responses to Social Stress."

181 *Stanford University affective scientist James Gross*: Gross, "Emotion Regulation."

182 *The human stress system shows a* threat-type stress response: Jamieson et al., "Capitalizing on Appraisal Processes to Improve Affective Responses to Social Stress."

182 *leads the body and the mind to prepare for* damage and defeat: Blascovich and Mendes, "Social Psychophysiology and Embodiment"; Sally S. Dickerson and Margaret E. Kemeny, "Acute Stressors and Cortisol Responses: A Theoretical Integration and Synthesis of Laboratory Research," *Psychological Bulletin* 130, no. 3 (May 2004): 355–91, https://doi.org/10.1037/0033-2909.130.3.355.

182 *Cortisol reduces inflammation in damaged body tissue*: Jamieson et al., "Capitalizing on Appraisal Processes to Improve Affective Responses to Social Stress"; Panayotis Fantidis, "The Role of the Stress-Related Anti-inflammatory Hormones ACTH and Cortisol in Atherosclerosis," *Current Vascular Pharmacology* 8, no. 4 (February 2010): 517–25; Michael W. Whitehouse, "Anti-Inflammatory Glucocorticoid Drugs: Reflections after 60 Years," *Inflammopharmacology* 19, no. 1 (February 2011): 1–19.

182 *being defeated tends to decrease testosterone*: Pranjal H. Mehta and Robert A. Josephs, "Testosterone Change after Losing Predicts the Decision to Compete Again," *Hormones and Behavior* 50, no. 5 (December 2006): 684–92, https://doi.org/10.1016/j.yhbeh.2006.07.001.

183 challenge-type stress response: Jamieson et al., "Capitalizing on Appraisal Processes to Improve Affective Responses to Social Stress"; Blascovich and Mendes, "Social Psychophysiology and Embodiment"; Jim Blascovich et al., "Social 'Facilitation' as Challenge and Threat," *Journal of Personality and Social Psychology* 77, no. 1 (1999): 68–77, https://doi.org/10.1037/0022-3514.77.1.68; Wendy B. Mendes et al., "Challenge and Threat during Social Interactions with White and Black Men," *Personality and Social Psychology Bulletin* 28, no. 7 (2002): 939–52, https://journals.sagepub.com/doi/abs/10.1177/014616720202800707; David S. Yeager et al., "A Synergistic Mindsets Intervention Protects Adolescents from Stress," *Nature* 607, no. 7919 (2022): 512–20.

183 *affective scientists seek to promote challenge-type responses*: Crum, Jamieson, and Akinola, "Optimizing Stress"; Yeager et al., "A Synergistic Mindsets Intervention Protects Adolescents from Stress"; Jamieson et al., "Capitalizing on Appraisal Processes to Improve Affective Responses to Social Stress"; Jamieson, Mendes, and Nock, "Improving Acute Stress Responses."

184 *Jeremy Jamieson, now a professor of psychology at the University of Rochester*: Jamieson is a collaborator of the author's and they have discussed these details many times during their collaborations dating back to 2012.

184 *one of Harvard University's top affective scientists, Dr. Wendy Mendes*: Mendes is now a professor at Yale University. "Wendy Berry Mendes," Department of Psychology, Yale University, accessed March 23, 2024, https://psychology.yale.edu/people/wendy-berry-mendes.

184 *Crum's research on the stress-can-be-enhancing belief*: Crum, Salovey, and Achor, "Rethinking Stress."

184 *Jamieson wrote a scientific article for research participants to read*: Jeremy P. Jamieson

et al., "Turning the Knots in Your Stomach into Bows: Reappraising Arousal Improves Performance on the GRE," *Journal of Experimental Social Psychology* 46, no. 1 (January 2010): 208–12, https://doi.org/10.1016/j.jesp.2009.08.015.

184   *see box 7.2*: Jamieson et al., "Turning the Knots in Your Stomach into Bows."

185   *Jamieson evaluated his scientific article's impact*: Jamieson et al., "Turning the Knots in Your Stomach into Bows."

185   *The other group consisted of older adults*: Jeremy P. Jamieson et al., "Reappraising Stress Arousal Improves Affective, Neuroendocrine, and Academic Performance Outcomes in Community College Classrooms," *Journal of Experimental Psychology: General* 151, no. 1 (2021): 197–212, https://doi.org/10.1037/xge0000893; Jeremy P. Jamieson et al., "Reappraising Stress Arousal Improves Performance and Reduces Evaluation Anxiety in Classroom Exam Situations," *Social Psychological and Personality Science* 7, no. 6 (August 2016): 579–87, https://doi.org/10.1177/1948550616644656.

185   *For the Harvard students*: Jamieson et al., "Turning the Knots in Your Stomach into Bows."

185   *In the community college experiments*: Jamieson et al., "Reappraising Stress Arousal Improves Affective, Neuroendocrine, and Academic Performance Outcomes in Community College Classrooms"; Jamieson et al., "Reappraising Stress Arousal Improves Performance and Reduces Evaluation Anxiety in Classroom Exam Situations."

186   *The reason comes from the power of appraisals*: Jamieson et al., "Capitalizing on Appraisal Processes to Improve Affective Responses to Social Stress"; Gross, "Emotion Regulation."

186   *is called the* transfer problem: J. Kevin Ford, Timothy T. Baldwin, and Joshua Prasad, "Transfer of Training: The Known and the Unknown," *Annual Review of Organizational Psychology and Organizational Behavior* 5 (2018); Brian D. Blume et al., "Transfer of Training: A Meta-Analytic Review," *Journal of Management* 36, no. 4 (July 2010): 1065–1105, https://doi.org/10.1177/0149206309352880.

187   *I got a call from Danielle Krettek Cobb*: In 2022, Krettek Cobb asked for and received permission from Google to publicly describe the work we collaborated on, featured in this chapter. A mention of our Google collaboration was also published here: "Online Mindset Training Protects Adolescents from Stress," *Nature*, (July 2022), d41586-022-01746–4, https://doi.org/10.1038/d41586-022-01746-4.

187   *four years before the public release of ChatGPT*: "Introducing ChatGPT."

188   *we developed the theory of synergistic mindsets*: Yeager et al., "A Synergistic Mindsets Intervention Protects Adolescents from Stress."

188   *growing out of Carol Dweck's research*: David S. Yeager and Carol S. Dweck, "Mindsets That Promote Resilience: When Students Believe That Personal Characteristics Can Be Developed," *Educational Psychologist* 47, no. 4 (October 2012): 302–14, https://doi.org/10.1080/00461520.2012.722805; Carol S. Dweck and David S. Yeager, "Mindsets: A View from Two Eras," *Perspectives on Psychological Science* 14, no. 3 (February 2019): 481–96, https://doi.org/10.1177/1745691618804166; Carol S. Dweck and Ellen L. Leggett, "A Social-Cognitive Approach to Motivation

and Personality," *Psychological Review* 95, no. 2 (April 1988): 256–73, https://doi
.org/10.1037/0033-295X.95.2.256; Daniel C. Molden and Carol S. Dweck, "Finding
'Meaning' in Psychology: A Lay Theories Approach to Self-Regulation, Social Perception, and Social Development," *American Psychologist* 61, no. 3 (2006): 192–203,
https://doi.org/10.1037/0003-066X.61.3.192; Yeager et al., "A Synergistic Mindsets
Intervention Protects Adolescents from Stress."

188 *Crum's stress-can-be-enhancing belief*: Crum, Salovey, and Achor, "Rethinking Stress."

189 *In 1993, biopsychologist Clemens Kirschbaum published*: Clemens Kirschbaum, Karl-
Martin Pirke, and Dirk H. Hellhammer, "The 'Trier Social Stress Test'—a Tool for
Investigating Psychobiological Stress Responses in a Laboratory Setting," *Neuro-
psychobiology* 28, no. 1–2 (1993): 76–81, https://doi.org/10.1159/000119004.

189 *Social stress refers*: Sheldon Cohen, Tom Kamarck, and Robin Mermelstein, "A
Global Measure of Perceived Stress," *Journal of Health and Social Behavior* 24,
no. 4 (December 1983): 385–96, https://doi.org/10.2307/2136404; Dickerson and
Kemeny, "Acute Stressors and Cortisol Responses"; Eefje S. Poppelaars et al., "So-
cial-Evaluative Threat: Stress Response Stages and Influences of Biological Sex and
Neuroticism," *Psychoneuroendocrinology* 109 (November 2019): 104378, https://doi
.org/10.1016/j.psyneuen.2019.104378; Brigitte M. Kudielka and Clemens Kirschbaum, "Sex Differences in HPA Axis Responses to Stress: A Review," *Biological
Psychology* 69, no. 1 (April 2005): 113–32.

189 *In the* cold pressor test: William Lovallo, "The Cold Pressor Test and Autonomic
Function: A Review and Integration," *Psychophysiology* 12, no. 3 (May 1975): 268–82.

190 *In the* carbon dioxide (CO_2) challenge: Jack M. Gorman et al., "High-Dose Carbon
Dioxide Challenge Test in Anxiety Disorder Patients," *Biological Psychiatry* 28, 189
no. 9 (November 1990): 743–57, https://doi.org/10.1016/0006-3223(90)90510-9.

190 *In our studies they're usually aged eighteen to twenty-three*: Yeager et al., "A Synergistic
Mindsets Intervention Protects Adolescents from Stress."

190 *dislike doing mental math in front of others*: Sian L. Beilock and Erin A. Maloney,
"Math Anxiety: A Factor in Math Achievement Not to Be Ignored," *Policy Insights
from the Behavioral and Brain Sciences* 2, no. 1 (October 2015): 4–12, https://doi
.org/10.1177/2372732215601438.

192 *in a 2022 study published in the journal* Nature: Yeager et al., "A Synergistic Mindsets Intervention Protects Adolescents from Stress."

194 *A follow-up experiment showed that both beliefs were important*: See experiment 4 in
Yeager et al., "A Synergistic Mindsets Intervention."

194 *each solitary mindset on its own yielded benefits in other studies*: David S. Yeager et al.,
"A National Experiment Reveals Where a Growth Mindset Improves Achievement,"
Nature 573, no. 7774 (August 2019): 364–69, https://doi.org/10.1038/s41586-019
-1466-y; Crum et al., "The Role of Stress Mindset in Shaping Cognitive, Emotional,
and Physiological Responses to Challenging and Threatening Stress."

194 *we gave the intervention (or a control) to ninth- and tenth-grade students*: See experiment 5 in Yeager et al., "A Synergistic Mindsets Intervention Protects Adolescents
from Stress."

195   *Dr. Cameron Hecht, a postdoctoral fellow at my research institute*: Cameron A. Hecht et al., "When Do the Effects of Single-Session Interventions Persist? Testing the Mindset + Supportive Context Hypothesis in a Longitudinal Randomized Trial," *JCPP Advances* 3, no. 4 (December 2023): e12191, https://doi.org/10.1002/jcv2.12191.

197   *an app that uses AI to give college-application advice*: The application is called ADVI and it was developed as a partnership between the private company Mainstay and a government entity called the Texas Higher Education Coordinating Board. "About Us," Ask ADVi, accessed March 23, 2024, https://askadvi.org/about/. The author has a small financial stake in Mainstay, and so this book will not comment on the efficacy of Mainstay's products.

197   *College applicants normally ask mundane questions*: Andrew Magliozzi, interview by the author, summer 2022.

199   *we asked our most reliable source of mentor-mindset wisdom, Sergio Estrada, to answer the texts*: A spreadsheet of approximately twenty-five text messages from students to advisers was sent to Estrada, without the human advisers' responses. Estrada answered eight of these first and they were discussed with the research team. Next, Estrada answered the remaining messages. This was done to test a broader hypothesis about whether AI could be trained on one body of text messages and then approximate future messages written by Estrada.

200   *In a study led by Michaela Jones and Mac Clapper*: Michaela Jones et al., "Assessing the Ability of Large Language Models to Generate Mindset-Supportive Advisor Messages" (working paper, University of Texas at Austin, August 14, 2023), https://osf.io/bqt4w/.

200   *Hawi told me*: Hawi interview.

Chapter 8: Purpose

202   *"A [person] who becomes conscious of the responsibility"*: Viktor E. Frankl, *Man's Search for Meaning* (New York: Simon & Schuster, 1959).

202   *Damon Munchus is now a leader in J.P. Morgan's machine-intelligence unit*: Damon Munchus, interview by the author, June 2022.

203   *Pearla faces this challenge in her math classroom*: Pearla (an alias), video interview conducted on my behalf by Meghann Johnson (a behavioral scientist who works in my research institute), February 2023.

203   *with just 14 percent of adults receiving four-year college degrees*: Analyses conducted with the American Community Survey, focusing on the county in which Pearla teaches, in June 2023: "American Community Survey (ACS)," US Census Bureau, accessed March 23, 2024, https://www.census.gov/programs-surveys/acs.

203   *only about 10 percent of eighth graders pass state tests at or above grade level*: Analyses conducted using the Texas Education Agency's official statistics: Texas Assessment Research Portal (Cambium), accessed March 23, 2024, https://txresearchportal.com/.

204   *called FUSE (Fellowship Using the Science of Engagement)*: Fellowship Using the

Science of Engagement, University of Texas at Austin, accessed March 23, 2024, https://fuse.prc.utexas.edu/.

205 *When we surveyed their students*: This survey was administered by the OnRamps program in January 2020, under the leadership of Jennifer Porter, and analyses were led by Matthew Giani, who at the time was the head of research for OnRamps. OnRamps, University of Texas at Austin, accessed March 23, 2024, https://onramps .utexas.edu/.

205 *we asked students in each year from fifth to tenth grade*: The results of this pilot survey were reported in the supplemental materials of this paper: Stephanie L. Reeves et al., "Psychological Affordances Help Explain Where a Self-Transcendent Purpose Intervention Improves Performance," *Journal of Personality and Social Psychology*, 120, no. 1 (July 2021), https://doi.org/10.1037/pspa0000246.

206 *adults tend to present young people with two sorts of rationales for learning*: Melanie Shanae Gonzalez, "Race, Socioeconomic Status, and Autonomy Support in the Classroom" (PhD diss., Austin, Texas, University of Texas at Austin, 2021).

206 *I recently attended the ASU+GSV Summit*: This conversation occurred at a dinner at ASU+GSV hosted by Schmidt Futures. "Why We Created ASU+GSV Summit," ASU+GSV Summit, accessed March 23, 2024, https://www.asugsvsummit.com /about-the-summit.

206 *due to the well-known phenomenon of* temporal discounting: Kai Ruggeri et al., "The Globalizability of Temporal Discounting," *Nature Human Behaviour* 6, no. 10 (October 2022): 1386–97, https://doi.org/10.1038/s41562-022-01392-w; Till Grüne-Yanoff, "Models of Temporal Discounting 1937–2000: An Interdisciplinary Exchange between Economics and Psychology," *Science in Context* 28, no. 4 (2015): 675–713.

207 *rewards/punishments in the future*: Daniel Kahneman and Amos Tversky, "Prospect Theory: An Analysis of Decision under Risk," *Econometrica* 47, no. 2 (March 1979): 263–92.

207 *young people in particular have a more "hyperbolic" rate of temporal discounting*: George Ainslie and Nick Haslam, "Hyperbolic Discounting," in *Choice over Time*, ed. George Loewenstein and Jon Elster (New York: Russell Sage Foundation, 1992), 57–92; Partha Dasgupta and Eric Maskin, "Uncertainty and Hyperbolic Discounting," *American Economic Review* 95, no. 4 (September 2005): 1290–99; David Laibson, "Golden Eggs and Hyperbolic Discounting," *Quarterly Journal of Economics* 112, no. 2 (1997): 443–77; Ariel Rubinstein, " 'Economics and Psychology'? The Case of Hyperbolic Discounting," *International Economic Review* 44, no. 4 (November 2003): 1207–16; "Why Do We Value Immediate Rewards More than Long-Term Rewards," The Decision Lab, accessed March 23, 2024, https://thedecisionlab.com /biases/hyperbolic-discounting.

207 *Don't eat the marshmallow now*: This is a reference to research on the "marshmallow test": Walter Mischel, Yuichi Shoda, and Monica L. Rodriguez, "Delay of Gratification in Children," *Science* 244, no. 4907 (May 1989): 933–38, https://doi .org/10.1126/science.2658056.

208   *a version of the temporal-discounting task that was more relevant to the macaques'*
      daily lives: Tommy C. Blanchard and Benjamin Y. Hayden, "Monkeys Are More Pa-
      tient in a Foraging Task than in a Standard Intertemporal Choice Task," *PloS One*
      10, no. 2 (February 2015): e0117057.

208   *by presenting them with rewards and punishments that are common in their daily*
      social lives: Eva H. Telzer, "Dopaminergic Reward Sensitivity Can Promote Adoles-
      cent Health: A New Perspective on the Mechanism of Ventral Striatum Activation,"
      Developmental Cognitive Neuroscience 17 (February 2016): 57–67; Eva H. Telzer et
      al., "Neural Sensitivity to Eudaimonic and Hedonic Rewards Differentially Predict
      Adolescent Depressive Symptoms over Time," *Proceedings of the National Academy*
      of Sciences 111, no. 18 (2014): 6600–605, https://doi.org/10.1073/pnas.1323014111;
      Kathy T. Do, João F. Guassi Moreira, and Eva H. Telzer, "But Is Helping You Worth
      the Risk? Defining Prosocial Risk Taking in Adolescence," *Developmental Cognitive*
      Neuroscience 25 (June 2017): 260–71, https://doi.org/10.1016/j.dcn.2016.11.008;
      Lydia Denworth, "Adolescent Brains Are Wired to Want Status and Respect: That's
      an Opportunity for Teachers and Parents," *Scientific American*, May 1, 2021, https://
      www.scientificamerican.com/article/adolescent-brains-are-wired-to-want-status
      -and-respect-thats-an-opportunity-for-teachers-and-parents/; Zara Abrams, "What
      Neuroscience Tells Us about the Teenage Brain," *Monitor on Psychology*, July 1,
      2022, https://www.apa.org/monitor/2022/07/feature-neuroscience-teen-brain.

208   *"We work together to get smart for a purpose"*: "More than You Think Possible," EL
      Education, accessed March 24, 2024, https://eleducation.org/resources/more-than
      -you-think-possible.

209   *A Mathematica evaluation study published in 2019*: "Mathematica School Design
      Study," EL Education, accessed March 24, 2024, https://eleducation.org/our-results
      /research-studies/mathematica-school-design-study/.

209   *students complete meaningful, real-world projects that are held to exceptional stan-*
      dards: Ron Berger, Leah Rugen, and Libby Woodfin, *Leaders of Their Own Learn-*
      ing: Transforming Schools through Student-Engaged Assessment (Hoboken, NJ: John
      Wiley & Sons, 2014); Ron Berger, Libby Woodfin, and Anne Vilen, *Learning That*
      Lasts: Challenging, Engaging, and Empowering Students with Deeper Instruction
      (Hoboken, NJ: John Wiley & Sons, 2016); "Models of Excellence," EL Education,
      accessed March 24, 2024, https://eleducation.org/models-of-excellence; "Attributes
      of High-Quality Work," EL Education, accessed March 24, 2024, https://eleduca
      tion.org/resources/attributes-of-high-quality-work/.

210   *Ron Berger is one of the architects behind EL Education's approach*: Berger, Rugen,
      and Woodfin, *Leaders of Their Own Learning*; Berger, Woodfin, and Vilen, *Learning*
      That Lasts.

210   *Berger told me*: Ron Berger, interviews and email correspondences with the author,
      September 2020–February 2024.

211   *The EL Education network of schools grew out of the popular Outward Bound pro-*
      gram: "EL Education - History," accessed March 24, 2024, https://eleducation.org
      /who-we-are/history.

211 *Outward Bound was founded by Kurt Hahn*: Wikipedia, s.v. "Kurt Hahn," last modified February 1, 2024, https://en.wikipedia.org/w/index.php?title=Kurt_Hahn&oldid=1201646310.

211 *Hahn's famous quotation*: Sam Silver, "20 Inspirational Quotes from the Outward Bound Readings Book," *Outward Bound Blog* (blog), March 31, 2020, https://outwardbound.org/blog/20-inspirational-quotes-from-the-outward-bound-readings-book/.

212 *coined the term* norm of self-interest: Dale T. Miller, "The Norm of Self-Interest," *American Psychologist* 54, no. 12 (1999): 1053–60, https://doi.org/10.1037/0003-066X.54.12.1053.

212 *Thomas Hobbes wrote his treatise* Leviathan: T. Hobbes, *Leviathan*, Barnes and Noble Library of Essential Reading (New York: Barnes & Noble Books, 2004).

213 *Miller cites a study of blood bank donations*: Dale T. Miller and Rebecca K. Ratner, "The Disparity between the Actual and Assumed Power of Self-Interest," *Journal of Personality and Social Psychology* 74, no. 1 (1998): 53–62.

213 *could invoke self-interested rationales to entice them to learn*: Gonzalez, "Race, Socioeconomic Status, and Autonomy Support in the Classroom."

214 *Youth obesity has been increasing for decades*: Boyd A. Swinburn et al., "The Global Obesity Pandemic: Shaped by Global Drivers and Local Environments," *Lancet* 378, no. 9793 (August 2011): 804–14; Mohammad H. Forouzanfar et al., "Global, Regional, and National Comparative Risk Assessment of 79 Behavioural, Environmental and Occupational, and Metabolic Risks or Clusters of Risks in 188 Countries, 1990–2013: A Systematic Analysis for the Global Burden of Disease Study 2013," *Lancet* 386, no. 10010 (December 2015): 2287–323, https://doi.org/10.1016/S0140-6736(15)00128-2; Emmanuela Gakidou et al., "Global, Regional, and National Comparative Risk Assessment of 84 Behavioural, Environmental and Occupational, and Metabolic Risks or Clusters of Risks, 1990–2016: A Systematic Analysis for the Global Burden of Disease Study 2016," *Lancet* 390, no. 10100 (September 2017): 1345–422, https://doi.org/10.1016/S0140-6736(17)32366-8.

214 *A person's diet has five times more impact on obesity than physical inactivity*: Forouzanfar et al., "Global, Regional, and National Comparative Risk Assessment of 79 Behavioural, Environmental and Occupational, and Metabolic Risks or Clusters of Risks in 188 Countries, 1990–2013"; Gakidou et al., "Global, Regional, and National Comparative Risk Assessment of 84 Behavioural, Environmental and Occupational, and Metabolic Risks or Clusters of Risks, 1990–2016."

214 *account for an outsize proportion of the problem*: Swinburn et al., "The Global Obesity Pandemic"; David A. Kessler, *The End of Overeating: Taking Control of the Insatiable American Appetite*, Reprint edition (Emmaus, PA: Rodale Books, 2010); Michael Moss, *Salt, Sugar, Fat: How the Food Giants Hooked Us* (New York: Random House, 2013).

214 *even a 1 percent reduction in hypercaloric food intake*: Y. Claire Wang et al., "Health and Economic Burden of the Projected Obesity Trends in the USA and the UK," *Lancet* 378, no. 9793 (August 2011): 815–25.

214 *developing a wide array of programs to change teenagers' food and drink choices*: Eric Stice, Heather Shaw, and C. Nathan Marti, "A Meta-Analytic Review of Obesity Prevention Programs for Children and Adolescents: The Skinny on Interventions That Work," *Psychological Bulletin* 132, no. 5 (2006): 667–91, https://doi.org/10.1037/0033-2909.132.5.667.

214 *examined the effects of all past programs*: Stice, Shaw, and Marti, "A Meta-Analytic Review of Obesity Prevention Programs for Children and Adolescents."

214 *Many conventional anti-obesity programs*: David S. Yeager, Ronald E. Dahl, and Carol S. Dweck, "Why Interventions to Influence Adolescent Behavior Often Fail but Could Succeed," *Perspectives on Psychological Science* 13, no. 1 (January 1, 2018): 101–22, https://doi.org/10.1177/1745691617722620; Christopher J. Bryan et al., "Harnessing Adolescent Values to Motivate Healthier Eating," *Proceedings of the National Academy of Sciences* 113, no. 39 (2016): 10830–35, https://doi.org/10.1073/pnas.1604586113.

215 *Food scientists in laboratories engineer ultraprocessed foods to be addictive*: Moss, *Salt, Sugar, Fat*.

215 *a failed launch of their Habit Heroes attraction*: Marni Jameson, "Disney Closes New Habit Heroes Exhibit after Criticism for Stigmatizing Fat Kids," *Orlando Sentinel*, March 1, 2012, https://www.orlandosentinel.com/2012/03/01/disney-closes-new-habit-heroes-exhibit-after-criticism-for-stigmatizing-fat-kids/; Piper Weiss, "Disney's Habit Heroes Accused of 'Fat-Shaming,'" Yahoo Life, February 29, 2012, https://www.yahoo.com/lifestyle/tagged/health/healthy-living/disneys-habit-heroes-accused-fat-shaming-232300194.html; "Disney's 'Tool of Shame': Florida Resort's Habit Heroes Attraction Closed after Being Accused of Stigmatizing Fat Kids," *Daily Mail*, March 1, 2012, https://www.dailymail.co.uk/news/article-2108811/Disneys-tool-shame-Florida-resorts-Habit-Heroes-attraction-closed-accused-stigmatizing-fat-kids.html.

216 *The Montreal* Gazette *ran the headline*: Misty Harris, "Disney Anti-Fat Attraction Called 'Horrifying,'" *Gazette* (Montreal), February 25, 2012.

216 *Epcot promptly shut the exhibit down*: Marni Jameson, "Disney Closes New Habit Heroes Exhibit"; "Disney's 'Tool of Shame'"; Sarah Boesveld, "Habit Heroes: Disney Shuts Down Anti-Obesity Exhibit after Critics Decry It for Being Insensitive to Overweight People," *National Post*, March, 2, 2012, accessed March 24, 2024, https://nationalpost.com/news/disney-shuts-down-anti-obesity-exhibit-after-critics-decry-it-for-being-insensitive-to-overweight-people.

216 *We changed the exhibit*: In this section I am only describing publicly available information about the revised exhibit. Kristen Kirk, "Habit Heroes Opens at Epcot's Innoventions," *Walt Disney World for Grown Ups* (blog), January 1, 2013, https://www.wdwforgrownups.com/articles/habit-heroes-opens-epcots-innoventions; "Disney World's Reworked Habit Heroes Attraction Opens," *AllEars.Net* (blog), January 22, 2013, https://allears.net/2013/01/22/disney-worlds-reworked-habit-heroes-attraction-opens/; "Habit Heroes Reopens with New Storyline, Characters and Games

at Epcot," *Attractions Magazine*, January 19, 2013, https://attractionsmagazine.com/habit-heroes-reopens-with-new-storyline-characters-and-games-at-epcot/.

216 *Newspapers praised the attraction's "kinder, gentler" approach*: Kirk, "Habit Heroes."

217 *Michael Moss's* Salt Sugar Fat: Moss, *Salt, Sugar, Fat*.

217 *took the form of an exposé of the food companies' manipulative marketing practices*: Bryan et al., "Harnessing Adolescent Values to Motivate Healthier Eating"; Christopher J. Bryan, David S. Yeager, and Cintia P. Hinojosa, "A Values-Alignment Intervention Protects Adolescents from the Effects of Food Marketing," *Nature Human Behaviour* 3, no. 6 (June 2019): 596–603, https://doi.org/10.1038/s41562-019-0586-6.

217 *The content of the article was factual and based on meticulous reporting*: David A. Kessler, *The End of Overeating*; Moss, *Salt, Sugar, Fat*; Jennifer L. Harris et al., "A Crisis in the Marketplace: How Food Marketing Contributes to Childhood Obesity and What Can Be Done," *Annual Review of Public Health* 30 (2009): 211–25.

219 *a* saying-is-believing *exercise*: Gregory M. Walton and Timothy D. Wilson, "Wise Interventions: Psychological Remedies for Social and Personal Problems," *Psychological Review* 125, no. 5 (2018): 617–55, https://doi.org/10.1037/rev0000115; Elliot Aronson, "The Power of Self-Persuasion," *American Psychologist* 54, no. 11 (1999): 875–84, https://doi.org/10.1037/h0088188; Joshua M. Aronson, Carrie B. Fried, and Catherine Good, "Reducing the Effects of Stereotype Threat on African American College Students by Shaping Theories of Intelligence," *Journal of Experimental Social Psychology* 38, no. 2 (March 2002): 113–25, https://doi.org/10.1006/jesp.2001.1491.

219 *you end up convincing yourself*: Aronson, "The Power of Self-Persuasion."

219 make it true: Bryan, Hinojosa, and I got the idea for this activity from the public health researcher and physician Dr. Tom Robinson at Stanford University.

219 *We call this a* values-alignment *approach*: C. J. Bryan, "Values-Alignment Interventions: An Alternative to Pragmatic Appeals for Behavior Change," in *Handbook of Wise Interventions: How Social Psychology Can Help People Change*, ed. Gregory M. Walton and Alia J. Crum (New York: Guilford Press, 2021), 259–85.

219 *by aligning the behavior with something people already care about*: Bryan, "Values-Alignment Interventions"; Kurt Lewin, "Group Decision and Social Change," in *Readings in Social Psychology*, ed. Theodore M. Newcomb and Eugene L. Hartley, 2nd ed. (New York: Holt, 1952), 330–44; Lee Ross and Richard E. Nisbett, *The Person and the Situation: Perspectives of Social Psychology*, 2nd ed. (London: Pinter & Martin, 1991).

220 *came from our analyses of testosterone levels*: Results described by Bryan in this chapter found in Bryan, "Values-Alignment Interventions."

221 The Outsiders, *a tragic young adult novel that ends in conflict and death*: S. E. Hinton, *The Outsiders*, platinum ed. (New York: Penguin Young Readers Group, 1967).

221 *Dr. William Damon, the author of* The Path to Purpose: William Damon, *The Path to Purpose: Helping Our Children Find Their Calling in Life* (New York: Simon & Schuster, 2008).

221 *In 2014, we published a paper showing that it could*: David S. Yeager et al., "Boring but Important: A Self-Transcendent Purpose for Learning Fosters Academic Self-Regulation," *Journal of Personality and Social Psychology* 107, no. 4 (October 2014): 559–80, https://doi.org/10.1037/a0037637.

223 *summarizes the purpose intervention's main argument*: Stephanie L. Reeves et al., "Psychological Affordances Help Explain Where a Self-Transcendent Purpose Intervention Improves Performance," *Journal of Personality and Social Psychology* 120, no. 1 (2021): 1–15, https://doi.org/10.1037/pspa0000246; Yeager et al., "Boring but Important."

224 *we asked them to complete the Academic Diligence Task (ADT)*: The ADT was developed by Sidney D'Mello and Angela Duckworth. The author helped with some of the framing of the task to participants and led some of the early data collection to evaluate the task, but D'Mello and Duckworth deserve the credit for inventing the task. Brian M Galla et al., "The Academic Diligence Task (ADT): Assessing Individual Differences in Effort on Tedious but Important Schoolwork," *Contemporary Educational Psychology* 39, no. 4 (October 2014): 314–25; Benjamin Lira et al., "Large Studies Reveal How Reference Bias Limits Policy Applications of Self-Report Measures," *Scientific Reports* 12, no. 1 (2022), https://doi.org/10.1038/s41598-022-23373-9.

224 *marshmallow test*: Walter Mischel, *The Marshmallow Test: Why Self-Control Is the Engine of Success* (New York: Little, Brown, 2015).

224 *In another experiment we conducted with 338 ninth-grade students*: This study, which is study 2 in our 2014 paper, was a true collaboration with Dave Paunesku, both in terms of writing the intervention and in terms of fielding the experiment via Paunesku's PERTS platform. Paunesku deserves much of the credit for this remarkable experiment. Yeager et al., "Boring but Important."

225 *Our purpose experiment*: It is important to note that there are many other experiments which have taken an approach that is similar to the one we took in the purpose experiments. These experiments asked participants to write about the relevance of their lessons (usually in science) and then showed that students performed better on those lessons over time. Those "relevance" experiments, which have been quite influential in the field, were developed in the laboratory of Dr. Judy Harackeiwicz, at the University of Wisconsin, Madison, and initially led by Judy's protégé Dr. Christopher Hulleman. Chris S. Hulleman and Judith M. Harackiewicz, "Promoting Interest and Performance in High School Science Classes," *Science* 326, no. 5958 (December 2009): 1410–12, https://doi.org/10.1126/science.1177067; Judith M. Harackiewicz and Stacy J. Priniski, "Improving Student Outcomes in Higher Education: The Science of Targeted Intervention," *Annual Review of Psychology* 69 (January 2018): 409–35, https://doi.org/10.1146/annurev-psych-122216-011725.

225 *how did Damon Munchus motivate his early-twenties employees*: Munchus interview.

226 *one of J.P. Morgan's top mentors to diverse, young talent*: "Damon Munchus," LinkedIn, accessed March 24, 2024, https://www.linkedin.com/in/damon-munchus-444b97/.

226 *seem to echo a similar refrain*: David Stillman and Jonah Stillman, *Gen Z @ Work: How the Next Generation Is Transforming the Workplace* (New York: HarperCollins, 2017).

227 *the most stable and meaningful sense of purpose had a* mix *of motives*: David S. Yeager and Matthew J. Bundick, "The Role of Purposeful Work Goals in Promoting Meaning in Life and in Schoolwork during Adolescence," *Journal of Adolescent Research* 24, no. 4 (July 2009): 423–52, https://doi.org/10.1177/0743558409336749; David S. Yeager, Matthew J. Bundick, and Rebecca Johnson, "The Role of Future Work Goal Motives in Adolescent Identity Development: A Longitudinal Mixed-Methods Investigation," in "Identity Formation in Educational Settings," special issue, *Contemporary Educational Psychology* 37, no. 3 (July 2012): 206–17, https://doi.org/10.1016/j.cedpsych.2012.01.004.

227 *researchers who study how anxiety interferes with the brain's functioning*: Sian L. Beilock et al., "More on the Fragility of Performance: Choking under Pressure in Mathematical Problem Solving," *Journal of Experimental Psychology: General* 133, no. 4 (December 2004): 584–600.

Chapter 9: Belonging

228 *"To sustain school success"*: See page 613 in Claude M. Steele, "A Threat in the Air: How Stereotypes Shape Intellectual Identity and Performance," *American Psychologist* 52, no. 6 (June 1997): 613–29, https://doi.org/10.1037/0003-066X.52.6.613.

228 *Christina, a college physics instructor*: Christina Markert (not an alias) is a professor of physics at the University of Texas at Austin and participated in our Texas Mindset Initiative program. "Texas Mindset Initiative—Postsecondary," Behavioral Science & Policy Institute, University of Texas at Austin, accessed March 24, 2024, https://txbspi.prc.utexas.edu/portfolio/texas-mindset-initiative-postsecondary/.

228 *Ingeboerg is a brilliant professional*: Ingeboerg (an alias), story told to the author, October 2022.

229 *Stanford University social psychologist Greg Walton*: Gregory M. Walton and Geoffrey L. Cohen, "A Question of Belonging: Race, Social Fit, and Achievement," *Journal of Personality and Social Psychology* 92, no. 1 (2007): 82–96, https://doi.org/10.1037/0022-3514.92.1.82.

229 *human beings have a basic need to belong and to be accepted*: Carol S. Dweck, "From Needs to Goals and Representations: Foundations for a Unified Theory of Motivation, Personality, and Development," *Psychological Review* 124, no. 6 (November 2017): 689–719, https://doi.org/10.1037/rev0000082; Roy F. Baumeister and Mark R. Leary, "The Need to Belong: Desire for Interpersonal Attachments as a Fundamental Human Motivation," *Psychological Bulletin* 117, no. 3 (May 1995): 497–529, https://doi.org/10.1037/0033-2909.117.3.497; Kipling D. Williams, "Ostracism: A Temporal Need-Threat Model," in *Advances in Experimental Social Psychology*, ed. Mark P. Zanna, vol. 41 (Cambridge, MA: Academic Press, 2009), 275–314; Edward L. Deci and Richard M. Ryan, "The 'What' and 'Why' of Goal Pursuits: Human Needs and the Self-Determination of Behavior," *Psychological Inquiry* 11, no. 4 (2000): 227–68, https://doi.org/10.1207/S15327965PLI1104_01.

229 *prefer to stare at faces and listen to human voices*: Anthony J. DeCasper and William P. Fifer, "Of Human Bonding: Newborns Prefer Their Mothers' Voices," *Science* 208, no. 4448 (June 1980): 1174–76; Anthony J. DeCasper and Melanie J. Spence, "Prenatal Maternal Speech Influences Newborns' Perception of Speech Sounds," *Infant Behavior and Development* 9, no. 2 (April–June 1986): 133–50; Andrew N. Meltzoff and M. Keith Moore, "Newborn Infants Imitate Adult Facial Gestures," *Child Development* 54 (1983): 702–09; György Gergely, Harold Bekkering, and Ildikó Király, "Developmental Psychology: Rational Imitation in Preverbal Infants," *Nature* 415, no. 6873 (2002): 755; Jacques Mehler et al., "A Precursor of Language Acquisition in Young Infants," *Cognition* 29, no. 2 (July 1988): 143–78; Olivier Pascalis, Michelle De Haan, and Charles A. Nelson, "Is Face Processing Species-Specific during the First Year of Life?," *Science* 296, no. 5571 (May 2002): 1321–23.

229 *mother's voice reading* The Cat in the Hat *versus a stranger's voice*: DeCasper and Fifer, "Of Human Bonding."

229 *Carol Dweck published an influential theory*: Dweck, "From Needs to Goals and Representations."

229 *Accepting interactions help babies survive*: Jeffry A. Simpson and Jay Belsky, "Attachment Theory within a Modern Evolutionary Framework," in *Handbook of Attachment: Theory, Research, and Clinical Applications*, ed. Jude Cassidy and Phillip R. Shaver, vol. 2 (New York: Guilford Press, 2008), 131–57.

230 *our need to be accepted becomes tied to our need to feel competent*: Dweck, "From Needs to Goals and Representations."

230 *the basis of earned prestige in a peer group*: Joseph Henrich and Francisco J. Gil-White, "The Evolution of Prestige: Freely Conferred Deference as a Mechanism for Enhancing the Benefits of Cultural Transmission," *Evolution and Human Behavior* 22, no. 3 (May 2001): 165–96; Eldon E. Snyder, "High School Student Perceptions of Prestige Criteria," *Adolescence* 7, no. 25 (Spring 1972): 129–36; Jerome H. Barkow, "Prestige and Culture: A Biosocial Interpretation," *Current Anthropology* 16, no. 4 (December 1975): 553–72; Joey T. Cheng et al., "Two Ways to the Top: Evidence That Dominance and Prestige Are Distinct yet Viable Avenues to Social Rank and Influence," *Journal of Personality and Social Psychology* 104, no. 1 (2013): 103–25, https://doi.org/10.1037/a0030398; J. K. Maner and C. R. Case, "Dominance and Prestige," in *Advances in Experimental Social Psychology*, ed. James M. Olson and Mark P. Zanna, vol. 54 (New York: Elsevier, 2016), 129–80, https://doi.org/10.1016/bs.aesp.2016.02.001.

230 *a breakthrough discovery made by Greg Walton*: Walton and Cohen, "A Question of Belonging."

231 *This process appears in figure 9.2*: Adapted from a figure developed by the author for the College Transition Collaborative's presentations, which was later published in several papers. David S. Yeager et al., "Teaching a Lay Theory before College Narrows Achievement Gaps at Scale," *Proceedings of the National Academy of Sciences* 113, no. 24 (2016): E3341–48, https://doi.org/10.1073/pnas.1524360113; Gregory M. Walton and Shannon Brady, "The Many Questions of Belonging," in *Handbook*

of Competence and Motivation: Theory and Application, ed. Andrew J. Elliot, Carol S. Dweck, and David S. Yeager (New York: Guilford Press, 2017), 272–93.

232 *New York University (NYU) fired Dr. Maitland Jones Jr.*: Stephanie Saul, "At N.Y.U., Students Were Failing Organic Chemistry. Who Was to Blame?," *New York Times*, October 3, 2022, https://www.nytimes.com/2022/10/03/us/nyu-organic-chemistry-petition.html.

232 *"teachers must have the courage"*: Saul, "At N.Y.U., Students Were Failing Organic Chemistry."

232 *he told the* New York Times: Saul, "At N.Y.U., Students Were Failing Organic Chemistry."

232 *Laura Janda, now a globally recognized professor of linguistics*: Anastasia Makarova, Stephen Dickey, and Dagmar Divjak, eds., *Each Venture a New Beginning: Studies in Honour of Laura A. Janda* (Bloomington, IN: Slavica Publishers, 2017).

232 *"all students deserve to be treated with respect"*: Laura Janda, "Treating Students With Respect," *Princeton Alumni Weekly*, December 9, 2022, https://paw.princeton.edu/inbox/treating-students-respect.

232 *according to the administration's report*: Saul, "At N.Y.U., Students Were Failing Organic Chemistry."

233 *home to some of the most advantaged people in the world*: According to Raj Chetty's analyses of tax returns and the intergenerational transfer of wealth via higher education, Princeton ranks as the worst Ivy League university for the largest share of students from rich families, tied for worst for the smallest share of students from poor families, and it is the worst in the "mobility index," which reflects the likelihood that a student was upwardly mobile after attending Princeton. About 44 percent of students at Princeton came from families in the top 5 percent of family income, while just 2.2 percent came from families in the bottom 20 percent of income. Regarding the latter, that's smaller than the proportion of students from families in the top 0.1 percent of income (which was 3.1 percent of the student body). Overall, just 1.3 percent of Princeton students entered the university coming from families in the bottom quartile of family income and ended up in the top quartile.

233 *inclusive excellence*: Sarah Brown, "Race on Campus: 'Inclusive Excellence' Is Everywhere. What Does It Mean?," *Chronicle of Higher Education*, February 8, 2022, https://www.chronicle.com/newsletter/race-on-campus/2022-02-08.

233 *author of the book* Cultures of Growth: M. C. Murphy, *Cultures of Growth: How the New Science of Mindset Can Transform Individuals, Teams and Organisations* (London: Simon & Schuster UK, 2024).

233 *culture of genius tends to create achievement disparities*: Elizabeth A. Canning et al., "STEM Faculty Who Believe Ability Is Fixed Have Larger Racial Achievement Gaps and Inspire Less Student Motivation in Their Classes," *Science Advances* 5, no. 2 (February 2019): eaau4734, https://doi.org/10.1126/sciadv.aau4734.

234 *a lovely study led by the London Business School social psychologist Aneeta Rattan*: Aneeta Rattan and Nalini Ambady, "How 'It Gets Better': Effectively Communicating

Support to Targets of Prejudice," *Personality and Social Psychology Bulletin* 40, no. 5 (May 2014): 555–66, https://doi.org/10.1177/0146167213519480.

234 *the well-known "It Gets Better" campaign*: "About Us," It Gets Better, accessed August 22, 2023, https://itgetsbetter.org/about/.

237 *But he wrote the textbook!*: M. Jones and S. A. Fleming, *Organic Chemistry* (New York: W. W. Norton, 2014).

238 *one of the most remarkable and influential papers*: Gregory M. Walton and Geoffrey L. Cohen, "A Brief Social-Belonging Intervention Improves Academic and Health Outcomes of Minority Students," *Science* 331, no. 6023 (March 2011): 1447–51, https://doi.org/10.1126/science.1198364.

238 *the follow-up analysis (conducted with Dr. Shannon Brady)*: Shannon T. Brady et al., "A Brief Social-Belonging Intervention in College Improves Adult Outcomes for Black Americans," *Science Advances* 6, no. 18 (April 2020): eaay3689, https://doi.org/10.1126/sciadv.aay3689.

239 *We ran three experiments simultaneously*: Yeager et al., "Teaching a Lay Theory before College Narrows Achievement Gaps at Scale."

239 *independent scholars replicated the effects*: Geoffrey D. Borman et al., "Reappraising Academic and Social Adversity Improves Middle School Students' Academic Achievement, Behavior, and Well-Being," *Proceedings of the National Academy of Sciences* 116, no. 33 (2019): 16286–91, https://doi.org/10.1073/pnas.1820317116.

239 *formed a large consortium with social psychologists*: Gregory M. Walton et al., "Where and with Whom Does a Brief Social-Belonging Intervention Promote Progress in College?," *Science* 380, no. 6644 (May 2023): 499–505, https://doi.org/10.1126/science.ade4420.

239 *made Walton's belonging intervention available for free*: "Social Belonging for College Students," PERTS, accessed March 24, 2024, https://www.perts.net/programs/cb.

239 *a kind of snowball effect*: Yeager et al., "Teaching a Lay Theory before College Narrows Achievement Gaps at Scale"; Gregory M. Walton and Timothy D. Wilson, "Wise Interventions: Psychological Remedies for Social and Personal Problems," *Psychological Review* 125, no. 5 (2018): 617–55, https://doi.org/10.1037/rev0000115; David S. Yeager and Gregory M. Walton, "Social-Psychological Interventions in Education: They're Not Magic," *Review of Educational Research* 81, no. 2 (June 2011): 267–301, https://doi.org/10.3102/0034654311405999; Geoffrey L. Cohen et al., "Recursive Processes in Self-Affirmation: Intervening to Close the Minority Achievement Gap," *Science* 324, no. 5925 (April 2009): 400–403, https://doi.org/10.1126/science.1170769.

239 *which psychologists call a* recursive process: Cohen et al., "Recursive Processes in Self-Affirmation"; Yeager and Walton, "Social-Psychological Interventions in Education."

239 *were more likely to get their hooks into the system*: Yeager et al., "Teaching a Lay Theory before College Narrows Achievement Gaps at Scale."

240 *"the final straw lifted from the camel's back"*: This characterization was shared with the author by Dr. Geoffrey Cohen during a meeting about a research project.

240 *Although the intervention seemed like a magic trick*: Yeager and Walton, "Social-Psychological Interventions in Education."

241 *What makes a good belonging story?*: See the belonging guide: G. M. Walton et al., "The Social-Belonging Intervention: A Guide for Use and Customization," Beta Draft, January 2017, http://gregorywalton-stanford.weebly.com/up loads/4/9/4/4/49448111/belonging_guide_overview-jan2017.pdf.

241 *a fellowship program we conducted during the 2020–2021 school year*: The Texas Mindset Initiative (TxMI) fellowship was enabled by the UT Austin College of Natural Sciences (Dean David Vandenbout and Assistant Dean Melissa Taylor) and was co-led by Dr. Kristin Patterson. "Texas Mindset Initiative—Postsecondary."

243 *The results of her storytelling amazed Christina*: TxMI has a video of Christina telling this story. It is available for viewing from the author and the Texas Behavioral Science and Policy Institute upon request.

245 *Moe, the bully who terrorized Calvin*: Bill Watterson, *The Complete Calvin and Hobbes*, (Kansas City, MO: Andrews McMeel Publishing, 2005).

245 *my collaborators and I published a paper that reviewed past studies*: David S. Yeager et al., "Declines in Efficacy of Anti-Bullying Programs among Older Adolescents: Theory and a Three-Level Meta-Analysis," *Journal of Applied Developmental Psychology* 37 (March–April 2015): 36–51, https://doi.org/10.1016/j.appdev.2014.11.005.

246 *When we analyzed the data*: Yeager et al., "Declines in Efficacy of Anti-Bullying Programs among Older Adolescents."

246 *sociologist Robert Faris*: Robert Faris and Diane Felmlee, "Status Struggles: Network Centrality and Gender Segregation in Same- and Cross-Gender Aggression," *American Sociological Review* 76, no. 1 (2011): 48–73, https://doi.org /10.1177/0003122410396196.

247 *they often use these skills to strike the right balance*: Rosalind Wiseman, *Queen Bees and Wannabes: Helping Your Daughter Survive Cliques, Gossip, Boyfriends, and the New Realities of Girl World*, 2nd ed. (New York: Three River Press, 2009); Rosalind Wiseman, *Masterminds & Wingmen: Helping Our Boys Cope With Schoolyard Power, Locker-Room Tests, Girlfriends, and the New Rules of Boy World* (New York: Harmony, 2014).

247 *Instead they look more like leadership-development programs*: Bruce J. Ellis et al., "The Meaningful Roles Intervention: An Evolutionary Approach to Reducing Bullying and Increasing Prosocial Behavior," *Journal of Research on Adolescence* 26, no. 4 (December 2016): 622–37, https://doi.org/10.1111/jora.12243; Joseph P. Allen, Susan Philliber, and Kathy Herre, "Programmatic Prevention of Adolescent Problem Behaviors: The Role of Autonomy, Relatedness, and Volunteer Service in the Teen Outreach Program," *American Journal of Community Psychology* 22, no. 5 (October 1994): 595–615, https://doi.org/10.1007/BF02506896.

247 *Carol Dweck is most well-known*: Carol S. Dweck, *Mindset: The New Psychology of Success* (New York: Random House, 2006); Carol S. Dweck and David S. Yeager, "Mindsets: A View from Two Eras," *Perspectives on Psychological Science* 14, no. 3 (February 2019): 481–96, https://doi.org/10.1177/1745691618804166.

247 *people can also adopt a growth mindset about personality*: Chi-yue Chiu, Ying-yi Hong, and Carol S. Dweck, "Lay Dispositionism and Implicit Theories of Personality," *Journal of Personality and Social Psychology* 73, no. 1 (1997): 19–30, https://doi .org/10.1037/0022-3514.73.1.19; Cynthia A. Erdley et al., "Relations among Children's Social Goals, Implicit Personality Theories, and Responses to Social Failure," *Developmental Psychology* 33, no. 2 (1997): 263–72, https://doi.org/10.1037/0012-1649.33.2.263; Benjamin M. Gervey et al., "Differential Use of Person Information in Decisions about Guilt versus Innocence: The Role of Implicit Theories," *Personality and Social Psychology Bulletin* 25, no. 1 (January 1999): 17–27, https:// doi.org/10.1177/0146167299025001002; Daniel C. Molden and Carol S. Dweck, "Finding 'Meaning' in Psychology: A Lay Theories Approach to Self-Regulation, Social Perception, and Social Development," *American Psychologist* 61, no. 3 (April 2006): 192–203, https://doi.org/10.1037/0003-066X.61.3.192; David S. Yeager and Hae Yeon Lee, "The Incremental Theory of Personality Intervention," in *Handbook of Wise Interventions: How Social-Psychological Insights Can Help Solve Problems*, ed. Gregory M. Walton and Alia J. Crum (New York: Guilford Press, 2021), 305–23; David S. Yeager et al., "The Far-Reaching Effects of Believing People Can Change: Implicit Theories of Personality Shape Stress, Health, and Achievement during Adolescence," *Journal of Personality and Social Psychology* 106, no. 6 (2014): 867–84, https://doi.org/10.1037/a0036335.

248 *some of the only experimental treatments proven*: Yeager and Lee, "The Incremental Theory of Personality Intervention"; David S. Yeager, Hae Yeon Lee, and Jeremy P. Jamieson, "How to Improve Adolescent Stress Responses: Insights from Integrating Implicit Theories of Personality and Biopsychosocial Models," *Psychological Science* 27, no. 8 (August 2016): 1078–91, https://doi.org/10.1177/0956797616649604; Adriana S. Miu and David S. Yeager, "Preventing Symptoms of Depression by Teaching Adolescents That People Can Change: Effects of a Brief Incremental Theory of Personality Intervention at 9-Month Follow-Up," *Clinical Psychological Science* 3, no. 5 (September 2015): 726–43, https://doi.org/10.1177/2167702614548317; David S. Yeager and Carol S. Dweck, "Mindsets and Adolescent Mental Health," *Nature Mental Health* 1, no. 2 (2023): 79–81; David S. Yeager, Kali H. Trzesniewski, and Carol S. Dweck, "An Implicit Theories of Personality Intervention Reduces Adolescent Aggression in Response to Victimization and Exclusion," *Child Development* 84, no. 3 (May/June 2013): 970–88, https://doi.org/10.1111/cdev.12003.

248 *growth mindset of personality intervention*: Yeager and Lee, "The Incremental Theory of Personality Intervention."

248 *a story about an adult who ran into someone who used to bully them*: The inspiration for this framing came from an experiment led by Aneeta Rattan. Aneeta Rattan and Carol S. Dweck, "Who Confronts Prejudice? The Role of Implicit Theories in the Motivation to Confront Prejudice," *Psychological Science* 21, no. 7 (July 2010): 952–59, https://doi.org/10.1177/0956797610374740.

248 *Hatred is a destructive and corrosive emotion*: Eran Halperin et al., "Promoting the Middle East Peace Process by Changing Beliefs about Group Malleability," *Science*

333, no. 6050 (August 2011): 1767–69, https://doi.org/10.1126/science.1202925; Amit Goldenberg, Tamar Saguy, and Eran Halperin, "How Group-Based Emotions Are Shaped by Collective Emotions: Evidence for Emotional Transfer and Emotional Burden," *Journal of Personality and Social Psychology* 107, no. 4 (October 2014): 581–96, https://doi.org/10.1037/a0037462.

249   *when Israelis and Palestinians thought the other group was bad and could never change*: Halperin et al., "Promoting the Middle East Peace Process by Changing Beliefs about Group Malleability."

249   *enter a cyclone of hatred*: David S. Yeager et al., "Adolescents' Implicit Theories Predict Desire for Vengeance after Peer Conflicts: Correlational and Experimental Evidence," *Developmental Psychology* 47, no. 4 (2011): 1090–107, https://doi.org/10.1037/a0023769.

250   *easy to scale up*: David S. Yeager et al., "A National Experiment Reveals Where a Growth Mindset Improves Achievement," *Nature* 573, no. 7774 (August 2019): 364–69, https://doi.org/10.1038/s41586-019-1466-y.

250   *tested this intervention with thousands of students*: David S. Yeager, "Texas Longitudinal Study of Adolescent Stress Resilience and Health, 2016–2019" (Interuniversity Consortium for Political and Social Research [distributor], 2022), https://doi.org/10.3886/ICPSR38180.v1; Jeni L. Burnette et al., "A Systematic Review and Meta-Analysis of Growth Mindset Interventions: For Whom, How, and Why Might Such Interventions Work?," *Psychological Bulletin* 149, no. 3–4 (March–April 2022): 174–205.

250   *one experiment we published in 2013*: Yeager, Trzesniewski, and Dweck, "An Implicit Theories of Personality Intervention Reduces Adolescent Aggression in Response to Victimization and Exclusion."

250   *experienced exclusion by peers in an online game*: Kipling D. Williams and Blair Jarvis, "Cyberball: A Program for Use in Research on Interpersonal Ostracism and Acceptance," *Behavior Research Methods* 38, no. 1 (February 2006): 174–80, https://doi.org/10.3758/BF03192765.

250   *showed 40 percent less revenge*: Here, aggression as measured by the amount of hot sauce allocated to the peer who excluded the participant, knowing that the peer disliked spicy foods. For more on this method see Joel D. Lieberman et al., "A Hot New Way to Measure Aggression: Hot Sauce Allocation," *Aggressive Behavior* 25, no. 5 (January 1999): 331–48, https://doi.org/10.1002/(SICI)1098-2337(1999)25:5<331::AID-AB2>3.0.CO;2-1. The online supplement of Yeager, Trzesniewski, and Dweck, "An Implicit Theories of Personality Intervention Reduces Adolescent Aggression in Response to Victimization and Exclusion" validated that the hot sauce allocation decisions were sufficient proxies for real-world aggressive behaviors.

250   *experiment we published in 2016*: This experiment was only possible because of the contributions of Dr. Hae Yeon Lee. Yeager, Lee, and Jamieson, "How to Improve Adolescent Stress Responses."

250   *Trier Social Stress Test*: Clemens Kirschbaum, Karl-Martin Pirke, and Dirk H.

Hellhammer, "The 'Trier Social Stress Test'—a Tool for Investigating Psychobiological Stress Responses in a Laboratory Setting," *Neuropsychobiology* 28, no. 1–2 (1993): 76–81, https://doi.org/10.1159/000119004.

250 *wallowed in damage and defeat*: Specifically, in our experiment we saw increased cortisol, decreased testosterone, and increased TPR in the control condition relative to baseline and relative to the treatment group. Yeager, Lee, and Jamieson, "How to Improve Adolescent Stress Responses."

250 *new study with more than a thousand ninth-grade students*: Yeager, "Texas Longitudinal Study of Adolescent Stress Resilience and Health, 2016–2019."

251 *improves long-run mental health*: Yeager and Dweck, "Mindsets and Adolescent Mental Health."

251 *independent scholars such as Dr. Jessica Schleider*: Jessica Schleider and John Weisz, "A Single-Session Growth Mindset Intervention for Adolescent Anxiety and Depression: 9-Month Outcomes of a Randomized Trial," *Journal of Child Psychology and Psychiatry* 59, no. 2 (February 2018): 160–70; Jessica L. Schleider and John R. Weisz, "Little Treatments, Promising Effects? Meta-Analysis of Single-Session Interventions for Youth Psychiatric Problems," *Journal of the American Academy of Child & Adolescent Psychiatry* 56, no. 2 (February 2017): 107–15, https://doi.org/10.1016/j.jaac.2016.11.007.

251 *surprised the clinical psychology community*: For a discussion of the comparisons between conventional clinical psychology treatments and therapies versus the single-session interventions that I developed, see Jessica Schleider, *Little Treatments, Big Effects: How to Build Meaningful Moments That Can Transform Your Mental Health* (London: Little, Brown, 2023).

Chapter 10: Inclusive Excellence

255 *"How do we retain and nurture these people"*: Keivan Stassun, interviews by the author, June 2016–February 2024.

255 *Josh Pepper said to his professor*: Stassun interviews, and Josh Pepper, interview by the author, September 2021. Stassun and Dan were also profiled in a segment on *60 Minutes*: "Recruiting for Talent on the Autism Spectrum," *60 Minutes*, October 4, 2020, https://www.cbsnews.com/news/autism-employment-60-minutes-2020-10-04/.

256 *Stassun has thirteen* Nature *papers*: "About Me," Keivan G. Stassun, Vanderbilt University, accessed March 24, 2024, http://astro.phy.vanderbilt.edu/~stassuk/about.htm.

256 inclusive excellence: Sarah Brown, "Race on Campus: 'Inclusive Excellence' Is Everywhere. What Does It Mean?," *Chronicle of Higher Education*, February 8, 2022, https://www.chronicle.com/newsletter/race-on-campus/2022-02-08.

256 *Frist Center for Autism and Innovation*: "All about Us," The Frist Center for Autism and Innovation, Vanderbilt University, accessed July 12, 2020, https://www.vanderbilt.edu/autismandinnovation/all-about-us/.

256 *Approximately 1 percent of the world's population*: "Autism," Newsroom, World

Health Organization, November 15, 2023, https://www.who.int/news-room/fact -sheets/detail/autism-spectrum-disorders.

257 *works as the communications director for Stassun's center*: "Claire Barnett," Vanderbilt University, accessed October 3, 2019, https://wp0.vanderbilt.edu/tedxvu/previ ousspeakers/claire-barnett/.

257 *In Claire Barnett's words*: Claire Barnett, "Why Autistic Unemployment Is So High," TEDxVanderbiltUniversity, posted on YouTube on January 2, 2020, https://www.you tube.com/watch?v=FVZu557_k04.

258 *Stassun's postdoctoral fellow Pepper told me*: Pepper interview.

258 *maintaining intellectual rigor while allowing logistical flexibility*: Katie Rose Guest Pryal, "When 'Rigor' Targets Disabled Students," *Chronicle of Higher Education*, October 6, 2022, The Review, https://www.chronicle.com/article/when-rigor-targets -disabled-students; Beckie Supiano, "The Redefinition of Rigor," *Chronicle of Higher Education*, March 29, 2022, News, https://www.chronicle.com/article/the -redefinition-of-rigor.

260 *focus on* inclusive excellence: Sarah Brown, "'Race on Campus.'"

260 *ranked all the scientific disciplines by conventional metrics for inclusion*: Sarah-Jane Leslie et al., "Expectations of Brilliance Underlie Gender Distributions across Academic Disciplines," *Science* 347, no. 6219 (January 2015): 262–65, https://doi .org/10.1126/science.1261375.

261 *Studies show that professional physicists*: Leslie et al., "Expectations of Brilliance Underlie Gender Distributions across Academic Disciplines."

261 *graduate programs in physics relied more or less exclusively on a* single number: Casey Miller and Keivan Stassun, "A Test That Fails," *Nature* 510, no. 7504 (June 2014): 303–04.

261 *Dr. Keivan Stassun lit this fire*: Katie Langin, "'GRExit' Gains Momentum as Ph.D. Programs Drop Exam Requirement," *Science*, November 29, 2022, accessed March 24, 2024, https://www.science.org/content/article/gre-exit-gains-momentum -ph-d-programs-drop-exam-requirement-amid-pandemic.

261 *we both spoke on a panel*: KIPP Foundation, "College Presidents Convening Panel— Keivan Stassun," posted on Vimeo in 2016, https://vimeo.com/178173553.

262 *Stassun's graduate program at Vanderbilt*: Research talk delivered in the Texas Behavioral Science and Policy Institute in Austin, Texas, in March 2022.

262 *when she published it in* Nature: Fabienne A. Bastien et al., "An Observational Correlation between Stellar Brightness Variations and Surface Gravity," *Nature* 500, no. 7463 (2013): 427–30.

262 *first-ever Black lead author of an astrophysics paper*: This and other statistics come from my interviews with Stassun and can be seen in KIPP Foundation, "College Presidents Convening Panel—Keivan Stassun."

262 *he pointed out a flaw in the* interpretation *of the GRE scores*: Miller and Stassun, "A Test That Fails."

263 *the quality of high school math teachers isn't evenly distributed*: Francis A. Pearman, "The Effect of Neighborhood Poverty on Math Achievement: Evidence from

a Value-Added Design," *Education and Urban Society* 51, no. 2 (February 2019): 289–307, https://doi.org/10.1177/0013124517715066.

263   *residential zoning, real estate, and property tax policies that go back a century or more*: Vega's high school, which has overall low math performance, was on a block of houses in San Antonio that real estate agents in the 1920s deemed unsellable for white buyers, which meant that loans were scarce and property value growth was stunted. There are many studies of the devastating structural origins of racialized inequality in America. One summary of the evidence, focusing on policies in the last century, is here: Richard Rothstein, *The Color of Law: A Forgotten History of How Our Government Segregated America* (New York: Liveright Publishing, 2017).

264   *When Laura Vega was a little girl*: All reporting on Laura Vega came from three interviews with the author, starting in September 2021, and three interviews with Stassun. Although Vega told the author the story about looking at the stars herself, a version of it was also published two years later: "First a Bridge Program Graduate, Now a NASA Astrophysicist," *APSNews*, January 2023, http://www.aps.org/publica tions/apsnews/202301/bridge.cfm.

265   *the school gets a three out of ten on the data-aggregation site GreatSchools*: Analysis conducted by the author using the GreatSchools website in June 2023.

265   *Schlegel specialized in analyzing the data*: "Eric Schlegel, Ph.D.," College of Sciences, University of Texas at San Antonio, accessed March 24, 2024, https://sciences.utsa .edu/faculty/profiles/schlegel-eric.html.

266   *eventually published in her field's top journal, the* Astrophysical Journal: E. M. Schlegel et al., "NGC 5195 in M51: Feedback 'Burps' after a Massive Meal?," *Astrophysical Journal* 823, no. 2 (May 2016): 75, https://doi.org/10.3847/0004-637X/823/2/75.

266   *Schlegel said*: "The Vaughan Family Endowed Professorship in Physics," University of Texas at San Antonio, accessed March 24, 2024, https://www.utsa.edu/en dowed/profiles/vaughan-family.html; "Laura Vega," College of Sciences, University of Texas at San Antonio, December 7, 2020, https://sciences.utsa.edu/spotlights /alumni/2020/laura-vega.html.

267   *over a quarter of a decade ago, Steele wrote*: Ronald A. Taylor, "A Degree Of Success: 'Stereotype Vulnerability' Being Overcome As Black Students Raise Their SAT Scores And Collect More Degrees," *Black Issues in Higher Education*, 13, no. 26 (Feb. 1996): 18.

268   *Dr. Franita Ware was a PhD student at Emory University*: Franita Ware, interview by the author, February 2023.

268   *article written by her professor Dr. Jacqueline Irvine*: James Fraser and Jacqueline Jordan Irvine, " 'Warm Demanders': Do National Certification Standards Leave Room for the Culturally Responsive Pedagogy of African-American Teachers?," *Education Week* 17, no. 35 (1998): 55–56.

268   *work of the anthropologist Dr. Judith Kleinfeld*: Judith Kleinfeld, "Effective Teachers of Eskimo and Indian Students," *School Review* 83, no. 2 (February 1975): 301–44, https://doi.org/10.1086/443191.

268   *Ware saw something surprising*: Franita Ware, "Warm Demander Pedagogy:

Culturally Responsive Teaching That Supports a Culture of Achievement for African American Students," *Urban Education* 41, no. 4 (July 2006): 427–56, https://doi.org/10.1177/0042085906289710.

268　*how Ware's 2006 article described the students' responses*: Ware, "Warm Demander Pedagogy."

269　*the sociologist Roger Shouse analyzed data from the High School and Beyond (HS&B) study*: Roger C. Shouse, "Academic Press and Sense of Community: Conflict, Congruence, and Implications for Student Achievement," *Social Psychology of Education* 1, no. 1 (March 1996): 47–68.

269　*federal government's National Center for Educational Statistics commissioned the study*: "High School & Beyond (HS&B)," National Center for Education Statistics, accessed March 24, 2024, https://nces.ed.gov/surveys/hsb/.

270　*Stassun said when I asked him about the origins of his inclusive-excellence work*: Stassun interviews. Also see Kevin Waldron, "Astrophysicist Keivan Stassun Wins 2018 AAAS Mentor Award," American Association for the Advancement of Science (AAAS), February 15, 2018, https://www.aaas.org/news/astrophysicist-keivan-stassun-wins-2018-aaas-mentor-award.

270　impostor syndrome: George P. Chrousos and Alexios-Fotios A. Mentis, "Imposter Syndrome Threatens Diversity," *Science* 367, no. 6479 (February 2020): 749–50.

271　*Stassun visited my lab at UT Austin*: Keivan Stassun, visit with the author, March 2022.

Chapter 11: Future Growth, Part One

278　*"Justice, justice you shall pursue"*: " 'Justice, Justice You Shall Pursue . . .' Deuteronomy 16:20," *Lerner School* (blog), September 3, 2019, https://lernerschool.org/2019/09/justice-justice-you-shall-pursue/.

278　*was California's most influential landscape architect of the twentieth century*: Marie Barnidge-McIntyre, "Ralph Dalton Cornell, FASLA," *Eden: Journal of the California Garden & Landscape History Society* 17, no. 4 (Fall 2014): 3–8; Brian Tichenor, "Ralph Cornell—California's First Landscape Architect," posted on YouTube by Claremont Heritage, April 23, 2021, https://www.youtube.com/watch?v=Psf71WjTb54; "The Landscape Designs of Ralph Cornell," The Huntington, November 12, 2017, accessed March 24, 2024, https://huntington.org/videos-and-recorded-programs/landscape-designs-ralph-cornell; "Ralph Cornell—Southern California Dean of Landscape Architecture," The Cultural Landscape Foundation, accessed March 24, 2024, https://www.tclf.org/news/features/ralph-cornell-southern-california-dean-landscape-architecture; Wikipedia, s.v. "Ralph D. Cornell," last modified March 17, 2023, https://en.wikipedia.org/w/index.php?title=Ralph_D._Cornell&oldid=1145140189.

278　*Olmsted, the designer of Central Park, in New York City*: Erik Larson, *The Devil in the White City: Murder, Magic, and Madness at the Fair That Changed America* (New York: Vintage, 2004).

278　*Cornell became the master architect for Pomona College and the University of*

California, Los Angeles: Barnidge-McIntyre, "Ralph Dalton Cornell, FASLA"; Tichenor, "Ralph Cornell"; "The Landscape Designs of Ralph Cornell"; "Ralph Cornell—Southern California Dean of Landscape Architecture"; Wikipedia, s.v. "Ralph D. Cornell."

278 *Torrey Pines' first-ever "dry ground park" in San Diego*: Ibid.

278 *including Beverly Gardens Park, Griffith Park, and the Franklin D. Murphy Sculpture Garden*: Ibid.

278 *I interviewed several of LA's leading landscape architects*: Brian Tichenor and Marie Barnidge-McIntyre, interviews by the author, June–July 2023.

279 *Professor Charles Baker*: Barnidge-McIntyre, "Ralph Dalton Cornell, FASLA"; "Ralph Cornell—Southern California Dean of Landscape Architecture."

279 *Cornell came from a poor family*: Tichenor, "Ralph Cornell"; Ralph D. Cornell et al., "Half a Century as a Southern California Landscape Architect" (Oral History Program, University of California, Los Angeles, 1970), https://static.library.ucla.edu/oralhistory/text/masters/21198-zz0009023k-4-master.html.

279 *Cornell would have run through a brick wall for him*: Cornell et al., "Half a Century as a Southern California Landscape Architect."

279 *eventually they published their art, accompanied by Baker's biological commentary, in academic journals*: Cornell et al., "Half a Century as a Southern California Landscape Architect."

279 *I once met a tattoo artist for rock stars at a bar*: This happened in February 2024 in Austin, Texas. The tattoo artist told me that he does not tattoo images from the same plants on Google Images, and instead looks at images from Ralph Cornell's illustrations.

279 *Cornell said in his oral history sixty years later*: Cornell et al., "Half a Century as a Southern California Landscape Architect."

280 *Brian Tichenor, one of today's leading LA architects, told me*: Brian Tichenor, interview by the author, July 2023. Also see Tichenor, "Ralph Cornell."

280 *Ruth Shellhorn was one of the only female landscape architects working in LA in the mid-century*: Louise A. Mozingo and Linda Jewell, eds., *Women in Landscape Architecture: Essays on History and Practice* (Jefferson, NC: McFarland, 2011).

280 *Dr. Daniel Lapsley is a professor of adolescent psychology*: University of Notre Dame, "Daniel Lapsley," Department of Psychology, University of Notre Dame, accessed March 25, 2024, https://psychology.nd.edu/people/daniel-lapsley/.

280 *He grew up in Pittsburgh*: This story about Lapsley came from personal conversations with the author and from a chapter written by Lapsley. Daniel K. Lapsley, "Strangers, Mentors and Freud," in *The Ones We Remember: Scholars Reflect on Teachers Who Made a Difference*, ed. Frank Pajares and Timothy Urdan, Adolescence and Education (Charlotte, NC: Information Age Publishing, 2008), 189–94. Lapsley fact-checked this information in the fall of 2023.

281 *Lapsley wrote*: Lapsley, "Strangers, Mentors and Freud."

281 *In a paper we published in 2017*: David S. Yeager et al., "Loss of Institutional Trust among Racial and Ethnic Minority Adolescents: A Consequence of Procedural

Injustice and a Cause of Lifespan Outcomes," *Child Development* 88, no. 2 (2017): 658–76.

283 *Its name in the scientific literature is* fade-out: Drew H. Bailey et al., "Persistence and Fade-Out of Educational-Intervention Effects: Mechanisms and Potential Solutions," *Psychological Science in the Public Interest* 21, no. 2 (October 2020): 55–97; Drew Bailey et al., "Persistence and Fadeout in the Impacts of Child and Adolescent Interventions," *Journal of Research on Educational Effectiveness* 10, no. 1 (January 2017): 7–39, https://doi.org/10.1080/19345747.2016.1232459.

285 *A poor score in calculus discourages students*: Treisman, in addition to his work as a calculus instructor, has also led policy initiatives to change calculus pathways in higher education, because it can be unnecessarily determinative of students' educational progress. Here are several reports from national efforts to do this; these reports also discuss the gatekeeping role of calculus in higher education. Karen Saxe and Linda Braddy, *A Common Vision for Undergraduate Mathematical Sciences Programs in 2025* (Washington, DC: Mathematical Association of America, 2015), https://maa.org/sites/default/files/pdf/CommonVisionFinal.pdf; Susan L. Ganter and William E. Haver, eds., *Partner Discipline Recommendations for Introductory College Mathematics and the Implications for College Algebra* (Washington, DC: Mathematical Association of America, 2011), https://maa.org/sites/default/files/pdf/CUPM/crafty/introreport.pdf; Charles A. Dana Center at the University of Texas at Austin, *Launch Years: A New Vision for the Transition from High School to Postsecondary Mathematics* (Austin, TX: 2020), https://www.utdanacenter.org/sites/default/files/2020-03/Launch-Years-A-New-Vision-report-March-2020.pdf; Pamela Burdman, *Degrees of Freedom: Diversifying Math Requirements for College Readiness and Graduation*, (Oakland, CA: LearningWorks, 2015), https://edpolicyinca.org/sites/default/files/PACE%201%2008-2015.pdf; Pamela Burdman et al., *Multiple Paths Forward: Diversifying Mathematics as a Strategy for College Success* (San Francisco: WestEd & Just Equations, 2018).

285 *The course is hard, fast-paced, and unforgiving*: An excellent description of the student perspective on freshman calculus appears in Paul Tough's chapter on Uri Treisman's class: Paul Tough, *The Inequality Machine: How College Divides Us* (New York: Mariner Books, 2021).

286 *freshman calculus is a gatekeeper*: Pamela Burdman and Veronica Anderson, "Calculus Acts as a Gatekeeper," *Inside Higher Ed*, September 11, 2022, accessed March 25, 2024, https://www.insidehighered.com/admissions/views/2022/09/12/admissions-offices-need-change-way-they-treat-calculus-opinion.

286 *Could it be a gateway instead?*: This problem framing was shared by Treisman and his collaborator (and the author's mentor) Tony Bryk, in their work reforming community college math, Anthony S. Bryk and Uri Treisman, "Make Math a Gateway, Not a Gatekeeper," *Chronicle of Higher Education*, April 18, 2010, https://www.chronicle.com/article/make-math-a-gateway-not-a-gatekeeper/.

286 *won the MacArthur Genius Grant*: "Philip Uri Treisman," MacArthur Foundation, 1992, https://www.macfound.org/fellows/class-of-1992/philip-uri-treisman.

286 *In the five years before he launched his workshops, from 1973 to 1977*: These and all other data about the emerging scholars workshops appear in a series of evaluation studies and theses that have evaluated and extracted lessons from the workshops. Uri Treisman, "Studying Students Studying Calculus: A Look at the Lives of Minority Mathematics Students in College," *College Mathematics Journal* 23, no. 5 (1992): 362–72, https://doi.org/10.2307/2686410; Philip Uri Treisman, *Improving the Performance of Minority Students in College-Level Mathematics*, vol. 5 (Washington, DC: Distributed by ERIC Clearinghouse, 1983), n17; Robert E. Fullilove and Philip Uri Treisman, "Mathematics Achievement among African American Undergraduates at the University of California, Berkeley: An Evaluation of the Mathematics Workshop Program," *Journal of Negro Education* 59, no. 3 (Summer 1990): 463–78; Eric Hsu, Teri J. Murphy, and Uri Treisman, "Supporting High Achievement in Introductory Mathematics Courses: What We Have Learned from 30 Years of the Emerging Scholars Program," in *Making the Connection: Research and Teaching in Undergraduate Mathematics Education*, ed. Marilyn P. Carlson and Chris Rasmussen (Washington, DC: Mathematical Association of America, 2008): 205–20; Rose Asera, "Calculus and Community: A History of the Emerging Scholars Program," *Report of the National Task Force on Minority High Achievement* (New York: College Board, 2001).

286 *But once Treisman implemented his workshops*: Treisman, "Studying Students Studying Calculus."

286 *According to one account*: Rose Asera, interview by the author, 2009.

287 *I spent two fall semesters watching Treisman teach freshman calculus*: The reporting in this chapter is based on over 150 hours of observations and interviews over 15 years. The author observed between one-third and one-half of Treisman's classes over two semesters in 2016 and 2017. Each class meeting was then debriefed with Treisman and, on occasion, with his teaching assistant Erica Winterer.

287 *In a focus group*: The author conducted this focus group on Paul Tough's behalf when the latter visited Austin in 2013; this is how Tough identified the student who was profiled in his magazine article: Paul Tough, "Who Gets to Graduate?," *New York Times Magazine*, May 15, 2014, https://www.nytimes.com/2014/05/18/magazine/who-gets-to-graduate.html.

289 *Uri Treisman was born in a mostly Jewish section of Brooklyn, New York*: Some of these details were informed by Paul Tough's excellent book and reporting; the rest came from the author's independent reporting and conversations with Treisman over fifteen years. For example, Tough also wrote about Louis the Butcher, but Treisman had independently told the story in this chapter to the author, with a different emphasis than appears in Tough's book. Tough, *The Inequality Machine*.

290 *A bite from a deadly pit viper*: A note for skeptical readers: This story sounds unbelievable, but the details have been confirmed by two sources and has appeared in print in several places before, such as Joanne Peeples et al., "Yueh-Gin Gung and Dr. Charles Y. Hu Award for 2019 to Philip Uri Treisman for Distinguished Service

to Mathematics," *American Mathematical Monthly* 126, no. 3 (March 2019): 195–98, https://doi.org/10.1080/00029890.2019.1551605.

290 *the legendary mentor and mathematician Leon Henkin*: Robert Sanders, "Leon Henkin, Advocate for Diversity in Math & Science, Has Died," *BerkeleyNews*, November 9, 2006, https://newsarchive.berkeley.edu/news/media/releases/2006/11/09_henkin.shtml.

291 *as I read Cornell's personal papers*: Cornell et al., "Half a Century as a Southern California Landscape Architect."

291 *the "architecture of the changing"*: Cornell et al., "Half a Century as a Southern California Landscape Architect."

291 *Cornell pointed to the example of planting redwood trees at Pomona College*: Cornell et al., "Half a Century as a Southern California Landscape Architect."

291 *the example of the great grassy lawn in the heart of Pomona College's campus*: Cornell et al., "Half a Century as a Southern California Landscape Architect."

291 *Landscape architects call this a* pathway of desire: Tichenor interview.

291 *he famously rode around the park on horseback for hundreds of acres*: Tichenor, "Ralph Cornell"; Barnidge-McIntyre, "Ralph Dalton Cornell, FASLA."

292 *Griffith Park is now considered a masterpiece*: Barnidge-McIntyre, "Ralph Dalton Cornell, FASLA."

292 *At UC Berkeley in the mid-1970s*: Uri Treisman, interviews by the author conducted between 2010 and 2024.

292 *This process yielded insights*: Treisman, *Improving the Performance of Minority Students in College-Level Mathematics.*

293 *no more than two Black students ever got above a B- in any semester that decade*: Asera, "Calculus and Community"; Hsu, Murphy, and Treisman, "Supporting High Achievement in Introductory Mathematics Courses"; Fullilove and Treisman, "Mathematics Achievement among African American Undergraduates at the University of California, Berkeley"; Treisman, "Studying Students Studying Calculus"; Kalyn Culler Cohen, "Giving Voice to Ideas: The Role Description Plays in the Diffusion of Radical Innovations" (master's thesis, Massachusetts Institute of Technology, 1999).

295 *many students have accumulated a kind of "math trauma"*: The author first heard this phrase from UCLA psychology professor James Stigler. Also see the work of Sian Beilock and Gerardo Ramirez: Sian L. Beilock and Erin A. Maloney, "Math Anxiety: A Factor in Math Achievement Not to Be Ignored," *Policy Insights from the Behavioral and Brain Sciences* 2, no. 1 (October 2015): 4–12, https://doi.org/10.1177/2372732215601438; Gerardo Ramirez et al., "Teacher Math Anxiety Relates to Adolescent Students' Math Achievement," *AERA Open* 4, no. 1 (February 1, 2018): 1–13, https://doi.org/10.1177/2332858418756052.

296 *"The required skill"*: Cornell et al., "Half a Century as a Southern California Landscape Architect."

297 *"It is never fair to judge anything in an incomplete stage"*: Cornell et al., "Half a Century as a Southern California Landscape Architect."

297 *Ivonne is beautifully profiled in Paul Tough's book* The Inequality Machine: Tough, *The Inequality Machine*; "The Campus Tour Has Been Cancelled," *This American Life*, March 12, 2021, https://www.thisamericanlife.org/734/the-campus-tour-has -been-cancelled.

297 *"My high school wasn't challenging enough," Ivonne told me*: Paul Tough profiled Ivonne in his book and in a later episode of *This American Life*. The author met and interviewed Ivonne in August 2020, when she was a teaching assistant in Uri Treis- man's calculus course her senior year, and the author was supporting Treisman's implementation of the synergistic-mindsets intervention (described in chapter 8). Tough, *The Inequality Machine*; "The Campus Tour Has Been Cancelled."

Chapter 12: Future Growth, Part Two

299 *"We are all better than we know"*: "Kurt Hahn Quote," A-Z Quotes, accessed March 25, 2024, https://www.azquotes.com/quote/910872.

299 *Having worked with KIPP on a few projects*: David S. Yeager et al., "Teaching a Lay Theory before College Narrows Achievement Gaps at Scale;" David S. Yeager et al., "Adolescents' Implicit Theories Predict Desire for Vengeance after Peer Conflicts: Correlational and Experimental Evidence."

299 *although KIPP students were getting admitted to college, they weren't graduating*: Rich- ard Whitmire, "How KIPP Learned the Truth about Its Students' College Comple- tion and Inspired Others to Do the Same," *Chalkbeat*, September 12, 2016, https:// www.chalkbeat.org/2016/9/12/21100341/how-kipp-learned-the-truth-about-its-stu dents-college-completion-and-inspired-others-to-do-the-same/.

300 *I once conducted a study with Angela Duckworth and Greg Walton*: Yeager et al., "Teaching a Lay Theory before College Narrows Achievement Gaps at Scale."

300 *described camp to me the first time she went*: This occurred one summer day in the mid-2010s when Steve Baskin took the author's family on a tour of the camp, which Scarlett attended.

300 *an analysis conducted by Donald Kamentz*: Kamentz described this analysis to the author in 2011. It was conducted with students attending the YES Prep charter schools. Unfortunately it was never published, and so it is not definitive, but simply suggestive.

301 *fascinating research conducted in the 1990s by psychologists James Youniss and Mi- randa Yates*: James Youniss and Miranda Yates, *Community Service and Social Re- sponsibility in Youth* (Chicago: University of Chicago Press, 1997).

301 *A 2014 meta-analysis of the same phenomenon*: Anne van Goethem et al., "The Role of Reflection in the Effects of Community Service on Adolescent Development: A Meta-Analysis," *Child Development* 85, no. 6 (November/December 2014): 2114–30, https://doi.org/10.1111/cdev.12274.

302 *several had interned in my research lab*: For example, Ahmad Saleh, who was an ex- cellent research assistant.

302 *Walton belonging studies*: Gregory M. Walton and Geoffrey L. Cohen, "A Brief Social- Belonging Intervention Improves Academic and Health Outcomes of Minority

Students," *Science* 331, no. 6023 (March 2011): 1447–51, https://doi.org/10.1126/science.1198364.

303 *Students wrote things like*: David S. Yeager, "Pilot Evaluation of the Effects of Summer Camp on College Enrollment," *Open Science Framework*, August 7, 2021, https://osf.io/362z5/.

303 *Baskin sponsored roughly one hundred campers on a full scholarship per summer*: Yeager, "Pilot Evaluation of the Effects of Summer Camp."

304 *I interviewed campers eight years after camp to try to find out*: These interviews were conducted from January to March 2023. During the interviews, the author did not disclose any association with Camp Champions until the end of the interview, in order to avoid influencing campers' responses.

304 *a notoriously outrageous freshman-orientation program called Fish Camp*: "Fish Camp," Texas A&M, accessed March 25, 2024, https://fishcamp.tamu.edu/.

Putting It into Practice

313 *who authored* Queen Bees and Wannabes: Rosalind Wiseman, *Queen Bees and Wannabes: Helping Your Daughter Survive Cliques, Gossip, Boyfriends, and the New Realities of Girl World*, 2nd ed. (New York: Three River Press, 2009).

315 *The parenting expert Dr. Becky Kennedy talks about*: Becky Kennedy, *Good Inside: A Guide to Becoming the Parent You Want to Be* (New York: HarperCollins, 2022).

322 *I witnessed a conversation between a young white woman in her early twenties and her mom, a baby boomer*: Conversation in Austin, Texas, March 2022.

324 *such as Black@Airbnb*: Airbnb, "Black@Airbnb Releases Employee Resource Group Manual," *Airbnb Newsroom* (blog), February 28, 2022, https://news.airbnb.com/employee-resource-group-manual/.

352 *the fast-friends protocol*: Arthur Aron et al., "The Experimental Generation of Interpersonal Closeness: A Procedure and Some Preliminary Findings," *Personality and Social Psychology Bulletin* 23, no. 4 (1997): 363–77.

352 *freely available online*: "36 Questions for Increasing Closeness," Greater Good in Action, accessed March 25, 2024, https://ggia.berkeley.edu/practice/36_questions_for_increasing_closeness.

355 *experimentally evaluated the peer-modeled-mindset approach*: Cameron A. Hecht et al., "Peer-Modeled Mindsets: An Approach to Customizing Life Sciences Studying Interventions," *CBE—Life Sciences Education* 21, no. 4 (December 2022): ar82, https://doi.org/10.1187/cbe.22-07-0143.

355 *Dr. Nicole Stephens evaluated an intervention*: Nicole M. Stephens, MarYam G. Hamedani, and Mesmin Destin, "Closing the Social-Class Achievement Gap: A Difference-Education Intervention Improves First-Generation Students' Academic Performance and All Students' College Transition," *Psychological Science* 25, no. 4 (2014): 943–53, https://doi.org/10.1177/0956797613518349.

358 *The mentoring committee*: National Academies of Sciences, Engineering, and Medicine, *The Science of Effective Mentorship in STEMM* (Washington, DC: National Academies Press, 2019), https://doi.org/10.17226/25568.

367   *Katy Perry's Super Bowl halftime musical*: Katy Perry, "Super Bowl XLIX Halftime Show," February 1, 2015, posted on YouTube by pntherpaw on February 3, 2015, https://www.youtube.com/watch?v=WmcWZ2Bzoho.

367   The Office: "The Office (TV Series 2005–2013)," IMDb, accessed March 25, 2024, https://www.imdb.com/title/tt0386676/.

Index

Note: page numbers followed by *f*, *t*, or *b* refer to figures, tables, or boxes, respectively.

Avid Reader Press, an imprint of Simon & Schuster, is built on the idea that the most rewarding publishing has three common denominators: great books, published with intense focus, in true partnership. Thank you to the Avid Reader Press colleagues who collaborated on *10 to 25*, as well as to the hundreds of professionals in the Simon & Schuster advertising, audio, communications, design, ebook, finance, human resources, legal, marketing, operations, production, sales, supply chain, subsidiary rights, and warehouse departments whose invaluable support and expertise benefit every one of our titles.

Editorial
Jofie Ferrari-Adler, *VP and Co-Publisher*
Carolyn Kelly, *Associate Editor*

Jacket Design
Alison Forner, *Senior Art Director*
Clay Smith, *Senior Designer*
Sydney Newman, *Art Associate*

Marketing
Meredith Vilarello, *VP and Associate Publisher*
Nicholas Rooney, *Marketing Manager*
Katya Wiegmann, *Marketing and Publishing Assistant*

Production
Allison Green, *Managing Editor*
Sara Kitchen, *Digital Workflow Specialist*
Alicia Brancato, *Production Manager*
Ruth Lee-Mui, *Interior Text Designer*
Cait Lamborne, *Ebook Developer*

Publicity
Alexandra Primiani, *Associate Director of Publicity*
Eva Kerins, *Publicity Assistant*

Subsidiary Rights
Paul O'Halloran, *VP and Director of Subsidiary Rights*
Fiona Sharp, *Subsidiary Rights Coordinator*

About the Author

DAVID YEAGER, PHD, is a professor of psychology at the University of Texas at Austin and a cofounder of the Texas Behavioral Science and Policy Institute. He is best known for his research conducted with Carol Dweck, Angela Duckworth, and Greg Walton on short but powerful interventions that influence adolescent behaviors such as motivation, engagement, healthy eating, bullying, stress, mental health, and more. He has consulted for Google, Microsoft, Disney, and the World Bank, as well as for the White House and the governments in California, Texas, and Norway. His research has been featured in *The New York Times Magazine, The New York Times, The Wall Street Journal, Scientific American,* CNN, Fox News, *The Guardian, The Atlantic,* and more. Yeager is the only developmental scientist to have won all three of the major awards for early career contributions to developmental psychology, and the only to have won "best paper" awards in four different fields: behavioral science, social psychology, developmental psychology, and education. Clarivate Web of Science ranks Yeager as one of the top 0.1 percent most influential psychologists in the world over the past decade. Prior to his career as a scientist, he was a middle school teacher and a basketball coach. He earned his PhD and MA at Stanford University and his BA and MEd at the University of Notre Dame. He lives in Austin, Texas, with his wife and their four children.